AMERICAN DREAMING

AMERICAN DREAMING

THE FILMS OF JOHN CASSAVETES
AND THE AMERICAN EXPERIENCE

RAYMOND CARNEY

UNIVERSITY OF CALIFORNIA PRESS

BERKELEY · LOS ANGELES · LONDON

University of California Press
Berkeley and Los Angeles, California
University of California Press, Ltd.
London, England
© 1985 by
The Regents of the University of California

Printed in the United States of America

1 2 3 4 5 6 7 8 9

Library of Congress Cataloging in Publication Data
Carney, Raymond.
  American dreaming.
  Bibliography: p.
  Includes index.
  1. Cassavetes, John, 1929–   I. Title.
PN1998.A3C3333 1985   791.43′0233′0924   84-58
ISBN 0-520-05099-1

Cover illustration: Figures of desire—Maria and Chet in *Faces*.

For

RICHARD POIRIER
DAVID THOMSON
JOHN CASSAVETES

I don't have a quarrel with studio executives. They're just there to make money. Thank God they are there. We need them. If you're a writer, you want to get published. If you're a laborer, you want to build a real building; you can't just mix mortar. My quarrel is with the artists. What have we done in an effort to find out who we are?

JOHN CASSAVETES

Where do we find ourselves?

RALPH WALDO EMERSON

CONTENTS

INTRODUCTION

The script was structured very carefully to set up a whole new [way] of thinking. *John Cassavetes*

This book is an appreciation of and a homage to America's greatest, yet most astonishingly neglected and misunderstood, filmmaker. John Cassavetes is known to millions of moviegoers as a character actor who has appeared in dozens of Hollywood films in the past three decades—from *Edge of the City*, *The Killers*, *Rosemary's Baby*, and *The Dirty Dozen* in the 1950s and 1960s to *Two Minute Warning*, *The Fury*, *Whose Life Is It Anyway?* and *Tempest* more recently. But what is less well known is that Cassavetes acts in big-budget Hollywood movies chiefly in order to be able to finance his own small-budget independent films between acting jobs. He is a one-man Hollywood studio, a spunky maverick who writes, directs, edits, finances, produces, and frequently acts in his own independent films.

It is a tribute to his enormous energy that over the past twenty-five years, though working almost alone at times, he has completed ten feature-length films that have made profound impressions on the audiences fortunate enough to catch them in their invariably limited and brief releases. They range from strange, eccentric romantic comedies like *Shadows* and *Minnie and Moskowitz*, to painful, intense domestic dramas like the critically acclaimed *Faces* and *A Woman Under the Influence*, to almost indescribable and unclassifiable extravaganzas of acting and emotion like *Husbands*, the cult favorite *The Killing of a Chinese Bookie*, and the recent *Gloria*. But it is impossible to describe Cassavetes' movies with a few adjectives or brief phrases. They are like nothing else in film, and their unsummarizable strangeness and intensity easily qualify Cassavetes for the title of America's most iconoclastic and least categorizable filmmaker.

It goes without saying, however, that filmmaking in modern corporate America is a big business like other big businesses, with little

1

allowance for, or tolerance of, mom and pop operations, so that it has been an uphill and lonely battle for Cassavetes all the way. Even after spending months or years writing, filming, and editing his movies, Cassavetes has, in almost every instance, had to spend additional months or years trying to get them distributed—peddling them from city to city, publicizing them with newspaper interviews and appearances on talk shows, and attempting to persuade theater owners and distributors to screen them.

Thus it is not surprising that many of Cassavetes' films are still almost entirely unknown to the average filmgoer. But it is perhaps sadder and more disappointing that, for a variety of reasons, they are seldom or never screened in big city revival houses or college film societies either, and that his work is still slighted or almost entirely ignored by most major American film critics. These pages are a modest attempt to address that situation. I take John Cassavetes to be America's most profound and interesting filmmaker, and his ten movies to be the most stunningly original sustained creative achievement in recent film. The book that follows is an appreciation of that achievement; but it is also simultaneously an indirect meditation on how such a lamentable state of affairs could have come to pass—how such truly extraordinary work could have been patronized, overlooked, or misunderstood for so long by so many alert and intelligent film viewers and critics. Insofar as Cassavetes' career and the egregious critical neglect of it intermittently raise larger critical, cultural, aesthetic, and intellectual questions about the adequacy of particular kinds of contemporary filmmaking, film reviewing, and criticism, I have not hesitated to take them up. Thus what follows is simultaneously a study of John Cassavetes' work in particular and a more general and oblique reflection on the predicament of the artist attempting to make it alone outside of the bureaucracies of conventional commercial filmmaking and reviewing.

As the almost universal critical silence or confusion that surrounds his work suggests, Cassavetes presents a special problem for criticism, which in itself is necessarily one of the central subjects of this study. Cassavetes' films are deliberately designed to repel and frustrate the application of the sort of methods and categories that are taken for granted in most contemporary film criticism and journalistic film reviewing. As the statement that heads this introduction suggests, and many of my discussions of particular films will indicate, the films are, in Cassavetes' words, attempts "to set up a whole new [way] of thinking" about experience, both in the movies and in life. They are, in effect, studies of the limits and possibilities of certain ways of thinking and knowing, and there is nothing more American about them than their distrust of the sorts of systematic ways of knowing that most criticism assumes to be valuable. The films are designed to criticize and resist static, formulatable ways of arranging and ordering experience. Like the characters in the films, the viewer of them must attempt to master a new way of knowing—a way of knowing that moves beyond the crudity and schematization of common psychological, social, or critical annotation. A viewer who would understand them must attempt to free himself from his own prefabricated structures and codes of understanding, including, but not limited to, the systems of meaning most critics look for and describe in a work of art.

Yet this is not at all to suggest that the films are in any way abstract or arcane intellectual or epistemological exercises. In fact, their apparent ordinariness and the domesticity of their plots and situations is probably one of the reasons that they have been underestimated or ignored by most sophisticated criticism. It is the essence of Cassavetes' technique that the particularity of the films never lets us even for a moment escape from the specific situations, characters, and the time-bound progress of the narrative into a realm of pure abstraction or transcendental theory. The films are radically, savingly, impure explorations of untranscendental predicaments. Thus, though my argument implicitly treats Cassavetes as our most challenging and "advanced" contemporary filmmaker, the films deliberately defeat abstract technical analyses and resist the sorts of formalist treatment usually reserved for "advanced" texts. Cassavetes' films engage large, profound issues and imaginative stances, as my specific discussions will indicate, but they always imagine them as inextricably involved with practical issues of human relationship and feeling. It is essential to an appreciation of their unique strengths to realize that the visionary and transcendental aspirations of the films and of the characters within them are never abstractable from the prosaicism of the ordinary life in them. The films document the career of transcendental impulses (on the part of both their characters and their author) passed through the resistance of assertively untranscendental situations. Which is to say, the films are thoroughly problematic, error-ridden, human expressions of life as it is actually experienced under the constraints of time, space, and society. Any criticism that would adequately describe them must attempt to be as human, humane, and practical as the films themselves.

The films resist being turned into esoteric, self-contained, self-referential "aesthetic objects," or into pure "texts" with a self-contained "textuality." Cassavetes' texts cannot be disengaged from multitudinous, everywhere impinging "contexts" of confused intentions, biographical events, social and psychological realities, and cultural and imaginative contingencies. Thus, in my discussions, biographical events in Cassavetes' life are incorporated into considerations of the aesthetic effects of his films. Cassavetes' sometimes muddled intentions and statements about his films are treated as texts coequal to the films themselves. The technological and bureaucratic constraints of modern filmmaking are treated as being inseparable from any consideration of the texts of the films that result. Historical, cultural, social, and moral issues are incorporated into discussion of what might otherwise be considered to be purely filmic matters. The forms of personality, performance, and expression in these films are more complex and subtle than anything describable by a more mechanical or formalist critical method. A description of these films in more purely cinematic terms—as a concatenation of semiotic structures, visual metaphors, or allegorical meanings—could only simplify, mechanize, and dehumanize the experiences and ways of knowing that Cassavetes' films explore.

But notwithstanding the contingencies and particularities of the experiences offered by Cassavetes' films, it would be an even greater injustice to them to approach them as if they were "realistic" or "naturalistic" texts in the line of Wyler, Zinnemann, Lumet, Pakula, and other postwar filmmakers. The assumption these filmmakers make is that "reality" consists of worldly facts and forces that ultimately make the individual imagination fairly powerless and unimportant. But Cassavetes believes the opposite. His films are designed to explode the structures of personality and plot and the simplified forms of confrontation and climax that such "realistic" films take for granted and define as "reality." The realities Cassavetes acknowledges are realities of desire and imagination that have little or no relation to the rather trivial collections of sociological and anthropological bric-a-brac that these other directors are interested in documenting on film and calling reality. The troubled, and troubling, expression in our culture of those realities (in Cassavetes' sense of the word) is the subject of all of his work.

Cassavetes' films are, in the largest sense, inquiries into the trajectory of the American dream in the local and inevitably hostile environments in which it is forced to express itself in modern America. They are explorations of the challenges and burdens of the essential American imaginative situation. That is why I have not hesitated to make frequent comparisons here between Cassavetes' work and analogous work in American dance, music, drama, fiction, and poetry, and have contrasted his work in several discussions with that of apparently similar work by important British and Continental artists. Such references to other arts appear in the text not in a covert attempt to dignify film studies in general or Cassavetes' work in particular, but in an honest effort to suggest some of the ways that what Cassavetes is doing in film has important analogues in other American art and equally important differences from work in other artistic traditions.

Though the pages that follow are only a beginning, the goal of tracing such connections and differences would ultimately be to establish some sort of rough road map of subterranean paths between artists exploring common imaginative territory. My assumption is that these American filmmakers, poets, novelists, choreographers, and musicians do to some extent inhabit a common social, psychological, historical, and imaginative terrain that it is the challenge of criticism to map and describe. There are important differences between the expressive capacities of the different arts, but too much of our contemporary compartmentalization of knowledge has arisen not because of a well-founded respect for such differences but simply as a result of the overspecialization and intellectual provincialism of academic criticism.

In this sense, Cassavetes' films and career may be said to matter less because of their uniqueness than because of their profound representativeness. Cassavetes' life and work are only the most recent, most powerfully articulated, and most exemplary response to what is an enduring American imaginative predicament. John Cassavetes is an American dreamer trying to keep alive a particularly American dream of imaginative freedom and free self-expression in the hostile environment of American bureaucratic filmmaking, just as his characters are American dreamers trying to keep alive their personal dreams and ideals amid the messes, confusions, and contingencies of their ordinary middle-class lives. It is the exemplary and recurrent Americanness of this dreaming and the complications it results in that makes it matter so intensely to us here and now. (I should add, parenthetically, that many of the connections between the work of John Cassavetes and that of other filmmakers, and between American film and other American art will be elaborated further in two companion volumes—one devoted to the work of Frank Capra in the 1930s and 1940s and another devoted to the silent films of Buster Keaton and Charlie Chaplin. They will expand the argument begun here and extend this study of the American cinematic imagination backwards to suggest, among other things, that the work of Chaplin, Keaton, Capra, and Cassavetes uniquely defines a central tradition in American film, a tradition that is a direct continuation in twentieth-century filmmaking of the energies of nineteenth-century American romanticism. Their work is a twentieth-century cinematic expression of impulses that were previously most powerfully expressed in earlier American painting, philosophy, and literature. It is in this great tradition of distinctively American ideals and aspirations that Cassavetes' work takes its place, and, as I will argue, it is as a continuation and extension of this imaginative tradition that the Chaplin-Keaton-Capra-Cassavetes line of filmmaking defines one of the indisputibly major lines of accomplishment in modern American art.)

That is to say, this is a study of a particular filmmaker and his ten films, but, like the films themselves, it is, as my title suggests, a study of something that might, for lack of a better phrase, be called American dreaming. Cassavetes' films are meditations on the career of the American dream at this point in our culture, and this book is, in the most general sense, an extended meditation on the dreamlike forms and forces that energize, and frequently confuse, American art and life. In particular, it is a study of some of the ways specific cultural forms and strategies of artistic expression (in American literature, dance, film, and music) work both to release the explosive dreamlike energies of the American imagination, and simultaneously to control the potential damage of the release, to limit the disruptions, to channel the wild, passionate, sometimes anarchic energies of the dream into socially, psychologically, and artistically endurable forms of experience.

Finally, though it is implicit in my argument and never surfaces in an explicit way, the notion of the film experience itself as essentially affiliated with the dream experience and drawing upon some of the special energies of the dream state is never very far from my considerations. It is not accidental that the land of the American dream in the economic, social, and imaginative senses of the phrase has also been the land of the American dream in Hollywood's sense of it as well. In America's pervasive forms of mass communication, the dream factory that is American filmmaking and the dream factory of American ideology and society are inextricably linked (as Cassavetes' *Minnie and Moskowitz* depends upon our understanding).

At the heart of the argument of the following pages is the premise that John Cassavetes' films, like all of the greatest and most daring American art before them, derive their particular power from their ability to tap the bewildering, unsystematic, disturbing, but potentially liberating energies of all of these sorts of American dreaming. But how the dream is made public and social and how the individual entertains the incredible possibility of actually living it in the real forms of personality, space, time, and narrative is too much to go into here and now. The reader interested in following out the complications and contradictions of daring to dream the impossible American dream is directed to the chapters that follow.

Writing a book of this sort, dealing with a filmmaker about whom little or nothing has been written in the past, has largely been a single-handed effort. However, several people lightened the load at various points. At a crucial juncture, the project was assisted by a grant from the National Endowment for the Humanities. Research was facilitated by the resourceful aid of Joan Allen and Judith Humphreys. Assistance, helpful information, or useful suggestions about the manuscript were provided on specific occasions by William Everson, Deac Rossell, Gerald Peary, Albert Johnson, Ernest Callenbach, Charles Silver, Jonathan Rosenbaum, Bruce Kawin, Tom Edwards, Warren French, Robert Morsberger, Frederick Crews, David Seachrist, P. Adams Sitney, Ted Perry, and Mary Corliss. Three former teachers also deserve mention for their initial encouragement and the continuing stimulation of their example: Reuben Brower, Stanley Cavell, and Erik Erikson. It is also a pleasure to acknowledge the help of Richard Kaye and Robert Fieldsteel of Faces International Films, Inc. I am grateful to the Museum of Modern Art and to *Film Quarterly* for illustrations.

But my most profound and personal debt, and one that goes beyond my capacity ever adequately to acknowledge or repay, is to the three men named in my dedication. By their lives and work this book was inspired; to them in all humility it is dedicated.

CHAPTER I

FREEDOM FROM STYLES
AND STYLES OF FREEDOM

What is wanted is not intensity of style but intensity of thought.
Henry James

We have to move beyond the current obsession with technique and camera angles. *John Cassavetes*

His face hasn't been featured on the cover of *Time* or *Newsweek*. His films are seldom screened and less frequently written about. To the average moviegoer his work is almost unknown. To film buffs and insiders he has become the Hollywood equivalent of Howard Hughes or Bobby Fischer—a living legend of cranky independence, eccentricity, and inaccessibility. But it is the argument of the following pages that John Cassavetes is one of the major creative artists of our generation, and that, though his films are hard to get hold of and many are seldom screened publicly, they are one of the monumental achievements of twentieth-century American art.

Even in an area so prone to overstatement as film criticism, this claim may seem excessive. The list of major, serious, or interesting American directors changes almost monthly, it seems; but in all the flux one thing remains constant—the omission of Cassavetes from almost everybody's list. Twenty-five years and ten films into his career as writer, director, financier, and sometimes actor in his own independent films, his work is still seldom screened at revival houses and is ignored by all but a handful of leading film critics. Even at this relatively late date in film scholarship, after a decade in which it seemed that a new book on Fellini, Hitchcock, or *Citizen Kane* arrived in the bookstores every month, there is still not a single volume on Cassavetes' life and work in print. Film encyclopedias and dictionaries that devote page after page to the work of European artists such as Truffaut, Godard, and Bergman, skim over his long and productive career in two or three

8

paragraphs. One searches in vain through the indexes and chapter headings of the standard recent histories of American film without finding more than a footnote or a one-sentence mention of his work.[1]

It is only natural to wonder why this situation should have arisen, especially considering the artistic poverty of the cinematic competition Cassavetes is implicitly up against, and the spiritual and moral meagerness of many of the films that do get a large share of critical and popular attention. The question of critical canon formation is a complex one, and there is a thick book still to be written on the history of twentieth-century intellectual and commercial fads, fashions, and favorites in the arts. But there are several obvious explanations for Cassavetes' position as odd man out both critically and popularly.

One can begin with his notoriously difficult personality and his steadfast refusal to work within the Hollywood system in any way. His uncompromising independence and fierce iconoclasm are the stuff of which traditional Hollywood legends are made (and traditional Hollywood careers unmade). Nor have his opinions and attitudes been calculated to win friends and influence people in positions of cultural power. He earned his reputation as "film's bad boy" in the late 1950s with a series of blistering attacks on the film and television establishment, and he has not backed down from a critical, commercial, or cinematic argument in the years since. But his scorn is not confined to a rejection of the bureaucracies of Hollywood; he has courted the affection of critics, film distributors, and audiences as little as he has tried to please producers and studio executives. What other director, while being interviewed by Pauline Kael for *The New Yorker* and its half-million influential, ticket-buying readers, would have dared to break off the interview halfway through (actually throwing Kael out of the restaurant where they were talking) because, according to him, she showed insufficient appreciation of the "artistic side" of his work? What other director would not only refuse to let many of his films be distributed through an outside rental agency but, holding sole ownership of them himself, would routinely turn down requests to rent them even from his own rental company? Nor does Cassavetes seem to have mellowed with age or neglect: as recently as three years ago, belatedly honored by the Los Angeles Film Exposition with a five-hour retrospective of his work, he boycotted the proceedings because the final screening schedule had not been cleared with him in advance.

Cassavetes himself perhaps best summarized his deliberately embattled position in his curt reply to an interviewer who pressed him to name some school or cinematic movement to which he and his work belonged: "I'm not part of anything; I never joined anything."[2] He is a "non-joiner," a fiercely independent maverick who has wasted no time or effort currying favor with studio executives, press interviewers, or film critics, though all three groups will admit that his charm and infectious enthusiasm can be overwhelmingly winning when he chooses to display them.

Notwithstanding his well-documented cantankerousness, however, the commercial and critical neglect of Cassavetes cannot be attributed entirely to the crotchets and quirks of his temperament. John Cassavetes would be the first to be able to name many directors even harder to get along with than himself who have thrived in Hollywood. Personality just does not count for all that much in the bureaucracies of contemporary film production, distribution, and publicity.

The independence that has sealed the commercial and critical fate of Cassavetes' films is not the independence of his temperament, but the independence of his aesthetic. The problem, in other words, is not that John Cassavetes the person is not a "joiner," but that his films refuse to be "joiners" of any of the fashionable and over-subscribed clubs within film studies. The important issue is not that he does not feel "part of anything" in the way of film schools, studios, unions, or production methods, but that his films deliberately rethink every critical and cinematic commonplace handed down from the hills of Hollywood since the days of Griffith. The result, since his films just do not look or feel like other movies, since they are precisely as far from looking like "Entertainment" as they are from looking like "Art," is, predictably enough, commercial rejection and critical incomprehension.

Few other directors so profoundly challenge the very concept of "stardom" and the organization of scenes and events around one or two central figures. Few expose the viewer to so much social and psychological mess, to so many competing points of interest within a scene. Cassavetes' films radically question the whole concept of the "well-made" or "well-composed" frame, scene, or work of art. Altman's calculated, controlled "layerings" of visual and aural planes of interest seem academic, mannered, and painterly compared to Cassavetes' bewildering human clutter of conflicting emotions, interests, and attitudes. No filmmaker since Dreyer has so daringly experimented with dramatic pacing and duration, and with such complexities of personal interaction. A viewer has to unlearn (or at least to rethink) so many assumptions about how a movie is supposed to look that cinematic sophistication can be an actual liability in appreciating Cassavetes' work. He has always felt the relative cinematic innocence of audiences outside the United States and their unfamiliarity with the prevailing Hollywood modes of packaging experience to be among the reasons his films have traditionally fared better outside this country than within it.

Cassavetes' problem getting attention from the most sophisticated filmgoers has been compounded by the degree to which his work is jarringly out of step with both the style and content of most other "significant" contemporary film. Not only is his loose and baggy photographic and narrative style the opposite of the elegantly photographed, tightly paced intellectual exercises of a Bergman or Antonioni, but the plots, characters, and situations in Cassavetes' films resist just the sorts of metaphorical and philosophical expansions that these directors and others have taught us to expect in important contemporary films. It has been an unspoken premise of most twentieth-century art since the time of Yeats, Pound, Forster, Joyce, and Eliot that ambitious modern masterworks must grapple with grand cultural themes.[3] Hollywood itself, when it has aspired to make a work of art with a capital A, has known the importance of an epical, preferably allegorical story. From *The Ten Commandments* to *Apocalypse Now* and *Heaven's Gate*, otherwise quite ordinary movies have offered abstractions and cultural pretensions as earnests of their importance and bribes to an audience's impatience with their length. Up to twenty or thirty years ago, however, American films largely escaped the burden of being High Art, and the best American movies were largely free of such cultural grandiosity. But whether through the influence of European cinema or of film schools on a new generation of writers and directors, that seems to have changed. Film, even American film, has become Art, and the assumption seems to be that it should emulate the techniques of other major modern art forms. Filmmakers as different as Kubrick, Altman, Malick, Coppola, Spielberg, and Lucas (to name only the most impressive examples) and films otherwise as wildly unrelated as *The Godfather*, *A Clockwork Orange*, *Nashville*, and *Star Wars* have in common their eminently discussible cultural generalizations.

So it is perhaps the very humaneness of Cassavetes' work that most successfully camouflages its importance. His work emerges out of an intertwined double tradition, theatrical in one strand and filmic in the other. But both traditions are profoundly opposed to the current apoc- alyptic aesthetic. Cassavetes' filmic antecedents lie in the German *Kammerspiel*, or "chamber play," films of the 1920s and 1930s with their simple domestic stories, long takes, and attention to the subtle emotional interactions of a small number of characters. His theatrical heritage derives from the work of Stanislavsky and Chekhov in the Moscow Art Theatre. The first tradition comes down to Cassavetes most powerfully in the work of Carl Dreyer, for which he has admitted his great admiration; the second comes to him through his own training at the American Academy of Dramatic Arts in the techniques of the Method, with its naturalistic depictions of delicate human relationships and its interest in capturing complexities of feeling as they are expressed in nuances of a character's tones, gestures, and movements.

In place of culturally allusive allegories about the alienation of Modern Man, the quest for meaning in a spiritual wasteland, or the moral condition of Western civilization, Cassavetes offers thoroughly domestic stories of ordinary middle-class families, narrations of unabstractable personal relations of husbands and wives, lovers and friends, parents and children. His films are small scale in more than their budgets and production crews; they are virtually microscopic studies of the course of specific human relationships. The interest lies in the minutely observed details of particular social situations, not in cultural posturings, apocalyptic confrontations, or metaphorical and metaphysical generalizability. While many ambitious filmmakers today seem to be trying to reproduce in film the clanking artistic technologies of a Joyce novel, or the cultural allusiveness and metaphysical abstractness of a poem by Eliot, Yeats, or Pound, Cassavetes offers something much more like the culturally shyer and more humane investigations of a Robert Frost, Eudora Welty, Elizabeth Bishop, or Anton Chekhov. (And as anyone who understands the true value of this second group of authors knows, this is far from being a limiting judgment on his work.) The metaphorical insistence of a Coppola film, the Olympian cultural aloofness of an Altman film, or the abstract stylistic tendentiousness of a Kubrick film would only make Cassavetes uncomfortable.

With his interests so firmly focused on the complex, local, human drama of his characters, it is not surprising that Cassavetes regards himself more as a writer quietly describing people and situations he has known than as the profoundly original cinematic stylist that he is. In fact, one of the most frequent criticisms of his work, and one Cassavetes has done nothing to deny, since he fancies it rather more as a compliment than as a criticism, is that his films have nothing to offer in the way of a coherent visual style or cinematic imagination. Nothing could be further from the truth, but it is not hard to see why his films lay themselves open to such a charge. What Cassavetes does lack, and in fact prides himself upon avoiding, is just what many film journal articles are devoted to describing: a style detachable from particular characters, feelings, and relationships, and discussible apart from them. His is a style in contrast whose entire purpose is to efface itself in the presentation of particular characters and situations. There are no "beauty" shots as ends in themselves, no painterly, pictorial compositions, in short, none of the stylistic tics that elevate the *auteur* above the material in which he works. The visual gaudiness of the contemporary tour de force so much in evidence since the rise to power of the color cinematographer is absent. Cassavetes' goal is the opposite of working out a complex or personal visual style in the *auteurist* fashion. His intention is to subdue the dyer's hand to the thing it works in. This is not to say that he has no style, but only that his style is organic and functional and entirely in the service of the experiences, situations, and characters in his films. Though his films may look styleless and undiscussible at first glance, like those of the neorealists, whose work his own so much resembles in places, it is a style that on repeated viewing reveals itself as a profound expression of knowledge about the complexities of human experience.

Neorealist art, however, never lent itself very well to close stylistic analysis, Marxist or sociological readings being only a way of avoiding the necessity of a detailed visual analysis. For similar reasons, it would be hard to think of a contemporary filmmaker whose style is less easily described with the traditional terms and methods of modern film criticism than that of Cassavetes. The sorts of things that form the backbone of most film analysis—the discovery and description of formal, abstractable, generalizable visual symmetries and patternings—are things Cassavetes' work deliberately avoids. Meaning emerges only out of the minute-by-minute course of a human interaction between two or more people. The patterned emphases and schematic organizations of material that are the basic rhetorical principles of most other films would only obscure the small, shifting, personal tones, rhythms, and relationships Cassavetes is interested in exploring. He works to protect his narratives from the encroachment of precisely the kinds of summarizing cinematic structures that most other films depend upon to generate and enlarge their meanings. As far as he is concerned, overarching metaphoric and narrative patterns would only betray the situations he is interested in studying. All of which is only to say that Cassavetes' avoidance of certain common stylistic and rhetorical patternings in film (like Frost's, Bishop's, or Welty's avoidance of them in literature) is more than a negative stance. It is not that Cassavetes dislikes carefully crafted, coherent, "well-made" films in themselves (as some of his detractors would charge), but that few directors have been more acutely suspicious of the inevitable betrayals and simplifications of cinematic styles, all the more so the portable, deployable, and extractable styles of so many recent "masterworks." As Cassavetes realizes, every stylistic arrangement is necessarily a lie about experience, an inevitable simplification of the full emotional, psychological, and social complexity of even an hour in the most ordinary and uneventful life.

Cassavetes has a fear of the systematization and stylization of experience. His distrust of fixed styles and systems of understanding situates him closer to classic writers of the American tradition such as Emerson, Twain, and James than to most contemporary American filmmakers. This great film stylist, like the great literary and artistic stylists preceding him, has a paradoxical fear of style itself—a fear that "styles" of expression are somehow intrinsically inadequate to express the self; a fear that "style" in itself inevitably represses the energies it exists to express and release. In the particular case of Cassavetes' films, it is the fear that a screenwriter's, director's, or editor's formal arrangements will invariably simplify and betray the more complex and less shapely forms of experience on behalf of which the film is made. But the "styleless style" is a fiction, however much American artists or characters have aspired to believe it. Henry James captures the paradox of the American attempt to go beyond (or without) style when, after Isabel Archer voices her conviction that clothes, no matter how elegant, cannot express her self, he has Madame Merle ask her if she wishes, therefore, to go naked. And Cassavetes' ideal of the "styleless style" leads him, like another Isabel, into the strangest pronouncements. One finds him telling Joseph Gelmis in an interview:

We have to move beyond the current obsession with technique and camera angles. It's a waste of time. How you shoot a film is a diversion. I think anybody can shoot a film. Look at the most commercial things in the world—television commercials. They're magnificently photographed. What are we wasting our time doing that for? It has nothing to do with life. Now we're making that a value. Pretty photography is part of our culture.[4]

Passing over the bizarre (and false) statements that "how you shoot a film is a diversion" and "anybody can shoot a film," I want to call attention to the peculiar statement about "life" near the end of this quotation. In the ordinary sense of the word, this too is nonsense. Commercials do not have "nothing to do with life"; they have everything to do with life today. One might argue indeed that no other contemporary form of expression has so much to do with our lives today, not even movies. But, of course, this is a misreading of what Cassavetes is saying. What makes this passage so interesting is the special meaning he is making the word "life" bear here and in a dozen other statements he has made. "Life" in this sense represents precisely everything that "techniques," "camera angles," and "styles" betray. And it is hardly surprising that in the many times he has used the word, he has never defined it more exactly than he does here. The "life" Cassavetes is interested in capturing on film is just what resists more precise definition in print or on film.

The energies his films are designed to release are the energies of "life" in this primitive sense, energies of personality and feeling not reducible to what he calls "styles," "techniques," and "angles." And the result is that Cassavetes invariably talks about a successful cinematic style in almost entirely negative terms. Style, to the extent that it is adequate, is paradoxically an effort of withdrawal and self-effacement. It is an effort not to destroy something (call it "life" or whatever) that Cassavetes imagines to be already present before style intrudes, before a cameraman, director, or editor comes on the scene. In the same interview, Cassavetes talks about making *Faces*, his first fully independent commercial feature:

In *Faces*, Al Ruban did the lighting, and I had a great operator who worked the camera. They had individual pride in their work. But they also realized they were part of an overall thing. It wasn't decisively important how beautiful their photography was. . . . The question was: "What are we working for?" And the obvious answer was that we were working for these *people* [i.e., the characters in the film]—we're not dealing with objects and walls—to look better. . . . [What we are interested in is] what these people are thinking, what they're feeling. And that's the drama of the piece. . . . It's as simple as that. . . . The idea was "How do we get to these people the fastest, quickest, most expedient way before that little feeling that they have disappears?" That's the important thing. . . . We were slaves to [the actors]. All we were there to do was record what they were doing. Much like an interview. You really want me to say something. So you've got to help me the best way you can to say something that will be interesting. And if I want to talk on and on and on and on, that's my way, and you've got to sacrifice your style.[5]

The director and cameraman become mere "recorders" and "slaves." The writing, sets, photography, and editing exist, in effect, only to make themselves invisible, utterly transparent to the "little feelings" that emerge on the set. "It's as simple as that."

What is most interesting about this conception of cinematic style, of course, is its absolute absurdity. Moreover, if this account of the filming of *Faces* were even roughly correct in its factual details, the 129 minute film would not have taken six months and three hundred thousand feet of film to shoot and almost three years of work to edit. As anyone who has ever taken home movies—and certainly John Cassavetes himself— knows, the transparency of style, the invisibility of the camera work, and above all the release of the "little feelings" are the most difficult of all stylistic illusions to achieve. The antidote to an obtrusive, manipulative, or artificial style is never an abandoning or renunciation of style but, on the contrary, an even more sensitive and carefully controlled style. Those "little feelings" Cassavetes and his cameramen may or may not have felt they were only "recording," as they watched the actors perform on the set, are only brought into existence (for a group of possibly bored, tired, or indifferent viewers sitting in a movie theater miles away and years later) by means of the most consummately crafted cinematic style.

There is, needless to say, no such thing as the sort of unmediated, unarranged, unstyled experience that Cassavetes is appealing to in this interview and in many others. We are only now beginning to see how thoroughly crafted, arranged, and stylized the films of the neorealists of the early fifties are. The films of the *cinéma vérité* filmmakers who followed them are equally far from being mere "records" or "documents" from "life." Though film has replaced the novel and then still photography as the art most powerfully capable of hiding the fact, its contents are always and everywhere contained; its *vérité* is necessarily and inevitably arranged by its *cinéma*. But Cassavetes is not lying to his interviewer, he is passing a necessary fiction on himself. However much we may regard the cinematic lie of the styleless style as bad aesthetics and worse practical filmmaking doctrine, it is a central and important fiction for his work. In fact, it is a fiction that underlies much American art, though there too it has been more honored in the breach than the observance. The interest of Cooper, Twain, James, and Faulkner in the child, the primitive, the ingenue, and the American Adam is an attempt to locate and celebrate some form of unmediated experience unconditioned by stylistic conventions and rules. But, as every sentence of their work testifies, there is no escaping style. Only through style is style even provisionally conquered. As Isabel Archer's experience tells us, and she herself learns, alien, threatening styles are never conquered through innocence, but only through a finer, subtler experience and knowingness.

Isabel Archer met Gilbert Osmond; Cassavetes' discovery of the pervasiveness of cinematic styles and stylizations and their inevitable encroachment on "life" took place upon the completion of his first film. *Shadows* was made as a deliberate and calculated experiment in capturing the "life" that Cassavetes was convinced had been squeezed out of contemporary Hollywood movies. As he once described it, it was made as an attempt to depict the "real lives" of "real people" that Hollywood avoided. But, not surprisingly, "style" turned out to be harder to get rid of than he had calculated.

Cassavetes spared no effort in making the first version of the film. He exposed over 60,000 feet of 16mm stock (roughly thirty hours of film, or a shooting-to-first-print ratio of 30:1) over an eight-week period in the middle of 1957. He then spent the next year and a half editing and redubbing (since almost all of the original direct soundtrack failed to be of usable quality). But he discovered that he was unable to escape the stylization of experience, no matter how hard he tried. When *Shadows* was screened at the end of 1958, many contemporary viewers criticized the film for its artless, grainy, hand-held camera work, but in Cassavetes' opinion, the problem with the film was not that it was too rough, too crude, or too unfinished, but the reverse. In his view, despite all he had done to avoid it, the film was still too "beautiful" and too stylized. As he harshly characterized it at the time: "[*Shadows*] was filled with cinematic virtuosity. . .with angles and fancy cutting, and a lot of jazz going on in the background."[6] As he would summarize years later, again very unfairly to himself and his film: "I had fallen in love with the camera, with technique, with beautiful shots, with experimentation for its own sake. . . . It was a totally intellectual film, and therefore less than human."[7] (One cannot help noticing that the concept of "humanness" functions here in exactly the absolute, honorific way the concepts of "life" and "feeling" functioned in the previous quotations.)

But *Shadows* also illustrated a necessary, if paradoxical, corollary to Cassavetes' distrust of style. If "style" inevitably threatens "life," true, honest, authentic "life" can never entirely be suppressed. Feeling and life are able, if only in the most marginal ways, to "survive" whatever stylistic "tricks" are played on them. And as much as he disliked this print of *Shadows*, Cassavetes was forced to recognize that "the one thing that came at all alive for me after I had laid *Shadows* aside for a few weeks was that just now and then the actors had survived all of my tricks. . . . They barely came to life."[8]

The important consequence was that he did not simply give up on this film or on filming in general. Even as *Shadows* was being hailed as a breakthrough by many in the New York film avant-garde, Cassavetes decided to scrap more than half the footage in the original print and raise more money to refilm and entirely reedit it in a second version. Eight new scenes were written and rehearsed (changes amounting to about half of the scenes in the film), 40,000 feet more of film were shot in two weeks of additional photography, and three more months spent in reediting, increasing the length of *Shadows* by almost half—from sixty minutes in the first version to eighty-seven in the second—before Cassavetes allowed the film to be rereleased, in the version we now have, at the end of 1959. Whatever Cassavetes may have intended, the second print of *Shadows* does not (and cannot) avoid style, but its excitement and interest are Cassavetes' effort to keep "those small feelings" "alive" in the hostile environment of "style."

Cassavetes' films, as the scrapping of the first version of *Shadows* and the making of the second version indicate, are energized by this quixotic quest for a "styleless style." What makes *Shadows* and the films that follow it so interesting is that Cassavetes' peculiar stylistic predicament, as a filmmaker endlessly negotiating the traps, conventionalities, and brutalities of cinematic styles, becomes the social and psychological situation of his characters as they try to keep alive the possibilities of life, humanity, and feeling in a world where every style of behavior and expression militates against them. Like their creator, his characters are on an exhilarating quest for freedom and life, even as they are doomed necessarily to express themselves within styles and networks of relationship that at their best will betray their aspirations and fail adequately to express their unappeasably ardent dreams and desires for free expression.

The films are chronicles of small-town, small-time American dreamers daring to question the conventions and compromises of middle-class life. If only for the duration of a wild weekend or a brief, passionate affair, they dare to dream of ideal love, freedom, adventure, or self-expression. But the unique strength of these films is that there is no filmmaker more aware of all the ways both life and art work to repress and frustrate such dreams. In Cassavetes' characters, overwhelming impulses of imagination and desire are passed through the infinite resistances of society, space, time, and action. Ideals of life and freedom are forced to run the obstacle course of style and society, and the social and stylistic resistances of the film form itself. The films are stories of characters forever in invigorating transit between authentic life and stultifying, prefabricated, predetermined styles of expression.

Not since Capra's great populist masterpieces have characters been simultaneously more constrained and yet potentially more free—more hedged round by a web of influences, pressures, and competing responsibilities, and yet given more margin and breathing room to work out their own personal styles of response to the fields of force arrayed around them. Like Hawks, Capra, and Huston (three essential presences in his work), Cassavetes is fascinated by the power of the individual to shape an eccentric and original performance within the most severe constraints and restrictions imaginable. But, more like Capra than Hawks or Huston, he is aware of how hard the process of triumphing over the forces massed against the freedom of the individual is, of how difficult it is to keep "alive" in a hostile, coercive, or indifferent world. No director lets in more of the mess of existence that compromises the individual, more of the confusions of feeling and tangled webs of relationship that test his freedom so severely. The result is that Cassavetes' films violate almost all of the elegant framings, pacings, and patternings of the conventional film. But some would argue that his work has its own eloquence, which puts most of the others to shame. It is an eloquence that emerges out of magically, miraculously unpredictable transactions between individuals in transit, that admits the full range of confusion, clutter, and mess that riddles our dreams, and that achingly captures the yearnings and frustrations of the American experience.

CHAPTER II

MAKING SCENES AND FORGING IDENTITIES
The Making of *Shadows*

The great impression, however, the one that has brought me so far, was another matter. . . . the presence at my side of my young cousin Marie, youngest daughter of the house, exactly of my own age, and named in honor of her having been born in Paris, to the influence of which fact her shining black eyes, her small quickness and brownness, marking sharply her difference from her sisters, so oddly, so almost extravagantly testified. It had come home to me by some voice of the air that she was "spoiled," and it made her in the highest degree interesting; we ourselves had been so associated, at home, without being in the least spoiled (I think we rather missed it:) so that I knew about these subjects of invidious reflection only by literature—mainly, no doubt, that of the nursery—in which they formed, quite by themselves, a romantic class; and, the fond fancy always predominant, I prized even while a little dreading the chance to see the condition at work. This chance was given me, it was clear—though I risk in my record of it a final anticlimax—by a remark from my uncle Augustus to his daughter: seated duskily in our group, which included two or three dim dependent forms, he expressed the strong opinion that Marie should go to bed. . . . It had been remarked but in the air, I feel sure, that Marie should seek her couch—a truth by the dark wing of which I ruefully felt myself brushed; and the words seemed therefore to fall with a certain ironic weight. What I have retained of their effect, at any rate, is the vague fact of some objection raised by my cousin and some sharper point to his sentence supplied by her father; promptly merged in a visible commotion, a flutter of my young companion across the gallery as for refuge in the maternal arms, a protest and an appeal in short which drew from my aunt the simple phrase that was from that moment so preposterously to "count" for me. "Come now, my dear; don't make a scene—I insist on your not making a scene!" That was all the witchcraft the occasion used, but the note was none the less epoch-making. The expression, so vivid, so portentous, was one I had never heard—it had never been addressed to us at home; and who should say now what a world one mightn't read into it? It seemed freighted to sail so far; it told me so much about life. Life at these intensities clearly became "scenes"; but the great thing, the immense illumination, was that we could make them or not as we chose. It was a long time of course before I began to distinguish between those within our compass more particularly as spoiled and those producible on a different basis and which should involve detachment, involve presence of mind; just the qualities in which Marie's possible output was apparently deficient. It didn't in the least matter accordingly whether or not a scene

20

was then proceeded to—and I have lost all count of what immediately happened. The mark had been made for me and the door flung open; the passage, gathering up all the elements of the troubled time, had been itself quite a scene, quite enough of one, and I had become aware with it of a rich accession of possibilities.   *Henry James*

Please don't make any scenes.   *Lelia to her boyfriend Tony, as she makes a scene with him in a taxi in* Shadows

John Cassavetes is the kind of character who it seems could only have stepped out of a John Cassavetes movie. He is a scrapper, a hustler, a happy improvisor, and a free and independent cinematic entrepreneur in the best sense of the words. He is a living embodiment of the American dream at work—a confident, self-reliant, self-made man whose artistic and intellectual idealism, optimism, and faith in the power of hard work are matched only by his characters' idealism, optimism, and faith in their ability to solve their emotional and social problems. He makes movies with the same plucky pragmatism they bring to the process of shaping their identities. If he is a cinematic entrepreneur, his characters are practical-minded social and psychological entrepreneurs—investing in their personal dreams, holding onto their investments as long as they can, selling out their commitments when they must, and trying to make a psychological or spiritual profit wherever possible.

His energies and talents are truly prodigious. In addition to his work as a film actor, writer, and director, Cassavetes has written, directed, and mounted productions of a number of his own dramatic works (as well as a remarkable production of a play, *Love Streams*, by the British playwright Ted Allan) in repertory theater companies of his own organization. He has supported himself in all these enterprises by writing occasionally for the screen and acting in just the sort of box office blockbusters his own films and plays are a reaction against. Many of the younger directors who began making films in the past decade have been called "independents" because they frequently act as their own producers and assemble their own crews for each of their films, but nobody making feature-length commercial films is an "independent" in the way Cassavetes is. Nobody even comes close. He might almost be said to define one possible extreme meaning of the word, writing, directing, photographing, editing, financing, distributing, and publicizing his own films. Add to that the fact that seven of them have featured either Cassavetes or his wife (Gena Rowlands) in leading roles, and that the rest of the parts are almost without exception taken by friends and relatives willing to work for little or nothing for the opportunity to be in one of his films, and it is not hard to see why he has been called the wild home movie man.

The scrappy independence and improvisatory resourcefulness of Cassavetes' cinematic entrepreneurship necessarily reminds one that he is himself the son of a spiritual, cultural, and economic improvisor and entrepreneur of sorts. Cassavetes loves to tell the story of how his father arrived in America from Greece at the age of eleven with no money, no connections, and no English but "I want to work and I want to learn" to try to fashion his own free and independent identity out of the influences and opportunities around him. He succeeded in working his way through Harvard, "made and lost millions" (as Cassavetes tells it) in his own travel business, and was eventually able to move himself and his family to just the sort of mildly prosperous and upwardly aspiring Long Island suburb where many of Cassavetes' movie families seem to live. From this soil spring Cassavetes' spunky independence, his Capra-corny faith in the basic pluck and ability of the common man, and his wide-eyed fascination with the bootstrap operation of fashioning a family, an identity, and a uniquely personal style out of whatever materials and possibilities come to hand.

The career of this self-made man has been as zigzaggingly unpredictable as the lives of any of the social and psychological entrepreneurs in his films. After bouncing in and out of several upstate New York colleges as a young man, he enrolled almost on a whim in the American Academy of Dramatic Arts in New York, one of the nation's oldest and finest schools of drama. (He facetiously told a *Playboy* interviewer that he had done it only because a friend said it was easy to meet girls there.) AADA, like most schools of drama in the United States at the time, was in the grip of the Stanislavskian or Method acting techniques of the sort the Actors Studio and its most famous graduate, Marlon Brando, had brought into the mainstream of American drama in the late forties.

Graduating in 1953, Cassavetes married a young stage actress named Gena Rowlands, whom he would cast as the leading lady of many of his subsequent films. He spent the middle years of the decade pounding the pavements of Manhattan with hundreds of other aspiring Method actors, playing occasional bit parts in films and on television, then still in its infancy. But Cassavetes was nothing if not ambitious, talented, and lucky, and the golden age of television acting was just around the corner. In his late twenties, between 1955 and 1959, he began experiencing the kind of success that the American dream is all about. Graduating from supporting to leading roles, he managed to get parts in almost all of the critically applauded live television drama series of the time, from "Kraft Theatre" to "The Twentieth Century Fox Hour" and "Lux Playhouse." At the same time, he worked his way up through a series of increasingly important film roles as well, going from minor roles in *Taxi* (1953) and *The Night Holds Terror* (1955) to major and starring parts in Don Siegel's *Crime In the Streets* (1956) and Martin Ritt's *Edge of the City* (1957). (Based on the teleplay *A Man Is Ten Feet Tall*, in which Cassavetes had also starred, *Edge of the City* was a sort of *On the Waterfront* melodrama in which Cassavetes played the Brando role opposite the evil Jack Warden.) By the age of twenty-nine, Cassavetes had already appeared in over a hundred television productions, been spotted by Hollywood as a young actor with box office potential, and been interviewed, photographed, and discussed in magazine feature stories (most prominently in *TV Guide* and *Look* magazine). As if all that were not enough to absorb his enormous ambitions and energies, he and Burt Lane had founded a New York drama workshop called the Variety Arts Studio on West 48th Street (at the site of the old Malin Studios) to train and showcase new talent.

In the language of press agentry, Cassavetes was on the fast track on his way to comfortable bankability. But it is characteristic and revealing that, flush with the kind of success that most other young actors only dream about, he felt frustrated, deeply dissatisfied with the roles available to him, and profoundly resentful of the studio system bureaucracies within which he was required to work. His independent temperament chaffed at taking orders from producers and directors who knew less about drama and acting than he thought he did, and all of his training at the American Academy of Dramatic Arts made him wince at the shallowness and superficiality of the roles available to a young actor. He had been trained in the Method creation of character and his subsequent films would be devoted to the most subtle explorations of identities in flux and crisis in contemporary film, and yet the creation of character was the one thing to which most of the melodramatic films of the 1950s were indifferent. Characters were stereotyped and locked into the most wooden and mechanical identities. Furthermore, in Hollywood's effort to steal television's audience, what possibilities of characterization that did exist were usually made secondary to emphasis on a suspenseful or action-heavy plot with a fast-paced succession of events to which even the best actors were kept too busy reacting to have the opportunity to do much acting.

Cassavetes' first foray into filmmaking was, in a sense, an attempt to break free from the kinds of films and the sorts of mechanical, prefabricated roles that were offered to him as an actor. But one must understand his position as an aspiring independent filmmaker in the context of two contrasting facts about independent work in New York in the 1950s. In the first place, Cassavetes was by no means operating in an artistic vacuum. New York was a hothouse of independent filmmaking from about the middle of the 1950s to near the end of the next decade. In that fifteen-year period, and principally in New York City, what has since been christened the American New Wave would be born, flourish, and subside (or move on to points West). When Cassavetes began *Shadows* in 1957, he was among the earliest of these independents, and certainly the most brilliantly audacious and creative, but he was by no means alone in his efforts.

But while acknowledging this groundswell of independent filmmaking, one must emphasize that the American New Wave and the particular filmmakers working in New York at this time were a notoriously unorganized group of artists. They had neither the financial solidarity of a Hollywood studio, the intellectual and critical cliquishness of the French filmmakers of the *Nouvelle Vague,* nor the sociological and political common cause of the Italian neorealists to unite them. Their work was accomplished largely as independently of one another as it was independent of Hollywood, which probably helps to explain why the dozen or so American independents working in narrative film in these fifteen years, though producing works that were they better known would be seen to rival those of any other movement in the history of film, have still not been studied with anything like the critical attention that has been given to the better-organized and more vocal trans-Atlantic cinematic movements. The American independents had neither money, polemics, nor politics to unite them. Like Cassavetes, they were the sort of mavericks who did not attach their names to manifestos or movements. Which is why, like the American jazz musicians who revolutionized the history of music in the twenties, thirties, and forties, these filmmakers are best understood in their sheer individualism and creative eccentricity, in the best sense of the words.

But once that is understood, it can still be valuable to locate Cassavetes and some of his fellow independent filmmakers in the force field of artistic relations and disjunctions that was New York City in the middle and late 1950s. In the first place, and despite the fact that its influence would probably be denied by all concerned, it would be hard to overestimate the impact both positively and negatively of the styles and technologies of the television programming of the time on both commercial and noncommercial filmmaking. While critics in the pages of *Sight and Sound* and *Film Culture* were only theorizing about the artistic potential of the "Kino-Eye," fifties television dramas, occasional documentaries, and news shows, precisely because they were made in such imperfect conditions—under extreme pressures of space and time, and often by young, inexperienced (and therefore inadvertantly iconoclastic) directors—were exploring the expressive possibilities of the long take, complex composition in depth, the elaborate sequence shot, rapid mobile reframings, and the simultaneous recording of several layers of live sound and action with a thoroughness beyond anything in Dziga Vertov.

On the other hand, it is easy nostalgically to overrate the innovativeness and interest of this same programming. The now legendary television dramas of the era (bracketed by Paddy Chayefsky's *Marty* on the one end in 1954 and Rod Serling's *Requiem for a Heavyweight* on the other end in 1962, with Reginald Rose's *Twelve Angry Men* in between in 1957) were almost without exception as artistically banal, safe, and pedestrian as the average "Masterpiece Theatre" presentation today. But such drama did provide occasionally creative opportunities for a small army of young and sometimes innovative Actors Studio and AADA-trained actors, writers, directors, and technicians, and brought them together in one city. It was in this fertile soil that future film directors Sidney Lumet, Arthur Penn, Delbert Mann, Martin Ritt, John Frankenheimer, and Irvin Kershner, and screenwriters Paddy Chayefsky and Abby Mann, to name only the best-known examples, began their careers on "Studio One," "Playhouse 90," "Goodyear Playhouse", and "Philco Playhouse." In the 1960s many would move on to Hollywood with their television-bred approaches to break the back of the hidebound studio and genre-film production methods that had so stunted Hollywood's growth in the fifties.

The television dramas of this period, with their skimpy production budgets, hurried schedules, tiny sets, and influx of Method-trained actors created, as if by accident, an American version of the old German *Kammerspielfilm*. Stories, settings, and events were simplified. Emphasis was placed on characterization. Because of limitations in production facilities, writers were encouraged to deal with the lives of fairly ordinary people in simple domestic surroundings. The exploration of character and personal relationships took precedence over plot and complexities of settings, lighting, and photography. But while *Kammerspielfilm* were typically photographed in medium- or long-shots, fifties television methods added the extreme close-up as a frequent expressive resource. Extreme close-ups simplified backgrounds, were fairly easy to light, and could add expressive punch to a pedestrian script. (For the same reasons, they were also used as a crutch by the poorer television directors to give their characters and their situations an intensity unearned by the true complexities of the narration or the acting.) It would be hard to overstate the impact of this *"Kammerspiel* in close-up" form of television drama on contemporaneous independent work in film. Cassavetes' first four films would have much more in common with these television dramas, with their prosaicism, their dramatic simplicity, intensity, and confinement to one or two sets, their mobile camerawork, their interest in ordinary people, and their use of frequent, extreme close-ups—Paddy Chayefsky's 1956 *The Bachelor Party* is an appropriate point of reference—than with the kinds of big-budget films Hollywood was making at the time.

The feature films Cassavetes (and most independent New York filmmakers) were watching in the fifties were not Hollywood films at all, but the films of the Italian neorealists. The great "art house" circuit of theatres that flourished in this country from the mid-sixties to the mid-seventies and many of the private and college film societies that exist today were only just being created in the late fifties. New York was a different place for seeing independent, uncommon, or foreign films than it is now. Only a handful of the very best known foreign films gathered enough financial and popular backing to be subtitled, shipped to this country, and find a theatre in which to be exhibited. But if one can speak of a happy result of such a lamentable state of affairs, it is that in the same years in which independent filmmaking was developing in New York, many of the classics of Italian neorealism were bursting on the innocent American eye with all the freshness and impact that they had had four, five, or six years before upon their first release in Italy.

Notwithstanding its "New Wave" appellation, American work of this period originated almost entirely independently of the French *Nouvelle Vague*. The much more relevant connection is with the work of the Italian neorealists. When asked what films mattered most to him at this period in his life, Cassavetes talked with excitement about *Umberto D, Bicycle Thief, Bellissima,* and *La Terra Trema.* (On the other hand, it is sometimes forgotten that *The 400 Blows*, which has been suggested by more than one critic as an analogue for *Shadows*, was released in this country three years *after* Cassavetes began work on his film.) If antecedents must be sought for an American artist's work (and it is an old sign of America's artistic insecurity that new work is invariably treated this way), the true antecedents of *Shadows, Too Late Blues, Faces*, and *Husbands* are buried in the paradoxical "poetic realism" of Zavattini, De Sica, and Visconti—in the strange, strong coloration of imaginative yearning and idealistic dreaming they impart to the forms and experiences of an invariably disappointing or impoverished "reality."

What is most interesting in the work of the Italian neorealists is only partly the superficial physical "realism" of the settings and narratives. The physical realism in these films is paralleled by an extreme stylization of narrative, characterization, and photography that communicates the pressure of imaginative realities at least equal to the material reality of the sociological facts represented. The neorealists were interested in the power of imagination to transform and transcend observed physical realities, and the tension between resistant sociological facts and attempted imaginative transformations of those facts is the central focus of their work. Considerations of imaginative enrichment and impoverishment are the true subjects of their films (and not considerations of literal enrichment and impoverishment, as is sometimes mistakenly assumed). No subjects are closer to Cassavetes' own work, or would have made a greater and more profound impression on him as a filmgoer.

But taken together both television *Kammerspiel* and Italian "poetic realism" seem altogether less important to an account of the genesis and development of Cassavetes' work in independent film than a third context in which it must be placed in the New York of the middle and late 1950s. Television dramas and the film work of De Sica and Zavattini may have crystalized Cassavetes' ideas about possible dramatic subjects, themes, and content for this work, but the most crucial discoveries a young artist makes are not thematic but formal and stylistic. As many a second film has proven, the discoveries embodied in novel or innovative subjects are soon exhausted and used up; the discovery of new styles and forms of expression represents the discovery of a new way of feeling and seeing, the discovery of a whole universe of possible contents that can never be exhausted. It was in the work of the New York "documentary" filmmakers of the middle and late fifties that Cassavetes discovered a possible style and form for the neorealist and

Kammerspiel interests in his work—a style that, as Cassavetes developed it, would prove limitless in its possible contents.

The development in the middle and late fifties of the Nagra portable tape recorder for direct sound recording and the blimped 16mm Arriflex for portable and hand-held camerawork resulted in a renaissance in American documentary filmmaking unlike anything since the early work of Robert Flaherty had launched the initial wave of interest in the documentary thirty years earlier. Specifically, the years between 1955 and 1963 saw the filming, among many other things, of Shirley Clarke's *A Scary Time* (1960), *The Connection* (1962), and *The Cool World* (1963); Lionel Rogosin's *On the Bowery* (1956) and *Come Back Africa* (1959); Morris Engel's *Lovers and Lollipops* (1955) and *Weddings and Babies* (1958); Bert Stern's *Jazz on a Summer's Day* (1959); *The Savage Eye* (1959) by Ben Maddow, Joseph Strick, and Sidney Meyers; Richard Leacock's *Davy* (1958), *The Children Were Watching* and *Primary* (both 1960); and *Pull My Daisy* (1959) by Robert Frank and Albert Leslie.

Cassavetes was conversant with the work of all of these filmmakers, and by his own account the work of the first three had a profound impact on him as a beginning director. At the least, this work offered him examples of privately financed and totally independent feature filmmaking using relatively portable equipment entirely outside of studio settings and studio systems of control. More profoundly, Clarke, Engel, and Rogosin initiated a stylistic revolution in the feature-length narrative film of which all of Cassavetes' subsequent work still has not exhausted the expressive potential. The genius of Clarke, Rogosin, Engel, and Cassavetes (and the first three learned as much from Cassavetes as he did from them, so I am in no sense suggesting a derivativeness in Cassavetes' work) lay in realizing (long in advance of Godard's related experiments) that documentary could describe a capacious, exploratory, interrogative style and not a narrow, polemical, or propagandistic content. (In the hands of filmmakers of less tact, delicacy, and loving tolerance for human foibles than Clarke, Rogosin, Engel, or Cassavetes, however, the tight close-ups, the unedited pauses, and the unblinking eye of the documentary camera can become a weapon. Godard's later work and most of the films of Fredrick Wiseman show how extremely hard it is to prevent documentary exploration from turning into documentary exploitation.)

The documentary style of Clarke, Rogosin, and Engel departed radically from the "poetic" photography, editing, and sound effects of earlier documentarists. Flaherty, John Grierson, and Willard Van Dyke had, consciously or unconsciously, emulated the styles of Hollywood film in their photography, lighting, and editing. In contrast, Clarke and the others strenuously refused to simplify human experience and the process of communication in the ways Hollywood films did.

Histories of the documentary give short shrift to Clarke, Engel, and Rogosin, if they are mentioned at all, because in the strict sense of the word none of them made documentaries. And that was their most innovative and suggestive quality. They (like Cassavetes in the apparently "improvised" scenes in his films that were in fact carefully rehearsed) were pseudo-documentarists. That is to say, they made their "documentaries" with characters, scenes, and stories that were actually scripted and rehearsed in advance (or refined through the process of repeated improvisation). Shirley Clarke's *The Connection* is only the most obvious example. As Polonius-like critics made uncomfortable by anything that stretched their critical categories or their minds a little were captiously eager to point out, *The Connection* was a Jack Gelber play masquerading as a documentary event. (Clarke filmed it as if the filmmaker and the crew had simply come upon the drug scene in the course of making a documentary.) *The Cool World, On the Bowery, Come Back Africa, The Little Fugitive,* and *Lovers and Lollipops,* to name the most important examples, all combine sections of documentary or pseudo-documentary footage with scripted actions and directed improvisations.

The result (and what must have made such work especially suggestive for Cassavetes with his AADA training, stage experience, and passionate interest in the expressive possibilities of particular acting strategies) was *cinéma vérité* that could analyze and develop complex characters and the small group interactions of several characters much more exhaustively and subtly than a true documentary ever could, limited as actual documentary was to events and actions that actually happened to take place in front of the camera crew and under the lights. At the same time, the documentary style and structure of such films opened up entirely new dramatic possibilities with respect to what could now be included on film as the record of an event, beyond anything in a Hollywood film. The mobile, eccentric movements of the documentary camera and live omnidirectional sound recording are superb examples of how apparent technical crudities could be converted into stylistic insights. They allowed a filmmaker to create and record a

polyphonic, layered reality, in which three, four, five, or more simultaneous events or interactions might be registered successively to be
pieced together by the viewer.

In addition, this form of documentary filmmaking changed the possibilities of film characterization. The creation and presentation of character could break most of the Hollywood molds so that, instead of being
tidily organized around a stereotypical set of qualities carefully presented in an initial series of scenes, characters could develop in less
programatic and simplified ways. The concentricity of Hollywood character development was replaced by the eccentricity of documentary
development, where competing, often conflicting, bits of evidence
about a character had to be carefully pieced together by the audience as
they watched the film. Characters could systematically indulge in various sorts of self-protective, self-concealing performances in the presence of the camera, which must be decoded before they can be read by
the audience. Rival and democratically equal characters in the same
film could compete for a viewer's attention and sympathy in ways that
the Hollywood star system, with its strict hierarchical ordering of actors
into leading, supporting, and bit parts and the accompanying rhetoric
of dovetailed close-ups, reverse shots, and long shots, always directing
a viewer's attention to the important place and the important actors in
each scene, could never allow.

But perhaps most importantly, the narrative structure of the documentary form itself and its abandonment of a rising and falling pattern
of action arranged around one or two central figures pointed the way
to free film from the monotonic pacing and plots of conventional melodramatic narrative, with its predictable patterns of climaxes and resolutions. Local eccentricities of narrative pacing and the irregular rhythms
of personal performance that are leveled and regularized by the
rhythms of orthodox Hollywood cutting patterns are let into the film.
Cinéma vérité style, in short, imparted a new density to each individual
shot and each individual character within it.

Evidence of the effects of these stylistic discoveries and of the new
expressive possibilities they offered Cassavetes are to be found
throughout *Shadows, Too Late Blues, A Child Is Waiting, Faces* and *Husbands*. But if it is important to understand Cassavetes' early work in the
context of experimentation in documentary filmmaking in the late
1950s, it is equally important to notice the filmmakers Cassavetes' work
turns away from, the stylistic experiments he deliberately chose *not* to
draw upon or to affiliate himself with. At the same time as the devel-

opments in documentary filmmaking described above, an even more prolific and articulate group of filmmakers was making films and conducting screenings in New York. They are the filmmakers generally grouped together under the rubric of the American avant-garde, whose unofficial history has been chronicled most ably in P. Adams Sitney's *Visionary Film: The American Avant-Garde, 1943–1978*. The film avant-garde has never been a monolithic or homogeneous group, and this is neither the time nor the place for a thumbnail sketch of the wranglings and power struggles between rival theorists and practitioners. Suffice it to say that, from around 1955 to 1965, a highly vocal and creative group of independent and theoretically sophisticated filmmakers gathered loosely together around the figure of Jonas Mekas (himself an extremely articulate and effective film theorist and critic as well as a filmmaker), the journal *Film Culture* (which published its first issue in January 1955 and of which Mekas was the editor, chief fundraiser, and principal writer), and the distribution resources of Amos Vogel's Cinema 16 and, subsequently, the New York Filmmakers' Cooperative (established in January 1961).

Cassavetes' relationship to these filmmakers was more than tangential. He was at the time (and still is) a close personal friend of Mekas's; he was nominally a member (though he never attended meetings) of Mekas's New American Cinema Group (founded in 1960) and knew almost all of the other filmmakers and actors involved with it; and, upon completion of *Shadows*, he was frequently mentioned in essays in *Film Culture*. Cassavetes was the first recipient of Mekas's Independent Film Award in 1959, an award that although it would go to what might be considered fairly conventional filmmakers for the two subsequent years (to Robert Frank and Alfred Leslie for *Pull My Daisy* in 1960 and to Richard Leacock for *Primary* in 1961) would subsequently become a Who's Who of the leading American avant-gardists (going consecutively to Stan Brakhage, Jack Smith, Andy Warhol, Harry Smith, Gregory Markopoulos, Michael Snow, Kenneth Anger, Robert Breer, and James Broughton in the years from 1962 to 1975). Furthermore, most of the earliest critical and commercial support for *Shadows* (and especially for the first version of the film, the one Cassavetes rejected as too "arty") came from Mekas and the group of avant-garde filmmakers and film theorists affiliated with *Film Culture*.

Cassavetes' initial connections with the filmmakers and theorists of the New York avant-garde were obvious and manifold. But one notices them only to have to attempt to explain the enormous gap that opened up almost immediately between his work and that of all of the "true" avant-gardists (i.e., everyone discussed in Sitney's book). The chronological turning point in Cassavetes' falling out with the New York avant-garde came at the end of 1959 with the release of the second version of *Shadows*. And his decision to go to Hollywood around the same time to star in the "Johnny Staccato" television series and subsequently to make films for Paramount was, needless to say, regarded as the last straw even by those who had tolerated the remaking of *Shadows*. Charges of commercial sell-out and betrayal were whispered everywhere, and, from that point on, the avant-garde have had no more interest in Cassavetes' work than he has had in theirs.

But it would be a mistake to interpret Cassavetes' falling-out with the film avant-garde as merely a matter of envy, misunderstanding, or conflict of personalities. It is not accidental that, like virtually every other such study, Sitney's book mentions none of Cassavetes' films except *Shadows*, and finds it difficult to conduct a sustained discussion even of that film employing the terms and categories applied to avant-garde film. In hindsight, Cassavetes' initial links to the avant-gardists around Mekas appear more and more to have been a case of mistaken identity. What the avant-gardists only gradually realized, and many film writers have still not understood, is that Cassavetes' work is as radically opposed to the entire avant-garde sensibility as it is to the forms of experience in a typical Hollywood film.

A comprehensive analysis of the aesthetic and cultural assumptions of the avant-garde filmmakers has yet to be written, and though this is not the place to attempt such an analysis, several aspects of the movement may be pointed out that should make it more apparent why Cassavetes could never have remained affiliated with it. In *Visionary Film*, Sitney masterfully describes what his title intimates—the essentially High Romantic impulse that informs and everywhere motivates avant-garde filmmaking. This visionary impulse necessarily takes many different forms in the work of particular filmmakers, but the common thread linking all of them, and in effect defining the avant-garde aspiration as distinct from that of other work in film, is an interest in special states of consciousness as they can be created and cultivated by the isolated, individual artist and expressed in the form of the unique, self-contained, self-referential aesthetic object. In their purest form, the works of these avant-gardists are expressions of dream states, trances, reveries, lyrical effusions, symbolic and mythopoetic visions, and other forms of transcendental experience essentially separate from the forms and forces of prosaic, ordinary life.

They are the filmic manifestation of the artistic movement that Frank Kermode in *Romantic Image* traces more generally in the forms of certain influential kinds of late nineteenth- and early twentieth-century symbolist and imagist poetry, painting, and criticism. As Kermode suggestively argues in a book that unfortunately never takes notice of intimately related developments in subsequent avant-garde film (and work in video much later in the century), this cult of the isolated, usually alienated romantic sensibility and this cultivation of unique visionary or transcendental "romantic images" can be traced back in artistic history to certain nineteenth-century readings of the work of Blake, Keats, Shelley, and several French and German poets, by influential English Pre-Raphaelites and many fin de siècle European painters, poets, and critics. Its earliest artistic manifestations were in British Pre-Raphaelitism and French *Symbolisme* of the nineteenth century, but its fullest flowering was in early twentieth-century symbolist poetry and certain forms of surrealism in the fine arts, all of which in the first three decades of this century came to energize what we now call European "modernism". To extend Kermode's argument beyond the point where he leaves off, one might suggest that it was via these modernist movements in the arts that European avant-garde filmmaking developed, crossed the Atlantic, and subsequently determined the contours of American avant-garde filmmaking, which as Sitney clearly shows has its deepest roots in European artistic traditions.

But the point of this cultural excursus is to emphasize that, from the very beginning Cassavetes' work has totally rejected the cultivation of this symbolist, visionary, and Romantic sensibility. The individual visionary impulse for Cassavetes must always be tested against the specific temporal rhythms and personal resistances of a social interaction. While the avant-gardists are devoted to making "lyrical" or "poetic" films, Cassavetes always forces the "lyrical" impulse (whether his own or that of a character) to negotiate the obstacles and constraints of a time-bound social narrative. The "poetry" must pass the test of living in a "prose" narrative and a "prose" world. Far from being a merely reactionary or conservative stance, Cassavetes' insistence on making films with characters and plots (in contrast to the avant-gardists' de facto rejection of such things in favor of allegiance to the solitary visionary impulse) is in fact a complex act of interrogation of the visionary impulse. Vision is forced into contact with the forms of personality, social relations, and temporal events, all the aspects of experience that resist conversion into vision. Vision must struggle with the nonvisionary.

It is implicit in my argument that there is something distinctively American in this attempt to make poetry live the life of prose, just as it might be argued that there is something more typically European in the avant-garde aesthetic position. If Cassavetes seems to make more conventional films than Stan Brakhage, Michael Snow, Peter Kubelka, or Ernie Gehr—that is to say, films that can never escape the entanglements of characterization, plotting, and social relationships—it is only that Cassavetes is much less blithely optimistic about the visionary prospects of human expression and everyday life. He has a characteristically American skepticism (some would call it anti-intellectualism or anti-aestheticism) about the capacity of the social "I" to express itself in terms of, or to live up to the aspirations of, the visionary "eye."

The remaking of *Shadows* represented Cassavetes' decisive turn away from the styles of the avant-gardists. He repudiated the visionary sensibility embodied in the "fancy" camerawork and editing of the first version to choose in the second to explore the situations and emotional lives of particular characters locked into a time-bound narrative form. That, in short, is why what the avant-gardists liked about the first version of *Shadows* was exactly what Cassavetes hated, and vice versa.

The tempestuous history of Cassavetes' brief affiliation with the New York avant-garde is quickly told. The first version of *Shadows* was screened at three free midnight screenings at the Paris Theater (to packed houses totaling over 2,000 viewers) in the fall of 1958. In a special ceremony on 26 January 1959, Jonas Mekas personally awarded Cassavetes *Film Culture*'s "First Independent Film Award" with a citation that was subsequently printed in *Film Culture*:

Since John Cassavetes' first film *Shadows*, independently produced by Maurice McEndree and Seymour Cassel, more than any other recent American film, presents contemporary reality in a fresh and unconventional manner, it rightly deserves the first Independent Film Award.

Cassavetes in *Shadows* was able to break out of conventional molds and traps and retain original freshness. . . . The situations and atmosphere of New York night life are vividly, cinematically, and truly caught in *Shadows*. It breathes an immediacy that the cinema of today vitally needs if it is to be a living and contemporary art.

In the months that followed, Mekas began an all-out personal campaign to rally support for Cassavetes' film. In a number of articles and
allusions to it, *Film Culture* heralded *Shadows* as one of the major American films of the era; Mekas wrote about the film in no less than four of
his "Movie Journal" columns in the *Village Voice,* and sang its praises to
thousands of listeners in public lectures and radio discussion pro-
grams. Never had Mekas or the New York avant-garde more warmly
welcomed a new filmmaker. But even as Cassavetes accepted Mekas's
praise and *Film Culture*'s Independent Film Award, he was working on
reshooting and reediting *Shadows.* When the revised version of the film
was given its world premiere screening through Cinema 16 on 11 November 1959, the profound philosophical and aesthetic split that exists
to this day between the two groups of independent filmmakers was
articulated. Mekas felt publicly embarrassed and personally angered by
Cassavetes' changes. On 18 November 1959 and 27 January 1960, he
wrote two scathing reviews of the revised film in his *Village Voice*
column, saying that he had been "ridiculously betrayed," and calling
the revised *Shadows,* among other things, "a bad commercial film, with
everything that I was praising completely destroyed." He compared it
unfavorably to Robert Frank and Alfred Leslie's *Pull My Daisy,* which
had had its premiere screening on the same night.

   In the weeks following Mekas's initial review, the letters column of
the *Voice* was largely given over to choosing sides in the dispute between Cassavetes and Mekas. Amos Vogel wrote in to side with Cassavetes. Ben Carruthers, one of the principal actors in *Shadows,* wrote
in to side with Mekas. Cassavetes himself jumped into the fray with a
letter to the *Voice* that broke publicly with Mekas, saying that he had
"blustered forth ridiculous accusations at the second version of the
picture."

   By the final issue of 1959, when the letters column of the *Voice* was
officially declared closed to further statements on the subject, the philosophical and artistic lines were drawn hard and fast. Frank and Leslie
would be awarded the Second Independent Film Award for *Pull My
Daisy,* and Anger, Conner, Snow, Brakhage, and other avant-gardists
would continue the trajectory of the High Romantic visionary aesthetic.
After his brief exposure to avant-garde filmmaking ideals that extolled
the centrality of the visionary "eye," Cassavetes utterly rejected the cult
of the poetic and the visionary, preferring instead to chronicle the
unvisionary mess and muddle of the social "I" trapped in events tran-
spiring in the real world of time, space, and society. (The accidental

conjunction of *Shadows* and *Pull My Daisy* on the same program offered an accurate summary of the differences between the two kinds of filmmaking. *Shadows*—in its second version—is an exploration of characters and narrative in real time and space that perfectly contrasts with *Pull My Daisy*'s evocation of an independent stylistic world of purely cinematic and literary times, spaces, rhythms.) As Cassavetes explained in his letter to the *Voice*, in remaking *Shadows* he restored the structures of narrative, characterization, and temporal organization that the first version of the film had abrogated, the very kinds of structure the avant-garde filmmakers were indifferent or opposed to.

Cassavetes' work in those years, along with that of Rogosin, Engel, and Clarke would represent the beginning of a line of independent filmmaking that unfortunately has yet to be chronicled with anything like the attention given the avant-gardists. Subsequent filmmaking in that independent tradition would include the immensely interesting work of Robert Kramer, John Korty, Elaine May, Paul Morrissey, James Ivory, and the late Barbara Loden. Like John Cassavetes, they would all reject the poetic highroad of the avant-gardists to choose rather to make their ways along the winding earthbound footpaths of narrative filmmaking, where there are no visionary escape routes around the temporal and spatial burdens and entanglements of mundane social and emotional life.

But to return to the genesis of *Shadows*, the production was launched with the audacity and iconoclasm for which Cassavetes would soon be famous (and infamous). It was during a talk show publicity interview for his most important part yet, the lead in *Edge of the City*, that his first independent production was born, early in 1957. Instead of talking up *Edge of the City*, Cassavetes astonished Jean Shepherd and the listeners of his "Night People" radio show by downplaying Martin Ritt's movie and instead outrageously proposing to the radio audience: "If people really want to see a movie about *people*, they should just contribute money"— to him, of course. No record of Cassavetes' fund-raising pitch survives today, beyond his own account of it, but if one can judge from the immediate results, his improvised performance that night as an entrepreneur and film producer must have been more interesting, creative, and persuasive than any of the creaky and schematic performances in the film he was supposed to be plugging. It was just the sort of spur of the minute performance a character in one of Cassavetes' films might be called on to make. When more than $2,000 in dollar bills came trickling into the station over the next week, Cassavetes' career as a fund-raiser, producer, writer, and director was launched.

There was no way Cassavetes could have known from that scrappily improvised beginning what he was getting himself into. *Shadows* would consume the better part of the next three years of Cassavetes' life: most of 1957 and all of 1958 being filmed and edited in its first version (the print of the film Cassavetes would repudiate); all of 1959 being rethought, reshot, reedited, and rereleased in its present form. The total budget for both versions ran only $40,000, a feat made possible only by using begged, borrowed, and rented lights, sound equipment, and a 16mm camera more often than not hand-held by Cassavetes himself. (As he later curtly told an interviewer, it was hand-held not out of any desire to be artistic or to imitate the French "caméra stylo" filmmakers, but simply because he could not afford a dolly.) Almost without exception, *Shadows* used unemployed actors from Cassavetes' own drama workshop and was loosely based on a series of dramatic improvisations he and his actors had been building scenes around there.

And the result of Cassavetes' efforts was, in his own terms, a film about real people, in real situations, a story at the furthest remove from the hyped-up Manichean melodramas Hollywood was obsessed with making in the late fifties, a film as unlike the cold-warish confrontations of good and evil in which Cassavetes had himself acted as possible.

It was no accident that Cassavetes' actors chose to play under their own names in the film. No small part of *Shadows'* sureness of touch is the result of its events and characterizations being in many ways almost indistinguishable from the off-screen experiences and identities of these young actors. It is the lightly comic narration of the experiences of two brothers and a sister living together in New York, and learning, as Cassavetes' apprentice actors themselves were learning, how to "play" the city in every sense of the word. Complicating their identities is the fact that the two youngest are blacks who pass for whites.

Hughie (Hugh Hurd) is the oldest. He is an aspiring black jazz singer learning how to negotiate business deals, how to write and rehearse a professional show, how to perform in front of an audience, and generally how to keep his artistic, commercial, and personal accounts in order in his relations with his business contacts, his friends, and his manager, Rupert (Rupert Crosse).

Ben (Ben Carruthers), the younger brother, is a harmless drifter who has read Jack Kerouac, wears black, slinks from corner to corner of a room, puts on sunglasses at night, and vulnerably and innocently

Explorations of identity
—*Hugh and Lelia*

postures through every possible variation on the angry young man about town, James Dean repertory of roles with his two white buddies, Denis and Tom (Denis Sallas and Tom Allen).

But the real "star" of this movie without stars, is the sister Lelia (played by Lelia Goldoni in one of the most comically outrageous performances in any Cassavetes film, a performance that makes *Shadows* the tiny comic masterpiece it is). She primps, preens, postures, and flirts through every social encounter of the film and steals every scene she appears in. Lelia goes through three coquettish flirtations in the course of the film. The first is with David (David Pokitillow), a tweedy, well-meaning, meek West Village intellectual who takes her to cocktail parties. From him she moves on to Tony (played by Nicholas Ray's son, Tony Ray), a callow, naive make-out artist, with whom she makes love on their second meeting. And she ends up dating Davey (Davey Jones), a black man alternately bewildered and bedazzled by her shenanigans. Lelia reminds a viewer of no one so much as one of the mysterious and fascinating young women painted by John Singer Sargent, or one of the brilliant young heroines in one of Henry James's early novels or stories. Like their creations, she is a figure too mercurial, too dramatic, and too imaginatively stimulating to be reduced to any one simple "identity." She is a consummate performer with a blithe confidence in her powers of making up ever-new roles and identities for herself as she goes along. She remakes herself and remakes the scenes she delights in creating as often as the impulse strikes her. But, just as in the work of Henry James, it is exactly the pains and problems created by such a radical commitment to one's own freedom that interest her creator. The rest of *Shadows* will be devoted to exploring the social and ethical constraints placed on a performer of such imaginative flexibility and prowess. (The serious subtext that runs through *Shadows*—though in this buoyantly high-spirited film it only surfaces in a few scenes—is that however brilliant Lelia's performances may seem to be, however much she may seem actually capable of changing her personal identity, she is utterly unable to affect the reality of her racial identity, and the facts of biology, family, and society that hem her in in a world that is not racially color blind.)

Cassavetes made *Shadows* as a reply to the melodramatic plots he had been confronted with as a actor, and no film more deftly debunks melodramatic constructions of reality. The way it does so is not by keeping melodrama out of the film, but by allowing it in and showing us the comic results. Tony, Lelia, and Ben in one scene or another could have stepped straight out of *Written On the Wind* or any other overwrought fifties melodrama. But the very point of *Shadows* is the inappropriateness of their melodramatic postures in this warmly personal film. Ben's rendition of a member of the Beat Generation is as ludicrous as it is affected. Lelia's self-dramatizations would look grand even on Greta Garbo or Joan Crawford. And Tony's clumsy machismo would embarrass Brando or Dean. *Shadows* is a dissection of the sorts of films and roles its characters (and its actors) would have grown up on. What links the stories of Lelia, Hugh, and Ben is that they are each, in their distinctive ways, learning how to "perform" in public. In the most practical sense, the subject of the film is what any of Cassavetes' young actors would themselves have studied most strenuously in both their professional and personal lives—how to hack a personal path through the jungle of styles, performances, personalities, and possibilities of expression available to them in New York City.

If one wanted to describe Cassavetes' films in terms of a formula (though, of course, the interest of any particular film is not in the general formula but in the characters' specific responses to their immediate situations), one might say that he is repeatedly attracted to moments when conventional, automatic roles, rules, and codes of behavior break down. Such moments, needless to say, may become times of extraordinary opportunity and growth (as they are in *Shadows*), or of crisis and tragedy (as they are in *Faces*), depending on a particular character's capacities of response to the loss of customary supports. During these "crises of identity" (in Erik Erikson's useful phrase) it becomes incumbent upon the individual himself to bring into existence whatever values or momentary stays against confusion there will be. *Shadows* is a film about just such a time of possibility and opportunity: a story of adolescents on the frightening, exciting brink of adulthood, exploring the possibilities of improvising an existence with the world all before them and everywhere to choose. Cassavetes significantly removes all adult figures from their world. There are no assured roles or easy role models from which to acquire unearned identities either by imitation or rebellion. In Max Lerner's brilliant characterization of the essential American predicament, the characters of *Shadows* are assertively thrust into a "moral interregnum." They are psychologically at sea, unmoored from all inherited values, with neither anchor, ballast, nor pilot for the course they must learn to navigate. *Shadows* gives us in microcosm a glimpse of the moral universe in which all of Cassavetes' subsequent films will be set, a new world where all the fixed relationships and identities of the old world have been thrown into flux and are up for appropriation, a brave new world where the work of creating and recreating oneself through performance is necessarily an unending, individualistic, bootstrap operation.

But lest that sound too dauntingly serious and abstract, it is important to emphasize that *Shadows* (like Fellini's *I Vitelloni*, to which it seems indebted) is at its heart a comedy, and most specifically a comic study of the excesses, ineptnesses, awkwardnesses, and embarrassments of these performances. But the true distinction of *Shadows* and the first indication of the greatness of this director is the gentleness and humaneness of the film's comedy. Where another director might have gone in for easy satire, or a self-protective smirk, Cassavetes' tenderly comic camera refuses to make a quick and dirty killing, or to take a cheap shot. His comedy (unlike Altman's, for example) is never a sneer of contempt or patronization, or a demonstration of his superiority to his characters. On the contrary, the comedy of *Shadows* (and of all of Cassavetes' work, for he is essentially a director of the sort of love and tolerance for human fallibility that finds its finest flowering in comedy) is a form of affection, a way of protecting his characters, of charming and amusing his audience out of sterner, more severely moral, and less flexibly responsive judgments about them. We cannot get mad at them because we are smiling so much of the time. We allow Tony, Lelia, and all the others such exemplary excesses of behavior because Cassavetes succeeds in making them so interesting and so entertaining even in their errors.

Cassavetes' patient, attentive close-ups and long scenes linger on their botched performances until we see deep in their eyes that *they* see their absurdity, too. Rather than merely attacking Hugh's clumsiness, Lelia's melodramatizations, or Ben's apparent smugness, Cassavetes makes us aware of the human consciousness and good intentions behind these frustrated efforts. The beauty of the film is in casting these immature actors (who probably would have been incapable of more subtly modulated playing) in the roles of these adolescents (who are uninterested in more subtly modulated playing). It is essential to the comic effect of the film and to our tolerance of these particular characters that they be young and immature; the effect would only be pathetic or farcical if we saw middle-aged or mature characters carrying on this way. *Shadows* deliberately focuses on figures who are assertively unfinished with their own process of figuration; characters still on the way to forming their characters: Hugh trying to cut a figure in the commercial world of business and professional performance; Benny trying out ideological and cultural stances; Lelia experimenting with personal and social relations. As much for the characters they play as for his young actors, *Shadows* is a study in the creation of character. What makes us tolerate (and even love) their mistakes is that these performers (both as characters and as actors) are at the age where experimentation and excess are still possibly the road to the palace of wisdom.

It was just this aspect of the film that most confused the initial

reviewers, who carped at the melodramatic excesses of particular performances and the awkward and unpolished quality of many of the
relationships in the film (for example, the pauses and hesitations built
into conversational exchanges, and the banality and clumsiness of
many of the relationships). What they failed to realize was that these
things were not accidental lapses in the film, but its very method and
interest. *Shadows* is a film that chooses as its explicit subject the awkwardnesses, excesses, and uncertainties in its characters' performances
with one another. The reviewers who objected to the unpolished,
unfinished, improvisatory quality of the relationships in the movie
(which they felt must have been the result of inadequate rehearsal,
directing, or scripting) failed to see that the unpolished, unfinished,
improvisatory quality of these lives is the point of the film. They were
watching the improvisations not of actors acting but of characters
living.

A more visionary, apocalyptic, or melodramatic cinema may want
(or need) to free its characters from accountability to the specific, time-
bound rhythms and pacings of particular human interactions, but for
Cassavetes the second-by-second timings of a human relationship are
everything. To remove the momentary awkwardnesses, hesitations, or
miscues in two or more characters' dealings with one another for the
sake of a picture that looked more polished, more finished, and more
tightly edited would be to change the nature of the event he is interested in recording. An ideal character is not someone who transcends
or rises above these personal rhythms of interaction, but someone who
learns to live within them, to make something of them. It is in this sense
that all of Cassavetes' characters are forced to be improvisors, and all
of his scenes are scenes of improvisation, as long as one remembers that
Cassavetes is interested not in the timings and pacings of an actor's
improvisations but the timings and pacings of an improvised human
relationship.

As examples of how improvisation works in the film, consider a
couple of the scenes in which we are introduced to Tony. (Quotation
from the spoken dialogue of *Shadows* necessarily leaves out much of the
content of any given scene—just as the quotation of only the dialogue
passages in a novel would leave out a large part of what is going on at
any time in it—but as long as one keeps in mind that Tony's words are
only one of several parallel "texts" present to a viewer at any moment,
the quotation is not entirely misleading.)

We first see Tony at a so-called sophisticated cocktail party at David's
place, a gathering of Village cognoscenti that is a comic set piece of

intellectual vapidity. He is clumsily trying to work his way into a conversation with any pretty girl in sight. First he tries to worm his way
into a ludicrous pseudo-intellectual discussion of "existentialism," a
word of which he obviously does not even know the meaning. Then he
sidles up to a beautiful blonde Marilyn Monroe type in a low-cut dress
who is sitting alone off to one side of the room.

Tony: Are you a writer also?
Blonde: Oh no. (*Wiggle. Squeal.*) Do I look like a writer?
Tony: I don't know anymore.
Blonde: I'm a dancer!
Tony: Oh a dancer! (*Pause.*) Wonderful! (*Pause.*) A ballet dancer?
Blonde: No . . . an exotic dancer.
Tony: (*Pause.*) Exotic?
Blonde: Don't you know what that is?
Tony: Not really. (*Pause.*) No.
Blonde: It's a kind of modern dance . . . but . . . more exotic!
Tony: That's great! I'll have to come and watch you some time.
Blonde: I'm not dancing right now. I'm going to have a baby in March.
Tony: (*Embarrassed.*) You . . . That's great. (*Pause.*) You're going to have a
           baby. Terrific. (*Pause.*) Congratulations. That's good news.
Blonde: We think so, don't we honey? (*Turning to her husband, whose voice is now
           heard on the soundtrack.*)
Tony: I think I'll just excuse myself and fix my drink a little.

The awkwardnesses, the long pauses, and the banality of Tony's come-
on are not the result of inadequate rehearsal or editing, but the point
of the scene.

Tony has better luck with Lelia. After meeting her at David's, he
arranges a rendezvous in Central Park for the next day, and as they
walk together later, he steers her to his apartment with the wonderfully
subtle approach: "Do you see where we are? . . .That's where I live,
number 7. Come on up. Have a drink. You know you're beautiful." As
they enter his apartment and he locks the door behind them, he plies
her with love talk so passionately sensitive as: "Don't you move. . . .
You know you've got the softest lips I've ever felt. . . . Love you, Lelia.
Love you, honey." In a moment that combines the comic clumsiness of
a scene by Billy Wilder with the poignant, romantic inarticulateness of
one by Nicholas Ray, Cassavetes has Tony clutching and pawing Lelia
so crudely that he almost sends them both tumbling on the floor with
their coats still on.

The film fades out prior to their making love, to fade back in on their
post-coital conversation. (Here, as in all of his future work, Cassavetes
is as indifferent to mere physical actions—in this case, the action of

making love—as he is fascinated by imaginative transactions—of making something of one's having made love.) The conversation that follows is a tour de force of awkwardness, inarticulateness, and insensitivity:

Tony: Lelia—Really, if I'd known this was the first time for you, I wouldn't have touched you.

Lelia: I didn't know it could be so awful.

Tony: (*Pulling her face over towards his, in order to try to comfort her by giving her a kiss.*) Don't be so upset, sweetheart, baby. It will be much easier next time.

Lelia: There isn't going to be a next time.

Tony: Want a cigarette, huh? Come on, have a cigarette.

Lelia: No.

Tony: I'm sorry if I disappointed you, I guess I did. (*Feigning hurt feelings.*)

Lelia: (*Rolling over and putting her head on him.*) I was so frightened. (*She smiles slightly to herself.*) I kept saying to myself you mustn't cry. If you love a man, you shouldn't be frightened.

Tony: (*Regaining his poise. On familiar territory.*) It's only natural. There isn't a girl in the world that wouldn't feel the same way. She's got to.

Lelia: (*Reassured. She looks at him.*) What happens now?

Tony: What happens? What do you mean what happens now? (*Worried. Beginning to lose his supreme masculine confidence.*)

Lelia: I mean, do I stay with you?

Tony: (*Almost frantic.*) Stay with me? (*He hesitates.*) You mean live with me?

Lelia: (*Calmly.*) Yes.

Tony: (*Scared. Tentatively.*) You . . .want . . .to?

Lelia: No. I want to go home.

Tony: (*Vastly relieved. In control again. He cuddles her.*) Okay, baby. (*Protectively.*)

Though his critics seem to have mistaken the one for the other, what obviously interests Cassavetes in a scene like this is not the improvisations of acting, but the improvisations of an uncomfortably intimate human relationship. It is in moments such as this that his use of this story with these actors seems to border on the inspired. We are watching characters learning to play parts—not Tony Ray and Lelia Goldoni learning how to play Tony and Lelia after making love, but Tony the character exploring how to play Tony the wise, male protector and consoler, and Lelia the character learning how to play Lelia the sensitive, hurt woman. (Incidentally, if there is any doubt about whether Cassavetes sees through Lelia's posturings in this scene as thoroughly as he sees through Tony's, it is dispelled by the shots that immediately follow the lines quoted: three successive lap dissolves of

Lelia striking the most hackneyed and melodramatic postures of the hurt woman. There are "arty" shots in the second version of the film, but they are never ends in themselves. Like these, they always comment on a character's merely rhetorical postures.)

It is no accident that Cassavetes sets his story on the movie block of 42nd Street, or that the first time we see Lelia alone (it is a scene in which Cassavetes makes a brief cameo appearance), she is staring at a movie marquee with a poster of Brigitte Bardot. Roles from forties and fifties films and novels flicker just behind each character's performance, like the neon flicker of the movie house posters they repeatedly pass in front of. *Shadows* keeps reminding us that this is the generation of Brando, Dean, Bardot, Kerouac, and Charlie Parker. It is the era of the sex kitten, the hipster, the jazz jammer, and the soulfully alienated actor. A large element of the fascination of *Shadows* is watching Cassavetes' young characters alternately blending into and asserting themselves against the same cultural and dramatic stereotypes that the young actors playing those characters are playing off and with.

Shadows recognizes the extent to which no cultural, sexual, or social performance is free, and that personal freedom can never simply be willed into existence. As the Times Square movie houses remind us (and these characters), a particular performance is always related to previous performances, and grows out of them; it can never escape their influence. Cassavetes' aesthetic of performance may have originated in an actor's insight into the preparation and rehearsal of a role, but it has profound moral and social implications that extend far beyond acting strategies. He realizes, as D. H. Lawrence understood, that there is no primitive (or transcendental) self to release or break free of influences—"only through a fine and delicate knowledge can we release our impulses." In Cassavetes' films, as in the great tradition of American literature, freedom is imagined not as a visionary escape from, or a transcendence of, the limitations of society, history, and biography, but as a subtler, deeper immersion in them; not as a flight from the particular impurities of experience, but as more complex recognition of them. Only in admitting the stylistic impurities of experience into one's performance, incorporating them into one's self, and not shutting them out, is a stylistic and imaginative mastery possible.

Reviewers in the late fifties and early sixties were quick to spell out the racial connotations of the title of this story of two blacks who pass for whites in a predominantly white world. But what they failed to see was that the question of racial identity is only a special instance of the larger question of human identity that runs through the film. All of the characters in *Shadows,* not just Ben and Lelia, are "shadows" in the Shakespearean sense of the word—pieces and shades of larger, unrealized possible identities. (It was obviously this sense of the word that Cassavetes and Lane had in mind when they initially gave their drama workshop the same name.)

Characters are repeatedly lapsing into shadows of previous characters, roles, and styles, and therefore shadows of themselves. Such is the complexity of these characterizations that they can even admit that they are half aware of and half embarrassed by their own role-playing. The first time we meet David, the writer and "intellectual" of the film, Ben is criticizing the "beat generation jazz" David puts in his novels. Of course, the only reason it threatens Ben (as we, he, and David all know) is that "beat generation jazz" is too close to the role he is trying to play in his own life. In each of their final scenes, the three principal characters explicitly or implicitly communicate an awareness that they have been playing roles, and their weariness with the whole process.

But one does not want to overemphasize the importance of these final recognitions. The three final scenes seem merely a formality, a technical device to end the film, and we have no reason to believe that Lelia, Ben, and Hugh will be any different in the time after the film has ended than they were in the time during which we got to know them. That is to say, there is very little of the formulaic "growth," "development," or "progress" in these characters that more traditional films train us to expect in the course of a movie. In fact, what makes the characters in *Shadows* so continuously interesting and prevents them from lapsing into mere "shadows" of previous cinematic and novelistic stereotypes is just Cassavetes' refusal to subject them to a simple pattern of development, consistency, or coherence. Ben, Lelia, Hughie, and Tony interest us precisely because their performances do not congeal into studies of "character," psychology, or development. They are not denied moments of zaniness, inconsistency, or improvisatory inspiration because these would violate some tidy, coherent, package of "character"—an entity, it is easy to forget, that exists only in certain forms of art and almost never in life. These characters keep interrupting their performances with precisely the quirks, hesitations, eccentricities, and swerves from pattern that a traditional studio production does its best to eliminate. Cassavetes' severest censure (in this and his subsequent films) is reserved for characters (such as the talent agent who books Hughie and the effete, pigeon-breasted intellectuals spouting

"existentialism" at David's party) who think they can define a destination for development, and who sell out their imaginations in order to
recline into the security of a fixed "character," identity, or style.

Cassavetes has said that he made *Shadows* as an experiment in freeing the actor from the tyranny of the techniques and technologies of
modern filmmaking:

> I had worked in a lot of films and I couldn't adjust to the medium. I found
> I wasn't as free as I could be on the stage or in a live television show. So for me
> [making *Shadows* was mainly an attempt] to find out why I was not free—
> because I didn't particularly like to work in films, and yet I liked the medium.[1]

The film was an experiment in liberating the actor from the fetters of
studio lighting, blocking, floor marks, and multiple short takes. But
these technical freedoms are the least important and interesting of
Shadows' accomplishments. The significant freedoms *Shadows* explores
are narrative and dramatic.

No director filmed in greater fear of stylistic betrayal of his
characters—whether the betrayal came in the form of a character's (or
actor's) enslavement to predetermined cinematic and social styles of
behavior, from the filmmaker's imposition of conventional photographic and editorial rhythms on a human interaction, or from the style
of the narrative itself, in the form of the coerced confrontations and
resolutions of the traditional melodramatic plot. When Cassavetes as-
serts that "the real difference between *Shadows* and any other picture is
that *Shadows* emanates from character while in other pictures the characters emanate from the story,"[2] he is doing more than playing verbal
games with the old artistic conundrum of which came first the person
or the plot. His elevation of character over plot (or what in another
context he calls "not bending the characters to the plot") is a way of
expressing his belief that the complexity and power of character must
in no way be sacrificed or simplified for the sake of the exposition and
development of a shapely plot. Cassavetes' goal is to let into film the
eccentricities and vagaries of individual impulse and desire, the "small
feelings" that are conventionally squeezed out of it by an attention to
the plot. (It is no accident that *Shadows* is scored to a jazz accompaniment rather than a standard romantic film score. The jazz musical
line of Charlie Mingus and Shaffi Hadi functions exactly like the anecdotal, shaggy, baggy plot line to avoid the neatly patterned tensions
and releases, the orthodox rhetoric of crisis and resolution of most
other films. In their place, Cassavetes demands something more like

the continuous acts of attention, adjustment, and response that a jazz jam session asks of its participants and its audience.)

While most films begin with certain predetermined dramatic conflicts and tensions and proceed in the process of photography and editing to eliminate any "slack" or "dead" material that stalls the pace of a confrontation or muddles its point, *Shadows* takes as its subject the very process of making drama in the face of distractions, resistances, and lulls. The hesitations, the awkwardnesses, the pauses, the false starts and the miscues of human interaction are not eliminated in rehearsal or edited out of the final print of the film. *Shadows*, in its primitive way, defines a central concern of all of Cassavetes' subsequent work: the effort, the time, and the difficulty of making a scene, of bringing about any dramatically significant moment between two or more people.

Shadows takes us surprisingly far into the territory *Faces* and *Husbands* will stake out and move in to explore—uncharted and rarely navigated areas beyond the straight and narrow road of the "well-made," fast-paced dramatic narrative where the people are less interesting than the plot. The schematic plots and pacings of the classic film script go the way of the studio's balanced two-shots, carefully alternated reverse shots, and sound-stage lighting. In their place, Cassavetes offers an aesthetic of continuous, inexcerptible, often unsummarizable and unbalanced movements and adjustments between groups of characters. That is why no film better captures the zany, unpredictable, and constantly revised relationships that take place between two or more characters unsure of themselves and each other. With his tenderly comic willingness to stay with their frequently long and rambling scenes, and a patience that is never merely anxious for resolutions or clarifications, Cassavetes is able to let in uncertainties, gaucheries, and distractions that would have been edited out of another film. They are there not out of some perverse glee at including what others would have cut, but because, in Cassavetes' view, these mutual adjustments and accommodations, this process of give and take, these endless revisions are the heartbeat of a living human relationship.

We feel the time in Cassavetes' movies more than we do in other films not because of their inordinate length (most of his films are roughly of feature length, and they feel "long" even in their first half hour), but because the predictable oppositions and simplifications of a melodramatic plot are not available as signposts to guide us through scenes. When we are denied the luxury of a navigational chart through troubled waters, every moment becomes as potentially important, interesting, and worthy of our attention as every other. A standard melodramatic plot provides a gyroscopic stability to a story, dampening certain oscillations and movements and reinforcing others. But Cassavetes' loose and baggy monsters refuse to indulge in just these sorts of narrative repression where characters are subjugated to events. The result is the most demanding film experience possible, an experience that denies any relaxation of attention from the moment-by-moment adjustments of personal relationships taking place before our eyes.

The most significant artistic breakthrough of *Shadows* is its repudiation of the Hollywood metaphysic of the star—its dethroning of the autonomous, self-sufficient figures brought into existence at the center of most previous Hollywood films. (As innocuous as it seems, the very concept of a leading man or leading lady, the idea of a star and of supporting players, smuggles into the classic film a whole philosophy of life and a way of organizing human relations around one or two preeminent individuals that is entirely foreign to Cassavetes' understanding of reality.) It is not accidental that the traditional Hollywood production is identified in the popular mind with the figure of the "star" who features most prominently in it. The Hollywood film of the thirties, forties, and fifties was the finest artistic flowering of decadent late nineteenth- and early twentieth-century Romanticism, with its sentimental cult of the autonomous, isolated ego. The Tennysonian or Virginia Woolfian ego, poetically swooning and suffering alone, consummately cultivating its exquisitely alienated sensibility, was brought back to life in the figure of the Hollywood "star." The Hollywood film represented a structure of meanings and relationships, a whole metaphysic of life if you will, designed to justify and perpetuate the star's isolated, glamorous, glorious existence. It is against this metaphysic that Cassavetes is reacting. The "star" and the sentimental, narcissistic aesthetic that conspires in his existence is dethroned in Cassavetes' films. At no point is one of his characters able to excerpt himself from the matrix of social, moral, and familial contexts in which he is embedded long enough to become a "star." That is not to suggest that the individual matters less to Cassavetes, but only that the individual's identity and destiny must be negotiated into existence in the course of a film. Identity or importance is not automatically conferred on anyone by virtue of his being given star billing and treatment. The corollary of this is that no individual is able to rise above the pressures, contexts, and influences in which the film everywhere embeds him. The individual is forced to function within a complex force field of personal, cultural, and stylistic interrelationships and interdependencies.

Cassavetes has spoken frequently of his admiration for the work of both Frank Capra and Carl-Theodor Dreyer, and one cannot help feeling that it was in watching these two masters of the cinematic construction of contexts that he found the inspiration for his own style. (It would be hard to think of two more apparently dissimilar artists whose works are more profoundly related.) From Capra, Cassavetes learned the possibilities of creating complex interpersonal narrative contexts around an individual, and some of the editing techniques that can make such contexts cinematically present in a scene. From Dreyer, he learned the expressive possibilities of the long scene and the long take in which pauses, gaps, spaces, and silences are not automatically trimmed out of a film. Capra's "overcutting" and Dreyer's "undercutting" at crucial dramatic moments in their respective films may seem to be mutually opposed techniques and contradictory lessons in filmmaking, but they are actually complementary. Both are ways of creating and elaborating pressures with which the individual figure must come to grips. Capra and Dreyer both teach a cinematic and personal lesson in the complex social, psychological, and physical contexts in which an individual performance must be shaped. They both taught Cassavetes the expressive possibilities of holding two or more figures together in a shot or scene in a dynamically unstable, unbalanced, and continuously changing composition of competing energies.

Whatever the improvisatory aspects of its narrative and acting, *Shadows* is a meticulously composed and edited film, shot by shot and minute by minute. What Cassavetes' careful photographic and editorial compositions communicate is how these performers are always and everywhere forced to pass their performative impulses through a matrix of rival styles, tones, and social, psychological, and cultural contexts that continuously impinge upon and resist them. Indeed, to call Cassavetes' young people "performers" is to suggest the extent to which they exist only in relationship to the specific and ever-changing audiences through which they circulate, like the successful comedians we see working their way from table to table through a nightclub audience in a scene early in the film, responding to the audience's remarks, and improvising comic routines as they go along.

For all the attention that has been paid to the extreme close-ups Cassavetes employs in *Shadows*, most critics seem to have overlooked the fact that he uses the close-up in a way diametrically opposed to usual cinematic procedures. It is used not to separate an individual figure from a largely undifferentiated background, to isolate him, or to elevate him over other figures (as in Hollywood filmmaking), but to embed him even more tightly in a group of democratically equal others. *Shadows* is a film of group interactions; and successive close-ups of each important character in each of the film's many groupings succeed one another so evenhandedly that the effect is to prevent any one character from becoming the star of a scene and absorbing a disproportionate share of the audience's attention. Take the scene of Hugh's abortive nightclub performance, for example. In the two- or three-minute section of the film in which Hugh is on stage trying to perform in front of a rude and indifferent audience, as we hear his voice and see his face in close-up several times, Cassavetes intercuts ten or fifteen separate close-ups and medium-shots of bored and inattentive members of the audience, the irritated owner of the club signaling to get him off stage, his manager Rupert trying to defend him, and, finally, the chorus girls coming onto the stage from the wings, forcing him to conclude his act. As their faces swirl around him in the final shots of the scene, the photographic effect heartrendingly summarizes his excruciating predicament. He is caught in the toils of forces competing for attention with him and ultimately drowning out his performance.

At other times, rather than exposing a viewer to a succession of sequential close-ups, Cassavetes will cram two, three, or four faces into one tightly packed and unbalanced shot (for example, the faces of Rupert and the piano player jammed together in one shot in extreme close-up as the two friends try to help Hugh polish his routine prior to his Philadelphia nightclub appearance; or Tony's and Lelia's faces side by side in tight shot after they make love in the scene of the dialogue quoted above; or the tensely crammed shot of the faces of Hugh, Rupert, and Ben in the scene in which Ben comes to borrow money from Hugh, described below).

The essential point to be made about the relentless intercutting of close-ups and the crowded frames of *Shadows* is that both techniques are at the opposite remove from the balanced two-shots and the relaxed and predictable shot–reverse shot patterns of the standard academy style. Two or three times the effect does not quite come off and ends up looking merely arty—like a sort of cubism for the masses (Georges Braque live on screen)—and reminds one of the contrived tight three-shots in John Huston's work, or of the turgid and tendentious close-ups of the judges' faces in Dreyer's *Joan of Arc*, effects Cassavetes could never have intended. But when it does work, this tensely dynamic editing and framing thrusts Cassavetes' characters into highly charged and unstable force fields of interpersonal pressures and influences. The repeated groupings and regroupings of characters, the editorial and social contexts created around each individual, and the tightly packed, asymmetrical frame space create a field of energies elaborated in space and time within which each individual exists and which he must learn to negotiate. The endless pressures Cassavetes puts on his individuals, the forces continually vying for their attention and for control over them, and these inescapable cinematic networks of relationship and influence are what makes Cassavetes' scenes seem so crowded and tensely full of pressures in comparison with the scenes in traditional Hollywood films, even though most of his films actually have fewer characters and certainly less melodrama than the standard studio production. The individual is put into competition with rival forms and energies around him as seldom before in the history of film.

But, of course, if it is by being pitted against these competing forces that an individual is tested in *Shadows*, it is in navigating a satisfactory course through the crosscurrents they produce that he may be said to thrive and prosper. Cassavetes imagines healthy, robust human relations not as a matter of similarities, agreements, and harmonies but as the result of a continuous, competitive play of differences. That is why *Shadows* is a film not of homogeneous but of heterogeneous groupings extending from the wildly mismatched threesome at its center to the strangely ill-sorted cocktail parties at its edges. One does not lose one's identity in this welter of styles, tones, and relationships, one is stimulated into fullest possession of it by boldly plunging forward into the fray. Virtue is never fugitive and cloistered in this world.

If the mobile, unbalanced interplay of styles and personalities in *Shadows* asks a lot of the attention of the audience in the course of the film, it is even more demanding of its characters. To be an adequate performer is to be fully capable of functioning in this continuously shifting narrative, social, and cinematic complexity. And by this standard, there are no adequate performers in *Shadows*. Only Hugh even comes close, and he not as a performer on stage (where he is quite rigid and unresponsive to the needs of his audience), but only at a few rare moments of sensitivity and awareness in the bosom of his family and in his personal relations with his manager, Rupert. The requirement is that one be someone who will not try to simplify, melodramatize, "edit," or hurry a scene to an enforced, restrictive, or repressive point or conclusion.

One must be able to live patiently in all the webs of cross-purposes, conflicting feelings, and mixed-up relations in which a given scene immerses its characters. Take, for example, the scene Hugh Hurd singled out to describe to an interviewer after the release of the film. Very early in *Shadows*, Ben, Hugh's younger "white" brother, comes to borrow money from him, the older "black" brother. Ben approaches Hugh when he is debating with his manager whether to take a low-paying job in a second-rate nightclub, knowing that he is being taken advantage of by the club owner:

The compromises I have to make as an older brother. In fact I compromise my whole life really, because I have this father thing with these kids, so I have to subject my personal—or professional—desires because of money, because of the necessity to protect them, to support them.

In fact, that's a very good scene where Bennie comes to ask me for money. I don't know whether we got it across—you know, it's so difficult for me to judge the picture, because I'm so completely and totally subjective to anything I do, I can't be objective about it. Well, in this scene, Bennie, who fights the love he has for me as his brother—he fights this continually—here he's forced to come to me for money. And with all the other problems he's got he would like to be proud of me as a brother, and he hears the man tell me that I have to take a second-rate job, and I compromise, I compromise because if I don't, no one else in the family is working. But of course he takes it personally, and as much as he needs the money, now he doesn't want to face me. So I take the money and I put it in his pocket. Now *I* have a problem, see; I feel like I'm buying him. The more I think about that script, the more involved it gets.[3]

The point of quoting Hurd's recollections is to suggest the complexity of even a very simple scene in *Shadows*. The moment this passage describes, this meeting between Ben and Hugh, takes up at most two minutes of film time, and the action that takes place, the borrowing of money, is never mentioned in the film again. At least this much is going on in every scene of the film. An awareness of, and an ability to respond to, this sort of complexity is required of every adequate performer in the film (and is what these young people only imperfectly or rarely achieved).

Furthermore, unlike the situation in a film with an orthodox melodramatic plot, the power to perform in *Shadows* is something only to be had in the momentary personal exertion of it. As Hugh Hurd's description of this scene suggests, adequate sensitivity and awareness of the field of forces around oneself is not something to be achieved once and for all, at one moment or another in the course of a film, but something that must be continually readjusted from minute to minute. Hugh no sooner gives Bennie the money he asks for than he has changed the field of forces between them and created a new dramatic "scene" whose possibilities and ramifications need to be worked out. There are no end-points, answers, or resolutions possible or imaginable in the aesthetic world of *Shadows*, only an endless series of transactions, a continuously revised series of new scene makings and new dramatic "problems." Every time a scene seems to be proceeding in a predictable direction or to a foregone conclusion, Cassavetes will deliberately throw it off course by having a new character unexpectedly enter, or by giving a new turn to the relationship of the characters already present. It is in this sense that one must understand his emphasis on the "problems" in the film when he was asked by an interviewer about the "theme" of *Shadows*. He replied that it was that "there is no problem that is not overcome and replaced by other problems."[4] This is not the doctrine of a pessimist, but of a dramatist. The point is that there are no crises, resolutions, or conclusions to be found or sought in the film (unlike the *On the Waterfront* melodramas he was reacting against). *Shadows* offers a way of thinking about reality other than in terms of destinations and end-points. Cassavetes asks us to imagine experience in terms of unending substitutions—with one dramatic "problem" relentlessly replacing another, one series of dramatic arrangements and accommodations endlessly correcting and adjusting the previous series of arrangements and accommodations. The exhilarating energy of all of Cassavetes' films and the invigorating, prototypically American appetency of their characters originate in this—that there can be no destination for desire in this world.

No relationship is allowed to stabilize, no judgment is allowed to congeal. In this respect, the anecdotal aspect of the film (the loose interweaving of the narrations of experiences in the lives of the three main characters) far from being a fault, is perhaps *Shadows'* most inspired quality. Any aspiration toward finality or resolution is undercut by the anecdotal succession of shifting transactions between the different characters, circulating through a seemingly inexhaustible series of repositionings in what seems like every possible combination of large and small groupings. Even the way the three central figures, Lelia, Ben, and Hugh, take turns soliciting our attention throughout the course of the film is an indication of how far Cassavetes is from investing all of his narrative capital in any one of them, or in any particular outcome of one character's actions. The narrative stays continuously in motion.

The energy of the film is an energy of revisions, corrections, and substitutions, not of narrative conclusions, psychological resolutions, or ideological end-points.

In freeing his narrative from the repressions of ordinary melodramatic plotting, pacing, and editing, Cassavetes has freed his characters, but in effect only freed them to the necessity of even more work, more awareness, and more sensitivity than would have been required of them in a more conventional narrative. The paradox that informs *Shadows* (and indeed all of his subsequent work) is that if characters have almost never been given such freedom to revise and reevaluate their performances, they have at the same time never been forced to be so continuously responsive to so many dramatic, personal, and social responsibilities, to so many changing narrative situations and dramatic "problems."

But the characters in *Shadows* are not poised halfway between responsibilities and freedoms. The film and the three main characters in it—especially Lelia—represent an exultant celebration of the possibilities of narrative, social, and psychological freedom. It is hard to remain unseduced by Cassavetes' and his actors' imagination of freedom in the film, to remain unresponsive to the endless willingness of these adolescent performers to revise and reassess their relationships, and to remain unimpressed by the film's youthful narrative energy and innocent appetite for movement and change. And yet this is exactly where one feels the gravest reservations about Cassavetes' aesthetic. Are he and his young actors not perhaps too ready to revise and review their lives and relationships; perhaps too willing to accept energetic fragmentariness as an end in itself? Have they earned their identities, or only counterfeited them? Are their roles and relationships too glibly put on and taken off to be true to the deeper psychological and social needs for stability and dependability in our lives? Is the celebration of continuously adjusted performances not perhaps an evasion of longer-term responsibilities and relationships that cannot be subsumed under a performative model? As I have been arguing, these characters live lives of improvisation not, or least importantly, in the dramatic or cinematic sense of the word, but in the existential sense: they lead inventive, unpredictable, interestingly extemporized lives. But a fundamental question must arise as to the adequacy of an improvisatory ethic or metaphysic. Can a marriage, a business commitment, or a mature adult relationship be lived as an improvisation? Cassavetes' celebration of American existentialism, for all of its comic buoyancy and optimism, has striking similarities to Norman Mailer's darker meditation on the philosophy of the hipster in *The White Negro*. But isn't there something rather adolescent and irresponsible in this emphasis on movement, change, and unfettered energy? Aren't the virtues that both Mailer and Cassavetes extol at this point in their careers too irresponsible, too fugitive, and too cloistered to be a philosophical basis for mature adult life?

One answer to such objections is that they are simply out of order. They force *Shadows* and its characters to be other than they are. The very point of Cassavetes' use of Lelia, Ben, Hugh, Tony, and the others is that his adolescent characters are free from the responsibilities and entanglements of long-term, adult relationships. The world is all before them, as it is before any young person. One can argue that it is perfectly appropriate that these characters should be given the vast liberties of experimentation, role-playing, and scene making that Cassavetes gives them, and that we should lovingly tolerate their endless improvisations and revisions of their performances the way we indulge any young person.

But even a teenager is expected to grow up, and we indulge him only insofar as his liberties of behavior are steps toward maturity. His excesses, improvisations, and adjustments are assumed to be in the service of a subsequent development toward more mature and enduring responsibility. That is to say, as much as we indulge *Shadows* as a youthfully exuberant film about youthfulness by a young and exuberant man, we are right to expect something more of his subsequent work. The refreshing excesses and liberties of performance of the characters in *Shadows* are not something Cassavetes can continue to present as ends in themselves in his later films. His characters and his aesthetics will have to grow up and grapple with more difficult situations. The films that follow *Shadows* must test the energy, imagination, and freedom of individuals against the complex responsibilities of mature adult relations. They must attempt the extraordinary task of reconciling the freedom, inventiveness, and eccentricity of personal performances with the temporal and causal burdens of a less anecdotal, more complex, continuous narrative form.

PERFORMING IN LIFE AND ART:
A NOTE ON IMPROVISATION

There's no such thing as a "good actor." [Acting] is an extension of life.
How you're capable of performing in your life, that's how you're capable
of performing on the screen.   *John Cassavetes*

In the first chapter I mentioned some of the reasons Cassavetes' work
has failed to achieve the critical and commercial recognition it deserves.
Its domestic subject matter and intensely personal situations have
counted against it in a film criticism heavily weighted toward the description and appreciation of the metaphorical, metaphysical, and
apocalyptic. But I neglected the aspect of Cassavetes' work that has
caused the most critical consternation and condescension: the apparent
interest in improvisation as an acting strategy in his films. No other
aspect of them has caused more critical confusion and probably done
more to delay the acceptance of his work among serious writers on film.
No other aspect of them has become more of an emotional and irra-
tional rallying cry for both his supporters and his detractors, or has
more encouraged the latter simply to dismiss Cassavetes' work out of
hand. Improvisatory art is not real art, the argument runs, and with
that one judgment the films are relegated to the limbo of critical indifference where reside other "interesting" but "nonartistic" events—the
Dadaist works of the early decades of this century, the be-ins and
happenings of the sixties, and recent audience-participation theater
and performative art. It is a common way of saving oneself the difficulty
of having to deal with any work of art, simply to define it out of
existence by means of such a category.

But in all fairness to Cassavetes' critics, it must be said that he
himself has done almost nothing to clarify the situation, or to explain
how or in what ways his works are or are not improvised. Consider the
example of his first film. The first version of *Shadows* concluded with the
following statement on the screen: "The film you have just seen was an
improvisation." Since the film was rehearsed for weeks in advance of
the filming in a series of dramatic workshop exercises led, and frequently partially scripted, by Cassavetes himself, the statement is not
strictly true; but it is not really false either, since actors were encouraged to develop their characters during rehearsals. However, as I have
already described in detail, Cassavetes subsequently withdrew this
version of *Shadows* from circulation, reshot and reedited over half of it,
rewriting dialogue and restaging whole scenes, and released a second
version, the one we have today. The surprise is that (out of some
keeping of faith with his actors? out of some allegiance to the original

impulse with which they had begun the film?) the second version ends with the same declaration: "The film you have just seen was an improvisation." When pressed on this point, Cassavetes stands by his statement that the film was improvised because "at no point was there a written script." But if the fact that the performers worked from spoken instructions and exercised liberties in interpretation defines improvisation, then almost every dance performance ever staged must be considered an improvisation. And even if we agree that the initial narrative of *Shadows* was "improvised," certainly the term does not apply in the same way to what the actors were doing after several weeks of rehearsals, or to what they were doing when they played the same parts in the second version of *Shadows* two years later. And even if one argues that the scripting and acting of *Shadows* were improvised, in what sense was Cassavetes' photography improvised? In what sense were the editing and scoring of the film any more spontaneous or less planned than those of hundreds of other films using hand-held cameras and extreme overshooting to cover a scene?

The point of asking all these questions is to suggest that perhaps it is the concept of "improvisation" that needs examination, especially insofar as the films following *Shadows* present even more complicated artistic situations than it does: Cassavetes, according to his own account, worked from carefully thought-out, detailed scripts in each of them, but at the same time never hesitated to change a line or detail during filming and editing. (As he explained in a typically unhelpful way to an interviewer who asked him to describe the process: "The lines were written down. The emotion was improvisation.")[5] In an effort to define what "improvisation" means as a criticism of these films—and it has been used against each of them—one can begin by dividing Cassavetes' critics into two camps.

The smaller, more easily dismissed group could be called the critical neoclassicists insofar as they believe that art should be completely "controlled" (a recurrent term in their criticism) and "pure"—that is, untouched by the personalities of participants or the accidents and contingencies impinging on the act of creation. Their ideal work of art is spared the compromises and confusions of contact with the world of real people, places, and events. Who could imagine Joyce, Flaubert, or Proust collaborating with an editor in changing and rewriting a passage? Would Wallace Stevens test out sections of his poems to gauge their effect on friends and the public and revise them according to their suggestions? Should John Milton have called in young Richard Bentley to edit *Paradise Lost* for him, and save him from mistakes? The very notion is laughable according to these critics. That would be artistic anarchy. This conception of the work of art is obviously much better suited to the discussion of a written text than it is to a consideration of the performing arts, which are fairly difficult to deal with in such absolute terms. That is probably why these critics tend to be less interested in the performing arts; but when they do think of them, their ideal is something like the text (and, significantly, not the performance) of the "well-made" play—complete in every word, specification of scenery and props, and stage direction, before casting and rehearsals begin.

Needless to say, no standard narrative film was ever made that way. Film, as has been noted to the point of annoyance, is an art that emerges out of compromises of collaboration, contingencies of staging, and revisionary impulses at every step of a production. Even a director as notoriously dictatorial and closed-minded as Hitchcock, walled-in behind his story-boards and "actors are cattle" philosophy, was known to be forced to compromise, revise, or improvise on a set. Which is why these critics can never take film quite as seriously as they would a well-made play, a piece of music, or a poem.

But the real problem is that not even these other things were brought into existence the way the neoclassicists imagine. Masters of drama such as Ibsen and Chekhov wrote with specific actors, actresses, companies, and stages in mind, and tried out things on audiences, friends, and companies before committing themselves to the final version of a text. Even at that point in the creative process, they were not averse to changing their texts in rehearsals, or after a few performances, depending on the reactions of actors, friends, and audiences. They were not all that different from a director improvising on the set, or changing his film in the editing room. As anyone who has ever leafed through a variorum edition of a poet knows, not even lyric effusions are written the way the neoclassicists imagine—not to mention a web of revisions and second thoughts as tangled as the various versions of Shakespeare's plays, with their repeated and specific reminders of the particular actors, settings, audiences, and performances they were initially staged for, and subsequently revised for in their different performances.

In short, the neoclassicist position can simply be dismissed as a naiveness about the creative conditions of almost all artistic activity. One suspects that the neoclassicists would be as appalled as they are with Cassavetes if they only knew the truth about the "improvisatory," "revisionary," and occasionally collaborative ways George Balanchine choreographed his ballets, Picasso painted his paintings, Stravinsky scored his symphonies, or Shakespeare wrote his plays.

That brings me to the second group of critics, a group more sophisticated about how works of art are really made. They realize that Hawks, Capra, Welles, and Renoir in Hollywood's Golden Age, like Bergman, Antonioni, and Fellini today, and like artists of any era, freely allow second thoughts, revisions, "improvisatory" insights, and collaborative revisions to adjust the course of their initial impulses. They realize that in the case of an art such as film, some of these second thoughts or self-corrections may come before a script is written down in draft form, some may come during the process of writing and rewriting, and some may come after it has been put together and is being rehearsed, filmed, or edited in post-production. And above all, they realize that it is rather silly and arbitrary to praise everything that happens prior to one point in this sequence as "creation," and to condemn everything that follows that point as commercial "compromise" or uncontrolled "improvisation."

But even this group of more sophisticated viewers seems to feel that Cassavetes has somehow overstepped the boundaries and gone too far in the way of cinematic improvisation. His films feel more radically improvised than those of other directors. They have concluded that Cassavetes works from an inadequate script and depends too heavily on an actor's ability to make up his lines as he goes along during filming, but they are mistaken. Cassavetes has never made a point of it, but the surprising fact is that after *Shadows*, he has always worked from scripts. His actors are encouraged to respond to the scripts and to make suggestions for the revision of them in collaboration with him where he and they are convinced changes are desirable, but in no case are they simply told to invent new scenes or to make up their lines as they go along.

Faces, Cassavetes' second independent production, was praised by some as an improvisational masterpiece and condemned by others as an improvisational mess for two years before Cassavetes proved both his admirers and detractors wrong by publishing the script his actors had worked from in a 319-page book. A comparison of the script with the released film reveals that the "improvisations" Cassavetes still insisted he had encouraged his actors to make were so slight that they were almost imperceptible—a reworded line here, a shortened phrase there—roughly equivalent to what one would find by comparing the written text of a typical theater production with the words actually spoken by the actors at a given performance. *Minnie and Moskowitz,* another shaggy, baggy movie, and one that in its rhythms feels for long stretches as if its actors are simply making up their lines, was in release for three years and likewise talked about exclusively in terms of the adequacy or inadequacy of its improvisational techniques, an approach to the film Cassavetes encouraged, before he published the script his actors had used, from which the finished film differs in only minor ways.

What is going on when films that were demonstrably not improvised (or were improvised only to the extent that all films are) are attacked for their excesses of improvisation? The fact that they are thought of as being improvised even when there is incontrovertible physical proof (namely, a shooting script) that they were not is an indication that what Cassavetes' critics are calling "improvisation" and responding to in his films has little or nothing to do with the acting strategies or methods of scripting he uses. What throws these viewers is not improvisation, but the impression of improvisation. It is not that Cassavetes fails to write out his scenes in sufficient detail; it is the kinds of scenes he writes that disturbs these critics. Though they are not improvised, the scenes Cassavetes scripts, blocks out, and rehearses in advance have as much of an "improvisatory" feel to them as actual improvisations by directors such as Hawks and Capra.

Even Pauline Kael (not an especially sympathetic audience to Cassavetes' films), after seeing *Faces*, sensed that improvisation was less a technique in Cassavetes' work than a form of performance:

When *Shadows* came out ... it was generally thought of as a group improvisation rather than a first film by John Cassavetes. But from bits of his two intervening commercially produced films (*Too Late Blues* and *A Child Is Waiting*), and now from *Faces*, in which he apparently had full control, it is clear either that he made *Shadows* or working on *Shadows* made his style.[6]

Cassavetes' characters, in *Shadows* and each of the following films, sound as though they are improvising their lines because the actors play them that way; but the improvisations are the improvisations not of theater, but of life. The critic's mistake is to think that he is watching an actor making up his lines, when in fact the hesitations, false starts, and changes of tone are those of characters muddling their ways through untidy relationships. Which is only to say that the films are not interested in displaying the relatively trivial improvisations of actors acting, but the profound improvisations of characters living. As long as Cassavetes' critics worry over the unimportant, and usually infrequent, presence or absence of the first sort of improvisation in his work, they will be doomed to miss the radical social, psychological, and dramatic importance of the second sort of improvisation. They will miss the extraordinary expressions it offers of characters making the best of messy, muddled, and untidily improvised existences. Improvisation, self-correction, adjustment, and endless reevaluation is not a sterile dramatic technique, but the central strategy for survival in these films.

For Cassavetes, an adequate personal performance can never be prefabricated or arranged in advance of the particular social, psychological, and dramatic demands of a situation. It must be assembled out of whatever materials come to hand in the moment, and is forced continuously to revise and adjust itself as it goes along. All the central characters in Cassavetes' films are compelled to become performers in this sense of the word: Lelia and Hughie, Chet and Jeannie, Archie, Harry, and Gus, Cosmo, and Gloria, and the others. Like Hughie in front of the hostile nightclub audience, these performers succeed or fail based on their instantaneous capacity to make something of their situations, and on their ability to keep themselves from being trapped, caught, or pigeonholed by those around them (or by the audiences who witness their performances in movie theaters). Like those extraordinary heroines in Henry James's work, from Eugenia to Maggie, Cassavetes' characters must learn to improvise a free self out of their performances, performances that (as in James's novels) become increasingly more difficult, complex, and imperiled as we move from one work to the next. To be capable of performing in this way is, in fact, for Cassavetes what it means to have a self worth saving, a self not limitable by pat critical or human categories of "character" or "psychology," a self capable of sufficient generosity of response and loving flexibility to be worth exploring on film. But the ramifications of that statement will take the rest of this book to spell out.

CHAPTER III

CHILDREN, CLOWNS, AND CON MEN
Working for Hollywood on *Too Late Blues* and *A Child Is Waiting*

[In 1964] I looked back at my accomplishments and I could find only two that I considered worthwhile, *Shadows* and *Edge of the City*. All the rest of my time had been spent playing games—painful and stupid, falsely satisfying and economically rewarding. *John Cassavetes*

In the three years following his completion of the second version of *Shadows*, from the end of 1959 to the end of 1962, John Cassavetes, like his immigrant father before him, rode the roller coaster of the American dream from rags to riches and back again. Reediting *Shadows* left him almost $20,000 in debt, and though he had it enlarged from 16mm to 35mm, the young filmmaker discovered to his surprise that commercial distributors were utterly uninterested in innovative, unusual, independent films. He was unable to recoup any of his loss. So he sent it abroad—where small-scale, small-budget, and unorthodox films have always had a better chance of finding appreciative, if small, audiences—and returned to full-time acting to pay the bills.

With a growing family (his first child was about to be born) and large debts, before he had quite finished editing the second version of *Shadows*, he accepted a lucrative, long-term contract in the title role of the "Johnny Staccato" detective series on NBC. It went on the air in October 1959. Never satisfied with being a passive participant in the creative process, Cassavetes asked for, and was given, an unusual amount of artistic control in the series. He supervised much of the filming and was given permission to direct five of the episodes, many years before men such as Alan Alda, Robert Redford, Warren Beatty, and Woody Allen would make the transition from actor to director seem commonplace. He later said of his directorial efforts on "Johnny Staccato": "I tried to do each one differently, hoping to develop some kind of style and technique."[1] But an inspection of the rather trite episodes reveals little of interest. Only two things stand out in his efforts: one technical and one narrative. The technical surprise is the indication of how familiar

Cassavetes was with many of the classic film idioms that he chooses to avoid in his later work. Hitchcockian extreme high and low angles, Wellesian vertical tracking, Ophuls-like 360° pans, classic two-shot framing, *film noir* low-key lighting, and half a dozen other rhetorical devices are tried out and discarded in one twenty-five minute episode. The narrative interest that emerges out of this haze of cinematic virtuosity, surviving the vapid murder mystery plots, is Cassavetes' attention to the psychological and social situations of his characters. His camera explores faces, postures, and glances between characters almost at the expense of allowing viewers to forget they are watching a whodunnit where clues and alibis are supposed to matter more than glances and facial expressions.

Meanwhile, *Shadows* quietly and modestly began to collect awards and gather small, but loyal, crowds at foreign film festivals. Marty Racklin, a Paramount executive, saw *Shadows* at a London screening and, after reviewing some of Cassavetes' work on "Staccato," thought he might have stumbled on to a studio executive's dream—a safely bankable director—though he would live to see how wrong he had been. Racklin's logic depended on a number of assumptions; but once they were granted, it was unassailable. If Cassavetes could make films on a shoestring budget (and *Shadows* suggested he could); if such films were critically in fashion (and the wild enthusiasm with which the second version of *Shadows* was invariably received by the critically sophisticated audiences of Amos Vogel's Cinema 16 and Lionel Rogosin's recently purchased Bleeker Street Cinema, the response of Mekas and the avant-gardists excluded, suggested that they were); if there was a commercial market for so-called serious and sophisticated pictures (and the modest success of several recent films such as *Twelve Angry Men, The Goddess,* and *Edge of the City* suggested there might be); and, finally, if Cassavetes would jump at the chance to break his contract with an inane murder mystery series to work for a major studio as his own writer, producer, and director (and he would)—then Paramount just might have the art house equivalent of a Roger Corman on their hands.

Cassavetes was flown to Los Angeles and offered artistic *carte blanche* provided he came in under budget and featured contract players, who were being paid anyway. It may not have been Hollywood heaven, but it was an offer too good to refuse. At the end of 1960, Cassavetes broke his contract with Universal and NBC and sat down with Richard Carr, a writer he had gotten to know on the "Staccato" series. In two days and nights over a weekend, as Cassavetes tells it, they wrote a screen-play called *Dreams for Sale* about an idealistic jazz musician whose high ideals come a cropper against the forces of commercialism around him and his own latent cynicism. Cassavetes gave it to Racklin and in a matter of weeks received approval on a production for the spring of 1961. It was a young entrepreneur's dream come true, but one that would, over the next two years, turn into a nightmare for Cassavetes. (The best thing that happened during the entire two-year period in Cassavetes' life was that, with the backing of a British film distributor, Lion International Films, he succeeded in getting a brief but wide-spread American distribution for *Shadows* in the winter and spring of 1961.)

Too Late Blues (as the released film was titled) starred Bobby Darin as John "Ghost" Wakefield, the young, talented, hopelessly idealistic leader of a jazz combo who would rather play "hot" jazz in charity gigs at orphanages and public parks than sell out to the commercialism of playing easy listening music for swanky clubs and record labels. But the film is strangely muddled, perhaps because the subject of an artist marketing his dreams to the establishment was too close to Cassavetes' own situation for him to see it objectively. The question of whether he himself had sold out by agreeing to work for Paramount was one that nagged him. The film's greatest intellectual strength is thus inseparable from its most serious dramatic weakness: Cassavetes' obvious ambiva-lence about his main character's idealism. The film refuses to make a clear case either for or against the ghostly figure of Ghost. Instead, it provides an open-ended, unresolved exploration of Cassavetes' own mixed feelings about commercial compromise: of the emotional and social problems of working within the system and the perhaps greater problems of trying to stand entirely outside it. But, however much we may admire the intellectual integrity and honesty of the film, in re-fusing to simplify such a complicated issue, *Too Late Blues* is finally unsatisfactory, confusing, and confused.

Ghost is a blend of Lelia, Ben, and Hugh from *Shadows*. He has Lelia's capacity for self-dramatization, Hugh's sense of the unreadiness of the world for his professional talent, and Ben's beat alienation. But *Too Late Blues* is a more ambitious and complex film than *Shadows*—even though its complexity is ultimately its undoing. Ghost is put in a much tougher, more exposed, and more difficult situation than any Ben, Hugh, or Lelia have to function in. He is a band leader, a full-time, professional performer, and that makes all the difference to how we (and others) judge his performances. Ghost's performances have serious economic and professional consequences from which the preening, posturing adolescents of *Shadows* were insulated. They could change their minds in the middle of a relationship or apologize or brazen their way out a misunderstanding, but a record company contract or a nightclub engagement cannot casually be renegotiated or rearranged with such liberties of improvisation.

The character Ghost most resembles in *Shadows* is Hugh, the aspiring jazz singer trying to get good bookings and make a living for himself and his manager. But Hugh is not first and foremost a professional performer in the way Ghost is. It is significant that Hugh's occupation becomes less and less important in the course of *Shadows*, while Ghost's becomes more and more important in *Too Late Blues*. We see Hugh performing professionally early in *Shadows*, but after that the only performances he gives that matter to the film are the personal performances of kindness, sensitivity, and understanding he stages in front of Lelia, Ben, and Rupert. As *Shadows* goes on, more and more of Cassavetes' narrative capital is withdrawn from the professional side of Hugh's life to be invested in the personal side. Hugh gradually shifts from performing as a professional jazz singer in front of an audience to performing as an older brother and friend in front of people he cares about. The shift is made explicit in the final scene in which we see him. Hugh himself chooses friendship over his career in the conversation with his manager in which he decides not to go on tour to Chicago, Cincinnati, or Arizona.

Ghost's dreams, on the other hand, are never able to remain personal. They are always up for sale. There can be no world of merely personal relations for him. There is no Rupert in his life, no manager who can be more important as a friend than a businessman. Even his sexual relations (with his singer Jess Polanski, played by Stella Stevens) are inextricably bound up with his professional career.

Ghost is forced to negotiate territory that the characters in *Shadows* never have to enter and that the earlier film as a whole backs away from. There are a few unpleasant or hostile characters in *Shadows*, but none of them ever seriously threaten the central characters about whom we care. Such was his own confidence that, almost without exception, Cassavetes could dismiss them with the sort of gently comic satire he directed against the pseudo-intellectuals at David's cocktail party. But Ghost has to contend with a scheming agent, sleazy recording studio executives, and others who cannot be controlled with easy satire.

However, the most serious threats to Ghost's powers of performance come not from the scheming agents and businessmen around him, but from his own doubts about himself. The finest and most subtle moments in this very uneven film are those in which Ghost is questioning his own purposes and ideals. He anticipates some of the most interesting characters in Cassavetes' later films in that his doubts and diffidences are expressed less in hesitation and uncertainty (like those of the characters in *Shadows*) than in a compensating flamboyance (like that of so many of the emotional con men who would follow him). For the first half hour of *Too Late Blues*, Ghost puts on a series of acts and routines that feign supreme confidence as a cover for his doubts about himself. He is a fount of wisecracks, pranks, and banter, but Cassavetes' camera searches his face to let us see how much it is just an act. When Ghost's saxophonist Charlie (Cliff Carnel) turns to him in the pool hall to plead that they are, after all, in their thirties and too old for fooling around and playing orphanages, Ghost's flow of patter stops, his poise evaporates, and his face shows his own awareness that he may be a little old for the kind of dreaming he indulges in. When his black friend Baby Jackson (who is obviously a successful commercial musician) gently teases him in front of others about the impracticality of his idealism ("He's got wonderful stories, like Mother Goose and Peter Pan"—the latter an ominous suggestion of the sexual deficiencies Ghost will show a few minutes later with Jess), Ghost has no snappy comeback.

It is at moments like this that the casting of Bobby Darin—a teen idol in his middle twenties, and not at all a commanding stage presence—seems almost inspired. Darin's weak, doughy face and his reedy, still faintly falsetto voice are exactly what are required to capture this mismatching of wildly impractical dreaming and insufficient practical dramatic power. With a deliberateness that is almost embarrassing, Cassavetes holds his shots on Darin's chubby baby-face one, two, or three beats too long in order to underline the weakness of his idealism. (He would use this technique of holding a close-up just a beat or two longer than a studio editor would consider acceptable in order to tease out an otherwise hidden feeling to best advantage in *Faces*.)

The most common mistake the initial reviewers of the film made was a failure to appreciate how truly original an experience Cassavetes was providing. Darin's acting is notoriously weak, and his inability to perform on camera in a more powerful and compelling way would have to be regarded as a dramatic failure in a more conventional film, but what his critics did not recognize was that Cassavetes was as aware of Darin's problems as they were, and turned his weakness into the subject of the film. The consequences of his inability to control a dramatic space, his incapacity to "make a scene" (as even Lelia could do) are what Cassavetes chooses to explore in his film. Both here and in his subsequent work, Cassavetes is asking his viewers to explore a world in which some of the standard ways of making drama are no longer available to the characters, a world that makes the melodramatic crises and confrontations of other films seem hopelessly old-fashioned.

The most frequently criticized aspect of the plot of *Too Late Blues* is thus perhaps its most interesting and innovative feature. What almost every reviewer of the film noticed and objected to was that for long stretches of *Too Late Blues* Cassavetes simply seems to abandon plot altogether to let Ghost and the characters around him "horse around" on camera. The first instance of horseplay occurs only a minute or two into the film. Immediately after the credits have ended, we see Wakefield's group, having concluded a charity concert, going off to a pool hall and bar to relax and get a bite to eat. For a full three or four minutes, the band members do nothing but tease the owner of the place with weird sandwich orders, steal drinks from his cooler, and clown around at the pool tables. It all seems especially zany and pointless here in the opening minutes of the film, when one is primed to expect a deft, dense exposition of plot and character. One might think the actors were improvising a routine left over from the rehearsals of *Shadows*, if the meticulously precise studio lighting, blocking, sound work, and matching cuts did not prove that it had all been elaborately scripted and rehearsed in advance. A few scenes later, Cassavetes does the same thing. Ghost takes Jessie, a girl he has just met, to a neighborhood bar and another four or five minutes at the beginning of the film are seemingly frittered away with Ghost, Jessie, and the bartender concocting a weird drink with which to celebrate the occasion and a series of toasts to anything the characters can think of—among other things, to courage (which, in terms of his narrative, Cassavetes shows no lack of) and to patience (which most audiences are by this point already greatly in need of). Then, only a few minutes later, Ghost and Jessie horse around a swimming pool in front of her apartment. And only a few minutes after that, we see Ghost's group clowning around on a baseball diamond the following morning.

Is this a case of a director merely indulging his actors or infatuated with Method improvisations (as was charged by critics of the film)?

Perhaps a clue to understanding these scenes is to be found by referring them to their sources in three earlier films. The pool hall horseplay and the clowning around on the baseball diamond are quoted almost verbatim from one of Cassavetes' favorite films, *Angels With Dirty Faces* (though in Michael Curtiz's film, the second scene is set on a basketball court and not a baseball diamond). The swimming pool scene is a version of the scene in *Rebel Without a Cause* when James Dean and Natalie Wood chase each other around the pool at the deserted mansion. Finally, many of the other incidents between Ghost and Jessie seem indebted to comparable moments from the courtship of George Bailey and Mary Hatch in *It's a Wonderful Life*. It is far from an accidental derivation. Ghost Wakefield is in the direct line of impractical, idealistic American dreamers extending from Curtiz's dead-end kids through Capra's George Bailey to Nicholas Ray's rebels—a figure not very far removed from Cassavetes himself.

But of the three influences on *Too Late Blues*—Curtiz, Capra, and Ray—Capra's is the most powerful and the one most worth investigating. Ghost is in many respects a character out of one of Capra's populist films. Like Longfellow Deeds, Jefferson Smith, or Long John Willoughby, he is an idealistic young man who is plunged into a situation that gets out of his control, and is forced to negotiate encumbering bureaucratic, political, and social entanglements. But Cassavetes' Ghost is more complex than any of Capra's prewar heroes and the appropriate comparison is to Capra's greatest postwar hero, George Bailey, a figure one feels sure Capra and America could have produced only after the trials and sacrifices of the war. What Ghost and George share is precisely the capacity for complexly self-conscious, self-aware playfulness that the more innocent, and at times priggish, earlier figures lack.

Like Wakefield, young Bailey is an idealistic improvisor, a lover of imaginative horseplay. One cannot help specifically noticing the similarity of the scenes of courtship in Capra's and Cassavetes' films. What goes on between Jimmy Stewart and Donna Reed is too similar to what happens between Bobby Darin and Stella Stevens in *Too Late Blues* for the resemblance to be merely coincidental. Capra chooses to further his couple's budding romance not with a solemn scene of courtship, but by having George and Mary fall into a swimming pool and walk home together in borrowed clothes. It is a scene significantly constituted of horseplay, role-playing, and seemingly pointless games and banter between the two lovers. They are both outlandishly costumed (Mary wears a bathrobe and George a football uniform ten sizes too big for him). They zanily sing an off-key duet of "Buffalo Girl," throw stones at a deserted house, and make wishes on its windows. And generally they self-consciously clown around playing farfetched romantic roles ("My lady, your train," Stewart says as he hands Reed the sash of her bathrobe, to which she replies that he may now kiss her hand). The one thing that is never expressed between them, though it is the real text of the scene, is their feeling of love for each other. (The neighbor who shouts down to Stewart: "Why don't you kiss her instead of talking her to death?" summarizes the strange obliquity that every viewer feels.)

And obliquity is the point of the comparable scenes in the Curtiz, Ray, or Cassavetes movies. These scenes express nothing more eloquently than the unplaceability of a character's desires in the normal structures of plotting and characterization. These films give us scenes in which plot is momentarily forgotten, scenes that have no point except the expression of personal energies that cannot find adequate outlet in the sort of actions a well-made plot provides for. Whether it is a scene of the dead-end kids carrying on in a pool hall or on a basketball court, of Dean and Wood horsing around a deserted swimming pool, or of George Bailey and Mary Hatch playing absurd dramatic games together, these scenes, in any strict sense of well-made drama, are dramatically excessive and gratuitous. They run on too long and relate too little to what comes before or after them in the narrative. They seem unmotivated and contribute little or nothing to the advancement of the plot events or the characterizations. They are overdone and superfluous. But far from being a fault, that is their very point. They are expressions of narrative and personal desires and energies denied more coherent, systematic and integrated expression, moments when more is going on than can be reduced to plot or characterization.

That is the function of these scenes in *Too Late Blues*, as annoying and long as they are. The unplaceability of personal energies either in the world of business or in the world of economical, action-advancing narrative is their very essence. If, for convenience, one labels Capra's George Bailey or Cassavetes' Ghost Wakefield "idealistic" (as I have been doing), it is this unplaceability of their energies to which one is referring. But for all Bailey's and Wakefield's performances and Capra's and Cassavetes' narratives have in common, it is just at this point that Capra and Cassavetes part ways. Capra ultimately comes down on the side of the necessity of channeling such energies into socially disciplined and narratively useful modes of behavior. Jimmy Stewart's role-playing and wish-making are converted into mortgage signing ceremonies. His imaginative building of castles in Spain is converted into the practical construction of row houses for the Martini's and others like them. But Cassavetes (like Ghost) is unable to make up his mind so firmly and decisively in favor of the values of cultural and emotional repression.

Before the temptations of sexual intercourse desublimate their relationship, Capra interrupts Donna Reed and Jimmy Stewart with the contrived announcement of the sudden illness of Bailey's father, but Cassavetes follows Jess and Ghost inside her apartment. Jess excuses herself to "slip into something more comfortable," while the camera holds on Ghost. Her reappearance in a scanty gown, draped alluringly off one shoulder, is an obvious invitation to Ghost to convert some of his excess imaginative and emotional energy into something more (or less?) than an imaginative commitment to her—to assume the practical responsibilities of making love to her. But it is a relation Ghost is unwilling to undertake. His sexually generated energies can apparently be expressed in every sort of performance but a sexual one. And what makes Cassavetes so radically different from Capra, who would certainly regard this as a victory for civilization and self-control, is that Cassavetes cannot make up his mind as to whether this is a moment of success or failure for Ghost. Cassavetes' refusal to follow Capra down the road of repression is what makes *Too Late Blues* both more muddled and at times more interesting than the comparable films by both Curtiz and Capra. Emotional repression, cultural sublimation, and the conversion of useless imaginative energies into socially beneficial forms of action become dramatic problems to be explored in *Too Late Blues* and not formulaic solutions to an imaginative predicament. Though the name he gives him must count as an implicit criticism of his failure to engage with the world, Cassavetes is, in the final analysis, unable to make up his mind about Ghost's ghostly idealism. And the corresponding uncertainty *Too Late Blues* induces in its viewers is both its greatest strength and its gravest weakness.

Cassavetes uses sexual intercourse (both the act of making love and the delicate conversational intercourse between two people that precedes or follows making love) in eight of his ten films (all but *A Child Is Waiting* and *Gloria*) just as he does here in *Too Late Blues*—as a kind of litmus test of a character's capacities for performance. Sexual intercourse (in both senses of the word) will be an opportunity for characters such as Richard Forst (in *Faces*) and Gus (in *Husbands*) to convert their visionary impulses into practical physical and social forms of expression. Sexual intercourse forces Cassavetes' American dreamers to confront and negotiate specific social, spatial, and temporal realities that check what would otherwise be their unlimited visionary expansions. For all its vaulting idealism, Cassavetes' vision (like D. H. Lawrence's in this respect) is essentially sexual and social. A successful performance, sexual or otherwise, must always be shaped against the resistance of another human being, never in solitude, and can never exist merely in reverie or imagination. It is just this supreme test of his powers to perform practically in the real world with one other human being that Ghost, like so many of Cassavetes' subsequent male characters, fails or evades.

But *Too Late Blues* is finally an unsatisfactory and confused film and, what is worse from the standpoint of pleasing an audience, a film that gets less and less interesting as it goes along. Cassavetes has said that with a bit more time to devote to this particular film, and a bit more experience with the bureaucracies of the studio system, he could have made a good movie out of *Too Late Blues*. But it is not true. The problems with the film could not have been remedied by refilming a scene or two or reediting. What Cassavetes was unable to see was that the deficiencies are not photographic or editorial, but are deficiencies in the fundamental structure of the film that could not be changed without changing the entire project. The central structural flaw is that Cassavetes creates two separate value systems (and characters who embody them) and is unable to bridge the gap between them, or to choose between them.

I want to describe the problem in some detail since, in the imaginative plate techtonics of Cassavetes' work, it is a fissure that will occur many more times. The fault line created by the frictional rubbing against each other of the two different sets of characters and value systems will energize Cassavetes' greatest achievements, though here it only succeeds in breaking his film into two pieces. On one side there are the impractical dreamers, the most notable of which is the ghostly, mercurial figure of Ghost with his vaporous idealism, his imaginative mobility, and his Actors Studio antics; on the other are the businessmen and punks who surround him, some of the most convincingly coarse, crass, and cynical parts ever gathered in one film. (The two most striking of the second group are Frielobe, a sleazy recording studio executive, brilliantly played by Val Avery, in the sort of role in which Cassavetes would cast him in four subsequent films, and Benny

Flowers, Ghost's manager, who is played with a wonderful blend of nervous mousiness and insinuating arrogance by veteran character actor Everett Chambers.) The problem—and it is a serious problem since it might be said to be the central dramatic situation of the film—is that Cassavetes is able to show neither the recording studio executives and business manager learning to respect or understand Ghost nor Ghost learning how to adjust and measure his performance enough to successfully negotiate the obstacles they place in his path. It is as if characters from two adjacent sound stages suddenly found themselves uncomfortably thrown together in the same film. Ghost arguing with Frielobe comes off like Peter Pan confronting Peter Lorre, a Walt Disney character plunked down in a Warner Brothers gangster picture. (We will see something like this again in Cassavetes' *Gloria*.) *Too Late Blues* conceives two radically conflicting imaginative worlds, but no way to reconcile them or negotiate a course between them.

Darin's situation as an actor caught in this schizophrenic dramatic predicament is a reflection of an imaginative schizophrenia—a war between idealism and cynicism—that will riddle and yet energize all of Cassavetes' subsequent work. But most specifically here it is evidence of his deliberate attempt as a young filmmaker to move beyond the world of *Shadows*, and its "all the world's a stage" innocence. Cassavetes tries to test his weak-kneed dreamer in the hard-boiled world of business compromises and contracts, but cannot see him through the situation he imagines him in. In this context, it is interesting to compare Cassavetes' original conception of the film with the final product. With Cassavetes' permission, Paramount issued the following publicity synopsis of the film prior to its release in the winter of 1961–62:

> *Too Late Blues*
> The story of an idealistic jazz musician, Ghost, played by Bobby Darin, who falls in love with a mediocre vocalist, an "easy" girl, Jess, played by Stella Stevens. In turn his ideals are shaken and his manhood challenged. Despondent, he "sells out" to a cheap record label, becomes a gigolo to the Countess, played by Marilyn Clark, loses his self-respect, and finds determination to return to his ideals. He finds Jess, a drifter and prostitute. Below the level of hope, Jess makes one last effort at love; singing "The Blues," Ghost's old song, she reinstates him with his old group. Jess departs. Ghost, accepting what is and what isn't, turns to his keyboard and "The Blues" begin again.

As this synopsis suggests, the final scenes are meant to show Ghost's process of growing up—ending a compromising contract, learning how to fight in order to save Jess, and rejoining his old group on more

Responses to alienation: self-creation or self-destruction?
—*Ghost and Jess perform the blues*

mature terms. But what is interesting is that in the final print of the film neither Darin nor Cassavetes can make these scenes work. Ghost's maturation remains contrived and unconvincing. (And it is surely significant that even the semi-sweet happy ending that this synopsis suggests was originally intended for the film was abandoned in the final print, which only shows Jess and Ghost standing on the periphery of the old jazz band, able neither to join it nor to renounce it.)

But if one can look beyond the commercial, critical, and aesthetic failure of this particular film, the unsatisfactoriness of *Too Late Blues* may be the most interesting thing about it. It shows us a writer-director divided by his double vision of experience and in effect destroying his film in his refusal to mute either side for the sake of compromise with the other. To the very end of *Too Late Blues*, Cassavetes cannot make up his mind between an allegiance to the irresponsible, improvisatory antics of Ghost and his unblinking recognition of the harsh reality of agents, executives, and money men, whose only desire is a blind instinct to exorcise all the "Ghosts" in their midst.

To make matters worse, the world of business and finance is, if anything, more convincingly rendered in the film than the world of free artistic imagination. Ghost's delicate, elusive capacity to "play" counts for virtually nothing next to the games of financial and sexual politics we see others around him engaged in. Cassavetes seems unable to convince even himself of Darin's power against the forces amassed against him. The film is finally torn in half by the incompatibility of its two visions, and Cassavetes' refusal to soften or compromise the alternatives. *Too Late Blues* is an attempt to force the idealistic adolescents of *Shadows* to mature their performances under the pressure of negotiating a world of alien and hostile others, but it is an attempt that fails.

One cannot help thinking back to a manifesto titled "What's Wrong With Hollywood" that Cassavetes issued in spring 1959, two years before he strangely found himself in Hollywood trying to do what he said could not be done, working on this "ultra low-budget picture" about Ghost Wakefield, another artist trying to reconcile the claims of individual expression with the rival demands of producers, businessmen, and managers:

> Hollywood is not failing. It has failed. The desperation, the criticisms, the foolish solutions, the wholesale cutting of studio staffs and salaries, the various new technical improvements, the "bigger picture," and the "ultra-low-budget picture" have failed to put a stop to the decline.
>
> The fact is that filmmaking, although unquestionably predicated on profit and loss like any other industry, cannot be made to please solely the producer's image of the public. For, as has been proved, this pleasure results neither in economic nor artistic success. . . .
>
> However the probability of a resurrection of the industry through individual expression is slim, for the men of new ideas will not compromise themselves to Hollywood's departmental heads. These artists have come to realize that to compromise an idea is to soften it, to make an excuse for it, to betray it.
>
> In Hollywood the producer intimidates the artist's new thought with great sums of money and with his own ego that clings to past references of box office triumphs and valueless experience. The average artist, therefore, is forced to compromise. And the cost of the compromise is the betrayal of his basic beliefs. And so the artist is thrown out of motion pictures, and the businessman makes his entrance.[2]

It goes on for several more paragraphs, but what is interesting is that this is a double vision of the inevitability of commercial "betrayal" and of the impossibility of artistic compromise as bleakly schizophrenic as that of the film that followed it, and that was done in by it.

Like *Too Late Blues*, "What's Wrong With Hollywood" is the formulation of an imaginative Catch-22, in which Cassavetes is himself a version of Ghost Wakefield, unable to express himself freely in the commercial bureaucracies of Hollywood and unable to express himself freely without them. In both his film and his essay, Cassavetes is unable to see a solution to the imaginative paradox Ghost is trapped in—how to reconcile free artistic expression with the forces of business and commerce that make free artistic expression available to the public. Capra, the supreme filmmaker of the American way of repression, was always able to suggest that the energies of the individual could be channeled into socially beneficial action, but Casavetes is unable to align the free expressive needs of the individual with the forms and forces of contemporary life.

That is why Ghost's most authentic expressions of his imagination and desires occur in scenes (such as the softball game or the horsing around making Jess a drink) that seem merely eccentric, irresponsible, and extraneous to the main events of the plot. Of course, eccentricity has a long and honorable history in American art and is a characteristic response to perceived entrapment by American artists from Twain and Whitman to Hawks and Huston; but the question Cassavetes and *Too Late Blues* are asking (without being able to answer it) is to what extent such eccentricity is only a form of escapism and irresponsibility. It is a question that haunts all of Cassavetes' subsequent work. Ghost is only one in a long line of would-be "free spirits"—beginning with Lelia and extending through Seymour Moskowitz in *Minnie and Moskowitz* more than ten years later—whose styles of "freedom" are at times troublingly indistinguishable from styles of irresponsibility and disengagement.

Cassavetes' ambivalence about these characters is mirrored in the forms of the films in which they appear, in a stylistic ambivalence that echoes the unresolved struggle in the characters between an allegiance to the values of free play and the need to organize desire into more focused and practical forms of expression. There is an unresolved struggle in his own consciousness between, on the one hand, an interest in play, eccentricity, and local expression of desire, completely unanswerable to larger systems of narrative organization, and, on the other hand, an allegiance to the rigorous narrative requirements of temporal and spatial unity, sequentiality, and closure, and an intense concern with thematic coherence and high moral seriousness.

But perhaps no entirely satisfactory resolution of the struggle is possible or desirable. Cassavetes is tracing the career of an impulse—an unappeasable aspiration toward absolute freedom and free expression—passed through the snares and nets of society and the repressive formal requirements of narrative. The value of his work is not to be sought in some putative resolution of these ambivalences or in some cessation of this struggle, but in the vigorous course of a career, the eccentric trajectory traced by an impulse locked in struggle with formal, psychological, and social forces that resist it.

Notwithstanding the commercial, critical, and artistic failure of *Too Late Blues*, Paramount signed Cassavetes to a five-picture contract at the conclusion of filming and turned him loose on his next project, *The Iron Men*, the story of an all-black World War II air squadron. Cassavetes again wrote it with Richard Carr. It was to star Sidney Poitier, with whom Cassavetes had costarred in *Edge of the City,* as the head of the squadron and Burt Lancaster as a war correspondent doing a story about them. But *The Iron Men* never got off the ground and the next thing Cassavetes knew, he had an offer to work with Burt Lancaster in another picture over at United Artists. *A Child Is Waiting* would star Lancaster and Judy Garland, be directed and partially written by Cassavetes (based on a screenplay Abby Mann had already successfully aired on television), and be produced by one of the three or four most powerful men in Hollywood at the time, Stanley Kramer. But the marriage between Kramer and Cassavetes, two enormous egos with enormously different temperaments, was one definitely not made in heaven. Their uneasy relationship came to an end one afternoon after principal shooting on the film had been completed and the editing process had just begun. After a heated argument with Kramer over the editing of the film, Cassavetes was summarily removed from the production crew (though his name was retained in the credits as director), fired by both Paramount and United Artists, and blackballed from subsequent studio work.

Since the script was largely by Mann, the final editing under the supervision of Kramer, and the finished film repudiated by Cassavetes, it is perhaps stretching a point to consider *A Child Is Waiting* as a Cassavetes film at all. But despite the best efforts of Kramer and his editors (and Kramer must have tried very hard to erase his imprint on the picture), *A Child Is Waiting* does still betray telltale signs of Cassavetes' approach.

In the first place, some of the acting, in particular the performance of Gena Rowlands as Sophie Widdicomb, the mother of one of the boys who lives at the home for the retarded in which the film is set, is at moments as emotionally nuanced and complex as Cassavetes' most mature work. Take, for example, the brief scene in which Sophie talks to a teacher at the home, who wants her to visit her child more often, of her inability to visit her boy there, "not because I don't love him, but

because I love him too much." After being forced to make this extremely painful and revealing admission to a complete stranger, she
runs to the window of the room she is in to glance out at her child
playing in the yard of the home, only almost instantly to withdraw from
her own impulse and run out of the building and get into her car. For
the duration of this short scene, Cassavetes generates a complexity of
cross-purposes between the mother, the boy, and the well-meaning,
but insensitive, teacher at the home (played by Judy Garland), and also
a complexity of feelings within Sophie Widdicomb herself, that are as
interesting as anything in his later films. It is a scene of mature emotional bewilderment and conflict recognizably from the hand of Cassavetes, even as it is more subtle, sensitive, and complex than anything
in *Shadows* or *Too Late Blues*. It is a moment more powerful in proportion
to the extent to which it is less histrionic, hysterical, and schematic than
the crises and confrontations in the earlier films.

In addition, there is a severity, simplicity, and avoidance of rhetoric
in the photography and blocking of particular scenes in which one also
feels Cassavetes' extreme respect for his characters. One can only imagine Kramer's (or his editor's) surprise at the discovery that Cassavetes
filmed many of the scenes with the highest emotional voltage only in
the equivalent of master or cover shots, with no close-ups, reverse
angles, or alternate camera positions to cut into them. The result even
in the final film is a visual and emotional restraint of which one is
certain that the editorializing and sermonizing Kramer—the Polonius
of film directors—would have been otherwise incapable.

But what stamps *A Child Is Waiting* most definitively as the product
of Cassavetes' imagination is simply its extraordinary affection for each
and every one of its characters. His affection, in particular, for the
children (most of them actual residents of the Pacific State Hospital for
the Retarded in Pomona) is so deep and sincere that for the first half
hour of the film, it actually deflects our attention away from the plot
and the supposedly more important adult characters around them.
Cassavetes seems almost to fall in love with these children, repeatedly
putting them in the foreground and center of a composition, and rele-
gating the nominal "stars" of the film as often as not to the background
or periphery of the frame. (One can only imagine how Kramer felt
about letting a bunch of amateurs, and kids at that, upstage box office
attractions Garland and Lancaster.) Cassavetes' democratic camera eye
(in which the actions and appearances of the children become at least
as important as those of the adults) functions as an implicit repudiation

The difficulty of creating a dramatic space within which
to stage a free performance
—*Burt Lancaster and the scene-stealing children*

of the very Hollywood star system he is supposed to be working in the
service of. Garland and Lancaster are cinematically put in their places,
implicitly told they are no more, and perhaps less, important to this
film than the anonymous children around them.

Cassavetes was fired, by his own account, because of his refusal to
use the film to mouth the sort of narrow, moralistic liberal platitudes
that Kramer was interested in presenting. According to Cassavetes,
Kramer wanted only to pull the heartstrings of his audience by telling
them how sad and worthy of pity these children were. But when you
respect the characters as individuals, as Cassavetes' photography does
here, it is impossible glibly to moralize or editorialize about them. The
faces he registers so lovingly in close-up cannot conveniently be made
into mere types or representatives of anything. Life at this intensity and
proximity cannot be cut to fit any of the easy patterns of melodramatic
or journalistic significance (at about the *People* magazine level of complexity) that producers such as Kramer so much pride themselves on.

But *A Child Is Waiting* is doing something much more complex and interesting than the typical Stanley Kramer production. A film with which it has superficial thematic similarities is Sidney Meyers' interesting independent documentary production *The Quiet One*, the story of a young Harlem boy whose situation is quite similar to that of Reuben Widdicomb. (Meyers had edited *Edge of the City*, where Cassavetes could have met him, assuming he had not already gotten to know him through Morris Engel or Lionel Rogosin.) But in its thoroughgoing rejection of the hierarchies and subordinations of standard melodramatic Hollywood plotting and characterization, Cassavetes' film has its most profound affinities with the work of Shirley Clarke. Clarke is, after Cassavetes himself, surely the greatest and most strangely neglected of American independent filmmakers. (Andy Warhol is not even in the same league with her.)

Specifically, *A Child Is Waiting* necessarily reminds the viewer of Clarke's *A Scary Time*, released in the preceding year. *A Scary Time* was another film commissioned for a narrow, propagandistic purpose that rose above its polemical occasion. It was funded by UNICEF to advertise its campaign to relieve world hunger, and was ultimately rejected as being too controversial. It is an extraordinarily sensitive and intelligent statement about childhood, and the vulnerability, fear, and dependency that are the flip side of a child's innocence, sensitivity, and idealism. It was just such an exploration of the borders of innocence and experience that Cassavetes attempted in his film.

It is astonishing how Cassavetes' imagination left its mark on the film Kramer finally released, even after it had been worked over by several other pairs of hands. The love of the particularity of faces, the patience with the unfolding of a human relationship, the restraint of the photography (contrasted to the emotional intensity of the subject), the democratic equality of treatment, and, above all, the supreme respect and fondness for individuals, which even dares to treat some of these retarded children comically, are almost as much in evidence here as in one of Cassavetes' own scripts. What *A Child Is Waiting* shares with *Shadows* and *Too Late Blues* is a loving generosity of response, a refusal to rush to hasty judgments about its characters, a willingness to entertain a multiplicity of personal viewpoints in any one situation, and a democratic belief in the equal cinematic importance of each individual. In short, Cassavetes was right when he told an interviewer that he could not "blame [Kramer] for taking the picture away, because it didn't fit his small, narrow viewpoint."[3] "All characters are created equal," the self-evident truth of this film and of almost all of Cassavetes' subsequent work, has never been received doctrine in Hollywood.

Kramer did not succeed in entirely erasing Cassavetes' imprint on *A Child Is Waiting*, but he did succeed in completely ending his career in Hollywood. At the beginning of 1963, Cassavetes was unemployed and (with Kramer against him) unemployable. He had gone in two years from being a member of the New York cinematic avant-garde to a wonder kid turned loose on the sound stages of Paramount, but now he found himself an outcast several steps lower than he was before he had arrived in Hollywood. His reputation as an unmanageable maverick was established with the studio heads for years to come, and his own worst fears about the studio system had been confirmed. He had taken a gamble in coming west, and in less than two years had lost everything. Ironically, back in New York, where he had begun, he was regarded as having taken the money and run—betraying independent filmmaking to sell his soul to Hollywood. (There were even desultory efforts on the part of some of the original cast and crew of *Shadows* to sue him for the profits they were convinced he had made on the film without cutting them in.) Any films he made in the future, he would have to make on his own.

CHAPTER IV

FIGURES OF DESIRE
Faces

At the beginning I had written a first draft that was two hundred and fifty pages long, and that wasn't even half the film. . . . Then we decided to film everything, even if the film lasted ten hours. We were happy to be shooting this film; we shot for six full months. So *Faces* became more than a film; it became a way of life, a film against the authorities and the powers that prevent people from expressing themselves the way they want to, something that can't be done in America, that can't be done without money. *John Cassavetes*

I want to start over again. —*spoken by Richard Forst to Jeannie Rapp in* Faces

What all three films preceding *Faces*, Cassavetes' first fully mature work, have in common is that each takes for its central figures young people whose performances are staged in the protected environments of childhood, adolescence, or young adulthood. We tolerate (and at times may even be charmed by) Lelia's histrionic excesses because of her youth; we forgive Ghost's idealistic impracticality because he is at the beginning, and not the end, of his career; we are amused and touched, and not irritated by the strangeness of the retarded children in *A Child Is Waiting*, because after all they are children and not entirely responsible for their actions. The untrammeled perceptions and performances of young people are a common post-Romantic subject (and one that has appealed particularly to American artists from Hawthorne and Twain to James and Faulkner) because their energies are temporarily freed from adult systems of control and arrangement. But the youthful performers in Cassavetes' first three films are unable to engage our most serious dramatic interest. The consequences of their actions and the constraints on their consciousnesses are simply not severe enough to elicit the most interesting possible performances. His characters' predicaments are not sufficiently serious and complex because their lives are still too much before them, too available to future revision and rearrangement. That is why each of these films, whatever the particular travails of its characters, is necessarily less than tragic in effect. Like Huck and Tom camping their way through American society and mores, Tony and Lelia are actors in an essentially comic situation.

All of which is to suggest the quantum leap Cassavetes makes in his fourth film. His characters and his work suddenly grow up, as he himself noticed in commenting on the difference between *Shadows* and *Faces* in conversation with Jonas Mekas:

[*Shadows*] dealt with youth, and there is no restriction on youth. But *Faces* deals with middle age, and in middle age there . . . are restrictions on behavior. A totally free behavior would become an indulgence in a picture like this; it would become destructive. So that to reveal middle age in all its complexities . . . and frustration, [*Faces*] must be more rigid, even in the acting itself.[1]

The characters in *Faces* are in the generation of the parents of the youths of *Shadows*. Extremes and excesses of behavior and feeling are still available to them, but are no longer so easily expressed or so readily accepted by those around them. As Cassavetes suggested in another interview, the newly felt restrictions and complexities in his characters' situations compelled him to find ways of registering smaller, more subtle, more complex, and more continuously changing feelings than he had to in *Shadows* or the other early work:

[*Shadows*] goes further than many other films. It is a film about young people, and you can say more [extreme] things about them than you can about older people, since young people themselves want to express themselves absolutely and continuously run the risk of losing themselves, even being killed. Young people like or dislike things and persons with no two ways about it; they always talk in terms of absolutes. On the other hand it isn't [as] easy to talk about middle-aged people, who change from one moment to the other according to their mood, their state of health, their memories, what happened to them ten years ago, or what will happen to them in ten years more, when they're dying.[2]

All of Cassavetes' films are about the necessary, if inevitably painful, explorations of personal styles, identities, and roles that allow a character to become a fully responsible and responsive adult. That is the explicit subject of *Shadows*—the process of exploring the possibilities of adequately sensitive performances in life and art. But *Faces* deals with a group of characters (everyone in the film, in fact, but Chet and Jeannie) who, in middle age, have never before dared to make such explorations. They missed both the growth and the growing pains of

Shadows' adolescents. They have apparently all their lives walled themselves into fixed styles and mechanical systems of relationship, and the long repressed impulses toward freedom and exploration return with a jolt in their mid-life crises.

Faces is a desperately dark film at the furthest imaginable remove from the playful liberties and irresponsibilities of the earlier work. *Shadows, Too Late Blues,* and *A Child Is Waiting* are stories of individuals beginning relationships, with almost everything still to be explored and achieved. *Faces* abruptly jumps decades ahead to the situation of Richard and Maria Forst, a married couple at the end of everything. It is not accidental that their marriage is childless, or that children and adolescents are absent from the film. Children represent an imaginative opening into the future, the possibility of new relations and future developments that is utterly unavailable here. It is as if Cassavetes had eliminated the little boy Reuben Widdicomb from *A Child Is Waiting* (and all the possibilities of change and growth his arrival at the hospital opens up to Judy Garland, Burt Lancaster, and his parents) and had chosen instead to focus on his mother and father alone, with nothing but their estrangement from each other as the subject of the film. The whole tone of *A Child Is Waiting* would have been altered.

Richard and Maria Forst are trapped—physically, emotionally, and imaginatively—in a situation from which there is no exit. In the course of *Faces*, they each strive desperately for some escape route, but it is obvious that the walls that hem them in and isolate them are just too high to be scaled. What makes *Faces* so exciting and such an extraordinary leap forward in Cassavetes' oeuvre is that the easy dream of freedom in the early work has given way to a tougher recognition of the sheer difficulties of its achievement. But this is not to say that *Faces* or any of the later work is any less passionately idealistic than *Shadows;* the exuberant, joyous dream of freedom that informs the early work (and of which Lelia may be taken as the paradigmatic expression) never dies or diminishes. But in *Faces,* and the films that follow it, it is pitted in combat to the death against emotional, psychological, social, narrative, and formal constraints that are more than its match. The dream of freedom, escape, and adventure is forced to negotiate every obstacle of society and consciousness that can be imagined to resist it.

It would be trivial to try to attribute this darkening and maturing of Cassavetes' vision to any particular experience he underwent in the years between the youthful optimism of *Shadows* and the harsh realism of *Faces*. One might simply say that he was growing up. But it is undeniable that many of the creative conditions of his own life had altered radically after his falling out with Stanley Kramer. Kramer was one of the most powerful men in a Hollywood studio system in its death throes, desperately clinging to its past powers and prerogatives, and no one hired anyone fired by him. Cassavetes has written about the years of visionary dreariness that preceded *Faces*:

> I stayed home, looked at trees, at my family, wrote several scripts, and learned patience. In 1964 I took a job running a company—a TV package company—in partnership with Screen Gems. After six months of that I looked back at my accomplishments and I could find only two that I considered worthwhile—*Shadows* and *Edge of the City*. All the rest of my time had been spent playing games—painful and stupid, falsely satisfying and economically rewarding. Then at the end of 1964 *Faces* was born, out of friendships and mutual dissatisfaction.[3]

Faces was originally conceived of as a play, because, as Cassavetes put it, "at the time . . . I thought the only freedom of expression left to the actor was the stage." But he quickly realized that its special qualities could only be communicated on film. He wrote an initial 250-page script, as he later recalled, out of "my recollections of people who had troubled my life." The Richard Forst character indeed seems remarkably similar to the Stanley Kramer Cassavetes had tangled with: a tough, shrewd, practical, supremely confident business executive (who in the first scene of *Faces* screens a film before cowed and sycophantic associates). But one of the supreme achievements of *Faces* is that, notwithstanding Cassavetes' bitterness and resentment at this time of his life, its characters are never less than human. They are never caricatured in order to make dramatic points. Though Cassavetes may have begun in "bitterness," "hysteria," and "hardness" (as he describes his feelings writing it in the introduction to the published script, a script that significantly was originally titled *The Dinosaurs*), it is typical and revealing that he could not stay that way. His is an aesthetic of inclusions and of opening oneself to experience, never of shutting it out. He may have begun *Faces* in a mood of dismissiveness and repudiation, but he finished it with nothing but sympathy and compassion for its doomed characters. He may have begun the portrait of Richard Forst as a study of men like Stanley Kramer who had troubled his life, but amazingly ended it by allowing that he himself was part of the portrait, too. That is why he could tell an interviewer that he had no malice when *Faces* was completed, and why, in his comments, he could describe the world of *Faces* not as someone else's world, but as his own and that of "almost everyone [he knew]." For Cassavetes, hell is never a place one puts other people:

Faces is a movie about the middle-aged, high middle income bracket people that are made fun of in our society. This is the White American society that certain social groups talk about all the time. One day I woke up and realized that I'm part of that society and almost everyone I know is. There's no sense pretending I'm back in New York in the early days looking for a job. I'm not. And I knew there was something to be said about these people and about their insular existence and about their place in a society that is frowned upon today. And we said it: we said it as honestly as we could, without malice, without anything but affection for these people.[4]

If Richard Forst resembles Stanley Kramer in some ways, he in other ways also resembles John Cassavetes' description of himself in the years preceding *Faces*. He is an eminently successful businessman who has spent his time "playing games—painful and stupid, falsely satisfying and economically rewarding."

Faces (like Albee's *Who's Afraid of Virginia Woolf*, which it resembles in superficial, but finally unimportant respects) deliberately confines itself to the narration of twelve hours in the disintegration of Richard and Maria Forst's marriage. The plot is as simple as it is symmetrical for both Richard and Maria. The film begins with Richard (John Marley) and a business associate Freddie (Fred Draper) carousing after a day of work at the apartment of Jeannie Rapp (Gena Rowlands), a high-class call girl. (From Ghost to Gloria, Cassavetes has selected the names of his principal characters with great care, so there is perhaps a reference in her name to Ginny Rappe, the call girl who was the pathetic victim in the Fatty Arbuckle scandal. But more likely her name was chosen as a combination of a diminutive form of Gena Rowlands' first name and a last name that signifies Jeannie Rapp's real métier. She is a mistress of the oldest profession, one even older than prostitution. She is a girl who has mastered the art of "rapping" with men, the art of putting them at ease and supporting their fragile and demanding egos—as a subsequently deleted long scene in a bar, included in the preview print of the film, showed. It is as an accomplished mistress of intercourse in this social sense of the word that Cassavetes is most intensely interested in her.) After leaving Jeannie's apartment, Richard returns home and stuns his wife Maria (Lynn Carlin) by suddenly asking her for a divorce and going off to spend the night at Jeannie's place. The rest of the film involves the simultaneous, futile attempts of Richard and Maria to find solace apart from each other. Richard sleeps with Jeannie and Maria sleeps with Chet (Seymour Cassel), a beach bum and drifter she meets in a bar the same evening. The scenes that follow alternate between Richard's and Maria's experiences apart from each other, trying to escape from the dead ends of their lives into a dream of new romance. But, needless to say, each attempt is futile. In the final minutes of the film, Richard returns home and he and Maria are alone together again, but more intensely alone than they have ever been. There are no resolutions, no conclusions, and nothing has really come of all the pain they have inflicted and felt.

The plot has been criticized as violating "plausibility," since, so the argument runs, it is too farfetched to assume that both Richard and Maria would be able to find sexual partners on the same night. The shortcoming of this criticism is not only its assumption that the plots of plays must be "plausible" to be intensely interesting—where would this leave most of Shakespeare, to name only the most obvious exception?—but, more importantly, its ignorance of the dramatic effect of the symmetry. The doubling of the plots in *Faces* is a strength of the film, not a weakness. What the doubling does here—as in Shakespeare—is to allow the viewer to become relatively indifferent to the sheer events and actions that transpire, plausibly or implausibly, and to heighten his awareness of the emotional and psychological meanings of the events. That is to say, since Richard and Maria each sleep with someone else on the same night, we are able to pay less attention to the event as a mere event in the plot and more attention to the different feelings and actions of two characters living through a similar experience. *Faces* is a film assertively less of events than of acts of consciousness.

To finance the $200,000 cost of *Faces*, Cassavetes acted in a series of films in the middle and late sixties—from relatively high-class pot boilers such as *The Dirty Dozen* and *Rosemary's Baby* to less self-consciously artsy productions such as *The Devil's Angels* and *Machine Gun McCain*, going from studio work during the day to hours at the moviola in his garage in the evening and on weekends. But no film could be less like these lurid, action-centered melodramas than *Faces*. Like Carl Dreyer, whose films he greatly admires, Cassavetes seems interested in actually minimizing the importance of plots, especially of the melodramatic sort, in his films. What my plot-heavy synopsis of *Faces* fails to emphasize is the extent to which the interest of the film resides in one scene after another of simple human relationships, and not in any particular "event" that generates these relationships or in which they eventuate. It is as if action and plot would only deflect the viewer's attention from the psychological, moral, and interpersonal events Cassavetes is interested in capturing on film. The most interesting moments in *Too Late Blues* and *A Child Is Waiting* were the moments between events, moments when perhaps nothing more was "going on" than a series of glances or looks between characters, and *Faces* is designed to maximize those moments and to minimize the trappings of action and eventfulness in the other sense of the word that only serve to get us from one such moment to the other. Cassavetes has discovered that to give his characters the sort of emotional and imaginative opportunities he is most interested in exploring, he virtually needs to immobilize them. To allow them the freest possible imaginative play and responsibility, he has to protect them from the coercions and distractions of mere events, something Samuel Beckett and Henry James both found necessary also. The often praised "realism" of *Faces* is not attributable to the complexity of its sociological or physical texture, but to the complexity of the trajectory of feelings, aspirations, and desires it traces.

Since Cassavetes is so frequently (and mistakenly) characterized as a careless "home movie" maker, it is worth emphasizing how tightly organized the writing and editing of *Faces* are. No film seems to have less slack material; every scene, and every second in each scene, counts as intensely as every other. The claustrophobic confinements of the characters and the density of the scenes are essential to its impact. *Shadows, Too Late Blues,* and (to a lesser extent) *A Child Is Waiting* have an anecdotal sprawl to their plots and their editing. They narrate sequences of events taking place over extended periods of time, and their narrative looseness and apparent casualness are inseparable from the youthfulness and insouciance of their attitudes. *Faces,* on the other hand, is a film of relentless temporal, spatial, and narrative compressions and juxtapositions. The entire film consists of only eight long scenes, and is restricted almost entirely to two small sets (Forst's home and Jeannie's apartment). There are only four principal characters (Richard and Maria, Jeannie and Chet), and a handful of supporting ones. And, most powerfully of all, the events that take place during the time of the film transpire in something weirdly like the "real time" such events would take to happen in life—a two-hour period late one night, and a half-hour period early the next morning.

The formal compressions in the film are as severe as the spatial and temporal ones. There are simply no extractable or excerptible moments—no big scenes or little scenes; neither high points nor low ones; no build-ups or climaxes in the predictability of which we can relax our attention. The effect is relentless and overpowering. At the end of the film a viewer feels almost as battered and overwhelmed as if he had himself lived through the two and a half hours of anguish trapped on the screen.

The most perceptive initial reviews of the film called its subject "sexual politics," but what they were responding to was not the content of the film but its very structure. *Faces* is perhaps the most brilliant exposition ever filmed of "sexual politics"—the endless, competitive jockeyings for position and power between male and female characters. But to say that its subject is *sexual* politics is to limit it unnecessarily. In the largest sense, *Faces* is a demonstration of the "political" nature of all human relations, sexual and otherwise, in its imaginative world. All of its experiences are "political" or power generated. There are *no* absolutes or fixities for its characters or its narrative to live up to. All of its values and its relationships are perpetually up for reappropriation and rearrangement. All of its experience is an experience of continuously readjusted power relations, of continuous renegotiations of human relationships. It is the extension of the American economic dream of free enterprise, of unrestricted laissez-faire democratic competition, into the realms of love and marriage, an American dream that turns naturally enough into a California nightmare.

Faces comprehends the America described over and over again by Tocqueville, Bryce, and Emerson, and summarized by Max Lerner when he wrote that "power pervades every phase of American society, which is not power-starved but power saturated."[5] Richard Forst represents the pragmatic American response to that situation. As the pun embedded in his name suggests, all relations in which he participates are "forced." He is a principle of plucky, opportunistic, American force, a will to power and control that eagerly and desperately fills the vacuum created by the absence of any other absolute principles of moral or social relationship. In an ungrounded, open, decentered, acquisitive society, he has made himself into a "vendible personality" (in Thorstein Veblen's phrase), and treats others likewise. In Max Lerner's formulation of the situation, he is someone for whom all relations have been charged, in the absence of any transcendental values, with "the power and violence of the acquisitive drive . . . as if the two circuits had become crossed, and the way Americans feel about money and success had got tangled up with the way they feel about love."[6] The result, *Faces* demonstrates, is psychic disaster.

The fierce competitive pressures present in the relations of any two characters to each other operate in the structure of the film as a whole. *Faces* is a film of inexorable editorial and imaginative contrasts, comparisons, and juxtapositions. It is not accidental that each of the eight major scenes is connected to what comes before and after it by a match cut that dovetails with the preceding or following scene (and usually comments ironically on it). Each moment exists only as it is tensely compared and contrasted with the preceding or following moment.[7] *Faces* is a film without a single fade or dissolve, not only between these eight long scenes but within them. It is a film that denies the viewer even the most momentary pause to extract a particular remark from the context of the other remarks and events within which it is situated. It is impossible to expand imaginatively within a particular moment outside of its competitive context, to linger romantically over a character's stance even for the brief duration of a fade-out and fade-in. The effect is temporally and emotionally relentless, and one of the reasons that the texture of experience in *Faces* is so hard to capture with excerpts from it.

Cassavetes will deliberately cultivate such a temporal constraint in his subsequent films, culminating in the extraordinary organizational achievements of *A Woman Under the Influence* and *The Killing of a Chinese Bookie*, in each of which almost the entire second half of the film takes place in something breathlessly close to the "real" time of the events narrated. (In *A Woman Under the Influence* in particular, Cassavetes devotes the final hour of the film to what is, in effect, one continuous scene, abridged with virtually no temporal "cuts" at all.) Far from "indulging" his performers or allowing them to "luxuriate" in their performances (charges frequently leveled against his work), he continuously pits them against temporal and formal constraints in all of the films from *Faces* on. While the rush of episodes in another film—say a comedy by Hawks—induces a temporary indifference to time, a suspension of belief in clock-time in order to establish an alternative fictional or cinematic "rhythm," Cassavetes' films do the opposite. As part of the responsibility of their performances, his characters must negotiate the tick-tock of the clock, the length of the audience's attention span, and the real time a scene takes to stage. This is, as I suggested previously, one of the respects in which Cassavetes' work, for

Vaulting dreams and desires boxed in by
inexorable formal, spatial, and social confinements
—*Richard, Jackson, and Stella*

all of its apparent experimental or avant-garde trappings, turns most
decisively away from most other recent work in film and video that falls
within these categories. With its jump cuts, strobe cuts, film loops,
patterned visual repetitions, and other fragmentations of temporal con-
tinuity and pacing, avant-garde and experimental work blithely treats
temporality and sequentiality as if they were mere compositional resources among others such as light, space, sound, and color. But for
Cassavetes, time (in its concrete manifestations as the time an emotion,
a humanly significant relationship, or a narrative series of events takes
to develop) is what necessarily chastens our compositional designs and
resists our visionary appropriations. Time is what our art must learn to
negotiate, not deny, escape, or reorganize. Time is what frustrates our
attempts to live the grand life of imagination and desire, but that is of
course a stimulation to artistic and worldly human endeavor and not a
discouragement.

The temporal burdens his characters must shoulder are of a piece with the other formal constraints of *Faces*: the physical confinements, the editorial juxtapositions, and the restrictions on the number of characters and scenes. Such constraints are Cassavetes' way of testing his characters. It takes enormous countervailing formal pressure to resist the self-expansions of these characters and their feverish imaginations of freedom. Out of the struggle between these formal constraints and the otherwise extreme performative freedom the characters are given comes the drama of Cassavetes' most extraordinary achievements.

The performances of his characters and Cassavetes' own performances as a writer, director, and editor are continuous struggles with timing—the timing of a scene, a relationship, or an event. That is why, in editing *Faces*, Cassavetes was obliged to adopt an unorthodox process of "block cutting" (in which whole scenes, many as long as thirty or forty minutes in running time were cut out of the film) instead of the normal process of "trimming." Cassavetes described the process in an interview (and his cuts may be traced in detail by anyone who is interested by comparing the released print of the film with the original script, which has been published):

[To start with] we had about 270 pages [of script], and that was about three-quarters of the film. We wrote it from that point as we went along. I think the whole script, when it was done, was something like 320 pages. A normal script today runs about 140 pages. Our first cut of *Faces* ran six hours. The version we ended up with runs two hours and nine minutes.

It was stupid of me to allow myself that kind of indulgence. . . . What people usually do [in this situation] is to "trim" a long film [i.e., cut short sections—pauses, lulls, dead spots—out of many different scenes]. But Al Ruban and I and Maurice MacKendrie, who edited *Faces*, all sat there and discussed what would happen if we did make certain trims. . . . And we came to the conclusion that each cut we made hurt the film. The timings of the people were real. And so, in altering the timings, we were altering the truth. So we were forced to make extremely large block cuts.[8]

In fact, the "timing" of the final print of *Faces* was so unorthodox that many of the initial reviewers suggested that the entire first half of the film should have been eliminated. The reason was that the pairing of Richard with Jeannie, and Maria with Chet, the central event of the film, insofar as it has one, does not occur until well into the second hour of viewing. (The two pairings do not occur until pages 248 and 294 of the 319-page published screenplay, or until more than three-fourths of the way through it.) But what these reviewers failed to appreciate was that Cassavetes was less interested in the mere fact, or event, of the pairing off of the two couples than in a record of the achievement of it.

The lowliest studio hack editor could have brought Jeannie and Richard, and Maria and Chet together by the middle of the first reel of *Faces*. But for Cassavetes a relationship is not a plot event but something that must be negotiated into existence, something that is only achieved arduously, slowly, and delicately over a period of time.

The two couples want to escape into dreams of romance, but the attainment of dreams is never that easy in Cassavetes' work. Society wars against the attainment of the individual dream. Romance, escape, and vision must be teased into possibility—a possibility the editorial, photographic, and narrative style of *Faces* questions. Richard and Jeannie, and Maria and Chet must run obstacle courses in order to attain even the most marginal moments of romantic intimacy; they must brave a seemingly endless series of alien entanglements before they can earn the right even to be alone in the same room together. Far from representing a strategic mistake in the editing of *Faces*, the sheer resistances these dreams of romantic escape meet with are the point of the film. With the exception of one very brief shot of Richard standing beside his pool table at home, and another in the first few seconds of the film as he walks into his office, the four principal characters are not allowed to be alone for a single second of *Faces*. Even a momentary release from social constraints would grant them too much individual imaginative authority and autonomy.

Consider all that must be lived through in this world of endless social competition and resistance to imaginative expansion. In the first scene of the film, Richard is in his office surrounded by ingratiating, flattering, manipulating junior executives. In the second scene, at Jeannie Rapp's, he must vie with Freddie for her romantic attention. In the next scene, he must compete with his wife's friend Louise (on the telephone) and Maria's stories of Louise's husband's infidelities. On his return to Jeannie's, he has to negotiate the distractions of two boisterous traveling salesmen and another call girl before he can even pair off with Jeannie. And it is no less arduous for Maria. After Richard asks for his divorce and runs off to see Jeannie, back at the Forst residence, Maria's friends—Florence, Billy Mae, and Louise—gather to jockey one another for social position around her and emotional preeminence over her now that her husband is gone (in an excruciatingly awkward and painful, yet comic, half-hour scene that was included in the first print of the film but cut from the second). Later, when Maria brings Chet back to her house for what is obviously intended to be a night of love, Billy Mae, Florence, and Louise again tag along, making it impossible for Maria even to have this moment alone with her lover to be.

FLORENCE: Have you tried those very sheer nightgowns?

LOUISE: Don't be a stupid ass.

FLORENCE: Well, there are ways . . . I wouldn't say this to anyone . . . but
        men get bored by sameness . . . A little of this . . . then maybe, he
        wants something else. So what does it hurt, give it to him . . .

BILLY MAE: Give it to him!

FLORENCE: Maybe you'll like it too--see? I went to a prostitute once . . .

LOUISE: Florence, don't be a stupid ass! You are a stupid ass, Florence!

FLORENCE: When I was having tough times with Louis . . . I almost fainted,
        there were so many sexual devices . . .

BILLY MAE: Thank you, Florence Henry.

MARIA: I repulse him . . . that's all. He wouldn't touch me . . . for anything.

FLORENCE: Have you tried?

MARIA: Everything.

FLORENCE: Maybe he didn't feel well.

LOUISE: That's kind, Florence, very kind.

FLORENCE: Well, I like men. Men are good, men are kind, men are right!
        Women are weak! There's got to be a reason for a man hurting a woman.

MARIA: He hates babies! He doesn't want a baby--is that reason enough? I've
        got a baby inside of me that wants to come out. Is that reason enough
        for you?

BILLY MAE: You poor baby.

LOUISE: He probably goes out two or three times a week.

BILLY MAE: Knock it off, sweetie.

LOUISE: It's true. Men cheat, or didn't you know?

FLORENCE (to MARIA): How did it end?

LOUISE: Florence, you've got to be the most insensitive person I've ever met.

MARIA: That's all right. Florence is Florence! She means well.

FLORENCE: Well, I do mean well!

LOUISE: Have you seen a doctor?

MARIA: A medical doctor or a psychiatrist?

LOUISE: Psychiatrist.

```
MARIA:    No, I don't think that's my problem.

FLORENCE: That's what psychiatrists are for.  I wouldn't say this to everyone,
          but I've been, and I tell you, I couldn't have made it without him . . .

LOUISE:   Freudian?

FLORENCE: No.

LOUISE:   The other kind are useless and, darling, don't argue.  I've been
          through the whole thing with the other kind.  It's Freudian.  It's sex.
          That's the problem and you'd better believe it.

MARIA:    It's having a child that's my concern.

LOUISE:   That's sex.  What do you think having a child is?  And I don't mean
          the intercourse . . . I'm talking about it, the child.  I don't mean
          that in a dirty way, or that there's anything conscious there, but after
          five years of analysis, you begin to understand the whole set-up.

BILLY MAE: Well, I've got three, and they're anything but sexual.

LOUISE:   I'm talking about Freudian.

BILLY MAE: Changing the diapers and all that, and listening to the screaming
          and the yelling . . .

LOUISE:   In the Freudian sense . . .

BILLY MAE: . . . and hearing that awful sound of "Mommy," that means trouble.

LOUISE:   It means you're needed.

MARIA:    I'm not going to any psychiatrist, that settles that.

FLORENCE: Well, anyway . . .

LOUISE:   It's done then, you're sure?

MARIA:    It's done.

LOUISE:   Darling, it never would have happened if you kept him in line.  Husbands
          aren't born, you know . . . They're made!

BILLY MAE: Now she's going to tell us about Fred . . .

LOUISE:   Fred behaves himself.  If I have to kill him, he'll behave.

BILLY MAE: Careful, Louise . . . One day . . . bang . . . you're dead, Fred!

LOUISE:   A woman is given insight.  Use it.  Train him.  Once they're trained
          they're fine.  Do you know that Fred dies to go to bed with me and we've
          been married fifteen years?

BILLY MAE: That's fifteen years of death.

LOUISE:   I have a double indemnity one hundred thousand dollar life policy . . .
```

The secret agendas of desire
—Obliquities of expression and endless competitive maneuverings for position

Maria's friends gather to comfort her after Richard leaves. Two pages from the script of
Faces, *completed in 1965. The entire half-hour scene from which this is taken was included in preview prints of the film, but was cut from the final version.*

What matters at these moments is not the mere physical presence of others, but the emotional awkwardnesses, the social unbalances, and the psychological asymmetries that must be negotiated and lived through. Cassavetes' film passages are "passages" in the other sense of the word as well—time-bound journeys through and around resistances that the individual can never hope to escape. No film experience is more of a rite of passage for both the viewers of the film and the characters within it through the difficult, complex web of social relations that surrounds the individual.

It is in this respect that the visual style of *Faces* is most revolutionary. One could possibly attribute much of the style of *Shadows* (many of its hand-held camera effects, for example) to the limitations of Cassavetes' equipment and novice crew, and the visual styles of *Too Late Blues* and *A Child Is Waiting* are hopelessly muddled by the studio production systems out of which those films evolved. *Faces* is the first film in which one can be sure that Cassavetes' stylistic results were his own. For all the tightness of his budget, he had enough time, money, and equipment to be in complete control of his stylistic choices. What is interesting is the completeness of his break with the syntax of the conventional Hollywood film.

Faces utterly renounces the two basic shot patterns of the standard studio film: the shot–reverse shot alternation of two talking heads for the analysis of a dialogue, and the alternation of objective and subjective (or point-of-view) shots for the analysis of events or actions. (It should be obvious, incidentally, that the first technique is only a special instance of the second.) Both techniques are so common in the syntax of the sound feature film that it is almost impossible to watch a film that does not employ them. But no mater how common they may be, or how much they seem merely to be neutral technical devices for constructing a film experience, what Cassavetes realized was that they have profound moral and social ramifications. The tyranny of even the most conventional stylistic technique is absolute, and perhaps all the more insidious when it seems as inevitable and invisible as these techniques. It is all too easy to forget that almost no dialogue in real life ever takes place with the rhythms, alternations, and limitations of attention that classical intercutting of two talking heads creates. It is all too easy to forget how subtly the point-of-view shot insinuates the validity and importance of sovereign, separate, individual points of view. Both techniques implicitly wrench the individual out of the contexts in which he exists and isolate and separate him from others.

It is no coincidence that both techniques are the warp and woof of the standard Hollywood film. They grant actors exactly the kind of imperial power to control and arrange a screen space around themselves that is the heart of Hollywood's romantic aesthetic. The star system of autonomous, individual egos exerting dramatic power over our perceptions *is* these shot patterns, and the very thing Cassavetes brings into question in his work. He has written that first and foremost "man is a social animal,"[9] and the problem with these shot patterns is that they inordinately limit (when they do not outright abolish) the range of relevant human society at any given moment in a film. The social relationships Cassavetes is interested in exploring cinematically are just too complex to be analyzed in this traditional grammar and to be expressed in this way.

Cassavetes' techniques of photography and editing work to reestablish the democratic contexts around any individual, to resist the individual's effort to isolate himself from, or to elevate himself above, the social group of which he is a part. In doing something as apparently simple as setting up his camera to one side of a group of characters (rather than at the imaginary vantage point of one or two of them) he instantly downplays the importance of any one point of view. In attending equally to each and every member of a group, he automatically abolishes the star system pecking order of other films. To say that this is a standard documentary camera technique takes nothing away from its radicalness when it is used in a nondocumentary situation—i.e., in a feature film with recognizable and consistent characters. The individual character is no longer able to control or dominate the visual space of the frame or the social space of a scene as in the traditional fictional film. He is everywhere put back into a series of elaborated contexts and relationships—physical, psychological, and social.

But this documentary photographic technique is rudimentarily present in Cassavetes' work in the three films before *Faces,* and if *Faces* did nothing more than this, it would not be the breakthrough it is. What Cassavetes discovers in *Faces* is an editing technique of contrapuntal cutting that does full justice to his photographic vision of human relationships. In the central scenes in *Faces* the basic documentary shot from off to the side is intercut with shots of close-ups of individuals within the scene, cut not with, but against, or in counterpoint to, the action or dialogue.

If Cassavetes learned some of the expressive potential of documentary styles of photography from the contemporaneous experimental and *cinéma vérité* work of Shirley Clarke, Morris Engel, and Lionel Rogosin, he learned more than a little about the possibilities of contrapuntal editing from the old Hollywood master who taught him so much else—Frank Capra. Though the cornball quality of Capra's plots seems unfortunately to have deflected critical attention away from the fact, there is no more original and inventive editor in all of classic film. Consider one of the greatest moments in Capra's (or anyone else's) work—the long scene in *Meet John Doe* during which Long John Willoughby (Gary Cooper) prepares for and delivers his national radio speech. (There are so many similarities between the editing and staging of this scene in *Meet John Doe* and the one in *Shadows* in which Hughie abortively appears on stage to attempt his nightclub routine as to establish beyond doubt that it made an enormous impression on Cassavetes.) Willoughby is being coerced into giving a speech he has not written and does not believe in and Capra's contrapuntal editing captures the full complexity of his situation. Any minute of the film at this point is assembled out of ten or twenty separate cuts, each of which provides a slightly different view of one of the contexts around Cooper and puts a slightly different kind of pressure on him either to go through with the speech or to abandon it. The result is a reversal of the traditional aesthetic of the Hollywood film. *Meet John Doe* in this sequence is a film that actually resists the stardom of its central starring figure. Capra's editing creates contexts that surround and dwarf Cooper—contexts that everywhere contain him and to which he is continuously forced to become responsive. Cassavetes' editing does the same thing throughout *Faces*.

Consider the strange, awkward scene in the Forst's living room about halfway through the film. Richard has left to spend the night with Jeannie, and Maria and the women friends who have gathered around to console her have just returned from the Whiskey-A-Go-Go where they went to cheer themselves up and pretend they could have a good time independently of their husbands. They have brought back with them a drifter they have met there, Chet, who will eventually spend the night with Maria. It is a typical instance of an absurdly, awkwardly asymmetrical situation of the sort that occurs many times in *Faces*: the women are close friends and have known one another for years; Chet is an absolute stranger. It is in the air that Maria will spend the night with him and yet no one dares to say it. The friends are all trying their best to be publicly supportive in Maria's time of distress, but we and they know the first thing they will do the next morning is get together to condemn her and to gossip about the scandalousness of the evening. It is a situation painful and awkward in the extreme, and one's heart goes out to Maria in the clumsiness of this attempt to be even temporarily free of her husband, as she anxiously, shyly, ineptly flirts with Chet and endures the glances of her three middle-aged friends. But Cassavetes is interested in more than misery under glass. He is attracted to moments of imbalance because they are also moments of possibility, moments when characters (and the actors who play those characters) are forced into new, unaccustomed expressive positions, and unforeseeable, unpredictable, unprovided-for relations. Asymmetrical, awkward moments offer possibilities of personal exploration and expression precisely because they deny us, the characters, and the actors the luxury of reclining into our conventional patterns of response.

As the scene begins, the ladies seat themselves around the periphery of the room, embarrassedly wondering who dares make the first move. Chet, the youngest in the group, and the outsider, is interestingly enough the most poised and comfortable of them all. He tries (unsuccessfully) to break the ice with comic banter. He is obviously good at picking up women for one-night stands, and confident of his abilities to put them at ease. He almost enjoys the challenge of it.

It is the sort of moment of unspecified possibility in which Cassavetes' films abound. There is no clear action or predictable event around which the characters may be organized, or in comparison with which the progress of the scene may be measured. There is no way to arrange this unbalanced group into easily demarcated sides or alternative points of view. The scene presents a web of continuously shifting pressures, influences, and relationships in which a standard shot–reverse shot analysis of the dialogue or the relationships would be useless or misleading. Consider a representative and unexceptional section of the script from pages 280–86 in the published final text of *Faces*. Instead of attempting to assemble the scene out of alternating shots of speakers and listeners engaged in conversation, moving from one isolated speaker to another, Cassavetes intercuts and edits together, in what are in all only two or three minutes of the scene, close-ups of over forty interrelated glances, responses, and adjustments of position among the five participants. Any one remark or gesture is situated in a matrix of complexly intermeshed reactions, tentative advances, and corrections of feeling. (Something approximating this complexity of editing was achieved momentarily in *Shadows* in the scene in which David, Lelia, Ben, Tom, and Dennis talk together at a table in a coffee shop. But what was lacking in *Shadows* in that scene, as well as in the scene involving Hugh's nightclub performance, was a social and psychological situation complex and nuanced enough to justify, and even demand, the detailed registration of four, five, or six sets of interrelated glances, tones, and facial expressions.)

Cassavetes' work (especially *Faces* and *A Woman Under the Influence*, with their severe spatial and temporal confinements) is frequently called stagey, but almost none of these effects would be available in an actual stage production of one of his scripts. A stage production puts a premium on the spoken word, but the real "text" of *Faces* is the series of glances and facial expressions that counterpoint the spoken words of the script and that only Cassavetes' close-up camera and contrapuntal editing is capable of registering. In fact, shot–reverse shot conversational exchanges in a more conventionally edited film—say a late Hitchcock picture—would probably lose less in translation to the stage than one of Cassavetes' scenes would.

Take half a page of dialogue from the scene discussed above—a typical sequence in *Faces*, and one that in its ordinariness could easily have been trimmed entirely from the film in the interests of brevity. But the fact that Cassavetes retained this moment and so many others similar to it indicates that it is just this sort of thing he is most intensely interested in exploring. The women around him have just asked Chet why he goes to places like the Whiskey-A-Go-Go to dance:

Chet:	. . . Hey, listen, man, it's a very good way to express yourself.
Billy Mae:	What do you mean?
Chet:	What?
Billy Mae:	I said, what do you mean?
Chet:	I said, like, take a guy my age. Now I've got to have some kind of release. Now do you want to—Well, I can't very well hold up a bank for kicks. That's against the law, right?
Louise:	Right.
Florence:	Right, Chetty.
Chet:	Everybody agrees with me. So right, what do you do?
Louise:	You dance.
Chet:	You dance. You have a few belts and go up to some chick's pad, then make it, baby.
Louise:	Make it?
Chet:	Just make it, baby. You out and lay down and . . . Or you can sit around and have a drag and think about what's wrong and all, you know.

Louise:	Oh, I know what you mean.
Chet:	I think you do.
Billy Mae:	Sure she does.
Chet:	Sure she does.
Billy Mae:	Well, Louise, Maria, Florence, this is it: the new generation, the one our husbands are frightened to death of.
Chet:	That's funny. Funny as hell.
Louise:	Billy Mae, how did you happen to get on the subject of our husbands again?

As the inanity, pointlessness, and repetitiousness of this conversation should indicate, what is going on here is not an exchange of information or a buildup toward some action, but a continuous process of jockeying for position among these characters. That is why these nineteen bits of dialogue, lasting only about a minute or so of running time, are accompanied by something like twenty separate close-ups of the faces of the five participants.

As in a scene by Pinter on the stage, what matters here is not the explicit content of individual statements, but the subtext of shifting power relations between characters. Near the end of this excerpt, when Chet, Louise, and Billy Mae each agree that they understand what has been said, it is not an exchange of information that is taking place, but a process of positioning *vis-à-vis* one another. We are watching a process of interpersonal negotiation, of the sort that goes on throughout *Faces.*

There are frequent close-ups in this process of contrapuntal intercutting, but Cassavetes' every effort is devoted to preventing the close-up from isolating a character and setting him apart from, or above, the group of which he is always (in Cassavetes' cinematic world) an equal member. (Note that it is not a question of whether a filmmaker intends to do this or not. A close-up has this effect independent of his desires. It spotlights one character even as it hides others. It inevitably separates a figure from its background and a person from a social context.)

The most common way Cassavetes defeats the isolating effect of the close-up is by counterpointing the sound track against the visual track of *Faces,* so that even as we are looking closely at one actor, we are hearing the voice of another off screen. At other times, Cassavetes will deliberately (and jarringly) fracture the boundaries of the frame itself to remind us of the simultaneous presence of others at any one moment. Even as we focus on one character within the frame, the foot, leg, arm, hand, or part of the body of that figure or another will extend out of or

intrude into the corner of the frame, reminding us of the web of connections and relations outside our view at any one moment.

Cassavetes' use of hand-held shots for 90 percent of *Faces* is another
way he prevents the frame space from rigidifying around a character.
(As he did not in *Shadows*, during *Faces* Cassavetes had the use of a
dolly-mounted Arriflex but, after watching the dailies, chose instead to
use a hand-held Eclair.) *Faces* would not even remotely be the same film
photographed with the fixed framing of a dolly or tripod. Fixed framing
rigidifies the space it defines, and shuts out everything outside the
frame. But Cassavetes' hand-held shots sweep through the space in
front of, behind, or around a character repeatedly to remind us of all the
spaces not included in any one instantaneous shot. And even when the
camera operator is not deliberately moving his camera, the frame
boundary in a hand-held shot erratically shifts just enough at any
moment to prevent the space inside the frame from rigidifying and
what is inside of it from cutting itself off from what is outside of it. The
person or group of people within the frame space is never allowed to
wall itself into an autonomous social, psychological, or emotional space
because the hand-held shot itself never creates a rigid, autonomous,
self-contained visual space. We are always and everywhere reminded
in *Faces* that we are watching only a part of the action, seeing things
from one particular and limited vantage point. We can never forget that
there is activity outside the frame as important as the activity within it.

Furthermore, even when a character is orthodoxly framed, in a
"well-composed," relatively fixed shot, with a clear margin of space
around him, Cassavetes will remind us of the context in which he exists
by having him listening to, looking at, or facing something or someone
outside the frame. (The most frequent form of this is to have a quick
movement of the character's eyes briefly register something going on
elsewhere in the room that we cannot see.) The result is that even in
close-up the individual has been dethroned as a sovereign, autonomous agent. Just as the character must, the viewer is forced to hold
two, three, or four separate social and imaginative spaces in contiguity
and competition with one another. (Similarly, Cassavetes' editorial
shuttling between Jeannie's apartment and the Forst's house builds the
process of visual and imaginative contextualization into the larger
structure of the film). The individual is never excerptible from a context. He is always reminded that he must be part of a larger society. The
social force field he must negotiate is made visually real and palpable.

The longer one watches a group scene such as this in *Faces*, in fact, the more central the schoolroom scenes of *A Child Is Waiting* become in an assessment of the development of Cassavetes' visual style. The shots of the groups of children in that film have the elegant asymmetry and energetic, unbalanced mobility of the composition of a painting by Degas. The moiling sea of the children's faces, the cluttered, interestingly unbalanced groupings, the ragged edges of the frames (with the childrens' faces, hands, or bodies continuously moving in and out of sight, breaking the boundaries of the rigidly fixed frame in that film)—all of these things probably taking place only because the retarded children of the hospital could not be controlled better or their placements blocked out more symmetrically and tidily—more and more seem to anticipate the nervous, fidgeting maneuvering for position of these characters caught together in an uncomfortable situation.

Sam Shaw, one of the great Hollywood portrait photographers, the producer of many of Cassavetes' films, one of his best friends, and the man Cassavetes credits with initially encouraging him to dare to write and direct his own work when he was just an unknown actor on Broadway, has described his framing in terms of a fascination with "fragments": "John doesn't like perfect shots. They'll set it up, and if it looks too good, he'll change it—stick a shoulder in front of the camera. He'll say, 'I don't want it beautiful.' . . . He's interested in fragments."[10] But it would be equally correct to reverse that observation, and argue that Cassavetes is less interested in "fragments" than in "wholes." What he distrusts about the "perfect" or "beautiful" shot is that it is a fragment that tries to masquerade (with its formal closure and apparent completeness) as a whole. What makes Cassavetes put the shoulder into the frame is not a lust for fragmentation as an end in itself, but a desire that the fragment always declare itself as a fragment and never pretend to be otherwise. Each shot reminds us that it is only a jigsaw puzzle piece of a larger, much more complex whole that can only be teased or juggled into existence through our experience in time of a whole series of fleeting, endlessly replaced fragments. The reason to avoid "beauty shots" is that the "beauty shot" presents itself as a final, summarizing, atemporal statement. It stops the timebound process of piecing things together, one after another, each piece repeatedly correcting and adjusting the placement of the last, that reflects the political nature of experience for Cassavetes.

As the title suggests, *Faces* is a film of close-ups and extreme close-ups, and characters repeatedly try to isolate themselves in a world of their own in the film. The successive close-ups register the enormous gaps of sympathy and incomprehension between characters. But, as I have been arguing, Cassavetes' photographic and editorial practice keeps reminding both them and us of their embeddedness in larger networks of relations. In the gathering of women discussed above, Maria Forst sits for almost the entire scene quietly off to the side of the group, almost without a line of dialogue. But such is the inclusiveness of Cassavetes' camerawork that even this silent and distant character does not drop out of the scene or our consciousness for even a minute. On the contrary, silent, distant, and shy Maria never ceases to be the psychological center of it. Cassavetes' camera includes her silence, stillness, and furtive glances toward Chet as much as it does the boisterous volubility of the others. No one point of view, however quiet, is allowed to be lost; no one point of view, no matter how raucous, is allowed to control or determine the course of a scene.

Cassavetes' scenes offer a continuous play of social and personal differences, contrasts, and comparisons as fluidly flexible and continuously adjusted as the actual play of jokes, stories, postures, and performances his characters engage in with one another. In place of isolable "actions" and "reactions," "speakers" and "listeners," "stars" and "supporting characters," *Faces* offers a choreographic complexity of human interrelations. And if one searches for a strict choreographic parallel in contemporary dance, it is specifically the choreography of George Balanchine and Paul Taylor that functions most like the choreographic movements and relations in Cassavetes. Balanchine's and Taylor's choreography is as far from the traditional romantic methods of scene making in dance, as Cassavetes' own aesthetic is from the traditional romantic methods of scene making in film. It is a choreography that denies the possibility of any one individual's arranging or controlling a scene around himself, a scene that fails to accommodate the rival needs of the others around him. Like his counterparts in contemporary dance, Cassavetes replaces the traditional (and audience pleasing) "star system" with an aesthetic of symphonically complex interactions and responsibilities within a social matrix from which an individual can no more exempt himself than he can dominate or control. The individual only matters, the performance only brings itself into existence in the continuous give and take of these relationships, in these unending shifts and recyclings of position.

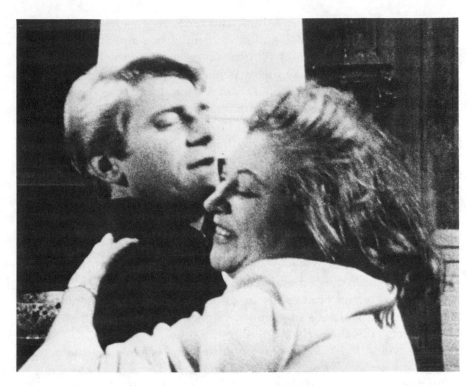

The anxious, eccentric movements of imagination and desire
—*Florence dancing with Chet*

Faces demonstrates an evenhandedness toward the complexity of human relationships and the moment-by-moment unfolding of an experience that extends right down to its avoidance of musical scoring. Orthodox romantic movie music, like orthodox romantic scene making and photography, inevitably elevates certain passages and individuals at the expense of others. Nothing could be less in sympathy with Cassavetes' purpose. When he does use background scoring in the films that follow *Faces*—with the important exceptions of certain parts of *A Woman Under the Influence, Opening Night,* and *Gloria*—like the contemporary choreographers whose work his own most resembles, he significantly chooses to use jazz musical scorings as different as possible from the Max Steiner cadences and pacings of the orthodox Hollywood picture. (Steiner occupies a place in film history analogous to that of Tchaikovsky in dance: a genius with the defects of his virtues, a creative force with the limitations of his strengths.) While most romantic film scoring by Steiner and others offers the filmgoer the comfort of

a predictable structure of rhythmic and tonal progressions and elaborately prepared crescendos and decrescendos of emphasis and emotion, Cassavetes' films and film music create the artistic illusion of
something much more like the excitement, energy, and opportunistic
spontaneity of an improvised jazz jam session. Cassavetes' scenes and
the occasional musical scoring in his soundtracks create a polyphonic
reality of eccentric syncopations and competitive, but oblique and unstressed, juxtapositions of rival rhythms, pacings, and emphases. The
unbalanced dramatic tensions, surges, and swerves of his work are
emphatically in the twentieth-century urban American idiom of the
music of George Gershwin, Louis Armstrong, and Charlie Parker, with
its radical rhythmic, tonal, and emotional experimentation, and not in
the implicitly European and late-nineteenth-century spirit of almost all
other feature film orchestration. Specifically, in four of the six films
following *Faces,* Cassavetes relies on the brilliantly eccentric and energetic, though unstressed and "cool," jazz scoring of Bo Harwood, in
which the musical phrases are as unpredictably syncopated and demanding of a listener's moment-by-moment attention as Cassavetes'
dramatic scenes themselves are.

Cassavetes, like Capra in his populist films, is exploring the possibilities of democracy and the ramifications of democratic interaction.
But democracy is studied in these films not in the superficial form of a
trite thematic statement or as a plot event, but as a style that can
transform the possibilities of all life. Democracy becomes a style of
consciousness and social interaction in their films that makes itself felt
in the rhythms of editing and the composition of each shot. There is an
evenhandedness and equality of treatment for even the most minor
characters and a distaste for stardom in both Cassavetes' and Capra's
work that one feels could only have originated in America. And yet,
perhaps because of the exalted democratic ideals of their makers, no
works of art are more aware of the potential difficulties and frustrations
of democratic relations. No films speak more eloquently of the inordinate responsibilities of democratic understandings of experience, of
the tendency of groups to overwhelm the individual, to deny the individual imagination any power over social realities.

A concern as profound and pervasive as that Cassavetes demonstrates for the complications and ramifications of democratic relations
does not simply appear out of nothing at a specific point in an artist's
career, so one should not be surprised to find signs of it in his earliest
work and attitudes, right from his initial discomfort with the Holly-

wood organization of experience around the forms of stardom and his dissatisfaction with the star vehicles he had to act in. *Shadows, Too Late Blues,* and *A Child Is Waiting* each in its own way may be read as an interrogation of the inadequacy of star-system posturings, and as a plea for democratic interaction. (*Shadows* gently and comically mocks its star-struck adolescents; *Too Late Blues* disturbingly wonders out loud whether the individual star can avoid being ground down in the mill of the ordinary and the commercial; and *A Child Is Waiting* mounts an implicit visual argument on behalf of demoting stars such as Lancaster and Garland in favor of a democratic equality of attention to the retarded children.) The films criticize those who would exempt themselves from the difficulty of democratic responsiveness to those around them. But Cassavetes' criticisms of undemocratic forms of experience in his first three films have merely the strength of their negativity. Nowhere in *Shadows* or *Too Late Blues*, and only fleetingly in *A Child Is Waiting*, is Cassavetes able to articulate a positive model of what mature democratic relations would look like. In none of them is he able to offer his viewers a sustained, positive stylistic alternative to the star system self-dramatizations and melodramatizations he is debunking. That mature style is brought into existence for the first time in *Faces*.

Characters are forced to be so thoroughly responsible to others around them, so democratically involved in the destiny of others, that one can count on the fingers of both hands the number of scenes in which a character is even allowed to be alone in Cassavetes' films. His films are sometimes called "talky," but that is not out of any special interest on Cassavetes' part in ideas or abstractions, but because talk is one way of converting what would otherwise be private, individual experience into public, social relations between characters. In *Minnie and Moskowitz*, one of the characters, Seymour Moskowitz, flies from New York to Los Angeles at one point in the film. It is an unimportant moment in itself and could have easily been done with ten seconds of stock footage of an airplane in flight. But so uninterested is Cassavetes in the mere mechanics of life (or plot), and, conversely, so fascinated is he with the way talk makes something out of what would be the mere mechanical motions of life, that he wrote and filmed a brief scene between Seymour and two fellow passengers on the plane even though the two characters Seymour talks to never reappear again in the film and the scene itself adds little or nothing to our knowledge of Seymour. Later in the same film (it is an extremely "vehicular" work, to borrow an adjective from Emerson), there is a short scene in which Seymour drives his pickup truck into a Los Angeles parking lot. One thinks that surely this is a moment Cassavetes cannot transform into a social occasion. But he does, by having an "argument" between Seymour's truck and a car ensue. Their brief difference of opinion is played out in a hilarious dialogue of beeps and honks on their two horns as each vehicle competes for a space in the lot. Everything from preparing a meal (in *Faces* and *A Woman Under the Influence*) to having sexual intercourse (in *Shadows, Faces, Husbands,* and *A Woman Under the Influence*) to being forced to commit a murder (in *The Killing of a Chinese Bookie* and *Gloria*) matters only insofar as it presents an opening to discourse, an opportunity for social interaction. In fact, for all Cassavetes' much vaunted fidelity to real time in *Faces,* and his distrust of "trimming," he has systematically cut all of Richard's many car trips back and forth from his home to the Loser's Club and from the Loser's Club to Jeannie's apartment. The reason is that Richard at these moments is solitary (as he is at no other time in the film) and therefore absolutely uninteresting to this filmmaker fascinated with social interactions.

"Experience" in these films is not something that one "has" or "feels" in privacy and isolation, as in the high Romantic sensibility. Rather, in a virtually Elizabethan sense, it is something that is exuberantly negotiated and socially performed into existence in the company of others. The enormous social complexity of relationships in these films is never merely oppressive or threatening to the individual, but is a stimulation to him, an invigoration to additional feats of performance. It is in this respect that Cassavetes' work differs so markedly from that of Robert Altman, which might be described with a superficially similar set of terms involving its Whitmanesque plentitude, questioning of the star system, and social complexity. The visual, aural, and narrative complexity in Altman's work seem in the service of a sensibility entirely opposite in nature to that of Cassavetes—as different as Edith Wharton or Theodore Dreiser are from Henry James. Altman's films depict personality on the verge of obliteration and extinction. To compare lesser creations to much greater, Altman's characters are more like Melville's Pierre or Pynchon's Slothrup, lost and half-smothered under layers of intellectual, bureaucratic, technological, and mechanical packaging. They can break loose only momentarily in the eccentric and fragmented forms of outrageousness, hysterics, rantings, tics, or self-caricaturings. But for Cassavetes, and this is his most Elizabethan quality, such entailments, complications, and networks of artificial relations are not to be wished-away, transcended, or nostalgically regretted, but to be embraced. It is precisely in negotiating various styles of relationship and networks of influence that the individual is brought into fullest and most robust existence. There is no greater believer in the power of the human spirit or in the supreme value of democratic interaction. The result is that even Cassavetes' most tragic films seem paradoxically more hopeful, more positive, and more life-affirming than Altman's comedies.

Faces is, of course, a tragedy, the record not of successful performers and performances, but of the excesses, crudities, and insensitivities of flawed performances and failed relationships. And just as it takes the mastery of a Balanchine to choreograph recognizable and unexaggerated human clumsiness in a dance, it takes a camera as patiently observant and an editing technique as precisely timed as Cassavetes' to make us fully aware of the mistakes, miscues, and mistimings of a social performance. *Faces*, as Cassavetes has pointed out, is a film about "timings"—the continuously readjusted timings of love and consideration and the missed timings of insensitivity, inconsideration, and misunderstanding. The subject of all of Cassavetes' work might in the most general sense be described as all that D. H. Lawrence meant by the phrase, "the adjusting of the oscillating, unestablished balance between two people who amount to anything."

No scene more poignantly captures "the trembling and oscillating of the balance," the "quickness" and "movement" of "living human relationships" (in Lawrence's terms) than the minute or so that follows the section of *Faces* discussed above. Chet is attempting to open up lines of communication with Louise, Billy Mae, Florence, and Maria by performing for them and inviting them to join with him in performance. He deliberately sings a comically off-color song to them ("Give me the red meat, baby"), but these women with their bouffant hairdos and their tailored suits are less embarrassed by the suggestiveness of the lyrics than by the suggestiveness of the moment—the sudden access of possibilities and emotions they sense, as they sit in a room with someone so different from their own husbands, at a gathering so remote from any of their own suburan kaffeeklatsches.

The episode that follows takes no more than a minute or two of film time, but it is typical of the emotional density of *Faces* that in that brief time a whole relationship between Chet and Louise is created, developed, and destroyed. From the preceding minutes of *Faces*, we have seen that Louise is an anxious intellectual who uses her considerable analytic powers to hold herself aloof from the rest of the group of women, but it is significant that even she is seduced into a momentary relationship with Chet. The script at this point reads as follows:

> *Chet leaves Florence and goes to Louise, trying to entice her to dance with him.*
>
> *Louise*: No.
> *Chet*: Come on.
> *Louise*: No.
> *Chet*: Come on, it's easy
> *Louise*: No.
> *Chet*: Right shoe, right shoe. Come on, Baby, Come on.
> *Chet*: (*singing to Louise*):
> Put on the red meat, baby.
> I want the red meat, baby.
> I like the rare meat, baby.
> No 'taters or no onions,
> All I want to do is tongue ya.
>
> That's it. Where are you . . . come here.
> *Louise*: No.
> *Chet*: Right here, baby, it's easy.
>
> I need the red meat, baby.
> That grooves me like the white meat, baby.
> Put it in the oven, warm it big and round
> Put it in the oven, eat it off the ground.
> Come and do the slip and slide,
> I ain't had no goodies since your grannie died,
> Put on the red meat, baby (*etc.*)
>
> *Maria rises, walks out and Chet stops and watches her.*
> *Louise*: I like the red meat, baby . . .
> *Chet*: (*quietly looking after Maria*): I think we're making fools of ourselves.
> *Louise*: (*startled*): What?
> *Chet*: Yeh.
> *Louise*: I'm making a fool of myself?
> *Chet*: Well, we are, yeh.
> *Louise*: (*indignantly*): Who are you to criticize me?
> *Chet*: I'm not criticizing, I was just saying . . .
> *Louise*: (*angrily*): Well, you don't have to tell me I'm making a fool of myself. Look, I know how to dance *my* way, I don't need you to tell me about it. I come from a musical background. I take care of my family of five. I have a college degree, and I don't need you to tell me I'm making a fool of myself.
> *Chet*: Will you . . .
> *Louise*: Don't touch me!

The words Cassavetes has scripted are deceptively simple and repetitive, but the emotional transactions at this moment are as complex as anything he has ever filmed. In this couple of minutes, Louise and Chet go from being strangers to incipient lovers, and back again to being enemies. The camera shows Louise making four separate advances and retreats as Chet sings his dirty little ditty to her. She goes from embarrassment and refusal to participate, to a strained self-conscious effort, to something like enjoyment and surrender, and then back to a revulsion against Chet and her own sexual impulses. In epitome this is what is going on each and every moment of this film—a timebound series of adjustments and transactions that will not sit still for the camera or the participants in the scene. *Faces* is a continuous calculus of infinite variations, and at a moment such as this one cannot help feeling how immensely far Cassavetes has progressed beyond the relatively cruder (but, in their more modest places, equally touching and effective) dances of doubt, hesitation, attraction, and repulsion that he choreographed between Tony and Lelia in *Shadows* and Ghost and Jessie in *Too Late Blues*. These slipping, sliding movements and frictional resistances between two people are the necessary dance of love for Cassavetes.

The continuous adjustments and readjustments of relationship are exactly what make *Faces* such a demanding viewing experience and a film that frustrates attempts to pin its characters down into predictable positions. Cassavetes was aware of how different this made the characters and events in *Faces* from those of other, more conventional films. As he told an interviewer:

The . . . script was structured very carefully to set up a whole new [way] of thinking so that the audience could not get ahead of the film. Most people think, "Oh, yes, this is what's going to happen in the next moment." What happens with *Faces* though is that . . . the film really bugs people because it doesn't fit any easy pattern of behavior.

Well, I don't know anybody who has an easy pattern of behavior. I know people who are just sensational one minute, and absolute bastards the next. Terribly funny one minute, and morose the next. And these moods come from specific things that I can't put my finger on because I don't know their whole life. And in two hours and nine minutes, we can't put their whole life on the screen. So I've got to depend on that [actor] to identify with his role enough that he can express those things. And to get it on the screen is something miraculous.[11]

What makes Cassavetes' characters so free, so full of possibility, so unovercome by the pressure of events and surroundings (so unlike

Altman's characters) is just his faith in their capacity to break out of patterns of behavior. Without this capacity, they would necessarily be overwhelmed by the formal, psychological, and narrative constraints of a film like *Faces*. No matter how unenviable their situations (and it would be hard to imagine a more pathetic scene than this bleak gathering of middle-aged women around this young drifter), Cassavetes holds out the possibility of freedom and renewal for each and every one of these characters. The balance is, in Lawrence's metaphor, always free to "oscillate." But, needless to say, the point of the conclusion of this excerpt from the screenplay is that Louise (like each of the other characters in *Faces*) ultimately flees from the oscillations of the balance—she puts her thumb in the pan and damps the frightening, stimulating, exposing interaction between herself and Chet. She becomes afraid of the possibilities that are opened up before her and retreats back into the comfort of a fixed, absolute position.

Faces repeatedly opens up Lawrencian possibilities of imbalance and oscillation that its characters ultimately retreat from. The mistake Richard and Maria make is not their infidelity to each other, their attempts to find love and independence in one-night stands, but their unwillingness to play the game without security, to take the full risks and responsibilities of freedom. They each spend the night with another person, but they are finally unwilling to make themselves vulnerable to that other person in an intimate human relationship. After wanting to break down the walls of reserve and reticence around them, they want to be able to withdraw to the safety of those same walls if pain intrudes. Each and every character in the film plays with the possibilities of free, new, unpatterned relationships and, like Louise, each and every one of them finally scurries back from the wildness that suddenly looms before him to the walled enclosures of empty social conventions and polite veneers. It is a pattern of behavior that we will see again in *Husbands*.

For all the endless possibilities of communication and readjustment that *Faces* continuously opens up, it is finally an anthology of failures of communication. The failures run the gamut of possible relations—from the opening scene in which a group of executives and PR men gather to screen a film with all the false familiarities, vapid politenesses, and empty critical cant of a Hollywood boardroom, to the bedroom scene near the end of the film after Jeannie and Richard have made love, where Richard shows himself only capable of uttering the same vacuous jokes, pleasantries, and polite chitchat to Jeannie that he has used to evade personal commitments throughout the film. For all the talk, talk, talk, of this film, there is, with only the rarest exceptions, no emotional communication at all between characters. The endless anecdotes, jokes, and banter are only a smokescreen of evasions and avoidances. That is why *Faces* is so far from being reducible to its screenplay. The words characters mouth are, in fact, the least of the processes of communication in the film. Under all the words is the film's true subtext—a photographic dialogue of glances and expressions that is where communication takes place, to the extent it takes place at all, in this film.

And yet *Faces* is never interested in mocking its characters. Their relationships are too fluidly alive and too open to unexplored possibilities for satire to be an appropriate or adequate response to them. Just as in *Shadows*, Cassavetes is interested not in hurrying but in postponing final judgment on his characters. Consider the long second scene of the film, when we see Richard and Freddie at Jeannie's apartment after they have picked her up in a bar after work. It is undeniable that , in the course of the scene, Freddie and (to a lesser extent) Richard are implicitly measured and judged by the standards of Jeannie's tact and sensitivity and found wanting. But the leisurely pacing, the continuous repositionings of the principals with respect to one another, and the endless adjustments and readjustments of relationships deliberately give Freddie and Richard a chance to explain and redeem themselves. We learn about Richard, Freddie, and Jeannie and form judgments about them the way they do with one another—gradually and hesitantly, in a series of surmises, guesses, and endless revisions. They no more stand still for our judgments of them than they do for one another. They play games, put on airs, experiment with attitudes, and make adjustments and corrections of relationship as they go along.

The choreographic metaphor I have been using is more than a metaphor in this scene. Cassavetes actually has his three characters dance with and for one another, and trade partners, in a deliberate process of choreographic variation. Jeannie dances with Freddie while Richard watches; Richard dances with Jeannie while Freddie watches; Richard and Freddie perform an old college routine while Jeannie watches; Jeannie does a striptease bump and grind while Freddie and Richard watch. None of the "strange irregular rhythms" of a human relationship are elided or abridged. Cassavetes preserves all of the incipient overtures and implicit rejections, the approaches and withdrawals, the moments of daring and afterthoughts of caution that defy more concise narrative or metaphorical summarization.

It is because he is so much a master of the timings of relationships that Cassavetes can be so discriminating about the insensitivities and mistimings of his characters. Nothing is a surer sign of inadequacy than the sort of inflexible, unresponsive, and repetitive performances most of the characters in *Faces* indulge in. The problem with the businessmen, salesmen, and suburban housewives of the film is that they cannot adjust their performances lovingly and sensitively enough in the presence of others. They can only, in the words Cassavetes applied to himself in the years before he made *Faces,* "play games—painful and stupid, falsely satisfying and economically rewarding."

Cassavetes' sympathies are infinitely more with the prostitute Jeannie Rapp and the gigolo Chet than with either of the groups they interact with: these businessmen with their manipulative, high-pressure tactics and mechanical humor; or these women with their prefabricated patterns of decorum and public standards of decency and virtue. What makes Chet and Jeannie more interesting than either of these groups is that they are "professional" performers in the best sense of the word, performers capable of continuously adjusting, reassessing, and correcting their performances in response to the needs of the people around them who make up their "audience." This capacity to adjust one's performance, to avoid rigidifying into any one pattern of behavior is, in effect, the definition of sensitivity and understanding in Cassavetes' moral universe. To the extent that characters are incapable of infinitely and indefinitely adjusting their tones, expressions, and words in a living and continuously changing relationship with one or more other persons, they are incapable of love.

No film since the work of Carl Dreyer holds up more intense possibilities of sensitivity and awareness even as it communicates the inability of its characters to realize those possibilities. The use of extreme close-ups in *Faces* communicates both the theoretical possibility of infinitely sensitive human communication and the practical, social unattainability of such sensitivity in ordinary life. Like Dreyer, Cassavetes is fascinated with the expressive possibilities of the human face and uses close-ups to register the most subtle fluctuations of feeling in characters' expressions; but the paradox is that precisely to the extent that characters' feelings are registered in close-up, *Faces* suggests how unavailable they are for normal social intercourse. In short, if

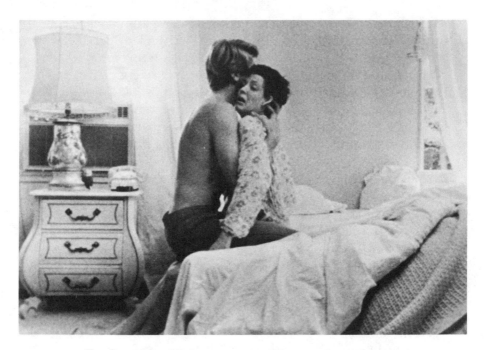

Tenderness and intimacy expressible in art but not in life
—*Maria and Chet*

Cassavetes' close-ups make us aware of nuances of feeling that we may
never have seen in film before, it is only by way of reminding us how
invisible such feelings are to the characters themselves, who lack the
microscopic sensitivity of Cassavetes' camera and the temporal alert-
ness of his editing procedures. The close-ups are necessary precisely
because the emotional signals of these characters are too delicate to be
broadcast longer distances without their aid (except in the distorted and
evasive forms of the hysterical jokes, skits, and laughs that run
throughout the film) and too weak to be received by any instrument
less sensitive, patient, and attentive than Cassavetes' camera. The
deepest lesson of the editing and photography of *Faces* is the profound
difference between our views of these characters' feelings and relationships and their own views of one another. There is finally no
bridge between its emotionally isolated, insulated, lonely characters
but the film itself and a viewer's own cinematically enriched consciousness.

That is why one can paradoxically argue that perhaps the most
poignant and touching moment of love in the entire film, the most

tender embrace, is one whose plangency and love is invisible to both of the characters involved in it. The moment I am thinking of is the nearly silent scene near the end of *Faces* when Chet is trying to revive Maria after her suicide attempt. The fact that it is a recapitulation of Jack Lemmon's efforts to revive the suicidal Shirley MacLaine in Billy Wilder's *The Apartment*—Lynn Carlin coincidentally even looks a bit like Shirley MacLaine—takes nothing from its achievement. Though it was the scene most frequently criticized in initial reviews of *The Apartment*, Cassavetes must have seen it for what it was, one of the most touching and complex moments in all of Wilder's work. It is the scene that crowns *Faces*.

A large part of the effect of the scene, as of many of the moments in *Faces*, is the result of its juxtaposition with what comes immediately before it. Cassavetes cuts from a brilliantly lighted breakfast scene between Richard and Jeannie at her place that, unlike the rest of *Faces*, was shot on plus-x-reversal stock, a close-grained film, for a pointedly "pretty" effect. It is a gorgeous scene full of the sounds of banter, jokes, and laughter between Richard and Jeannie (however hollow it all is). The film cuts from that to sudden silence and a stark, shadowy glimpse through the bedroom doorway of Maria's body lying on the bathroom floor, shot with grainy, plus-x-negative film "pushed" in processing. The grotesque pantomime that follows for the next eight minutes as Chet tries to revive Maria has for a sound track only the noises of Chet's slaps, grunts, and curses, and then the final sound of Maria vomiting up the pills she has swallowed. But there is strangely more care, more true intimacy, and more tenderness at this moment than at any other time in all of *Faces*, though the sensitivity, care, and tact in this scene do not, strictly speaking, originate in Chet and Maria, and exist not in their relationship, but in the relationship of Cassavetes and the audience to them at this point near the end of *Faces*.

But the whole point of *Faces* is the necessity of continual readjustment of all relationships within it and all relationships to it. The scenes in *Faces* will no more stand still for our critical appreciations of them than they will stand still for the characters' social and emotional appropriations of them. For a relationship, social or critical, to stop changing would be for it to be doomed to die for Cassavetes. Endless negotiation is the only certainty in this temporally, psychologically, and emotionally relentless experience. That is why, as touching as the scene between Maria and Chet is, Cassavetes will not let us imaginatively expand within it. We cannot pause over its poignancy or pathos even for the length of a fade-out.

Maria comes to, but rather than feeling gratitude or love for Chet, who has literally saved her life, her initial reaction is a feeling of shame, violation, and hatred for him. (The author of "You Touched Me" would have understood the swerves of feeling, and so much else in this film, though Cassavetes shows no sign of an indebtedness to, or even an awareness of, D. H. Lawrence.) But Maria does eventually warm to Chet and at the very moment when, still pale and shivering, she starts to snuggle up against him on the bed, Cassavetes again pulls the rug out from under the viewer with an even more abrupt tonal shift. All of the emotion that has accumulated between Maria and Chet is suddenly dissipated by a cut to a shot of Richard unexpectedly pulling into the driveway, getting out of the car, and comically dancing and singing ("I'm ready") to himself as he enters the house. That is followed by a bizarre static shot from the bedroom window of Chet making a Harold Lloyd escape across the roof of the house, leaping onto the garage roof, and bounding across the lawn and down a hill out of sight. And then this comic silent movie escape is itself capped with Richard's sudden tirade of anger and abuse at Maria as he condemns her for being unfaithful to him.

There is no need to belabor the ironies and hypocrisies of the situation that are obvious to every viewer. But it is these tonal shifts and sudden reversals that leave everyone gasping at the end of this film and make more schematic descriptions of the abstract shape and structures of *Faces* (or talk about its irony) seem so inadequate. The point of these tonal lurches is precisely that Cassavetes is denying us (or these characters) any possibility of a fixed, resolved, mechanical relation to these experiences. Dependable, monotonic patterns of response—the sort of things most serious film viewers go to a film in search of—are the very things Cassavetes is attempting to move us and his characters beyond.

If one is determined to draw a moral or point from the excruciations of *Faces*, it is that the only salvation lies in the renunciation of all systematic and mechanical relations to experience, critical or social. The alternative Cassavetes offers is a timebound aesthetic of continuous, infinitely sensitive adjustments and negotiations between any two people who care about each other. But, as I have already said, this is a standard of awareness, sensitivity, and improvisatory openness to the complexity of any moment for which only Cassavetes' own camerawork and editing can stand as a sufficiently sensitive and loving example.

Chet and Jeannie, the professional performers in the film, intermittently demonstrate the capacity for continually revised sensitivity, for endlessly adjusted performance, that is the ideal of behavior in *Faces*. But the real hero of the film, the greatest, most sensitive, most aware performer in *Faces* is not a character in it. It is John Cassavetes, the creator of the film, whose scripting, photography, and editing are in themselves a paradigm of the endless labor of loving awareness and inclusiveness that none of the characters even comes close to matching. The quality of consciousness offered by the artistic experience of the film is higher than anything realizable or expressible in the lives of the characters within it or in life in the world outside of it. No more than in the work of Henry James, can life live up to this exalted artistic imagination of it.

CHAPTER V

IN DREAMS BEGIN RESPONSIBILITIES
Husbands

Husbands depicts the American man without any camouflage.

These three men are forty-year-old kids. They're happy. They do whatever they want to. It's our night out, the way we'd like to take our night out. We'd like to take people on our trip with us, to break all the conventions that bug us, without being moralists about anything. . . .
  The hope of course is that people stay crazy. It's really no fun to work with sane people, people who have a set way of doing things. . . . That's also the reason I'm looking forward to playing with Peter Falk and Ben Gazzara. We don't care what the problems will be. As long as we stay crazy. If we became all nice people who are very polite, we'd never get along together. Because basically we're bums. I mean, I'm basically a bum. I know a lot of my enemies would agree with that too. But I don't think that's such a bad thing. I think it's more fun. I think I probably have the philosophy of a poor man. You know, like maybe I'd steal the pennies off a dead man's eyes. *John Cassavetes*

The final minute of *Faces* is a summary of all of the imaginative immobility, emotional paralysis, and mechanical insensitivity the preceding two hours and eight minutes document. Cassavetes holds a fixed camera on Richard and Maria Forst sitting separated by the length of the stairs, boxed in by the floor, walls, and ceiling of their home as tightly as they are boxed in by the four walls of the static frame. If they are momentarily together in the frame, they are lifetimes apart in the experience of the film we and they have just lived through. Cassavetes denies them even the final, excruciating luxury of having their differences explode into apocalypse or melodrama. Even as they sit there, they begin again the deadening cycle of social rituals that their only hope had been to escape. They pass cigarettes and matches back and forth, but there is no more personal communication for them in those gestures than there is possibility of a release from their solitary confinement together. As the house lights come up in the theater, they walk off in opposite directions, out of the now empty frame, more estranged, frustrated, and unable to express themselves to each other than ever before.

The films Cassavetes makes after *Faces* are, one after another, explorations of the possibility of escape from the confinements, isolation, and failures of expression that *Faces* documented. In their different ways, *Husbands, Minnie and Moskowitz,* and *A Woman Under the Influence* are attempts to break the stalemate and paralysis, to imagine some escape for his characters from bleak entrapments and hysterical failures of communication. But as Cassavetes knows (to quote an aphorism of Robert Frost's) "the best way out is always through." That is to say, the way out of the Forst home is not to be found in a sudden wild escape, or by eliding and avoiding the problems *Faces* raised, but by plunging more deeply into them, by living through everything yet again.

After his two disastrous studio productions, the festering resentments of his years of underemployment, and the long, dreary months spent mending 16mm sprocket holes and tediously editing the film alone at home—*Faces* made John Cassavetes' reputation. At the age of thirty-nine, he proved to the world, and perhaps to himself, that the freshness and originality of *Shadows*, nine years before, had not been a fluke. And *Faces* was a popular success as *Shadows* had never been. It joined the select ranks of those few fully mature recent films (along with two or three films by Antonioni, Fellini, and Kubrick, and his own subsequent *A Woman Under the Influence*) that have even temporarily entered the American vernacular and contributed, in however small a way, to shaping mass consciousness. Though necessarily less than a box office blockbuster, *Faces* repaid its modest cost and left Cassavetes with spare change. (*Playboy* magazine, on the basis of the initial critical raves the film gathered, predicted it would gross $8 million, but Cassavetes was never to see even a fraction of that amount.) But the film did accumulate a small following in a few major American and Canadian cities, and unprecedentedly garnered the praise of almost every important American film critic (with the predictable exception of Pauline Kael, who is indifferent to precisely the human values Cassavetes' films most esteem). What Andrew Sarris was to write eight years later was true in 1968: "If [Cassavetes] had never done anything else since *Faces*, his place in film history would be secure."[1]

The making of *Faces* marked the end of a period in Cassavetes' life, a time of frustration, neglect, and unhappiness that is reflected in the tone of the film. But, more importantly, its success marked the beginning of another period. In the six years between 1969 and 1975, Cassavetes would perform the unprecedented feat of almost single-handedly putting together four major independent feature-length productions—*Husbands, Minnie and Moskowitz, A Woman Under the Influence* and *The Killing of a Chinese Bookie*—each film more extraordinary and ambitious than the one before it.

When he persuaded Peter Falk and Ben Gazzara (a former classmate at the American Academy of Dramatic Arts) to make *Husbands* with him, he was riding high on the crest of the wave *Faces* had created. He was able to bankroll the production to the tune of a million dollars, a budget five times what he had been able to spend on *Faces* (though he and Hollywood were still keeping their distance: the money came from an Italian financier), and was able to switch from the grainy black and white of 16mm stock to wide-screen technicolor. But the differences between *Husbands* and *Faces* are traceable to more than a sudden access of money and cinematic resources. As if finding himself (in addition to his characters) at an imaginative dead end after the intensity and pain of *Faces*, in both *Husbands* and the film that immediately followed it, *Minnie and Moskowitz*, Cassavetes chooses a perspective and story as different from *Faces* as possible.

In place of *Faces*' clockwork mechanism of match cuts, temporal and editorial compressions, and claustrophobic narrative confinements, Cassavetes writes two rambling, picaresque road stories where time seems hardly to exist. In place of *Faces*' bottomless repressions and performative sublimations (where none of the characters—not even Chet or Jeannie—seem able or willing to express their true feelings), he imagines possibilities of sincere, expressive volubility and prolix camaraderie. In place of shopworn and repetitious social routines, he offers his characters possibilities of novel situations and new encounters. In place of entrapments, fixations, and paralyses, he offers the spectacle of characters endlessly on the move in high-spirited pursuit of escape, adventure, and freedom.

Even the style of the narrative, photography, and editing has changed; it is as if Cassavetes had suddenly got a whole new optical system for his camera, or were looking at everything through the opposite end of the viewfinder. At a superficial approach, the differences between *Faces* and *Husbands* are as striking as they are affecting. (Even if, to a trained eye, and after further acquaintance, the characters and scenes in *Husbands* have an ominous similarity in their deeper structures to those in *Faces*. One concludes that if *Husbands* is an exorcism of the world of *Faces*, it is one that in its insistence on its differences from *Faces* disturbingly testifies to the power of the spirits it tries to expel.)

The film is the story of three rather ordinary, upper-middle-class, married, middle-aged buddies suddenly forced to ask questions about their lives, loves, and relationships—questions they have been blissfully unaware of in their moderately prosperous and unreflective existences before the start of the film. Faced with the unexpected death of their closest common friend, Archie (Falk), Harry (Gazzara), and Gus (Cassavetes) go off on a four-day combination wake and binge to try to come to grips with the youth they suddenly realize they have lost and, in their own profoundly inarticulate ways, to try to assess the meanings of "life, death, and freedom" (as the subtitle of the film phrases it). After twenty years of security and happiness, living comfortable, sheltered existences in a Long Island suburb, the bottom of their lives suddenly falls out. These three grown-up little boys run off to taste the life they feel they have somehow missed out on all along. And in their sudden, infantile attempts "to grab for all the gusto they can," they are as clumsy, crude, and stupidly passionate as characters in a beer commercial. They dash off to Manhattan to play basketball and go swimming in an athletic club. They go on a drunken bender and end up in a neighborhood bar conducting an absurd singing contest in which patrons have to prove (by singing!) that "true feeling" and "true love" are not dead. Then, on impulse, they fly to London together, throw money around like the crassest of American tourists, and finally pick up girls at a swanky gambling casino for a little extracurricular sex and excitement, "to dare to take a chance" with life (as Archie puts it) for the first time in their lives. In short, they (and Cassavetes) do everything imaginable to try to break the cycle of entrapment that in ten years will turn each of them into a version of Richard Forst in *Faces*.

But as much as *Husbands* needs to be regarded as an imaginative response to the entrapments and repressions of *Faces*, only a purist would pretend that the practical aspects of Cassavetes' situation and the technical resources newly available to him as a filmmaker have nothing to do with the changed narrative situation of the characters in the film. His access of cinematic possibilities corresponds exactly to their access of narrative possibilities. The wide-screen 35mm photography frees the characters from the grainy, boxed-in feeling of *Faces*. The professional lighting and sound equipment at Cassavetes' disposal for the first time allow him to move his characters through spaces—both outdoor locations and vast interiors—that were previously unavailable to him or them. And none of the aesthetic possibilities of technicolor are lost on him either. The brilliant yellow taxicabs, the lush aquamarine swimming pool, the rich red velvet and green felt of the gambling casino suggest all the delights of sensuous reality, all the pleasurable possibilities of taste, touch, and vision that were utterly unavailable to the characters of *Faces*.

In fact, it is only by contrasting *Faces* with the two films that immediately follow it that one can fully appreciate the mysterious and deep relationship between expressive opportunities and achievements in Cassavetes' work. While making *Faces*, his own financial and cinematic resources were almost as pinched and narrow as the social and psychological resources of his characters. The limitations and constraints on his filmmaking capabilities of lighting, staging, and photographing a scene almost exactly paralleled the spiritual and social limitations and constraints in the lives of his characters. The sensuousness, movement, and picaresque quality of the subsequent films—their radical imaginative differences from *Faces*—are traceable as much to technical differences in Cassavetes' equipment and production methods, and to this new-felt power as a director, as to any fundamental change in his artistic sensibility or attitudes. The basic fact to be accounted for is that the same man with virtually the same artistic consciousness made films as apparently different as *Faces* and *Husbands*. A term such as "development" (if it ever explains anything) simply will not account for the difference between two such different looking works released only a year apart. The difference between *Husbands* and *Faces* is a lesson in the complexity of artistic "intention," a lesson in the complexity of the different contexts within which any work generates its meanings and from which it takes its origins.

The opening minutes of *Husbands* begin where *Faces* left off—with a vision of a crowded world of boisterous, superficial conviviality. The opening of the film is a series of still photographs of the four friends clowning around together and posing for the camera in their bathing suits at a poolside party. The soundtrack is flooded with the noises of busy, loud friendliness. If one did not hear in these sounds just the faintest echoes of the hollow laughter, and see in the postures and poses of these grown men just the slightest reminder of the falsely hearty camaraderie of the businessmen of *Faces*, one would seem to be in the happiest, healthiest, and best of all possible worlds. Of course, one does not want to force a connection between the two films. The bright primary colors of these photographs, the airy, spacious, out-doorsiness of the poolside setting, the relaxed, sensuous, un-embarrassed bodies of these paunchy men, half naked in their swim-suits, all tell us how far they are from the confinements, repression, and cover-ups of the characters of *Faces*. But these men are trapped and deadened in certain ways too. Just as they are visually confined in the still photographs, they are psychologically hemmed in by their cocky masculinity, their sureness of themselves and their positions. Just as they are aurally enveloped in the comforting party noises of the sound-track, they are protected and sheltered from the realities of their own emotions. In fact, as the rest of *Husbands* will be devoted to showing, their growth has been stunted in some of the very same ways Richard and Maria Forst's was. Money, possessions, a comfy home, and petit bourgeois politenesses protected the Forsts from having to acknowl-edge certain emotional and psychological realities too. *Faces* is about the day when all the walls come tumbling down, and so in its own way is *Husbands*.

The difference between the two films is that Archie, Harry, and Gus do what Richard and Maria never quite dared. When the ceremonies of innocence are drowned, they launch out on a truly dangerous voyage of emotional exploration, a journey that will carry them beyond all the comforts, complacencies, and emotional shelters of these initial snap-shots. It is not exactly that these three men are braver or more auda-cious than Richard and Maria, but that they are not as polished, refined, practiced, or eminently successful in their evasions of life as Richard and Maria were. What saves Archie, Harry, and Gus is para-doxically their clumsiness, their crudity, and their boyish inarticu-lateness. They stumble their way into emotional and psychological tangles that glib, poised, unctuous, always-ready-with-a-joke Richard, or shy, demure Maria would have avoided. And in their lapses and falls is the possibility of self-discovery and growth that Richard and Maria could never experience.

In this sense, *Husbands* is Cassavetes' return to the territory and the leisurely rhythms of the emotional explorations of *Shadows*. Archie, Harry, and Gus are, in effect, a glimpse of Hughie, Ben, and Lelia twenty years later. But, needless to say, that intervening twenty years makes all the difference. While the tentative, awkward, emotional ex-plorations of the adolescents in *Shadows* were essentially comic, the excesses, crudities, and confusions of these middle-aged men are disturbing and painful. *Husbands* is a film Cassavetes labeled a comedy (in the subtitle of the picture), but it is less and less comic as it goes along, more and more pathetic and bewildering as these three men, arrested at the stage of adolescence, try to badger, cajole, and analyze long suppressed and forgotten feelings into existence.

The self-conscious and self-centered adolescents of *Shadows* could at least pursue their emotional explorations in a straightforward manner. They were still close enough to their feelings to take them seriously and approach them directly. That possibility is not available to these middle-aged men. Games and play are apparently their only avenue back to their feelings—as if they had to regress to the actual behavior of adolescence to feel things that they have not allowed into their consciousnesses since adolescence. Joking, teasing, competing, game-playing, role-playing, and having fun—"playing" in all of its senses—is an important activity in all of Cassavetes' films, but in none more so than in *Husbands*. Playing a scene or a role, playing with, or against, another character, playing with imaginative possibilities, while still playing within certain rules and boundaries, is a way of momentarily freeing oneself from the tyranny of habit and of releasing oneself to possibilities of discovery.

And yet, as Cassavetes' introduction to *Faces* acknowledges, and as much of *Husbands* implicitly recognizes, playing can also be a form of evasiveness, a matter of "games—stupid and painful, falsely satisfying, and economically rewarding." The playing of Richard and Freddie, and McCarthy and Jackson in *Faces* is mechanical, repetitious, and self-protective, the opposite of a process of openness, exploration, and discovery. The central question the viewer of *Husbands* has to answer is, to what extent is the playing in *Husbands* only another version of the "stupid and painful" playing of *Faces*, and to what extent is it a bona fide form of exploration in pursuit of self-discovery? The most disturbing and puzzling thing about *Husbands* is Cassavetes' refusal to provide an easy answer. Cassavetes seems almost as uncertain as his three husbands about the value of all the playing they indulge in in the film; it is not for nothing that he casts himself as one of them. Playing has become problematic, as it never was in *Shadows*. In that film, playing (as in the case of Lelia's compulsive melodramatics) was at times exasperating, but it was always viewed as a creative activity, an overflowing of performative energies in and of themselves healthy and desirable. By the time of *Faces* and *Husbands*, Cassavetes recognizes that fresh-faced American innocence, jokesiness, and exuberance may be only a more subtle form of indifference and unresponsiveness to experience.

The scene immediately following the opening still photographs exposes us and the husbands to one of the things the smug suburban world of pool parties had shut out: death. Cassavetes suddenly cuts to the silent immensity of an outdoor cemetery interment service and (in one of the very few crane shots in his entire work, but one absolutely necessary in communicating the sudden smallness and lostness of his three main characters) an overhead shot of the stunned and dwarfed figures of the three husbands as they work their clumsy ways through the sea of mourners.

The gatherings of friends, relatives, and neighbors here and at the preceding pool party are the last crowds we see in *Husbands*. For the next three days and two hours and twenty minutes of film time, Cassavetes deliberately propels his three survivors outside all the nourishing, protecting, muffling encirclements of the middle-class Long Island society they have probably never before wanted or dared to venture beyond. In the scenes following the funeral scene, Cassavetes pulls his camera back to isolate his three men within large, deserted, and anonymously impersonal visual spaces: horsing around drunkenly on a nighttime city street (where even the local wino comically goes out of his way to avoid them); sitting together in an empty subway car whizzing under the streets of New York, comically spouting platitudes on the meaning of life, death, and professional sports; playing basketball in a cavernously empty and echoing indoor basketball court; and splashing around in a deserted indoor pool. The spatial isolation and social estrangement are deliberate. Harry, Gus, and Archie are men who have been protected, surrounded, and swaddled all their lives. They have probably never had to question a single one of the premises or practices of their comfy existences. The death of their friend leaves them suddenly bereft, alone, outside the walls, stripped of defenses, and thrown on their own psychic resources.

"O to break loose, like the chinook/salmon," the opening of Robert Lowell's magisterial poem "Near the Ocean," is the unexpressed aspiration of Cassavetes' inarticulate middle-class husbands. But as Lowell recognizes, even as he voices the desire, the poet who can imagine such an aspiration, and articulate it in such masterful poetic form, is precisely one whose human consciousness will forever prevent him from "breaking loose" into the sheer freedom and animality of the salmon.

Likewise *Husbands* is, as it were, Cassavetes' equivalent of Lowell's doomed recognition. It is at one and the same time Cassavetes' most passionate expression of the desire "to break loose," and his most poignant recognition of the impossibility of ever attaining that visionary aspiration.

The various sorts of social and imaginative enlargements explored in *Husbands* are inextricably intertwined with the various sorts of visual and cinematic enlargements of perspective and shifts of scale Cassavetes plays with during the film. Harry, Archie, and Gus begin dwarfed by the vast, empty spaces of the first few sets (the graveyard; the basketball court on which they play, photographed in extreme long shot; the echoing, hollow space of the swimming pool in which they race). They proceed gradually to sets shot predominantly in medium distance in which social interactions count for more, and in which they are gradually forced into contact with other characters (surrounded by others on the street, and in the bar during their singing contest). Their scope of movement is gradually enlarged until it extends to the sudden jet flight to London; but then it is contracted again as they encounter the difficulties of escape from their emotions and their pasts. The uncontrolled displays of adolescent energy in athletic contests and drunken carousing in the first half are, as it were, necessary to allow them to loosen up old, long-unused muscles and emotions, as a sort of training session for the more complex and challenging exercises of adult social and sexual relations that will be demanded of them in the second half of the film. Their initial physical attempts at free movement within the space of the frame and the limits of reframing embodied in Cassavetes' fairly static camera set-ups are trivial and limited in the New York scenes of the film, but are necessary as practice for the much more complex social movements they will attempt later in the London scenes of the film.

Husbands is a difficult, demanding, and frequently painful film, and Archie, Harry, and Gus function at such a relentless pitch of emotional desperation and exposure that it is not hard to see why they easily qualify as Cassavetes' three least-liked protagonists, or why Cassavetes has been criticized for overindulging them and failing to see through their childishness. Archie, Harry, and Gus behave with the offensiveness of drunken fraternity brothers at a beer bash in a number of scenes. Their flight from family and friends, their drunken bender in Manhattan, and their London sexual escapades are irresponsible and escapist. They mock and bully one another, abuse strangers, and try to badger and cajole intimacy and feeling into their relationships. They are immature, insensitive, and self-centered. But, Cassavetes suggests, so is most of white, middle-class, male American society, and so were the characters in *Faces*, who only appeared less childish because they were more repressed and less willing to confront and expose their own immaturities. Cassavetes' goal is neither to present ideal characters nor to take refuge in an easy criticism of less than ideal characters, but simply, lovingly, to accept these men as they are, insofar as they are willing to expose and honestly investigate their own inadequacies.

To criticize Cassavetes or these characters for their shortcomings (as almost everything written about the film finally does) is to overlook two significant realities. First, one cannot ignore that it is only the husbands' naiveness, immaturity, and emotional childishness that make any journey of discovery possible at all. The characters in *Faces* are too burnt out and cynical ever to have attempted, or profited from, the same sort of effort. It is as if Cassavetes can see his way clear to break an escape route, however crude, out of the repressions and enclosures of the previous film only by indulging the characters of *Husbands* to the extreme of their outrageousness. More importantly, however much one may dislike Harry, Archie, and Gus as persons, one must recognize that *Husbands* is much more than the sum of their individual characters. Cassavetes' camerawork and scripting generate complex recognitions and experiences (for both his characters and his audience) out of a particular character's crudest and most immature behavior.

That is to say, the three husbands in *Husbands* can indeed be irresponsible and escapist in intention without the film in which they are characters being guilty of being irresponsible and escapist. In their common revulsion from the whiff of mortality, Archie, Harry, and Gus do perhaps want nothing more than to renounce their adult responsibilities and to indulge themselves in childish games and play for a few days. They do aspire to become little boys again (and are fatuous enough to believe that such a thing might be possible). They do want to live the life of the senses and escape the ties that bind them to larger, more demanding, enduring emotional and social obligations. It is easy to see why Cassavetes' scripting and camerawork, which lavishes so much time and space on these men and gives them so many opportunities to play out their scenes of irresponsibility, should seem a silent partner to their escapism. But what makes *Husbands* the opposite of silly and self-indulgent is the way Cassavetes' scripting and directing so complexly qualify and test the escapist intentions of these men. His camerawork and narrative continually remind us of how impossible any escape is, and, what is more important, what enormous effort is required for the achievement of even momentary freedom. For all the "husbands'" (even the title of the film refers Archie, Harry, and Gus to a qualifying social context that it is impossible for them to escape) overstrenuous protestations of their freedom from responsibilities, *Husbands* keeps reimplicating them in obligations and responsibilities to one another, to the people around them, and to themselves.

Serious, brooding Harry runs to London to escape his wife, but brings her along in his feelings no matter how far he flies from Long Island. To the embarrassment of his comely call girl and his friends, he mentions her at the most inappropriate moments—after making love to his girl, and when she starts to give him a back rub (which, Harry interjects, his wife used to do for him, too). Archie, an assistant travel editor at the *New York Times*, but the most comically unworldly and provincial of the three, tries to soothe his young Oriental date by singing. But the songs he chooses to sing, maybe the only songs he knows, are two nursery rhymes he sings to his kids at bedtime. There is no escaping the past and one's own biography. Even Gus, the coolest and most polished of the three, who protects himself from emotional involvement with his date behind a veneer of evasive jokesiness and Don Juanish charm, who wants only to have a good time on this trip to London, falls in love with her despite himself by the end of the film. Gus had thought he could escape emotional commitments, but Cassavetes shows he was wrong.

So interested is Cassavetes in the contexts and restraints placed on the assertions of freedom by his three characters that *Husbands* is, for long stretches, a film virtually without close-ups. Close-ups would grant the characters the moral and psychological autonomy and the dramatic importance that it is the point of the film to call into question. Even when the husbands are clowning around on the sidewalks of New York early in the film, Cassavetes holds his camera far enough back to let us see the faces of bystanders looking at them as a necessary reminder of how far they are from having the world to themselves. When faces are not peeking at his husbands from the edges and backgrounds of the frame, Cassavetes uses a middle distance pan that moves slowly and almost indifferently back and forth from character to

All dressed up with no place to go
—*Archie, Harry, and Gus pretending to be free*

character to deny any one character the chance to arrange a scene around himself. The slowly panning camera, with a mind of its own and its firm and evenhanded denial of any special, personal point of view on a scene, reminds us that no individual point of view is privileged in Cassavetes' moral universe. Every individual is embedded in a context. One thinks of Barbara Loden's reply to an interviewer who asked her about the absence of point-of-view and shot–reverse shots in *Wanda*. Loden replied that she always "saw [Wanda] *in* something, surrounded by something." There are no point-of-view shots or conventional shot–reverse shots in *Husbands*, and only a handful in all of Cassavetes' work because, like Loden, he always sees his characters "*in* something, surrounded by something" that they can never for a moment get out of. (Cassavetes could have learned this panning technique and its capacity to "place" an individual within a larger framework of social interactions from any number of *cinéma vérité* filmmakers, or from Dreyer's *Ordet*, but it is probably at least as likely that he stumbled onto its possibilities in simple revulsion from the false intimacies and confinements of the close-ups in *Faces*.)

Two of the most remarkable uses of the pan are in the scene in Gus's office just prior to the husbands' flight to London, and, twenty-four hours later, in the gathering of the three men and their three ladies in a London hotel room. In the first scene, Gus returns to his office for a few minutes in the middle of *Husbands* briefly to resume his "identity" as a dentist (though he is dirty, smelly, and still unshaven after his two-day binge in New York, and it is just such automatic and un-achieved "identities" that a scene such as this is designed to question). Cassavetes sets his camera in a documentary placement in front of his four actors. From left to right we see and hear: Archie in the back of the office impatiently trying to convince Gus to leave with him; Gus work-ing on his patient, trying to put her at ease; the female patient lying in the dental chair and occasionally laughing hysterically out of ner-vousness and anxiety when Gus touches her; and a kindly nurse hold-ing the patient's hand and trying to calm her down. It is an odd assort-ment of characters, to say the least, gathered in a tiny space, and as the camera pans slowly back and forth in the middle distance, each takes a turn at soliciting our attention and making his or her presence felt. Each momentarily holds our interest in the center of the frame, only subsequently to relinquish it as the arm or leg of another character moves into the space of the frame, or the voice of another character becomes audible on the soundtrack, and the panning camera non-chalantly continues on its deadpan course amid the giggles, screams, twitches, and dangling arms and legs. It is a scene of leisurely surveyed chaos as uncanny in its effect as the mannered madness of the Marx Brothers packed into a stateroom at sea. The humor and strangeness come precisely from the photographic evenhandedness. The scene refuses to sort itself out before our eyes, to allow Archie and Gus (who are, after all, the stars of the film) to control or dominate it. It refuses to relegate the anxious patient or the genial, supportive nurse (neither of whom appears in the movie again) to minor roles within it. Even the tones cannot be sorted out. Is this a comic moment or a serious one? There is no way to say. But the result is an enormous complication of our sense of interrelationships and mutual responsibilities.

Cassavetes' pan here (like Dreyer's in *Ordet*), which is all the more emphasized by the wide-screen format of the film, is a way of impli-cating his husbands in unexpected involvements and responsibilities at the very moments in which they think they are free from such things. The second scene in which the potential of the pan is exploited for maximum effect takes place in the hotel room to which the three hus-bands bring their London dates. Cassavetes' camera moves slowly and independently back and forth across the figures of the three men and three women gathered in Archie's room as they go through the clumsy formalities of pairing off for sex in their separate suites. One after another, we see: Gus busily ordering an overelaborate meal from room service to cover the awkwardness; Harry, prone on a bed sobbing and brooding over his failed marriage; Archie clumsily trying to cross-examine his "inscrutable" (his description of her!) Oriental date; Mary (played by Jenny Runacre in her screen debut and perhaps the greatest performance of her career) nervously fidgeting on the bed; and Pearl (a talented, "professional" performer in the oldest profession in the sense in which Jeannie Rapp was) trying to put everyone at ease. Cassavetes' pans, picking up on every nervous tic and clumsy adjustment in the room—a room, furthermore, backed with mirrors, so that several parts of it seem to be visible at once, no matter where the camera is pointed—remind us how little escape into "pure" sexuality there can be for these husbands embedded in a social (and visual) matrix of such extreme complexity.

Archie, Harry, and Gus may have intended their four-day binge and escape to London as a flight from the emotional complications of their Long Island lives; they may think they can flee back to the un-encumbered pastoral passionateness of boyhood games and the adolescent sexual athleticism of one-night stands, but what Cassavetes' framing and narrative make us aware of is how little escape there can be from the complications of adult relationships and consciousness. The husbands' efforts to lose themselves in boyish purities of feeling interest Cassavetes only to the extent that they comically plunge them into larger, more complex, and more perilous entanglements. What critics of the characters' escapism failed to see was that Cassavetes was in the text ahead of them, already critically scrutinizing and commenting on the essential impossibility and undesirability of escapism.

Each of the husbands wakes up from his dream of easy freedom (which meant merely "license" to them when the film began). They each literally wake up one morning and realize that all the social and emotional involvements they had thought they could so easily leave behind them in Long Island have been brought with them to their London hotel rooms. Harried, henpecked, sentimental Harry flies from the bizarrely encircling toils of his mother-in-law and wife (whom he has earlier tried to threaten and throttle into tenderness) to an even more bizarrely encircling relationship in his hotel room at the end of the film, surrounded by a surrogate mother-in-law, wife, and daughter, who understand him no more than the women he left behind at home do. Twelve hours after Archie and Gus have declared their immunity to the blandishments of a jaunt to London (they are only going "to tuck Harry in bed and return"), they have each fallen head over heels in love with the girls they have picked up.

If Cassavetes' boy-men embark on their binge with utter faith in the romantic myth that the child is father of the man and in their easy ability to recapture and be restored by the child in themselves, they end up with a chastening double recognition: not only are they incapable of leaving behind the responsibilities and burdens of their manhood, but more importantly, the emotional openness, exposure, and vulnerability of "boyhood" are in some respects more dangerous and disturbing to them than the adulthood they are trying to escape from. In the concluding minutes of *Husbands*, the final thing Archie and Gus flee from is, in fact, their own frightening freedom. The final escape of the film is ironically enough their flight back to the safety, the predictability, and the enclosure of their Long Island families.

These psychological reversals and complications of attitude are what make *Husbands* such a difficult and potentially disorienting film, especially for a viewer trying to get a simple critical handle on Archie, Harry, and Gus. What makes the film difficult and Cassavetes' attitudes so hard to fathom is that he seems to affirm two radically contrasted and incompatible impulses. If the first impulse that informs *Husbands* corresponds to the quest for an unfettered, uninhibited freedom away from the restrictions of social roles and obligations, the second corresponds to the fear of the same prospect and a desire to affirm the importance of enduring relationships and responsibilities. If Cassavetes' first impulse expresses itself in *Husbands* as the wildness, play, and mischief (of his characters, scenes, and narrative itself), the second expresses itself in the intrinsic conservatism of the values his film ends up affirming: those of love, marriage, and the family. If the first tendency stimulates the flight of discovery away from home and family at the beginning of the film, the second requires a return home for Archie and Gus (and the creation of a home away from home for Harry) at the end of the film.

This double impulse is the very heartbeat of the life-giving pulse of Cassavetes' work. To those who ask whether Cassavetes is for or against the behavior of the three husbands, one can only reply that he is affirming with absolutely equal intensity *both* their radical flight from family and responsibility at the beginning of the film, *and* their conservative return to family and responsibility at the end. Or, to put it more precisely, neither are recommended as fixed *positions*, but both are endorsed as imaginative *movements*. What makes *Husbands* (and Cassavetes' work in general) so bracing and so exciting to watch is that it is made up not of attitudes or positions, but of unceasing movements of exploration. Rather than articulating a particular position or stance, the effect of the film is more like that of an Alexander Calder mobile with its parts forever on the move, dynamically pulling against one another. Every tone and impulse is pitched against an opposite; every movement levered against a counter-movement.

The divided feelings of the film are summarized by the last scene in which the three men appear together, in the weird ceremony of parting improvised at the last minute by Harry. To the tune of "Dancing in the Dark," the three husbands dance with three strange women in Harry's room, mismatched with one another and their partners in every way. The three men are, in effect, attempting to stage a deliberate "scene," to improvise a work of art that will summarize and fittingly conclude their experiences together. But their ceremony of farewell to one another and to their ill-conceived attempt to recapture their youth and freedom is as confused about itself as the whole film. The scene lurches between being idiotic and absurd in some respects and being quite touching and noble in others. Like the American experience itself, *Husbands* is an unstable mixture of feelings about freedom and self-sufficiency. And like the screwy ceremony staged by the husbands, the whole film is constructed of scenes that attempt to turn themselves into epiphanies—moments of pure truth and feeling outside of time, space, and society—only, without exception, to be comically or pathetically disrupted by the forces of time, space, and society they seek to exempt themselves from. In this sense, the whole film is an anxious, unbalanced ebb and flow of invigorating transactions between the real and the imaginative, an insatiable, unending transit between the impure realities of home, family, and social responsibilities and the dream of a purer, finer world elsewhere of art, imagination, and freedom.

At the end of the film, Archie and Gus fly back to New York, load up on toys at the airport as bribes to their families, and after much pausing and delaying, with wandering steps and slow, reluctantly take their solitary ways up their respective driveways. Cassavetes' camera follows Gus up his driveway, where no more than three paces along, he is confronted with a crying daughter and a scolding son, who immediately picks a fight with his sister, tells his father, "Boy, are you going to get it!" and begins wailing for his mother. And then, as Gus proceeds up the driveway and around the back of his house following his children, in the most jarring conclusion of any of Cassavetes' films, the very instant he rounds the corner of the house, Cassavetes cuts to blackness and ends the film, as if to jolt us with a reminder of all the walls that have been absent for the previous two hours.

If this ending really were saying (what many critics and viewers took it to mean) that Gus has returned only to be entombed once and for all within the four walls of his home, it would be a profoundly depressing film, with an ending not very different in implication from the fixed-camera prison with which *Faces* ended. If, on the other hand, the ending were arguing one final time for escape from such enclosures to games of adolescence, barroom badgering, and casual pickups, *Husbands* would be a trivially escapist film (as even more critics and viewers took it to be). But the point of *Husbands* is that it affirms neither going home nor leaving home. It affirms no fixed positions whatever. It begins with an abrupt moment of movement and transition and ends with an equally startling moment of movement and transition. Hard pressed to say what such an ending ultimately affirms, one can only reply that it endorses change and dialectical movement. It endorses the possibility, the necessity, the vital importance of unfinished discovery, exploration, and transit between any two fixed points. *Husbands* offers as a philosophy of life only the prospect of unending movement, risk, and change: the stimulation and risks of unplanned excursions away from home, and the stimulations and risks of counter-movements back home as well.

An interview Cassavetes gave to *Life* while he was still in the process of scripting and rehearsing *Husbands* suggests how unable he himself was to make up his mind about his characters:

> The job that has to be done here is for three men to investigate themselves—honestly, without suppression. The minute you settle down and say, that's it, I'm closing shop, I know what I am, then you're a man, no longer a man-child. Is it really better to be a man-child than a man? I don't know.[2]

The film that resulted suggests how far from journalistic rhetoric that final question was. Cassavetes really could not make up his mind, and *Husbands* is that rarest of all films, a bona fide "exploration" (all the rarer in the tendentious late sixties and early seventies, when so many films paid lip service to the value of investigation just before they raced headlong toward their own foregone conclusions). It is a film of unbalanced puzzlements and oppositions at the furthest remove from the ideal texts of most film criticism of the past twenty years, texts that contain tendentious symbolic foreshadowings, mirrorings, and stylistic accentings of prefabricated meanings, mass produced for mass consumption. Like the much admired films of De Palma, Altman, and Kubrick, such texts offer truly dazzling (but ultimately empty) ingenuities of metaphor and pattern as substitutions for actual explorations of human feeling and experience. Instead of offering a poised, dramatically distanced vision insulated from the pressures of real time, space, and society, *Husbands* presents only swerves of feeling and conflicts of attitudes that cannot be controlled, contained, or cleverly ordered into a wonderfully explicable, overarching pattern.

We need a film criticism that will do justice to films that cannot be neatly reduced to semiotic patterns and structures or complex visual metaphors. It is the critical obsession with such ingenuities of structure as ends in themselves, as they manifest themselves in ingenious visual conceits, mechanically repetitive patternings, and icily detached aesthetic control that has led to the absurd overvaluation of the work of Alfred Hitchcock and of many of his film-school epigones. The phenomenon is analogous to that decried by Robert Lowell twenty years ago in the writing of poetry and the sterilely analytic literary criticism that had been developed to explicate it. Lowell noted that critical discourse was attracted to the complexly explainable and teachable work of art to the exclusion of more mysterious, more exploratory, and usually more profound work that resisted easy analysis and explication:

It seems to me we've gotten into a sort of Alexandrian age. Poets of my generation and particularly the younger ones have gotten terribly proficient at these forms. They write a very musical, difficult poem with tremendous skill, perhaps there's never been such skill. Yet the writing seems divorced from culture somehow. It's become too much something specialized that can't handle much experience. It's become a craft, purely a craft, and there must be some breakthrough back into life. . . . Any number of people are guilty of writing a complicated poem that has a certain amount of symbolism in it and really difficult meaning, a wonderful poem to teach. Then you unwind it and you feel that the intelligence, the experience, whatever goes into it, is skin deep. [But another kind of poetry] is exploring.[3]

Why can't we find a way of talking about film not in terms of mechanical ingenuities of arrangement and structure, but as an act of human exploration of humanly important experience? A description of film in that way could never be satisfied with the registration of the ways it fulfills or defeats genre expectations, with a notation of its sociological "importance" or representativeness, or with the description of a series of visual structures, repetitions, and patterns within it. Is it too audacious to suggest that once criticism began to move beyond these reductive and mechanical approaches, the whole canon of "great" directors and "masterpiece" films might be turned upside down? If this seems unduly harsh on recent film criticism, the near total critical neglect and incomprehension of John Cassavetes' work over the entire span of his twenty-five year career (with the notable exception of the brief burst of enthusiastic reviews *Faces* prompted in the popular press) is sad testimony that something has gone radically wrong somewhere.

Husbands is film as a strategy of sincerity; film as a process of exploration and discovery (for Cassavetes, the writer and director, as well as for his actors and characters—it is no accident that his statement above about the film implicitly conflates all of them). This is film as a series of opposed and ultimately unreconciled imaginative movements and endless adjustments. And if we were not all so indoctrinated by the exaltation of dramatic "control" and "distance," we would see that there is nothing wrong with that.

But, having said all this, one may still remain uncomfortable with *Husbands* and feel it to be an unsuccessful film. In the terms of the *Life* interview, the shortcoming of the film is that Cassavetes fails to create the man-child he is so interested in understanding. We see Archie, Harry, and Gus sometimes behaving like men in the film, and more frequently like children, but do we really continuously see the child in their manliness or the man in their childishness? Or, to put it another way, their childishness and manliness do not seem sufficiently related in their own consciousnesses for them to interest us fully. The modes of adult behavior and immature behavior never quite seem to come close enough together in any character's actions or consciousness. The alternative styles of experience and consciousness that *Husbands* formulates—the alternatives of play versus responsibility, freedom versus family, flying to London versus staying at home in Long Island, being a boy versus being a man—are too starkly opposed to each other for either alternative to be completely compelling as a model of behavior. In life such modes of behavior are always more implicated and involved in each other than they are here.

One can understand, without relishing the fact, that perhaps the craziness, extremity, and excessiveness of *Husbands* was the only way out of the entrapments, burdens, and paralyses of *Faces* for Cassavetes.

The husbands' wild unpredictable lurches into absolutely infantile or pointlessly aggressive behavior do succeed, in a weird and discomforting way, in liberating potentially healthy and salutary energies that had not been so clearly and powerfully expressible in his earlier work. But *Husbands* succumbs to the problem that beset *Too Late Blues*. It liberates an enormous range of narrative and personal energies—of emotional intensity, performative inventiveness, and imaginative yearning—that it then finds unplaceable in the larger structures of its characters' lives or organizable within the film's narrative development. Cassavetes ultimately does not know what to do with them in terms of the structures of society, personality, or narrative progress (which is why the three husbands are relentlessly on the move emotionally but seem to get nowhere, and why the film itself sadly seems at one and the same time to be both breathlessly plunging forward and maddeningly, repetitiously standing still).

Perhaps Cassavetes' own intuition of his failure to solve the narrative and social problem embodied in *Husbands* is the reason he was unable to put the film down after he finished it. Though he usually moves immediately from one project to another and in his own words "doesn't ever look back," he has commented that he could not get *Husbands* out of his system after he made it. While waiting for its release, he wrote a novel based on it, a manuscript that still sits in his desk unpublished. And the extensive speaking tour he went on with Falk and Gazzara to publicize the film at the time of its release was by his own account—and to the infinite annoyance or amusement of the talk show hosts the three men met—"an attempt to continue the film" because he "didn't want it to end." Even today, more than ten years later, he talks of *Husbands* as the film of all of his work that still interests him most.[4] It is assuredly *not* his best film; but it is the film in which certain positive possibilities of free adult performance for the first time clearly become cinematically conceivable (if not realizable in a fully mature and satisfying way). The films that follow would be repeated attempts to find some place for the unplaceable energies that continued to agitate him after *Husbands* was completed.

The contradictions, inconsistencies, and swerves of feeling in *Husbands* are exhilarating proof of the honesty and integrity of Cassavetes' efforts to bring the man and the child together without falsely compromising either position, and without the one being allowed merely to neutralize the other. But the final schizophrenia of *Husbands*, its tendency to formulate opposed, alternative stances, is evidence that he still had not been able to imagine a response to the dead ends of *Faces* that was not largely escapist, irresponsible, or impulsive. Cassavetes' renewed efforts to bring the man and the child together in one character, to make a character who would neither be overcome by domestic and personal responsibilities nor have to flee from them into escapist irresponsibility, would be the start of his next film.

CHAPTER VI

LOVE ON THE RUN
Minnie and Moskowitz

Minnie and Moskowitz was written for the screen. The first draft took approximately two and a half weeks to put down on paper. It was written for some friends to perform. The basic story came out of certain remembrances of loneliness. The need for family and love, friendship, and an understanding between certain people that you like and love. . . .

The screenplay calls all these problems lies—makes the past the past and the present now. It evades the insanity that life subjects us all to—places two people in a position to need each other. And in my mind, like life, gives them another chance.   *John Cassavetes*

If *Faces* represented an imaginative dead end or burial ground for Cassavetes, it also represented an extraordinarily fertile plot for further cultivation. The two films that follow revisit particular characters or situations in *Faces* in search of a way out of its high-walled maze of mechanical and insensitive behavior. In *Husbands* and *Minnie and Moskowitz*, Cassavetes attacks the problem piecemeal, with two almost opposite approaches. *Husbands* takes the two buddies of *Faces*, Richard and Freddie, makes them three (for the sake of the stimulating asymmetry and the improvisational possibilities it opens up), and instead of restricting them to a half-hour fling with Jeannie, gives them whole days together and opportunities of movement and exploration unavailable to Richard and Freddie. But, as we have seen, that does not quite solve the problem, so he then reverses his strategy. After trying to free *Faces'* two home-bound men, he tries in *Minnie and Moskowitz* to find a home for its two free spirits, Jeannie and Chet.

The problem is that although Jeannie and Chet represent the only possibilities of mature, sensitive performance in the world of *Faces*, their performances can never amount to anything in that world. Chet can no more pair off permanently with Maria than Jeannie can with Richard; they realize that as well as we do. And further, Jeannie and Chet paired off permanently with anyone else, or with each other, would cease to be Jeannie and Chet as we know them in *Faces*.

140

Cassavetes' question in *Minnie and Moskowitz* is whether there can be a future for characters like Jeannie and Chet, apart or together, in any possible relationship.

Minnie and Moskowitz are Jeannie and Chet, and *Minnie and Moskowitz* is Cassavetes' attempt to give the two doomed star performers of *Faces* a chance on their own, away from the repressions, confinements, and paralyses of that film. Here Cassavetes gives the Jeannie and Chet characters all the opportunity in the world to work out a relationship between themselves and to create a society hospitable to their needs.

This is not to ignore the fact that *Minnie and Moskowitz* is a comedy. Cassavetes has described it as his "entertainment" movie; and most critics who have addressed themselves at all to Cassavetes' work regard it as his lightest, most frivolous, and least serious film, and consequently dismiss it as being unworthy of critical attention. But that is to ignore its central place in his body of work. The fact that Cassavetes would choose to make an outright comedy at all at this point in his career should tell us that *Minnie and Moskowitz* may be a little more than a routine entertainment film. For all the humor in the film, one cannot help detecting a desperation in its laughter, a betraying urgency in Cassavetes' insistence that he is making a film as superficially different from *Faces* as possible. It is hard not to feel he protests a bit too much.

If, as I am arguing, *Minnie and Moskowitz* is at the center of Cassavetes' attempt to revisit and rebuild the disintegrated relationships and failures of communication with which *Faces* ended, it is especially appropriate that it is the first in a series of films in which he works to revisit and rehabilitate his own relationship with the Hollywood traditions he had previously been reacting against. Whatever their other virtues, the relationship of *Shadows*, *Faces*, and *Husbands* to the orthodox Hollywood tradition is almost entirely a negative one. These films, in effect, give us a glimpse of what filmmaking might have been like if the intimidating precedent of Hollywood's patterns of pacing, plotting, and editing had never existed. One obviously feels the presence of Capra, Ray, Curtiz, Wilder, and other Hollywood filmmakers in them at moments, but they are even more indebted to independent American filmmakers such as Shirley Clarke, Lionel Rogosin, and Morris Engel, all three of whose influences are felt frequently in *Shadows*, *Faces* and *Husbands* (for example, the visual and acoustic clutter of the barroom scene in *Husbands* seems to be right out of the comparable scene in Rogosin's *On the Bowery*). But the rhythms of *Minnie and Moskowitz*—both the rapid-fire clip of most of the dialogue and the accelerated pacing of the editing—transports us with a jolt back into the cinematic world of Preston Sturges, Howard Hawks, Leo McCarey, and late thirties and early forties comedy in general. Cassavetes begins a creative dialogue with the Hollywood whose forms and styles he had previously been content merely to repudiate and reject. It is no accident that the three films following *Husbands* engage three of the most durable and important genres in the Hollywood repertoire: the screwball comedy, the domestic melodrama (or women's "weepie"), and the gangster movie of the particularly dark postwar variety the French have christened *film noir. Minnie and Moskowitz, A Woman Under the Influence,* and *The Killing of a Chinese Bookie* (which, taken as a group along with *Faces,* constitute the most stunning sustained achievement in recent film) go back to revisit the territory Cassavetes had simply struck away from in his earlier work.

Cassavetes' return to orthodox Hollywood genres (and the tight plotting, editing, and characterizations such genres imply) represents an implicit recognition of his need for formal constraints on his imagination, and his characters' needs for formal constraints that resist the expansiveness of their performances and their imaginations. But it also represents a more personal biographical recognition as well. There may be a new generation of directors out there somewhere, nursed on Antonioni and Bresson, Tanner, Akerman, and Schlöndorff, for whom Hollywood is only a word and not a felt presence in their work or on their imaginations, but Cassavetes is not one of them. He is, after all, a New York boy. He was raised on Capra, Hawks, Bogart, Charles Boyer, and Jimmy Cagney. (His comments about Cagney are especially suggestive insofar as they hint at Cassavetes' fascination with the sheer power of personal performance even as a young boy, a fascination that would animate his acting and directing many years later: "He was my childhood idol, the guy most responsible, I suppose, for getting me into films. I loved him . . . Cagney played a man you didn't want to see die. Whether he was right or wrong he was a guy who could stand up to life and to as many gangsters as would come up against him; he was the toughest guy I'd ever seen. . . . He set up a terrific force on screen; he always portrayed an average guy who could somehow knock down giants. He was almost like a savior to all the short guys in the world, of whom I am one.")[1] His favorite films were then, and still are, *Angels With Dirty Faces, Mr. Smith Goes to Washington, Algiers, It's a Wonderful Life, Public Enemy, Bringing Up Baby,* and *Casablanca.*

Hollywood is too much a part of his experience ever to be merely repudiated or ignored (even as brilliantly as he does it in *Faces* or *Husbands*). That is why the three genre films that follow *Husbands* must be understood, in this most exhilaratingly inclusive of filmmakers, not as a compromise, a retreat, or a softening of his adversary relationship with Hollywood, but as a larger, finer act of inclusion, as a return to, and exploration of, his own origins and antecedents. They are occasions not of giving up his independence, but of enriching and deepening his dialogue with the forms of Hollywood experience in ways that are denied a more dismissive position. They are films that will play with and against the limitations of Hollywood genres and genre-governed characterizations, the forms of experience created by the films in Cassavetes' life. And in many ways they represent, as I will argue, Cassavetes' reviewings and revisitings of characters and scenes from his own earlier films.

It is appropriate that the first of the three should be the movie that of all of his work is most about movies, a movie about the kinds of movies that shaped his and our imaginations and the America of his childhood. *Minnie and Moskowitz* (as the oxymoron of the title suggests) locates itself squarely in the tradition of screwball courtship comedy, which, though its dramatic origins may be traced to Shakespeare's *Midsummer Night's Dream* and before, found its finest filmic flowering in the Hollywood of the 1930s and early 1940s in films otherwise as wildly dissimilar as *It Happened One Night*, *The Thirty-Nine Steps*, *It's a Wonderful World*, and *His Girl Friday*. And as different as these particular examples might seem, the form has remained almost untouched from Shakespeare to Hawks. It is at one and the same time one of the most rigidly rule-governed and conventional and (largely for that reason) one of the most self-conscious and self-aware of genres.

Screwball comedy is, as Stanley Cavell's *Pursuits of Happiness* indicates, one of Hollywood's most complex and sophisticated dramatic forms. Perhaps that is because it is the only Hollywood form built around a paradox: it is essentially a romantic form, showing the development of a growing attachment between two people, and yet it is simultaneously antiromantic insofar as it always pokes fun at the couple and their relationship. It was because of that antiromantic quality that it flourished most abundantly in the hands of the toughest-minded and least sentimental directors of Hollywood's golden age—directors such as Hawks, Sturges, and McCarey, who were entirely undeluded by the Hollywood romantic styles of their day and whose films frequently debunked (a post-modernist critic would say "deconstructed") the reigning cinematic rhetoric of love, romance, marriage, and happily-ever-afters. Thus it is fitting that Cassavetes, who is paradoxically both one of the most yearningly idealistic and romantic of contemporary directors and at the same time one of the most tough-minded, skeptical, and unsentimental, should be attracted to screwball comedy to initiate his dialogue with Hollywood.

Hitchcock handcuffs Robert Donat and Madeleine Carrol together, Capra and Riskin put Gable and Colbert on adjacent bus seats, and Hawks ties Rosalind Russell to Cary Grant with a piece of telephone wire and a fast-breaking story, but the basic premises of the form are the same. The drama is almost exclusively limited to a society of two—a man and a woman with independent, strong personalities who are thrown together by circumstances beyond their control. The more differences between them, the screwier and more interesting the comedy that can be generated. If they are from different social, political, intellectual, or economic backgrounds, good. If they actually dislike (or hate) each other, better (which is why, as Cavell noticed, so many of these comedies begin with previously divorced couples or those whose marriages are on the rocks). And if all of the above and a few more differences are thrown in for good measure, best. In its most common form, the man and woman are thrust together on the road, on the lam, pursued by police, villains, or relatives, or hard-pressed by fast-changing events they cannot prevent or affect, so that their differences have an optimal opportunity of flowering and flourishing in protracted arguments, struggles, and silences. Screwball comedy is the form above all others that thrives not on the romantic harmonies, similarities, and swoonings that are the trademarks of most other Hollywood love stories, but on the discovery and exploitation of differences, disagreements, and misunderstandings between its reluctant lovers. But, of course, the power of no dramatic form is merely formal, and these comedies only entertain and interest us so intensely because they so effectively mimic the forms real sexual relations take in our culture. The explosive verbal and physical combat of these situations and the clumsiness of these courtships is only satisfying because it so effectively (if exaggeratedly) captures the rhythms and tones of the emotional, psychological, and social tug-of-war that takes place in any robust sexual relationship. (That is what we mean when we say that these comedies feel more "realistic" than Hollywood romantic films, notwith-standing the fact that they are every bit as selective, conventional, and artificial as films within the straight romance genre.)

Thrown together, the man and the woman are set on a forcible exploration of their differences and misunderstandings, so that the films inevitably become processes of negotiation—negotiations con-cluded only when each character begrudgingly acknowledges his ad-miration of, and desire for, the other. The important point is that it is not in spite of but because of this process of discovery and exploration of differences, disagreements, and misunderstandings that each part-ner comes to appreciate the other's wit, strength, and resourcefulness in adversity. It is because of all the arguments that their initial distrust or revulsion turns (almost against the characters' wills) into love.

The form achieved its happiest expression in the series of Fred As-taire and Ginger Rogers musicals (the first of which, *Flying Down to Rio*, antedates Capra's *It Happened One Night* and Hawks's *Twentieth Cen-tury*, the customary starting points for discussions of the genre). Though not relying as heavily on physical comedy as some of the other screwball comedies do, the Astaire and Rogers musical situates itself squarely in the screwball tradition by taking as its central subject the comic awkwardnesses, ineptnesses, and errors of a man and a woman learning how to partner each other. The genius of the dances Astaire choreographed (and their relation to this tradition) was his recognition that partnering does not mean erasing or ignoring differences between the man and the woman, but just the opposite. As Astaire and Rogers, almost alone of all film dancers, were able to demonstrate, partnering means making something out of these differences and resistances, something more sexually and socially exciting than could ever emerge out of harmonies and similarities.

And that is why screwball comedy was a natural choice for Cas-savetes. The continuous emotional, psychological, and social nego-tiations and misunderstandings that take place in a screwball comedy are, in a comic vein, exactly what he had already been exploring in the interactions of his characters in *Shadows*, *Too Late Blues*, *Faces*, and *Husbands*. The comic misunderstandings between Minnie and Seymour in *Minnie and Moskowitz* are the exact equivalent of the endless com-petitive play of differences (of style, tone, and point of view) that take place between the adolescents of *Shadows*, the musicians of *Too Late Blues*, or the three boy-men of *Husbands*. They force characters to test their identities and capacities of performance against the resistances of each other character with whom they are in social and performative competition.

These are the formal qualities *Minnie and Moskowitz* shares with virtually all other romantic screwball comedy films. But a vital distinction remains to be made. Though the genre is almost always treated as if it were monolithic and homogeneous (Cavell's book is an example of this assumption), screwball comedy, as it was in fact practiced by the major Hollywood writers and directors, actually takes two quite distinct and practically opposed forms. They may roughly be described as "idealistic" screwball comedy on the one hand, and "pragmatic" screwball comedy on the other. The idealistic form is represented by the work of Chaplin, Astaire and Rogers, Capra, and, finally Cassavetes; the pragmatic strain by that of Ben Hecht, Lubitsch, Noel Coward, W. S. Van Dyke, Hawks, and Sturges—to lump together an odd assortment of actors, writers, and directors who indicate the range of possible achievement in each form. There are, however, obvious areas of overlap between them and each sub-genre contains elements of the other.

Frank Capra once described his films as the rubbing against each other of idealism and pragmatism, and though all screwball comedy to some degree depends on the conflict of ideals and ideal-eroding realities, the two forms I am discriminating come down on opposite sides of the fence in their respective preferences either for ideals or for pragmatic accommodations. Hawks and Sturges, the two greatest practitioners of the pragmatic form, corrode and question ideals in the course of their films and gradually replace them with flexible, illusionless, and inventive pragmatic social arrangements between characters. Capra and Cassavetes, the two great practitioners of the idealistic form, in effect do the opposite. They work to make imaginative space for ideals that ultimately call all mere social and practical arrangements of affairs into question. (In the rival cases of Sturges and Capra, at least, this is not merely a tidy theoretical contrast. Sturges's output, virtually picture by picture, is an explicit reply to, and comic inversion of, the value system in Capra's work.)

But if one calls filmmakers such as Capra and Cassavetes practitioners of a special idealistic (or romantic) form of screwball comedy, as the previous statement by Capra suggests, their work does not neglect pragmatic realities. The comedy in *Minnie and Moskowitz* (like the drama in all of Capra's and Cassavetes' work) embodies a jostling, exciting competition between the most romantic and exalted conceptions of the individual's imaginative powers and the jarring recognition of all the physical, emotional, and social restraints on imagination, idealism, and visionary expansion. Understood in this way, *Minnie and Moskowitz* is descended from Shakespearean high comedy (as it is enacted for example, in *A Midsummer Night's Dream* or, in a fairly different form, in *The Tempest*) in which exalted ideals of love and romance are pitted against, and triumph over, temporal, spatial, social, and linguistic realities that resist them. Were this same Shakespearean sensibility not evident in so many other American works of art, one might, in fact, call Cassavetes' faith in the potential imaginative prowess of the individual—in the power of desire and imagination in performance to transform reality—a throwback to the drama of the English Renaissance and English poetry of the seventeenth century. From the beginning, however, the American imagination has had more affinities with the imaginative audacities of the renaissance spirit than with the ironies, burdens, and self-puzzling doubts of post-romantic English and European artistic positions. The extraordinary claims Cassavetes makes for the stylistic powers of performance to change the world are a recurring dream of the potency of the individual imagination in American art. That is the cultural context in which the "idealistic" or "romantic" form of screwball comedy that he is continuing must be understood.

But, as I have suggested, this is not to say that the majority of American screwball comedies are of this idealistic form. Quite the contrary. The rival directors I have named made careers out of questioning, corroding, and displacing these ideals in their work. I cited Shakespearean drama above as an example of high comedy in the idealistic or romantic form, but it is important to emphasize that Shakespearean high comedy is quite different from what is usually described as "high comedy" in post-Shakespearean drama and twentieth-century film, most of which falls into the "pragmatic" category as I am defining it. The smart chat and leisure-class protagonists of a Noel Coward play or a film in the Van Dyke *Thin Man* series are in the same tradition as the Hecht-Hawks-Sturges line of comedy in which dextrous social arrangements and unromantic practical accommodations are the supreme goals. More exorbitant and less pragmatic ideals and imaginative claims on reality are proffered only to be adjusted and compromised into an adequate social stance. Typically, the protagonists of Coward, Van Dyke, Hawks, and Sturges are (like their authors) either too sophisticated and "wise" to harbor romantic ideals and "illusions," or too worn out and battered. Indeed the feeling with which one leaves the overwhelming number of screwball comedies in this pragmatic tradition is precisely that one has just participated in a process of destruction in which no ideals or romantic values have been left standing. Every form of idealism has been wittily called into question, every value (except for flexible, resilient pragmatism) has been playfully negated or caustically corroded. (This is so far from being regarded as a shortcoming of such films that it is what is most frequently praised in the work of Hawks, the greatest master of this sort of comedy, by his most sophisticated critics.)

It is against this background that the romantic comedy of the Chaplin-Capra-Cassavetes tradition (to reduce it to the names of its three most powerful post-Shakespearean practitioners) must be appreciated. In this tradition it is not that ideals are not questioned or tested (they are), but rather that they will not go away or their disruptive force be eliminated, no matter how much trouble they cause the characters and their authors.

With its uneasy lurches between ideals and realities, the idealistic form of screwball comedy is perfectly suited to the expression of the troubling double vision of life that informs all of Cassavetes' work: the endless war each of his films documents between his virtually operatic idealism and what he himself calls his "deep cynicism." This double vision is at the heart of the American experience, most powerfully articulated in prose by the work of Emerson, and summarized by him as the unbridgeable split between "the two lives, of the understanding and the soul."

Cassavetes' (and Emerson's) position is a far from comfortable one. The split between "the two lives" in the idealistic form of screwball comedy has an effect exactly opposite to what Andrew Bergman in *We're In The Money* says is the function of all screwball comedy (in a statement that has unfortunately become the *locus classicus* for all discussions of the form):

Simply stated, the comic technique of these comedies became a means of unifying what had been splintered and divided. Their "whackiness" cemented social classes and broken marriages; personal relations were smoothed and social discontent quieted. If early thirties comedy was explosive, screwball comedy was implosive: it worked to pull things together.[2]

This is the commonly accepted view of the function of screwball comedy, in which the comedy facilitates the interplay and gradual integration of disparate personal styles, classes, and energies into the social matrix. But it is only adequate to describe that form of comedy as

practiced by Hawks and Sturges, in which no higher values matter
ultimately than the practical, pragmatic integration of each of its interestingly different individuals into a society that weaves these various
styles, tones, and actions into one well-knit fabric of continuously adjusted social relations. It fails egregiously as an adequate description of
the work of Capra (which Bergman is mistakenly trying to characterize
in the above quotation), or any of the other makers of idealistic screwball comedies.

In their work something more like the opposite of social integration
or harmonization is taking place. As in so much other American art, the
inevitably exorbitant claims of desire and imagination (usually embodied in one or two central characters) "explode" all unquestioned
social roles, conventions, agreements, and identities (to use Bergman's
term). Rather than integrating characters into the social fabric through
the play of conversational differences (as happens in pragmatic screwball comedy, which in this sense is a descendent of the novelistic
comedy of Fielding or Austen), the Chaplin-Capra-Cassavetes line of
comedy does the reverse. The destinationless desires it articulates, the
wild dreams it releases, the unappeasable imaginative energies it stimulates make *all* merely pragmatic or social forms of integration irrelevant and unsatisfactory. That is the most profound significance of
Cassavetes' choice of this form of romantic comedy for *Minnie and
Moskowitz*. While Hawks and Sturges (like Austen or Fielding) are ex-
amining the adequacy of particular social styles, manners, and forms in
their films, Capra and Cassavetes are questioning the adequacy of all
possible or conceivable social arrangements of desire. Once this is understood, it will be seen that Cassavetes' turn toward screwball comedy
in *Minnie and Moskowitz* is not a retreat from the crises of the expression
of imagination and desire documented in *Faces* and *Husbands*, but a way
of plunging even more deeply into an exploration of them.

What Wylie Sypher says about the effects of the comedy in
Shakespeare's *Henry IV* may serve as a description of the effect of the
comic events in *Minnie and Moskowitz*:

Falstaff proves what Freud suspected: that comedy is a process of safeguarding
pleasure against the denials of reason. . . . Man cannot live by reason alone or
forever under the rod of moral obligation, the admonition of the superego. In
the person of Falstaff the superego "takes a holiday." The comedian is the self
behaving as prodigal and bohemian. [In Freud's terminology,] the comedy is
an essential pleasure mechanism. [It] is a momentary and publicly useful resistance to authority and an escape from its pressures; and its mechanism is a
free discharge of repressed psychic energy or resentment through laugh-

ter. . . . Its purpose is comparable to the release of the dream, except that the dream is private and asocial, whereas the comic uproar is "infectious."[3]

Sypher's invocation of Falstaff and Freud in the same context usefully suggests the degree to which a particular form of comedy may be hostile to all social structures of integration and understanding, as Sypher implies Falstaff is. The identification of Falstaff with the energies of the id (or what I would call the energies of unappeasable desire and imagination) makes clear the inadequacy of Bergman's whole analysis of this comedy merely in terms of initial social disruptions and subsequent social restorations of order. Falstaff, like Seymour Moskowitz, represents a principle of disruption deeper than the temporary disruption of society. He represents a permanent imaginative disruption that criticizes *every* possible form of social arrangement, not merely some particular set of social forms or characters against which he may seem to be reacting.

The drama in both this example from Shakespeare and the idealistic forms of screwball comedy is, in Sypher's terms, an examination of something much deeper than a character's social disruptiveness. Seymour Moskowitz and Falstaff are "prodigals and bohemians" in social terms, but Shakespeare and Cassavetes are interested much less in those aspects of their characters than in their imaginative bohemianism and prodigality. Seymour Moskowitz's most profound subversion of the society of *Minnie and Moskowitz* originates not in the fact that he is a footloose hippie or unambitious car parker, but in that he is a daydreamer and a free-spirited romantic. That gets him into much deeper water than social or economic irresponsibility ever could. The public "release of the dream," and the complications of that event, might be said to be the subject of all of Cassavetes' (and Chaplin's and Capra's) work. What Freud knew, but Bergman ignores, is that the disruptive energies of publicly released dreams may do the opposite of promoting the "fantasy of social unity" described by Bergman.

But Capra was the last major Hollywood filmmaker to dare to make this disruptively idealistic form of comedy. In the late 1940s and the 1950s, Hollywood comedies increasingly contented themselves with the shallow, contrived, bland social harmonizations of Doris Day, or with the mild and ultimately unthreatening lunacy of Jerry Lewis and Danny Kaye. True anarchic wildnesses of American imagination and desire left the field of film comedy altogether to find very different forms of expression in *film noir* and the postwar "woman's picture"—

not accidentally the two cinematic genres Cassavetes would be attracted to in the two films that followed *Minnie and Moskowitz*. Cassavetes
is renewing his encounter with Hollywood, after the disaster of *A Child
Is Waiting*, on his own terms. He would pick up where Capra abandoned the field after 1948, to explore the territory and rewrite the
history of the three major genres of postwar American film in his own
vein. Just as Minnie and Seymour are forced to make something loving
out of their arguments and bickerings, he would lovingly make something out of his own differences, disagreements, and arguments with
the traditional forms of Hollywood film.

Minnie and Moskowitz is in many ways a study of how directors such
as Hawks, Capra, and Cukor, and performers such as Grant, Hepburn,
Bogart, and Bacall (these last two are mentioned more than once in the
film) have shaped our language of love and courtship, even as it is an
analysis of all the ways in which life is different from the movies. The
power of movies to form and inform our lives is a felt presence in much
of Cassavetes' work—from the 42nd Street film marquees that frame
and fascinate the adolescents in *Shadows* to the references to Ingmar
Bergman in *Faces*—but *Minnie and Moskowitz* is far and away Cassavetes' most cinematically self-conscious film. It may begin in the old
world of New York City, but Cassavetes uses New York in the intro-
ductory section of the film only to indicate everything that the rest of
Minnie and Moskowitz will leave behind. Seymour flies to the West Coast
and virtually all of the rest of the film is set on the fantasy island strip
of never-never land bordered by Sunset and Wilshire Boulevards and
the grand old movie studios in the heart of the heart of Hollywood.
References to movies, movie stars, and movie situations abound. But
Minnie and Moskowitz is the opposite of the artsy, hermetic, life-begins-
and-ends-in-the-movies film that movies-for-movies'-sake critics extol.
Cassavetes realizes that it is only by successfully anatomizing and,
where necessary, mocking the old Hollywood forms of love and human
relationship that he can earn the authority to assert an authentic
worldly alternative to Bogart and Bacall in his film. Only by meticulously dissecting, criticizing, and discarding false forms of cinematic
glamour can he clear and protect a sufficient cinematic space for the
very different sort of glamour of his delicate, unstable, breakable pairing of these two lovers.

There is one other cinematic antecedent for *Minnie and Moskowitz* of
a very different sort, which deserves notice. The similarities between
certain aspects of Cassavetes' film and Barbara Loden's *Wanda* are so

striking and profound as to merit a few words of mention, especially if they encourage anyone to go back and look again at Loden's neglected small masterpiece. *Wanda* was released in the fall of 1970 about three months before Cassavetes began work on *Minnie and Moskowitz*, which was written in January and February of 1971, filmed in April and May, and released in December of that year. Not only are there superficial similarities of characterization and plot, in that both films center on mismatched couples thrust together on the run and endlessly on the move down the road (in a car in one case and a truck in the other), but one cannot help feeling that Loden's film pointed the way for the much more important stylistic breakthrough of the new kinds of editing and sound work Cassavetes would employ in *Minnie and Moskowitz*. Loden's film (photographed and brilliantly edited by Nicholas Proferes) uses an extraordinarily full and layered sound track to create a world of extreme density and complexity around the central characters, and uses certain kinds of editorial ellipses to jump rapidly and unpredictably between scenes to create a feeling of extreme rush and haste. Cassavetes would use both techniques in *Minnie and Moskowitz* for the first time in his work. (Incidentally, though influences are always unfathomable, many of the clipped, hurried editorial rhythms in certain scenes of chase and pursuit in a later film by Cassavetes, *The Killing of a Chinese Bookie*, also seem indebted to some of the brisk editorial pacings of the bank robbery scenes in *Wanda*.)

In the most profound sense, both *Wanda* and *Minnie and Moskowitz* are studies of the possibilities of personal movement in complex, changing environments. That is to say, the importance for Cassavetes of Loden's and Proferes' work with sound and editing in *Wanda* was that it showed Cassavetes a way to explore the relation of personal styles and the alien contexts within which styles are enacted and tested. Both films are about the interaction of personal styles and hostile environments, and further, about the interaction of the different styles of their two central characters—their different rhythms of personal relations, their different senses of timing, and their different styles of acting (both as characters and as actors). Both films are, in short, about the possibilities of productive synchronization and creative counterpoint of personal styles and timings that might be said to be one possible definition of a loving relationship.

Like Wanda and Mr. Dennis in Loden's film, Minnie and Seymour begin with every difference and incompatibility between them Cassavetes can invent. In one corner is Minnie Moore (played by Gena

Battle-scarred idealists—
A Minnie Moore with all the values in the world but no place to put
them. Seymour Moskowitz . . . a footloose, practical, uncomplicated
American dreamer.

Rowlands) a prim, proper, WASPish, L.A. County Museum worker.
She is delicate, shy, emotionally vulnerable, and a shell-shocked veteran of past love combats that have been much less than loving and
(breaking the first rule of the comic form) much more than verbal. She
is scared, battle-scarred, and gifted neither with the sharp-tongue of
Claudette Colbert, the scrappiness of Rosalind Russell, nor the coolness under fire of Lauren Bacall.

   In the other is Seymour Moskowitz (played by Seymour Cassel) a
fitting adversary to Minnie, opposite to her in every imaginable way.
He is a loud, brash, Jewish, walrus-mustachioed, over-the-hill hippie
who parks cars for a living, spills food on himself when he eats, and has
longer blonde hair than Minnie does. In the course of the film, they
meet, fall in love, and eventually admit their passion to each other and

marry, but the destination they ultimately reach is obviously much less interesting to Cassavetes than the twists, turns, and bumps of the journey itself. The ending of the film is hurried, glib, and almost perfunctory. It is the obstacles, road blocks, and detours that must be negotiated in the running of the course that matter to him and to us—just as the final, elaborate, perfectly danced production number in a Fred and Ginger musical only matters because of all we and they have lived through to get to it, all the strange, awkward, uncomfortable dances of learning to partner that have preceded it.

But Minnie and Seymour inhabit a world fallen far from that in which Fred and Ginger accidentally stepped on each other's toes. In Cassavetes' zany, comic updating of the rituals of courtship, the elegant ceremonies of East Coast high society have been superseded by the casual brutalities of the L.A. singles scene. The *Town and Country* living rooms of Cedric Gibbons and the Big White Sets of Van Nest Polglase have been struck and replaced by the gaudy glare of neon-lighted fast food joints and the dark dinginess of side-street parking lots. The demure verbal exchanges of polite couples ensconced in swanky suites at big hotels have given way to the contemporary craziness of one night stands in noisy motels. While Hawks, Capra, and Curtiz (whose *Casablanca* is mentioned twice) more often than not spirited their romancing lovers off to exotic, pleasure palace night clubs, or at the very least to a house or forest in Connecticut, where reluctant admiration had time and space in which to bloom, Cassavetes forces his hot-house romance to bud and blossom in cheap restaurants, parking lots, and the front seat of Seymour's pickup truck. Even Minnie's and Seymour's bedrooms offer no escape from the insanity of Hollywood and Santa Monica Boulevards, where almost all the rest of the film takes place. Beeps of horns, screeches of brakes, and noises of rushing traffic impinge on them in their most private moments in this, Cassavetes' most complexly layered soundtrack. In the film's rare lyrical interludes, the music Minnie and Seymour dance to comes neither from piano players named Sam nor from the hundred and one strings of the MGM Studio Orchestra, but from their own off-key singing or over the static and hiss of Seymour's truck radio, interrupted by news reports of murders, wars, and weather.

The difference between the sets, situations, and pacings of *Husbands* and those of *Minnie and Moskowitz* is instructive and significant. *Husbands* deliberately protected its characters, coddled them even, in ways that Cassavetes refuses to do in this film. The cavernously empty bas-

ketball court, indoor pool, and subway car, the sequestered suite of
rooms they occupy in the London hotel, and the almost deserted gambling casino where they pick up their dates were places of protection
and seclusion, places where Archie, Harry, and Gus could explore
themselves and one another free from distractions and disturbances. It
is more than as a joke about tourism in Britain that Cassavetes has it
rain the entire time his three husbands are in London. Rain is a way of
simplifying his characters' situations, because it keeps them indoors
and off the streets. They are insulated from the workaday world and
from distracting contacts with strangers, the better to conduct their
emotional and psychological explorations uninterrupted and unim-
peded. The very pacing of the scenes in *Husbands* is an effort to coddle
his three characters. The film (as many audiences have groaningly
complained) deliberately grants the men enormous time and space in
which to explore and explain themselves, as far as possible from the
temporal imperatives of plot and the urgency of action. (So well does
Cassavetes do it that there has probably never been an audience that
wished *Husbands* a minute longer or more leisurely than it already is!)

That is to say, *Husbands*, like almost all films, deliberately synchro-
nizes the pace of its narrative events, its characters' actions, and its
actors' performances in order to maximize the possibility of the particular sorts of dramatic events it is most interested in. *Husbands* in particular is a film of leisurely, retarded rhythms, just as Hawks's *His Girl
Friday* is a film of crazily accelerated rhythms. In the one film, medita-
tive, brooding characters give slow, reflective performances in scenes
that seem to run on forever. In the other, fast-talking characters give
frenzied performances in a fast-paced narrative of rapidly changing
events. Each film creates and maintains its own temporal momentum.
Characters from one could never appear or function in the other. But
that is just what changes in *Minnie and Moskowitz*. The rhythms and
pacings of scenes, characters' performances, and the narrative itself
become as eccentrically syncopated as Bo Harwood's jazz soundtrack to
the film (which, incidentally, gets wonderful mileage out of the exqui-
site goofiness and ragged elegance of Louis Armstrong's "Skid-Dat-
De-Dat," which is used, appropriately enough, as Seymour's theme
song in the opening minutes). It is impossible either for the viewers
watching the film or for the characters living it simply to coast with the
rhythms of a scene. Scenes slow down one minute, only to accelerate
out of control the next. Fast-paced characters interract with slow-paced
ones. The pacing of a scene is sprung free from the individual rhythms

of the characters within it. Characters are not coddled or protected within a special, sacrosanct temporal universe. Like the outrageously interrupted and intermittently resumed credit sequence to the film itself, in which Cassavetes' credit as writer and director suddenly pops up between two scenes somewhere around ten minutes into the movie, all ordinarily dependable temporal expectations have been put on edge. Rhythms have become desynchronized. A large part of a character's task in *Minnie and Moskowitz* will be simply learning how to live in the alien pacings around him, learning how to synchronize his rhythms with the rhythms of one other human being for the time it takes for a relationship to develop.

But with all of its rhythmic syncopations, its eccentric accelerations and decelerations, its conflicts of rival pacings, its added beats and missing beats, the one thing that can be said about the overall timing of *Minnie and Moskowitz* in comparison with Cassavetes' previous work is that it is fast, much faster than anything else he had ever done. Genre film that it is, it has the hurried feel of the Hollywood comedies it imitates. Even in its slower moments, it will not allow its characters (or its director) the exploratory liberties the husbands of *Husbands* had. In its particular narrative and social world, long, uninterrupted per- formances with understanding or sympathetic others have become an impossibility. There can be no escape for its characters to the barroom, ballroom, or bedroom of the imagination here. There is no refuge for the traumatized ego in buddy-boy friendships, shared fantasies, and relaxed narrative rhythms. For the first time in Cassavetes' work, the rhythms of the film approximate the eccentric, brisk, abrasive rhythms of the world in which the film is set and in which the characters must function.

The general rapidity of the film is established in the opening. In the first ten minutes, we are exposed to something like ten separate scenes, the longest (Seymour's encounter in a restaurant with a derelict pan- handler called Morgan Morgan) only two or three minutes in length, the others a minute or less each. (Remember that *Faces* had only eight scenes in its entire two hours and nine minutes, and that scenes ran on so long in *Husbands* that many members of the audience never sat past the halfway point in the film.) But the accelerated cutting and pacing in *Minnie and Moskowitz* is not an attempt by Cassavetes to mollify his audience or to sell out his film to box office receipts; it is a recognition of the changed nature of the material. Long scenes have become a luxury Cassavetes and his characters can no longer afford. *Faces* and

Husbands were documents of the leisurely (if painful) progress of a series of intimate human relationships. One could appreciate the experience of watching them, no matter how uncomfortable particular emotional discoveries might be, because one could be humanly grateful for the sheer time and opportunity to watch people work through a relationship in such detail and complexity. But the rhythms of *Minnie and Moskowitz* communicate a radically changed situation. Scenes are short and truncated. It is a film of gaps, abrupt elisions, and jump cuts. Relations have suddenly become hurried and fugitive. Even love has been put on the run in this world of social, sexual, and cinematic hustle.

Everything is speeded up. It is no wonder that Seymour has been driven to a camouflaging, self-protective flamboyance and Minnie to shell-shocked withdrawal in a world where human encounters are so hectic, abrasive, and evanescent. One of the scenes that sums up much of the frenzied, manic corrosiveness of the film is Minnie's blind date with Zelmo Swift early in the film. The name Cassavetes gives him and the description of him he included in the introduction to the published screenplay of the film suggest some of the brutalizing acceleration, breathlessness, and pressure of the scene in which he takes Minnie out to lunch:

> A Zelmo Swift has been driven crazy by business—dating girls for lunch and hurling blind emotions, crudely colored by his inability to forget himself, what he is, what he's done, the vast chambers of experience that he has gone through. In the end Zelmo Swift is an insane mechanic of credit cards, a manipulator of momentary emotions, constantly blackmailing, pressuring anyone he indiscriminately comes into contact with.

We have seen his sort before in the businessmen, agents, and salesmen of *Shadows, Too Late Blues,* and *Faces.* He takes his place in a long line of emotional hustlers and psychological con men in Cassavetes' work, but he is more than an additional example of Cassavetes' ability to work up brilliantly individualistic dialogue. He is a representative of all that is wrong with almost all of the relationships in *Minnie and Moskowitz.* Zelmo is too harried and frightened by an unprotected relationship, too much in retreat from the susceptibilities and exposures any intimate human commitment entails, ever to allow himself to become vulnerable to another human being. But rather than withdraw from human contact altogether, he chooses to feign communication and self-disclosure, while concealing himself behind an impenetrable smoke screen of canned anecdotes, mechanical jokes, and sham confidences. Zelmo is an emotional blackmailer who will agree to a relationship only if he can dictate all the terms in the deal. His lunch-time conversation with Minnie is one of the most awkward and embarrassing ever filmed:

Zelmo: Minnie, tell me about yourself.
Minnie: I can't.
Zelmo: You can't tell me about yourself?
Minnie: No, I can't.
Zelmo: Well, let me tell you . . .

. . . .

Zelmo: Let's see, you have a mature sense of humor . . . you like jokes, you're very romantically inclined. Is that true?
Minnie: Yes, it's true. All of it.
Zelmo: You're very artistic . . . even intellectual. You don't take romance lightly. If you fall in love with a man, it has to be for keeps.
Minnie: True, true, absolutely true.
Zelmo: You're very sensitive and delicate. You shake when you're upset and you're very gentle when you're moved. That's it. That's all I know about you.
Minnie: What shall we drink to?
Zelmo: Oh, I forgot to say that you're modest. There isn't one person out of a million that would not smile when you're talking about them . . .

. . . .

Zelmo: . . . You're very easy to talk to, Minnie. You look like you care about me. That's a terrific quality you have—a rare quality. I think those people that can listen endlessly are much more fascinating than the people that talk.
Minnie: Zelmo.
Zelmo: Look at your eyes. They're all moist. You're so sensitive. This is a rare quality to have today.
Minnie: Zelmo.
Zelmo: I'm a very lonely man. I'll tell you frankly, Minnie . . . not you, but someone . . . if I could find someone . . . it could be you . . . if I could find someone that would have your qualities . . . that if I touched her hand she would not pull it away if you know what I mean . . . .

Cassavetes is par excellence the filmmaker of the necessity of continuous adjustments in human relations, and Zelmo's sin above all others is his attempt to turn a relationship into a one-way street. Like the derelict Morgan Morgan's attempt to "adopt" Seymour in an earlier scene (whether Seymour wants to be adopted or not does not enter into his calculations) and Minnie's married boyfriend Jim's efforts to fix the scope and meaning of their relationship unilaterally, Zelmo's goal is to dictate not only the terms by which he is defined, but also the terms by which Minnie must define herself.

Zelmo is a figure who reappears throughout Cassavetes' work because he represents the dramatic negation of, and antithesis to, every positive performative value Cassavetes is interested in. As his conversation with Minnie indicates from beginning to end, his goal is to limit the possibilities of free performance and expression by making all personal styles subservient to predetermined forms, roles, and structures of experience. For Zelmo all of life and every individual he meets must be assimilated to his preordained categories of understanding and analysis. As such, he is a recurring nightmare inversion of the American dream, in which freedom of expression is absolutely circumscribed and constricted by fixed, preexisting forms and styles that resist all attempts to make them humanly responsive to the eccentric, idiosyncratic pressures of desire and imagination. It is a nightmare that has seized the imaginations and momentarily possessed the works of the greatest artists of the American tradition—from Hawthorne and Melville to Twain, James, Thomas Pynchon, and Stanley Elkin—and from which they, like Cassavetes, struggle to awake.

Like the figures in their novels James and Hawthorne most feared, Zelmo is a vampire of other people's experience. He would suck the secret mystery and unpredictability out of life in order to assimilate it to his fixed theories, categories, and received systems of relationship. This emotional blackmailer imprisons by knowing, and therefore destroys the possibility of an unpredictable, uncontrolled, free relationship. He demands nothing less as ransom than the sacrifice of the other person's independent selfhood. When Minnie, embarrassed and uncomfortable beyond endurance, will not pay up or play by his rules and his rules only, the only response available to him is to declare all-out war in an escalation of violence and abuse:

Zelmo: I can't seem to make you feel what I'm feeling. It's very hard.
Minnie: Very hard.
Zelmo: Oh, did I tell you my wife died, so I'm not divorced.
Minnie: Zelmo?
Zelmo: What?
Minnie: I don't want to hurt you.
Zelmo: How could you hurt me?
Minnie: Everything you're saying to me is very painful to you.
Zelmo: I made you uncomfortable . . .
Minnie: Zelmo, I have absolutely no interest in you personally. All I wanted was to go to lunch.

Zelmo: Not one dirty thing did I say. Not one off-center thing did I say . . . Always with blondes. They got some kind of Swedish suicide impulse in them.

. . . .

Minnie: Zelmo?
Zelmo: What?
Minnie: I'm already in love with someone.
Zelmo: What are you telling me that for? You tell me you're in love with someone else. What does that mean? I took you out, I was sorry for you. Bleach blonde hair, $90 a week worker . . . I wanted to take you out. Give you a little education. Let you understand that there's some kindness in the world. Don't tell me you're in love with someone— what do I want to hear that for?

These two sequences are less than a page apart in the screenplay, and only minutes apart in the film. Relationships in this world are initiated, developed, and destroyed within minutes.

The rhythms of human interaction have shifted radically from the previous films. If *Shadows, Too Late Blues, A Child Is Waiting, Faces,* and *Husbands* offered slow simmers of human relations, *Minnie and Moskowitz* puts its characters in a pressure cooker. In comparison to its co-erced feelings and forced reactions, even the misery under glass of the earlier films seems half preferable and certainly more humane. The earlier films are, after all, documents of the generation that came to maturity in the Eisenhower years. Their explorations and excru-ciatingly long scenes are synchronized with the painfully retarded pace of the emotional excavations of those years. The world of those films is a world of repressions, sublimations, and evasions of emotional honesty, but it is also for those reasons a safer and less turbulent world. Its emotional explorations were snail-like in pace, but that was testi-mony to how much time characters were able and willing to spend together. Intimacies, discoveries, and personal confidences were slow and difficult, and frustrated by the repressiveness of the age and the ubiquitous chaperonage of others; but the individual was also in a less vulnerable and exposed position. If wholesale denials and sup-pressions of basic emotional needs meant that individuals could never rise very high in intimacy with others, silence and repression also constituted a safety net that guaranteed that an individual could never fall very far into pain or shame either.

Cassavetes' technique in both *Faces* and *Husbands* was, in effect, to pull the safety nets out from under his characters, to expose them for the first time to the hazards and stimulations of unsupported, un-protected, unsanctioned relationships and identities. But *Minnie and Moskowitz* goes much further than that. The safety net of surburban lies, evasions, and self-protective social gatherings is not available even as a point of departure for Minnie and Seymour. Characters have been liberated from the repressed fifties into the free-for-all sixties. Cassavetes' characters have never before appeared to be so free—free from the pressures of peer groups, suburban codes of behavior, endur-ing attachments and obligations (in both real time and screen time), and the conservative and repressive institutions of marriage, family, and work. But the result is the opposite of comforting. *Minnie and Moskowitz* is Cassavetes' most zany, outrageous, and comic film (and many critics have failed to see more than that in it). It is a wild and woolly film populated with crazy, footloose drifters, hippies, and swinging singles. But it is also Cassavetes' most disturbingly manic, hectic, and frenzied film. If its characters are liberated from the usual middle-class hang-ups and institutions of his other films, they also constitute a gallery of his most vulnerable, exposed, and battle-fatigued figures, denied even the stifling families and homes of *Faces* and *Husbands* to retreat back into. If they are his most candidly voluble and comically expressive group of characters, they are also his most frightened, frantic, and abusive. If they are given the greatest freedom of movement and the widest pos-sibility of sexual liaisons of all of his characters, it is because they are one and all on the run from the pain of past associations and commit-ments. The styles of the late sixties have replaced those of the middle fifties, but progress remains to be proved. Relationships and identities have become catch-as-catch-can. There is neither time nor opportunity in this world for two people to get to know each other, to work through a long-term relationship together, to learn and grow together. "Scenes" (in both senses of the word) transpire too hurriedly. Individuals are thrust together too intimately, too quickly. Emotions are too close to the surface, and each individual too exposed to danger and too vulnerable to injury. We have entered the high-pressure, high-risk, low-profit world of singles bars, street corner hustles, and one-night cheap thrills.

The New York we glimpse in the first few minutes of *Minnie and Moskowitz* is a hurried, crowded, threatening society in many ways. But it is at the same time an old world society in which even the forms of alienation and loneliness have fairly human contours and dimensions. One can be lonely in a crowd in New York, too, but at least there are sidewalks along which to walk. People eat their food in restaurants

ZELMO: You're very sensitive and delicate. You shake when you're upset and you're very gentle when you're moved. That's it. That's all I know about you . . .

The wine is poured.

189   MINNIE: Well, what shall we drink to?

ZELMO: O, I forgot to say that you're modest. There isn't one person out of a million people that would not smile when you're talking about them. Did you know that? When I was a kid I used to say, "You know, there's something about you"--and there would be immediate interest. How come you called me? Listen, when you called me, what made you call me?

MINNIE can't answer.

190   ZELMO: That's okay--I understand. Your bone structure's interesting, too. Your hair . . . the way you dress . . . the shape of your mouth . . . I would say that you're Slavic. Or Swedish. What are you?

MINNIE: I'm English.

191   ZELMO: Oh, English, of course. Minnie, I don't know what to say. I don't go out very often. I'm actually scared of women. I suppose you must be frightened of men, too. So, I don't talk to them often . . . women. I say, "hello," "hello, how are you?" But I'm very interested in the arts; the arts: ballet, opera, theatre, concerts. I like poetry: Keats, Shelley, Byron, Shakespeare, Swinburne, Wordsworth . . . I like them. I've been reading since I'm twelve years old. I wear glasses now, I've read so much.

192   MINNIE: That's funny. I would have taken you for a businessman.

ZELMO: I hate business, Minnie. It's funny, 'cause I'm a fairly rich man, but I hate making money. I don't know what to do with it. I get up in the morning, I ask myself, Zelmo, what am I gonna do with my money? I give it to charity, I give it to friends. I buy a big house, take a vacation--from what, I don't know?? I'm not married anymore. I was married to a woman that was . . . a very rare woman, we had no children . . . it didn't last . . . not very long . . . I made a mistake on our wedding night . . . personal stuff, you know. You're very easy to talk to, Minnie. You look like you care about me. That's a terrific quality you have--a rare quality. I think those people that can listen endlessly are much more fascinating than the people that talk.

193   MINNIE: Zelmo.

194   ZELMO: Look at your eyes. They're all moist. You're so sensitive. This is a rare quality to have today.

MINNIE: Zelmo.

ZELMO: I'm a very lonely man. I'll tell you frankly, Minnie . . . not you, but someone . . . if I could find someone . . . it could be you . . . it could be someone that would have your qualities . . . that if I touched her hand she would not pull it away if you know what I mean.

195   MINNIE; Please, we should order . . . it's very late.

ZELMO: Aw, don't feel bad, please. I really have no right to put you on
        the spot like this, Minnie.

MINNIE: Zelmo, I think we should eat.

ZELMO: You're so delicate looking . . . look at your hands . . . they're so
        expressive. I can tell everything you're thinking by the way you're
        flicking your fingers there.

MINNIE: They have an interesting menu here. I really like this place.

ZELMO: Minnie, I got to tell you . . . my problem is that I have hair down
        my back, and on my chest, and down my arms . . . but not on my legs--my
        legs are very smooth. I don't know why I'm telling you this. . .

MINNIE: That's all right. I'll have the veal piccata.

ZELMO: You look at a man like me, Minnie, and what do you see?

MINNIE: I see a very nice man who's taking me to lunch.

196   ZELMO: I can't seem to make you feel what I'm feeling. It's very hard.

MINNIE: Very hard.

ZELMO: O, did I tell you my wife died, so I'm not divorced.

MINNIE: Zelmo?

ZELMO: What?

MINNIE: I don't want to hurt you.

ZELMO: How could you hurt me?

MINNIE: Everything you're saying to me is very painful to you.

ZELMO: I made you uncomfortable.

MINNIE: I am uncomfortable.

ZELMO: I could see that you were uncomfortable.

MINNIE: Zelmo, I have absolutely no interest in you personally. All I wanted
         to do was go to lunch.

ZELMO: Not one dirty thing did I say. Not one off-center thing did I say.

MINNIE: Zelmo, I want to go. I'm terribly sorry.

ZELMO: Always with blondes. They got some kind of Swedish suicide impulse in
        them. Took a girl out to lunch once--the next thing you know she wants
        me to kick her. I said--me kick you--for what? What's that supposed
        to be. . . something? (he looks around and catches the waiter's attention)
        Check--may I have the check, please?

The relentless deformations, distortions, and coercions of desire
—All the emotions in the world but no place to put them

*A sequence from Minnie's and Zelmo's blind date for lunch. Two pages from the final
script of* Minnie and Moscowitz, *completed early in 1971.*

sitting down indoors. Cocktail hour conversation standing in one place is possible. All that has changed utterly in the brave new world of Los Angeles. Life and movement have become mechanized, and relationships have become frantic and frenetic. We will not see Seymour walking down a sidewalk again for the rest of the film. Sidewalks will become another place on which to drive. The luxury of sitting down in one place to eat a meal away from the hustle and noise of the street will not become possible until the very end of the film. After living all of his life in and around the city, Cassavetes left New York for good in 1959 at the age of twenty-nine, about the same age Seymour seems to be in *Minnie and Moskowitz*. The film is, in a sense, an examination of all of the possibilities of life that were given up in that move away from the old world, and a survey of all of the imaginative possibilities that suddenly, confusingly, excitingly became available in the move to the new.

Perhaps the most disturbing aspect of *Minnie and Moskowitz* is how precarious the identities of individuals are, as if merely holding onto a recognizable, unique self had become problematic in this brave new world of infinite flux. Identities seem continuously on the verge of erasure or of being absorbed into one another. The film itself becomes a kind of visual and acoustic echo chamber as it goes along, so that Minnie, Seymour, Zelmo, Jim, and Dick Henderson weirdly start speaking one another's lines, playing one another's parts, and repeating one another's scenes. The effect is dizzying. It is as if anyone can turn into anyone else, or be polarized by these force fields of powerful relations into a new identity. Minnie no sooner escapes from Zelmo under the protection of Seymour, than Seymour whisks her off in the cab of his truck to a hot-dog stand and starts shouting at her and berating her in public in almost exactly the terms Zelmo did. Minnie sings "I love you truly" to Seymour at the end of the film in the same circumstances and in the same room in which she sang the same song to Jim at the beginning of the film. Morgan Morgan confides in Seymour in a painful scene early in the film, and Minnie confides in Seymour in a subsequent scene and uses some of the same phrases Morgan did. Seymour and Dick Henderson mouth each other's lines about protecting Minnie and not wanting to hurt her, and then both hurt her. Seymour peels away from Minnie in a parking lot in front of a disco exactly as Zelmo peeled away from her in the restaurant parking lot where she met Seymour. But there is no need to multiply examples. *Minnie and Moskowitz* is a virtual fun house of mirrored repetitions, doublings and redoublings, echoed and rhymed scenes, shots, and lines. (The most extreme example is the doubling of Jim's departure from Minnie's apartment early in the film, strange beyond all description. Cassavetes prints two takes of the same scene, unedited, back to back, transforming the rather routine lovers' farewell into an assertively filmic, *acted* event—that is to say, transforming an otherwise merely social moment into a moment in which one is made aware that an artificial, acted role is being constructed, put on, and played.) The whole film is a lesson in how easily (and frighteningly) roles and lines can be put on or taken off, transferred and passed along from one actor to another, how no one is fixed unalterably in a unique, immutable identity.

In L.A. where style and form are everything, maybe content has become obsolete and old-fashioned. There is perhaps no content left to be contained by the style, no identity apart from the momentary role. Relationships have become so harried, events so fugitive, identities so fluid, and Minnie and Seymour so vulnerable (and successive men and women so interchangeable in their love lives) that neither viewers nor characters can decide what the "real" people behind all the impersonations are, or if it means anything to ask for a "real" person. Is Seymour Humphrey Bogart, Claude Rains, Rick, Sam Spade, Zelmo, Dick, or Jim? The answer is that he is momentarily capable of being any or all of them, though to say that is to recognize how much more fluid, interesting, and alive he is than all of them. (In fact, in the scene discussed below, the climax of the film actually depends on Seymour physically changing his identity and appearance by cutting off the mustache that has hitherto been the single most salient aspect of his appearance.)

And yet as Cassavetes says in his introduction to the published text of the film: "The screenplay calls all these problems lies." Cassavetes later said that he made the film because he "couldn't understand why two people would get married anymore,"[5] but Minnie and Seymour do get married. In the hectic, harrying world he has created, they do learn to partner each other, and it is a partnering the more exhilarating for all the obstacles they learn to negotiate and the resistances they eventually surmount. There is no home for the heart or imagination here where everything is on the move. In his extraordinary essay "The Poet," Emerson calls all adequate expression "vehicular and transitive, and good as ferries and horses are for conveyance, not as farms and houses are, for homestead," and it is a metaphor that Cassavetes' film, as it were, literalizes. All adequate personal expression and relationships are forced to become as "vehicular" as Seymour's swerving, U-turning, constantly moving pickup truck, in which most of Minnie and Seymour's relationship develops. Minnie and Seymour must learn to live within the rhythms of this relentless stylistic and temporal movement if they are to survive at all. Indeed, their very abililty to stage an extended scene together (something *Shadows, Faces,* and *Husbands* took for granted) becomes a positive achievement for which we become grateful. Minnie and Seymour succeed (to the small extent they do), as Cassavetes himself does in this film, not by resisting or shutting out the rhythms and contents of the world in which they are forced to exist, but by converting the energies and pacings around them into principles of their own action.

Minnie and Moskowitz is a turning point in Cassavetes' search for a way out of the sterilities and frustrations of *Faces.* Amid the litter of failed and frustrated performances that surround his two central characters, he finds a way of imagining an extended two-person performance that is neither largely impulsive, immature, and irresponsible (as in *Shadows*), evasive, egocentric, and mechanical (as in *Faces*), nor bullying, escapist, and self-regarding (as in *Husbands*). What had in previous films been the excessive and potentially self-destructive energies of youthful idealism, mid-life frustration, or sentimental escapism, are for the first time converted into the give-and-take of a healthy, developing sexual relationship. For the first time, Cassavetes is able to imagine a society hospitable to the fully alive self. It is the smallest and most marginal of all possible societies—not the "society" of psychological con men and hustlers Minnie and Seymour circulate through in the course of the film, but the society they themselves, and only they, constitute. As small and marginal as the achievement is, it represents a personal triumph for this most tough-minded of filmmakers, and one of the exciting moments in recent film.

This is, of course, not to argue that in *Minnie and Moskowitz* Cassavetes softens his stance and treats Minnie and Seymour more sentimentally than his previous characters. In a review at the time of the film's initial release, Gavin Millar made the relevant discrimination between the toughness of Cassavetes' work and the comparative "indulgence" of a director as great as Fellini:

> In a strange way, the comparison should be with Fellini. . . . *Minnie and Moskowitz,* like *Giulietta of the Spirits,* is a film about the director's wife; and beyond that, like all of Fellini's films, it's about fantasies of escape. [But] the

difference is that Fellini indulges his fantasies, while Cassavetes doggedly worries at them.[6]

The toughness, the sincerity, and the supreme accomplishment of *Minnie and Moskowitz* is the earnestness and relentlessness of Cassavetes' "worrying" of his two characters and their situation, not to mention (since the characters themselves are endowed with almost as great an intelligence and sensitivity as their creator), Minnie and Seymour's "worrying" of their own relationship.

The comic device of making Minnie a rather shy, withdrawn WASP and Seymour a boisterous Jewish hippie is only another way of guaranteeing the maximum possible "worrying" of their situation. That they be as free as possible to worry each other and to worry themselves are Cassavetes' goals. In the service of the second of these, it is necessary that they simply be the most perceptive and self-reflective of all of his characters to date. One of the major limitations of Lelia and Tony in *Shadows*, of Richard and Maria in *Faces*, and of Archie, Harry, and Gus in *Husbands* is that none of them is able to remain worried deeply or continuously enough. Whether the refuge from worry is suicide, a return back home, or a retreat from emotional involvements into jokes, games, or melodramatics, each character wants nothing more than to stop worrying, to stop the disturbing (and enlightening) oscillations, tremulations, and turbulences of a living relationship. But for Minnie and Seymour on the other hand, with all the safety nets, refuges, and escape routes removed, there can be no avoiding worry; there is no way for them to evade or deny their troubling of each other and of themselves. Indeed, they gradually come to realize that in these techniques of trouble (to adapt a phrase from R. P. Blackmur) lies the only possibility of a fully alive relationship with each other.

Needless to say, for Cassavetes, as for D. H. Lawrence, such "worryings" and "troublings" of the individual's dreams are more than an aesthetic stance, more than a way of making interesting art; they are a belief about the nature of all healthy social interactions and relationships. So it should not come as a surprise that Gena Rowlands admitted at the time of the film's release that there were emphatic similarities between her cinematic courtship by Seymour and her actual courtship by Seymour's creator. Or that any number of Cassavetes' characterizations of his own married life perfectly describe the fictional relationship of Seymour and Minnie. Take this comment on his marriage, made by Cassavetes two years before *Minnie and Moskowitz* went into production:

In the beginning of our marriage I made a bargain [Gena] would fight me to the bitter end and I would fight her to the bitter end and the bargain never has been broken. Together we lead a magnificent, unassembled, emotional, and undisciplined life. I can't think of anyone with whom I would rather argue or love than my wife.[7]

"Unassembled, emotional, and undisciplined"—one would be hard pressed to think of three adjectives that better describe Seymour's relationship with Minnie. That is why it is important that the roles Minnie and Seymour play in the course of *Minnie and Moskowitz* are not fixed or predetermined by the broad categories (e.g., WASP and hippie) by which they are identified at the beginning of the film. In the course of the film, they are educated to the possibilities of other roles and relationships, to the extent that at one point Minnie and Seymour even reverse roles. (She arranges a surprise ice-cream party at a soda fountain, and he momentarily considers the event too outlandish.) A character is only interesting and adequate for Cassavetes to the extent that he can be "worried" or "troubled" out of his rigidities in this way, to the extent that he can stay on the move and learn to change and adjust his performance in the process of give-and-take with another character.

The antitheses of Seymour and Minnie in the film are Morgan Morgan, Jim, and Zelmo Swift, who, frustrated and frightened beyond movement and flexibility, devote all of their energies to clutching onto the marginal and inadequate characters they already have. But if their desperate effort were simply to hold on to their own characters, they would not be nearly as dangerous and destructive as they are. As Minnie says at one point in the film, their real threat is that they also try to possess the soul, mind, and body of everyone they meet. They are out to absorb everyone around them into their own catalogue of fixed categories and characterizations.

But as much as Minnie and Seymour struggle to resist absorption by the Zelmos, Morgans, and Jims in their lives, they resist the sort of critical footnoting to which most other film characters yield themselves. They refuse to be fixed, impaled, and "known" by a viewer in the same way that they refuse to lie down and yield to the unilateral demands of the emotional terrorists in the film. There is no more psychologically and sociologically astute filmmaking, but it is for this reason that Cassavetes' films inevitably foil the sort of standard psychological analysis that demands that a character or situation stand still for exegesis. Cassavetes has a virtually Jamesian fear of analysis, insofar as any

analysis, however subtle, is always an attempt to freeze a characterization or relationship out of time, change, and movement, and to limit
its possibilities. That is why this most psychologically subtle of all
contemporary directors (and of previous directors only Chaplin, Capra,
Renoir, De Sica, Dreyer, Ozu, and a few others deserve even to be
compared with him) can at the same time fear psychological analysis so
much as to insist with more than moderate passion: "I refuse to let
myself or my characters seek refuge in psychology either for purposes
of motivation or character analysis."[8]

Though it never summarizes itself so crudely, in the largest sense
Minnie and Moskowitz is an exploration of the possibilities of free movement in a world in which character is always in danger of being simplified into "character" and desire is always in danger of being restricted
to a destination. It is a film about the possibility of movement in a world
that craves fixities. Specifically, it is about two characters' attempts to
free themselves from the fixities and impalements of all analytic systems of understanding and relationship (and not only from systems of
understanding imposed upon them by others—Minnie's most difficult
task is to free herself from her own categories of analysis, categories
such as "romance," "true love," and "heroism" that Hollywood has
defined and drummed into our consciousnesses). To be free in this way
is for the first time to be capable of living fully in the mess and flux of
contemporary existence.

Cassavetes, in effect, charts two possible responses to the contemporary mess and muddle into which his characters are thrust: on the
one side, the rigid categories of Zelmo Swift and Morgan Morgan, and
on the other, the mercurial partnering of Minnie and Seymour. One
does not want to be too hard on the first group, and Cassavetes himself
humorously disarms them in the film beyond the point of their being
seriously threatening. Their form of psychological absolutism surfaces
intermittently at times of stress and confusion in the American experience. In earlier eras they might have been religious zealots, McCar-
thyites, or ideological purists or reformers of many sorts. Their desperate clutchings at psychological, social, and moral absolutes, their
terror-struck impositions of spiritual law and order are last-ditch emotional stands against what they must view as the encroachment of
chaos around them. But Cassavetes' sympathies are obviously all on
the other side, on the side not of screening out the confusions of
movement, mess, and time, but of learning to live with them; on the
side not of eradicating the "unassembled, emotional, and undisci-

plined" in experience, but of finding a style of living (and of film-making) adequate to an appreciation of them.

Cassavetes' formulation of the two alternative responses to experience in *Minnie and Moskowitz* is so close to William James' division of philosophers into the "tough-minded" and the "tender-minded" that it is worth quoting James at some length. As the following passage indicates, James even uses the same rhetorical strategy Cassavetes does to comment ironically on what he would call tender-mindedness (and what Cassavetes would call Zelmo Swiftism and Morgan Morganism). The American genius for mockery was seldom more effectively put to use. James mocks the attempt in art, life, or philosophy to escape into categories and abstractions that would "support, tie, and unify" experience with a description of tender-mindedness as parodically outrageous as Cassavetes' comic presentation of Morgan Morgan and Zelmo Swift:

> Something to support the finite many, to tie it to, to unify and anchor it. Something *un*exposed to accident, something eternal and unalterable. The mutable in experience must be founded on immutability. Behind our *de facto* world, our world in act, there must be a *de jure* duplicate fixed and previous, with all that can happen here already there *in posse*, every drop of blood, every smallest item, appointed and provided, stamped and branded, without chance of variation. The negatives that haunt our ideals here below must be themselves negated in the absolutely real. This alone makes the universe solid. This is the resting deep. We live upon the stormy surface; but with this our anchor holds, for it grapples rocky bottom. . . . This is Reality with the big R, reality that makes the timeless claim, reality to which defeat can't happen. This is what men of principles . . . think themselves obliged to postulate.[9]

It is a criticism many contemporary filmmakers, critics, and viewers might do well to take to heart. While they continue to scurry around in quest of something outside the flux of a film experience, some timeless excerptible moment of transcendence, or fixed, immutable structure or pattern, Cassavetes (like William James) offers only the unanchored, fluctuating timebound movement of experience. If Minnie and Seymour are on a metaphorical or literal journey in the course of *Minnie and Moskowitz*, it is one without any conceivable or desirable destination; if they are making a relationship, it is a work of making that will never be done. In James's reply to tender-mindedness (which he calls "rationalism" in the following quotation), he actually uses two of the same metaphors that Cassavetes does in *Minnie and Moskowitz*. For the Jamesian pragmatist, there is no "home" to run "home" to (more than Seymour's vehicular home), and no security beyond turning "tramp and vagrant" (as tramp and vagrant as Seymour's mother feels him to be):

To rationalists this describes a tramp and vagrant world, adrift in space, with neither elephant nor tortoise to plant the sole of its foot upon. It is a set of stars hurled into heaven without even a centre of gravity to pull against. In other spheres of life it is true that we have got used to living in a state of relative insecurity. The authority of "the State," and that of an absolute "moral law," have resolved themselves into expediencies, and holy church has resolved itself into "meeting houses." Not so as yet within the philosophic classrooms. . . .

For pluralistic pragmatism, truth grows up inside of all the finite experiences. They lean on each other, but the whole of them, if such a whole there be, leans on nothing. All "homes" are in finite experience; finite experience as such is homeless. Nothing outside the flux secures the issue of it. It can hope salvation only from its own intrinsic promises and potencies.[10]

But of course this is not to suggest that there is any direct relationship between William James and John Cassavetes. Cassavetes would probably scoff at this linkage of his name with that of a nineteenth-century philosopher. The connection, in fact, would be that much less interesting and less important if Cassavetes had read James's discussion of "homelessness" and "vagrancy" and merely decided to work out some of his vehicular metaphors and attitudes cinematically. No, the relationship of the two men is much deeper and much less deliberate than that.

Both men are involved in a more profound relationship than that of intellectual influence. They are products of a common culture and share a common heritage. As James's odd reference to "salvation" in the last sentence of this quotation suggests, they are both inheritors of the capitalist form of Protestantism that began to make itself felt in both England and America around the middle of the seventeenth century. In the Puritan forms in which it translated itself to this country, it placed extreme burdens on the individual by denying him any possibility of reclining into historically, institutionally, or culturally received values. In its Calvinist manifestations, the result was that "salvation" was only to be had through a moment-by-moment exertion of "work." That is the intellectual legacy James and Cassavetes share. It is the American ethic of unceasing creative "work"—not only the work of laboring in factories and mills, but more importantly, the work of making meaning in life and the burden of continually having to renew and recreate meaning. What came to America as a uniquely Puritan view of the necessary form of man's relations with God—as a series of continuous worryings, adjustments, and self-scrutinizing corrections of relationship—has become in the work of both James and Cassavetes the exemplary form of man's relation to the universe, to other men, and to himself.

The point of *Minnie and Moskowitz* is that an adequate style of relationship can never be "inherited" from a previous generation, or automatically appropriated from the forms of daily life, as Zelmo and Morgan tyrannically assume. It is something that the individual must labor to bring into existence. Cassavetes' films are demonstrations of the enormous and never-ending work involved in improvising into existence a style of personal performance that will maintain its sensitivity and responsiveness in a world everywhere threatened and trivialized by mechanical, inherited, repetitive, and unexamined forms of discourse and personal relationship. *Shadows, Too Late Blues, A Child Is Waiting,* and *Faces* constitute largely negative efforts at purging mechanical and received forms of performance. They are efforts at analysis, deconstruction, and exorcism. But with *Husbands* and, to a greater extent, *Minnie and Moskowitz* and the films that follow it, Cassavetes begins to reconstruct and rehabilitate the families that were absent or grossly inadequate in the earlier films. But, as Cassavetes knows and these films demonstrate, the negative effort of exorcism and parody can never be entirely separated from the positive effort of assertion. It is only in proportion to one's ability to cut away dead areas of human relationship and forms of consciousness that one makes a space for proposing, tentatively and hesitantly, areas of possible growth and development.

But the task is not easy and Cassavetes' efforts to capture moments of creativeness and freedom in these films, as alternatives to merely making his scenes and characters subservient to the prefabricated forms and forces of contemporary life, are always fugitive and inevitably leave themselves open to attack by critics who expect a film to mirror precisely those conventional values and forms of experience Cassavetes is questioning. A character as extravagant, eccentric, and zany as Seymour (or Mabel in the film that follows this one) is always going to seem merely self-indulgent, excessive, or irresponsible to critics for whom social and narrative stabilities will always have an authority superior to the authority of the eccentricities of individual desire. Such critics can call Cassavetes' characters unrealistic and exaggerated only because the realities they acknowledge are the very psychological and social structures that Cassavetes' films encourage us not to accept but radically to question. (A student of mine once criticized Shakespeare's tragedies from the same standpoint, arguing that Lear, Othello, and Hamlet were all unrealistic, exaggerated, and excessive characters. The reply to that is, of course, that it is not Shakespeare who is at fault, but the playgoer's impoverished sense of reality, which limits it to what is socially and psychologically coherent, orderly, and organizable.) Such critics (and they include almost everyone who has dealt with Cassavetes' films in the past) are more interested in affirming the importance of social integration and harmonious interaction than in acknowledging, as Cassavetes is, the sheer insatiability, wildness, and eccentricity of desire and imagination. Like the student critic of Shakespeare, they have unconsciously internalized the repressive aesthetic and social structures Cassavetes' works are deliberately created to explode. The imaginative claims his films expose us to are always, and necessarily, at odds with, and disruptive of, the stable, articulatable, consistent, definable structures of society and conventional narrative form.

This "adventure of insecurity" (it is William James's phrase describing his own philosophy of life, but owes as much to Puritanism as it does to Pragmatism) might be the subtitle for *Minnie and Moskowitz*, or for all of Cassavetes' work, for that matter. The continuous swerves and adjustments of tone and plot in his work are devoted to destroying the false securities characters and audiences inevitably fall into, and to releasing impulses that make the "adventure" of exploration, discovery, and creation possible. In lieu of known quantities and predictable destinies, Cassavetes deliberately celebrates the possibility of endlessly adjusted transactions. Take the longest scene in *Minnie and Moskowitz* as an example. In one continuous scene (disregarding three brief ellipses), Minnie and Seymour zigzag from hurt feelings and lovers' quarrels in a parking lot, to a fist-fight with a friend of Minnie's in which they are both knocked out, to an attempted suicide (Seymour is going to stab himself with scissors for love of Minnie, but cuts off his mustache instead), to Seymour's proposal of marriage to her, to a lovers' duet and phone calls to their mothers from Minnie's bedroom. The very essence of the scene is the swerves and shifts of feeling Cassavetes mixes together, so that nothing in a human encounter is predetermined or predictable; in this tramp and vagrant universe, every moment is on the move, and everything is up for revision. We move from serious drama to tragedy to comedy to farce and back again in a matter of minutes, as no director since Billy Wilder has dared to do with such abandon.

That is what makes Cassavetes' scenes and their effects so hard to summarize and potentially so disorienting to an audience (or a reviewer) prepared only for an evening of "comedy" (in the case of *Minnie and Moskowitz*) or "serious drama" (in the case of most of the other films). Films, scenes, and relationships refuse to stabilize (or congeal) this way. But the "adventure of insecurity" that Cassavetes offers his characters (and his audiences) is, as James well knew, a two-edged sword that asks at least as much in new responsibilities as it grants in new freedoms. On the one hand, characters (and actors) are denied the luxury of reclining into a prefabricated mood, atmosphere, or tone in even the briefest scene, which means that in a virtually Puritan sense they can never relax or stop working. On the other hand, the outcome of any encounter is so free of any aesthetic or emotional predestination or predetermination that one feels that characters have never before been given such opportunities to make up their own destinies and outcomes as they go along. The unique quality of Cassavetes' films is summarized precisely by the simultaneous blessing and curse that this adventure of insecurity confers on his characters: never has the freedom of characters been so enhanced, and yet never have characters been so heaped with endless responsibilities. (Or to explain it in an entirely different way in cinematic metaphors: the neorealistic toughness, worry, and "insecurity" Cassavetes injects into all relations is almost exactly counterbalanced by his Capra-corny idealism about the nearly infinite powers of the individual to "redeem" himself and those around him.) That doubleness is what makes these films simultaneously so bracing and so exhilarating (even in their most tragic moments).

All of which goes to suggest why *Minnie and Moskowitz* is one of the toughest, most unsentimental, and most self-critical comedies ever made. Cassavetes shows an almost Shakespearean willingness to include moments of brutality and violence that resist his own comic intentions and his film's romantic rubric. There is a recognition of everyday loneliness, sadness, failures of communication, and outright cruelty that repeatedly interrupts and punctuates even its most lyrical interludes, until it seems that Cassavetes courts the destruction of his own film. Time after time, it threatens to tear itself to pieces, to contradict its own comic premises. It is almost a convention of the comedy-romance genre that the destruction, violence, and cruelty associated with the world outside the lovers' protected realm is sealed off from their awarenesses; lovers' quarrels take the place of real violence. But not so here. There are no sanctuaries or protected forms of relationship.

There is no sacrosanct sound-stage space within which Minnie and Seymour can let down their guards and get to know each other. In terms of genre traditions, it is as if *film noir* bullies walked the same streets and sets where Fred and Ginger learned to dance. Every time *Minnie and Moskowitz* takes the most hesitant dance step toward romance land, Cassavetes interrupts it, criticizes it, and wrenches it back to the world of fights, arguments, and both verbal and physical violence.

Sexual relations are not privileged encounters and opportunities of escape from the turmoil of the world here (as in most romantic films), but (as in *film noir*) are an extension of the stupidity, destruction, and waste of other human relationships. John Cassavetes appears in a cameo role as Jim, one of Minnie's former lovers, to beat and humiliate her in a fight early in the film. A few minutes later (in the scene already quoted) Zelmo Swift shames and badgers her on their lunch date, before getting into a fist-fight with Seymour, who is parking cars in the restaurant lot. Later still a friend of Minnie's knocks out both her and Seymour in an absurdly misguided attempt to protect her from Seymour. Sexual relations are not an escape from the insensitivities of the world, they are the ultimate refinement of them into techniques of personal torture. Here, as in *Faces*, the men Minnie dates are as much hustlers, manipulators, and con artists in their emotional and sexual affairs as they are in their business and financial affairs.

Minnie and Seymour successfully negotiate more hurdles and obstacles than any of Cassavetes' previous protagonists and still manage to keep their dream alive. But the film ultimately gets Cassavetes and Seymour and Minnie into deeper water than he knows how to navigate them or himself out of. When even the most receptive theater audiences are repeatedly brought up short by the film's bracing lurches of tone and feeling, it is not surprising that Cassavetes is unable to see his characters through to some satisfactory conclusion to their disturbing, disorienting, and continuously demanding cinematic predicament. In the end, he damps down the oscillations, reins in the lurches, and chooses to save appearances and keep his film from tearing itself apart. In the final few minutes of the film, Seymour proposes to Minnie, they meet their future mothers-in-law in a hilarious meal in a restaurant, are married in a quickie Hollywood chapel service, and are left at the end to live apparently "happily ever after."

The conversation with the mothers in the restaurant and the outrageous marriage ceremony are probably the funniest scenes Cassavetes has ever written, and the ones audiences walk out of a theater remembering most vividly and hilariously. But the comedy, Cassavetes' inspired narrative zaniness at this point in the film, is just the problem. These scenes are funny exactly insofar as they erase almost all of the social, personal, and emotional confusion that has led up to them. They have enough humanly complex comic material for a whole film by another filmmaker—Robert Altman has in effect extrapolated a whole film from the same fairly thin joke Cassavetes' wedding ceremony employs—and they would do another film proud. It is not the quality of the comedy that is objectionable, it is the fact that in this film, at this moment, sustained comedy is an evasion of more important issues. Cassavetes has had to stoop to a comic trick, an aesthetic sleight of hand, to get himself and his characters out of his film. In a filmmaking career of ever greater capaciousness and ever more daring inclusions (and up to this point *Minnie and Moskowitz* has managed to include more than any film that preceded it), these scenes are Cassavetes' least expected course of action. They are a series of subtly systematic exclusions, a sequence that elides and evades the (admittedly wild and perhaps finally unorganizable) energies the rest of the film releases.

Cassavetes moves his camera in for cleaner, less cluttered close-ups; the composition of particular group shots is simplified; the sound track is made less complex; the rhythm of the film begins to stabilize, and the tone settles into a bland geniality. Characters who had previously never stopped moving, suddenly start to "sit still" for Cassavetes' scenes and his camera set-ups, both literally and metaphorically. The battle between form and impulse that made earlier scenes interesting is over; good photographic form has triumphed almost completely over the wildness of individual impulse.

Cassavetes once described *Minnie and Moskowitz* as a "pure fantasy," and perhaps that is the criticism an admirer of the earlier sections of the film would level against the final five or ten minutes of it. There is nothing wrong with fantasy, but one wants it less "pure" than these final scenes give it to us. The discrepancy between the last shot Cassavetes' shooting script stipulated, and the last shot he actually filmed and released communicates not only the invigorating "impurity" of the fantasy he originally imagined, but also the subtle escapism of the ending he chose to use in the final print. The plot is identical in both versions of the film: Minnie and Seymour get married, and the film immediately jumps ahead in its last minute to show them with their burgeoning family five or six years later. But the difference is in Cassavetes' imagination of that final scene. In the version in the shooting script, we eavesdrop on a typical moment in their lives at home:

Annihilating all that's made
To a green thought in a green shade

CUT TO:

EXTERIOR Backyard—Day.

It's a patio type arrangement. A little grass, a little mortar. A chair with Minnie's mother on it. A chair and a pair of sunglasses for Mrs. Moskowitz. Several young kids ranging in ages from two to five patrol the yard. Minnie sits next to her mother and Seymour plays with the kids. There's a radio turned on very low and there's classical music on it—FM, of course. The film credits commence. We feel the relationship of a middle-class, American, anti-liberationist, typical, normal, fraught-with-problems, happy couple with both mothers-in-law. The conflict of how the children are to be raised, the love, and the lack of loneliness—is felt.

But how different the final filmed version is. It, too, cuts from the wedding ceremony to a scene several years later in a backyard, but it is nothing like this. The patio with "a little grass, a little mortar" has been transformed into a lovely, lushly green, shrubbery-enclosed yard. The FM radio music has been replaced with a jazzy, polished soundtrack of the sort the whole film after the opening credits has been defending against. The drab, ordinary day, with just the most subliminal hint of ominousness in the children's "patrol" of the yard, has changed into the festivity of a birthday party celebration complete with brightly colored presents, treats, costumes, and balloons.

A literal-minded viewer might want to know where all that grass and shrubbery found room to grow in this world paved previously only with asphalt, concrete, and formica. Someone as factual as Mrs. Mosko-witz might want to ask what Seymour does for a living to pay the mortgage and support a family in such style in or around L.A. (Mrs. Moskowitz in fact does ask Seymour about his employment plans in the earlier scene in the restaurant, but when Seymour gives an absurd answer about going to work in a bigger parking lot, Cassavetes de-pends on our laughing and not taking the question any more seriously than Seymour does.) One might wonder whether the kids are to be raised as Jews or Protestants. (It is a question raised by the final sen-tence of the shooting script, and one Mrs. Moskowitz also asks in a scene that was cut from the final print of the film.) Do the kids have to walk across Wilshire or Santa Monica Boulevard to get to school, or does Seymour drive them in his pickup truck? Where is Seymour's ubiquitous pickup in this final shot, anyway? But there is no need to be so trivially factual and literal-minded. Even an imaginative viewer feels the way virtually every problem the preceding 100 minutes of film staked out as its territory has been forgotten here. Any viewer feels the sleight of hand in transporting Minnie and Seymour suddenly to a green world, when green has been the one color conspicuously absent up to this moment. The screenplay intended a much more subdued and qualified ending, but all "conflict," everything "fraught with problems" has disappeared in Cassavetes' final print. The film ends up denying its own insights. The sexual awkwardnesses, insensitivities, fears, and excesses (which are a necessary part of even the healthy relationship of Seymour and Minnie) are simply wished away.

Not that Cassavetes is unaware of his compromise. The use of a zoom to move in and out of this scene on tiptoe as it were (a technique unprecedented in his other work), the unsynchronized sounds of the party, the musical scoring, and the stylized coda form itself, which then blends into the final credit sequence, are all confessions on his part that he has moved into a world different from that of the preceding film. In this movie about movies, a movie that unendingly criticizes movies, we have moved back into the world of the movies, into a world of purely cinematic arrangements and balances, a world of "pure" fantasy. It is true that the birthday party we catch a glimpse of in this scene is

interestingly disorganized and energetically busy with visual and social
activity, but a birthday party, however anarchic, is an occasion just too
tame and domesticated to summarize such a wild and occasionally
frightening film fittingly. Seymour wears an Indian headdress, but the
problem is that in this scene, it is only a form of costuming, a party
get-up. His earlier, stimulating primitivism, his ethnicity, his frequently violent and always disruptive energy have been made safe,
sublimated into the jokesy metaphor of a cardboard costume hat. It is
a purely formal ending for form's sake, as perhaps the rose-colored
glasses Cassavetes has Minnie wearing in that final minute admit.

The very best one can say of it is that, bland as it is, this "happy
ending" emphatically does not succeed in erasing the emotional and
physical violence and wildnesses of feeling that came before it. It pours
oil on the troubled waters of the preceding film, but it is testimony to
the power of Cassavetes' film up to this moment that the storm of
experience we have lived through cannot be quelled or forgotten that
easily.

But this is not to suggest that Cassavetes should have substituted a
relentlessly tough ending instead—say an ending in which Minnie and
Seymour are somehow reexposed to the likes of Morgan Morgan or
Zelmo Swift. The problem is that neither Minnie nor Seymour, even
with the help of the other, could withstand the pressure of such narrative treatment. Even the original screenplay recognizes that they
must be cordoned off from the world of the preceding film, sheltered
in the lap of the suddenly created family. Minnie and Seymour need to
be protected from the harshness and crudity of the preceding film; they
need to be segregated in a backyard and orchestrated off to a happily-
ever-after Cinema Land. They are simply too weak to withstand the
trials and tribulations of the earlier film, even after their marriage. But
to say that is only to acknowledge once again the imaginative weakness
at the heart of the film.

After 100 minutes of tough-minded, bracingly comic exploration of
the trenches, landmines, and battlefields of sexual warfare, perhaps it
is unfair to complain when Cassavetes declares a hilarious cease-fire. A
filmmaker of lesser genius would never have gone this deep into the
battle at all, before beating a hasty retreat. But the problem with the
ending in either version of the film is indicative of a fundamental
imaginative problem that haunts all of the previous work. In the implicit metaphors of *Minnie and Moskowitz*, Cassavetes cannot find a way
to bring together the free movements of Seymour's truck, with its

continuous swerves and U-turns, and the stabilities, immobilities, and responsibilities of the final scene of family life. The result is a kind of artistic schizophrenia in which Cassavetes wants to honor both the jaunty, improvisatory impulses of the moment (generally associated with Seymour) and the long-term obligations and relationships of love, marriage, and domesticity (generally associated with Minnie).

It is an imaginative schizophrenia not unlike that which ends up splitting *Husbands* into two opposing parts, home and escape. The adventure of the London excursion seems just too far removed from the ordinary lives, responsibilities, and occupations of the husbands to make Gus's return at the end entirely satisfactory. Like contemporary Huck Finns lurching from one extreme to the other, from an extreme of freedom to an extreme of obligation, Cassavetes' husbands have no tenable middle ground in which to live their daily lives. (Which is to say, Cassavetes fails to be able to imagine such a middle ground except as some unspecified point at which the two extremes communicate with each other.) That is the problem for Minnie and Seymour as well. *Minnie and Moskowitz* lurches between opposite states, and can find no inhabitable "home" for its ideal performers. Not until his next film, *A Woman Under the Influence*, will Cassavetes succeed in integrating romantic love and the harsher realities of sexual relations. Not until then will he be able to imagine a "home" for his characters' most robust and life-affirming performances. Not until then will he be able to imagine a society in which the most energetic personal performances can be healthily accommodated, a society that is neither the larger society of *Minnie and Moskowitz*—an ego-destroying world of con men and hustlers, from which love must always flee—nor the society that is the smaller society of the film, the society Minnie and Seymour constitute at the end of the film, two figures on the run from the rest of the world.

Minnie and Moskowitz was photographed by Arthur J. Ornitz, a friend of Cassavetes' and a cinematographer who has a long and distinguished career as a "realistic" photographer (as distinguished from, say, the Zsigmond-Kovacs school of prettified photography—American Impressionism for the coke-and-popcorn crowd—that has usually been in the ascendent in Hollywood). Ornitz was the photographer on Shirley Clarke's *The Connection* and John Cromwell's *The Goddess*, two films that impressed Cassavetes immensely when he was just beginning his own work. His documentary-style photography was used to occasional interesting effect in both *Requiem for a Heavyweight* and *The Boys in the Band*, and its stylistic origins may be traced back to Ornitz's actual documentary work with Joris Ivens in *Power and the Land* in 1940. During most of *Minnie and Moskowitz*, his *cinéma vérité* styles of lighting and camera placement perfectly counterbalance the extreme romanticism and idealism of the story and characters. At rare moments even *Minnie and Moskowitz* indulges in some isolated "beauty shots" of its own, but they are different from the "beauty shots" in other films in that they are present only to be criticized or critically put in their place here. Photographic prettiness exists in one scene only to be disrupted by the underlighted graininess of the next. The Vermeer lighting in a couple of scenes in Minnie's bedroom, the rosy tones in the lighting of Irish's basement apartment where Seymour spends the night at the beginning of the film (in a scene that was cut from the final print), and the bucolic final backyard scene present only fleeting, and finally illusory, possibilities of rest, relaxation, and comfort (for both the characters involved in those scenes and for the audience viewing them). Pretty shots represent imaginative moments of composition and lyrical composure that last only momentarily in this world of constant rush and pressure.

If there is a single image that summarizes both the special strengths and the peculiar limitations of *Minnie and Moskowitz*, it is the brief parody of Stanley Kubrick's *2001* that occurs about two-thirds of the way through Cassavetes' film. Despite Minnie's best efforts to resist Seymour, and Seymour's own incredibly clumsy efforts at courtship, they have by this point, almost against their wills, drawn closer together. At the first moment of abandoned, unselfconscious intimacy between them, Cassavetes suddenly cuts to a shot of Minnie and Seymour cruising down Hollywood Boulevard at night, silhouetted in the dark and framed in the cab of Seymour's truck. Strauss's "Blue Danube Waltz" swells on the soundtrack, and as the camera picks up the colored reflections of the neon lights of the avenue slowly moving along the windows of the truck, the illusion and the consummate beauty of the shot is complete. Seymour's old pickup gliding through Los Angeles at night has become a vehicle fully as inspiring and majestic as the grandest of Kubrick's spacecraft in *2001*.

But it is representative of the differences between Cassavetes and Kubrick that while Kubrick in the original of this moment chooses to revel in the technological wonder of spacecraft and spacesuits, Cassavetes (whose rare special effects are more like Fellini's in this respect, in that they extol the power of the human spirit and not the power of technology) is less interested in the vehicle than in the people inside,

Enchanted voyages of the imagination and bumpy returns to earth
in Seymour's pickup truck/spacecraft

and is less interested in the pickup truck/spaceship as a vehicle of
transportation than as a vehicle for the release of the human imagination. Ornitz's camera first tracks behind the truck, then tilts to the
stars, and then finally arcs slowly around it (as, at that point, his lovers
sit parked in the lovers' lane on Mulholland Drive). Amid all the razzle-
dazzle of the fancy camerawork and the wittiness of the visual allusion
(so rare and untypical in the work of such a strenuously unrhetorical
filmmaker), we never forget that Cassavetes is less interested in objects
than in the objective correlative of an emotional state. It is Minnie's and
Seymour's grand celestial love that is being celebrated, and not their
director's wit, special effects, or powers of allusion.

It is one of the most exciting and exhilarating moments in all of
Cassavetes' work, and yet, like the ending of the film, it is a moment
that, tellingly, is able to affirm Minnie and Seymour's romance only by
temporarily insulating them from the shocks and jars of the world in a
bubble of steel and glass, even as the scene insulates itself within the
self-contained wittiness of a purely cinematic reference to another
movie. The point the scene makes, even if Cassavetes was not fully
aware of it, is far from comforting. It is only when his two lovers are
protected—in the dark, shared fantasy world of a movie house, in
Seymour's truck, or in the fairy-tale world of the ending—that they are
truly safe to let down their guards and love. And, as Cassavetes obvi-

ously realizes, even the space-capsule impregnability of Seymour's truck can provide only the most temporary and fleeting refuge for romance.

This lyrical interlude lasts for only a minute or two in the film; nothing can stand still for longer than that here. As the crane shot swoops around the space-capsule cab one final time and then slowly tracks in on Minnie and Seymour inside, Seymour suddenly snaps off the radio, the Strauss stops, and we see Minnie sitting pensive and distant at the other end of the front seat. Just when we (and they) most want to be able to fulfill our romantic fantasies, to expand imaginatively in this gorgeous moment, Cassavetes suddenly brings us up short and reminds us that this is a world without romantic (or cinematic) refuges, a world of endlessly troubling and threatening transactions.

CHAPTER VII

MASTERING THE INFLUENCES
A Woman Under the Influence

We are social animals and . . . the nature of living is defined not by money, political power, and the like, but by virtue of the fact that we are social beings. *John Cassavetes*

Cassavetes' small success in partnering Minnie and Seymour in *Minnie and Moskowitz* was achieved only at the cost of an immense simplification of their predicament and of his narrative. Unable to find a way of including Minnie and Seymour in the larger society of the film, he gradually withdraws them from it, until in the last fifteen minutes or so he is finally forced to wish away almost all of the social, sexual, and emotional pressures that the preceding hour and a half have accumulated. The society Minnie, Seymour, children, and mothers-in-law make must be cordoned off from the earlier pressures in order to survive. But to notice this is less to criticize *Minnie and Moskowitz* than to appreciate its special place in Cassavetes' career.

What Cassavetes does in the final minutes of *Minnie and Moskowitz* is only a particular instance of a more general process of imaginative regression exemplified in both of the films that follow *Faces*. D. H. Lawrence has written that the "true myth of America" and the progress of American artistic development is "backwards from old age to golden youth," and something like what Lawrence describes is going on as Cassavetes moves from *Faces* through *Husbands* to *Minnie and Moskowitz*. As if he felt as overwhelmed and as trapped as his characters at the end of *Faces*, Cassavetes begins to search back in time for a situation that allows an opening out of the dead end of that film. In *Husbands*, he moves back in time from a marriage at the end of its tether, from which no escape is possible for its victims, to three men in their middle years. Harry, Gus, and Archie are lucky enough to be jolted out of their routines by the death of a friend at a point just before they have hardened into the robotic behavior of Freddie and Richard. Then in

Minnie and Moskowitz, Cassavetes moves to the still more severely simplified situation of a couple at the beginning of a relationship, a couple for whom the past may be wished away entirely because it does not exist for them as a couple. It is a process of radical, but apparently necessary, imaginative retrenchment. Searching for a way out of the maze of *Faces*, Cassavetes in effect traces a path back to the younger, smaller, and less complicated world of *Shadows*, where his own career began. But, of course, as Cassavetes realizes, the lesson of *Minnie and Moskowitz* is that he and his characters cannot go home again. Minnie and Seymour cannot live the lives of Lelia and Tony, any more than the man who made *Shadows* is the same as the one who made *Minnie and Moskowitz*. They and he are too battle-scarred, too war-weary, and too clear-sighted to entertain again even for a moment the starry-eyed idealism of the earlier film.

But that leaves Cassavetes and his characters in an unenviable predicament, stranded somewhere between the dreams of *Shadows* and the despair of *Faces*. He is finally unable to see Minnie and Seymour through the predicament in which he imagines them. Or, to formulate it another way, if Seymour and Minnie are his attempt to free Chet and Jeannie Rapp from the confinements of *Faces*, to give the two most healthy and sensitive performers in that film a chance on their own, away from its claustrophobic enclosures and repressions, he finds in the process of freeing them that he is still unable to imagine them as members of a society larger than the one they themselves constitute. His free spirits, in order to be free, must remain solitaries despite his best efforts to place them in the world.

All of which is ultimately to argue for the importance of *A Woman Under the Influence* in Cassavetes' canon. After the assertive simplifications of *Husbands* and *Minnie and Moskowitz*, he dares to revisit the complex, fully adult world of *Faces*, with its social constraints and physical confinements, once again. *Faces* examines a relationship in its final day, when it is too late to save it. *Minnie and Moskowitz* takes the easier course of presenting a relationship in its initial days. But *A Woman Under the Influence* plunges headlong into the most complex situation of all—a relationship somewhere in the middle of everything. Cassavetes creates a couple caught halfway between the wondering, puzzled love of Minnie and Seymour and the alienated desperation of Richard and Maria. It is as if, in his own recognition of how he had evaded the necessary complexities of Minnie's and Seymour's relationship in the final frames of their film, Cassavetes deliberately forced himself to return to their marriage ten or fifteen years later; or aware of how much had been left out of *Husbands*, he had dared to follow Gus around that corner and back into the home the whole previous film had only alluded to.

A Woman Under the Influence thrusts us into the very middle of a marital mess in which we and the characters are denied even the small consolations of endings or beginnings. For the Longhettis, as in most of life, there is no more possibility of a fresh start than there is of a tragic conclusion. There is only living in the middle of everything, in the perpetual middle of an endless muddle of feelings and relations.

If Nick and Mabel are a version of Seymour and Minnie ten years later, the first blush of love has rubbed off the romance, and the jazzy charm of Seymour and Minnie's mad courtship has given way to the realities of long hours of work, complaining relatives, and the everyday responsibilities of life. Seymour's jaunty old pickup has been traded in for a clunky family station wagon large enough to hold mother, father, and three school-age children. The small luxury of eating out in fast food palaces has given way to inexpensive spaghetti dinners for family and friends at home (around a dining-room table fitted out several times in the film with a rickety card table extension for friends and visitors). Minnie's attractive apartment has been given up for a cramped, confined, but comfortable and thoroughly middle-class home full to overflowing with children, relatives, and neighbors. And, most importantly, the two central characters have been ground down in the mill of the ordinary. Flamboyant, eccentric, creative Seymour has been replaced by Nick Longhetti (Peter Falk), a clumsy, easily flustered, if generally well-meaning, construction worker. Spunky, independent, if battle-fatigued, career woman Minnie has been replaced by Mabel Longhetti (Gena Rowlands), less sure of herself than Minnie ever was, and half crazy from the confinement and tedium of days spent indoors waiting for the children to return from school and nights spent alone waiting for Nick to return from overtime.

For the final film of his marriage trilogy, Cassavetes significantly chooses a couple halfway between the enchanted days of the whirl-wind courtship of *Minnie and Moskowitz* and the claustrophobic confinements and failures of communication of the couple in *Faces*. Nick and Mabel are forced to live through everything that was finally avoided by *Minnie and Moskowitz*—a past that cannot be wished away, children that tie them to an unspecified future, and, above all, a nearly overwhelming network of friends, neighbors, relatives, and co-workers that cannot be run away from or walled out with shrubbery. In many respects, they are caught in the same maze as Richard and Maria Forst—boxed in by commitments and obligations, harried by irrevocable past decisions, future responsibilities, and oppressive social standards of behavior, tangled in crises of fidelity and failures of understanding and communication. And yet the artistic, moral, and personal triumph of the film is Cassavetes' ability to see Nick and Mabel through it all. Not swerving away from these complications and responsibilities for one moment, in fact embracing them, he imagines, as he could not at the time of *Faces*, the possibility of saving them and of them saving themselves through the labor of love.

The astonishing complexity of *A Woman Under the Influence* is, in fact, the result of its peculiar double lineage. The symphonic and operatic scoring and the scenes of passionate lovemaking dangle dreams of personal fulfillment as intense as anything in *Minnie and Moskowitz*, even as the ringing telephones, the clinging children, the confinements of the house, and the encircling toils of friends and relatives restrict and threaten the individual as much as in *Faces*. The accomplishment of *A Woman Under the Influence*, as with the greatest of Capra's work, is that it finds a way to hold idealistic dreams of freedom and the oppressive toils of responsibility simultaneously in mind. Nick and Mabel succeed in negotiating the most arduous course of obligations and commitments Cassavetes has ever imagined, and yet somehow survive to avoid the fate of Richard and Maria.

Imaginative growth of the sort that *A Woman Under the Influence* represents is inseparable from a corresponding stylistic growth. In *A Woman Under the Influence*, Cassavetes finds a way to move beyond the stylistic as well as the social and psychological limitations of his earlier work. In this process of stylistic development, nothing is more worth watching than what happens to the close-up. The extreme close-up was a sort of visual trademark of his early work, but Cassavetes chose to use it less and less frequently by the time of *A Woman Under the Influence*. He gradually withdraws his camera in the films following *Faces*. The medium- and long-shots of *Husbands, Minnie and Moskowitz*, and *A Woman Under the Influence* are attempts to enlarge the visual and social spaces characters can inhabit, to allow them more freedom of movement and bodily disposition, even as they paradoxically make them responsible for, and responsive to, larger social involvements and commitments. If *Husbands* and *Minnie and Moskowitz* as a result seem at times to grant their characters too much freedom at too low a cost, *A Woman Under the Influence* resoundingly justifies the previous experiments.

In its editing and photography as well as in its script and direction, *A Woman Under the Influence*, in effect, pulls back from its characters to allow them more breathing room, even as it imagines them embedded in a more complex matrix of social, familial, and emotional "influences" than ever before. The paradoxical combination of confinement and openness that the film explores is summarized in Cassavetes decisions to film within the acute visual, psychological, and physical confinements of a real home (as *Faces* was filmed) and yet to use the longest possible lenses and most distant camera set-ups possible within those spaces (as *Faces* did not).

In an interview after the world premiere of the film at the 1974 New York Film Festival (he was unable to get commercial distribution for it until rave reviews from several New York critics stimulated distributors to take a second look), Cassavetes indicated his awareness of the human ramifications of what might otherwise seem to be merely a technical photographic decision. His goal was to prevent his characters in this film from being smothered by the sort of entrapments that had overwhelmed them in *Faces*:

> The location could have been a serious problem. At first everyone said, "How can you do a picture where 80% of it happens in the same house?" I think that's one reason we had such difficulty financing the picture; it didn't seem to have enough openness. But . . . we used long lenses and wide angles.
>
> One of the reasons we used long lenses especially for all the work in the house, was to avoid a feeling of confinement. So much of the picture takes place in the Longhetti house there's a real danger of getting a feeling the actors are locked in by the camera. The long lenses meant the camera could be far away and the actors wouldn't be constricted by its proximity. And after a while, the actors weren't aware of the camera. It seemed to work very well, very easily.[1]

More than any films since those of Dreyer, Capra, and Renoir, Cassavetes' work has taken the complex algebra of social relations as its subject, but here he outdoes himself in his ability to make cinematic room not only for the small groups of principal characters that people his earlier films, but for a description of the interconnected lives of an entire extended family and their circle of acquaintances. (The two films that followed, *The Killing of a Chinese Bookie* and *Opening Night*, would take even larger, more complex and amorphous social groupings as their subjects.) His operatic and symphonic musical scoring, star-system casting, and narrative put more emphasis than ever before on the particular individual consciousnesses of Nick and Mabel Longhetti, but his long-shots embed them in social matrices more complex than those in any of his previous films. Nick and Mabel are inextricably woven into a web of near and distant, personal and impersonal, public and private relations, with each other, their three children, two mothers-in-law, two fathers-in-law, a family doctor, a dozen or so of Nick's co-workers, and numerous friends, neighbors, and strangers. The film is an exploration of these shifting relations and their effect on the individuals involved. That is its "plot."

That is one of the things that makes Cassavetes' work so different from most other recent film. Most other American films of the past twenty years automatically equate drama with "plot," action, and movement through space. The result is an inevitable simplification of the possibilities of personal drama. Relationships are black and white; sides for or against a character are delineated; and causality is reduced to the simplicity of a linear sequence of events. By minimizing action, plot, and movement in his films, Cassavetes restores to personal relations a lifelike social complexity and a psychological interiority. The inner lives and subtle social relations of characters become important again (as they have not been in most American film since the late 1940s). These characters' adventures and the events of their lives may seem dull compared to the endless movement and rapid pace of most "action-packed" Hollywood film situations, but that is because for Cassavetes there is no adventure greater than an imaginative journey, and no event more earthshaking than an emotional scene. Once one becomes attuned to the complex excitements of those inward adventures and social events, the mere eventfulness of the other sort of film seems bland and dull in comparison.

But at the same time, no films are less like the marathon encounter sessions of Bergman, Tanner, or Rohmer either. After viewing *A Woman Under the Influence*, Andrew Kopkind aptly contrasted it with Bergman's *Scenes From a Marriage*, which was in release at approximately the same time:

Bergman's couple do nothing but intellectualize their relationship, discuss its every nuance, explore every metaphor they've invented to avoid real life. Mabel and Nick act out everything the Swedes discuss. But not one moment of intellectualization creeps into these American scenes. Unlike Bergman's middle-class professionals, Cassavetes' working-class characters have no illusions that they can talk their way out of the traps they're in.[2]

It is not that Mabel and Nick have no illusions about "talking their way out of traps" (whatever that means), but that their director is less

interested in individual verbal and symbolic arrangements of experience than Bergman is, and more in social and interpersonal arrangements. Both Bergman's and Cassavetes' films can be talky, but the
difference is that while talk is an intellectual, and often solitary, medi-
tative activity in a Bergman film, it is an essentially social event in a
Cassavetes' film. The individual verbal analysis of feelings and behavior matters much less for Cassavetes than the relative tones, styles, and
relationships his characters assume with each other. If the starting
point of a Bergman film is the individuality, isolation, and aloneness of
a character, in a Cassavetes film it is his nature as a social being, unable
to withdraw himself from relationships with others (whether he wants
them or not). Language is one of the ways Cassavetes' characters establish and adjust their social relationships with one another, but it is no
more important than the expressions on their faces, their positions in
a group, or their distances from one another in a room.

Notwithstanding the ordinariness of their backgrounds and the relative crudity of their linguistic skills, as Mabel Longhetti goes through
a nervous breakdown, confinement in a mental hospital, and return
home, and Nick tries to understand it all, Cassavetes offers us and his
characters one of the most ennobling and inspiring educations in the
meaning of love ever filmed. Nick Longhetti is "a man," in the words
of the publicity synopsis released with the film "who's happy with his
work, content with his life, and ignorant of the personal dimensions of
the woman he loves." Mabel is a sensitive, loving housewife and
mother who painfully feels the absence of romance and excitement in
her life, and her husband's failure to express love and appreciation. A
Woman Under the Influence is little more than the narration of two extended episodes in their lives together, separated by the six-month
period of her hospital confinement. So uninterested is Cassavetes in the
mere mechanics of chronological narration that (against the advice of
almost everyone who previewed the film in rough-cut) he actually uses
a "Six Months Later" insert to separate the two sections of the film.
What is interesting is that most audiences side with Cassavetes. If the
film works for a viewer at all, it has educated him so well by this point
to care only about emotional and personal "time" that the insert appears and passes away without a rustle of objection.

Since this is arguably Cassavetes' most important film, and yet one
that is infrequently seen (Cassavetes owns and holds the only available
prints), a brief synopsis of the plot will be useful. The film begins with
Nick finishing up work at the end of the day and Mabel at home making

preparations for what is obviously a special weekend they have long planned to spend together. Perhaps it is their wedding anniversary or a "second honeymoon." Mabel packs the kids off in the family station wagon with her mother and goes inside to wait alone in the strangely empty house for Nick's return. But a municipal emergency at the last minute keeps Nick at work all night and it is hours after their planned date that he even has the courage to call her and tell her he will not be able to make it. A despondent Mabel, with nothing to do and no place to go, wanders into a local bar, gets drunk, and, only half knowing what she is doing, ends up spending the night with another man in her bed. The next morning, in his awkwardness and embarrassment at having to face Mabel alone, Nick invites a dozen or so co-workers to come along with him for breakfast at his house. Later that same day, we see Mabel meeting her children at the school bus stop and giving a zany backyard party for her own and neighboring children. Nick suddenly arrives home (he has become aware that Mabel spent the night with another man), fights with her and a next-door neighbor he finds in the house, and precipitates her nervous breakdown. After a long, painful scene, Mabel is finally committed to an institution, during which time we see Nick trying to play at father and to get to know his kids for the first time. Finally, six months later, Mabel returns home to a typically ill-conceived and insensitive party of friends and relatives gathered together by Nick to welcome her back. After friends and relatives leave, under pressures no less extraordinary than those that caused her breakdown in the first place, Mabel tries to kill herself by slashing her wrists in front of her family. Nick stops her and the film ends with the two of them tucking the children in bed and picking up the pieces of their lives together.

But *A Woman Under the Influence* is not summarized very well by a list of events such as this. It is a film of repeated gatherings of people; and in fact a better sense of the subject and texture of the film might be communicated simply by listing some of the gatherings of friends, family, relatives, and strangers that take place during the course of it: Nick with his co-workers gathering in a tavern after work; the workers gathered together for a spaghetti breakfast at Nick's house; a neighbor named Mr. Jensen and his children joining Mabel and her children at a party in the Longhettis' yard; her children, her mother-in-law, her husband, and the family doctor gathered around Mabel during her nervous breakdown; the friends, neighbors, and co-workers Nick gathers together for the party on Mabel's return; the group of close relatives who remain with Mabel after the others leave; and, above all, the gatherings and regatherings of Nick, Mabel, and their three children as a family throughout the film.

A Woman Under the Influence is Cassavetes' most powerful film and the one, along with *Faces*, that has affected audiences most deeply. Its extraordinary impact is probably attributable to two factors. The first is the particularly severe way it articulates the double vision that informs all of his work. The rival claims of the would-be free, autonomous individual and the competing forces of the society of which the individual is only a member have never been more starkly contrasted. The second reason for the power of this particular film is the archetypically American form the contest between the individual and society takes. Though Cassavetes never generalizes or abstracts Mabel's predicament in such a way (and though the forms her struggle takes are embedded so deeply in our culture and the ways we understand ourselves that they are hardly recognizable as "forms" of experience at all), Mabel enacts the imaginative struggle of some of the most central figures of the American tradition.

At the risk of schematizing a film that is the opposite of schematic, let me try to describe the two starkly opposed and archetypically American imaginative poles between which the extraordinary force field of *A Woman Under the Influence* is generated. At the center of the film is Mabel, Cassavetes' most gloriously lyrical character. She is a visionary and a dreamer in the Emersonian tradition, a heroine with a freedom of consciousness and a richness of imagination that Henry James would have appreciated. But Cassavetes makes her something more than Emerson or James would have conceived of when he makes her a mother and wife as well. She is not only a visionary and dreamer for herself but the maker of imaginative worlds for others; she is the source of dreams for her children, her husband, and her friends. Her dreams become biological, social, and familial realities.

But if we designate Mabel and the extraordinary (virtually operatic) imaginative energies she is capable of generating as one pole of the film, the astonishing thing Cassavetes does with this Emersonian, this Jamesian figure is to thrust her into the center of a world of pressures, influences, and circumscriptions as relentless and inescapable as anything Theodore Dreiser or Edith Wharton might have imagined. Mabel is at the center of endless gatherings of people, surrounded and hedged round on every side by insensitive, incomprehending others, forced to negotiate layer after layer of "influences."

Creative differences: rival styles of making scenes
—Attempting to make a home for the imagination

The reason one invokes such powerful artistic precedents to describe the forms of experience in this film is not to try to exalt Cassavetes' work with high-toned literary references, but to indicate the ways it taps into the central imaginative force field of American experience, one that was most clearly articulated by these authors. Though Cassavetes never metaphorizes or allegorizes Mabel's predicament the way Coppola, Kubrick, or Altman might have done (and it is essential that he does not), the impact of her experience is a result of its resonance with the fundamental forms of American experience. Mabel necessarily raises the question of the dream of America itself: the question of the destiny of the free individual imagination negotiating the practical forms and forces of time, family, and society; the question of what becomes of the glory and the dream when they are brought back to the world of real human obligations and interactions.

In a search for cinematic antecedents, one is forced to imagine a hybrid cinema compounded of the very different filmic worlds of Carl Dreyer and Yasujiro Ozu. Mabel is a character with the imaginative yearning of Gertrud, the interpersonal sensitivity and flexibility of Inger, and the performative capacities and playful inventiveness of Anne (the heroines of Dreyer's *Gertrud, Ordet,* and *Day of Wrath* respectively). But rather than being given the relatively free imaginative rein Dreyer gives his extraordinary women, she is immersed in a world with the social density and complexity of the extended families that populate an Ozu film. Notwithstanding its Dreyer-like heroine, *A Woman Under the Influence* is the film of all Cassavetes' work that most reminds the viewer of the social and familial confinements of an Ozu film. Its *shomin-geki* (literally, "family-drama-film") structure, with its repeated ceremonies of greeting, gathering, talking, and parting; its floor-level camera placements; the horizontally composed framing; the house Cassavetes chose to film in, with its horizontal timberwork and sliding door partitions between rooms; and even the course of whole scenes, such as the last five minutes of the film, which seems a carbon copy of the last five minutes of Ozu's *The Flavor of Green Tea Over Rice,* all advertise *A Woman Under the Influence* as both implicitly and explicitly indebted to Ozu. The film presents a stunning conflation of two usually disparate realms of experience, Dreyer being as thoroughly situated in the high romantic tradition as Ozu is staunchly neoclassical in his values and interests.[3] The goal of *A Woman Under the Influence* is to bring together these two very different worlds of visionary transcendence and familial embeddedness.

But what makes the film such a complex examination of Mabel's predicament is precisely its refusal to schematize itself into two contrasting positions as I have just done. Cassavetes refuses to sort out Mabel's situation into an opposition between "romantic individualism" and "classical responsibilities." He refuses to formulate her predicament by contrasting the "dreaming visionary" with the biological mother, or to oppose the imagination of the individual to the social claims of the family. The Americanness of the film is nowhere more evident than in its refusal to admit that the classic and romantic visions of the individual's role and responsibilities are irreconcilable. (America itself was, after all, an attempt to reconcile the two visions, to find a classic form for the romantic impulse, to bring the dream of lyrical poetry into the world of prose documents.) Dreams do not carry us beyond or above ordinary life. They count only in the world, and individuals matter only insofar as they are capable of being contributing members of a community. The central impulse of the film is a rejection of the romantic myth of the isolated, autonomous artist or individual cultivating his private consciousness in opposition to society. If such a fiction was ever an adequate description of the relation of the self and society (and even as Byronic a writer as Byron gives every evidence that it was not), Cassavetes suggests that it is hopelessly inadequate to account for the trajectory of romanticism in this country and the forms of contemporary experience. The individual vision must always and everywhere negotiate the influences of society. There is no escaping influences or pressures, and even to aspire to do so dooms one to victimization by the forces one seeks to escape.

In even more detail than the previous films, *A Woman Under the Influence* argues that personal freedom is not achieved by attempting to break away from influences into a less compromised, purer, more autonomous selfhood, but by making oneself vulnerable to them, by plunging into them, navigating them, and if possible mastering them. The mistake characters in *Faces, Husbands,* and *Minnie and Moskowitz* make, in their different ways, is to believe that pressures can even temporarily be renounced or escaped. What *A Woman Under the Influence* tells us is that there is nowhere to run to avoid them. The influences that envelop and temporarily overwhelm Mabel, far from being attempts by a hostile world to stifle or frustrate her, are expressions of love and concern for her by her relatives in her own home. To be free from these pressures and influences would be to be less than fully alive; only the drifters or derelicts in these films are free in this way, because they are not quite full members of the human community. The dream of escaping influences, present even in *Minnie and Moskowitz,* is a pastoral myth and delusion; the most we can hope for is that the influences be negotiated successfully—both in their offering and in their receiving—with the utmost tact, sensitivity, and love.

Cassavetes follows Mabel and Nick back into the home to which the endings of *Husbands* and *Minnie and Moskowitz* only allude. The performer must bring his performance back home and test it against the claims of family, children, relatives, and neighbors. The challenge is to find a style of domestic performance that will neither tear apart home and family nor allow itself to be smothered or limited by home, family, and community. In this conception of it, the home ideally thus becomes a theater larger and more challenging than any other, within which the most energetic performers can stage their most daring performances, and the very opposite of the place of shelter, confinement, retirement, and sexual and social repression that it came to represent in the Hollywood "women's" films of the 1940s and 1950s to which *A Woman Under the Influence* seems superficially similar. The home, for Cassavetes, is a place where the most exciting and complex energies of creative human interaction can be liberated.

That is also the important difference between Cassavetes' work and that of Nicholas Ray. Ray not only generally made a profound impression on Cassavetes as an actor and beginning filmmaker in the late 1950s, but much of the conception of *A Woman Under the Influence* is indirectly indebted to Ray's *Rebel Without a Cause* (with Mabel in the dramatic situation of James Dean's Jim Stark). Cassavetes' film explicitly pays homage to Ray's at several points (compare the "Stand up for me, Dad" line and the context in which it is said in both films). There are essential similarities between the sensibilities of Cassavetes and Ray. Both filmmakers are historians of the suffering of the individual with an imagination too energetic and eccentric to be understood or appreciated by the society around him. And, even more interestingly, both filmmakers use theatricality and the excesses of performance as an outlet for excesses of imagination and feeling that have no more socially useful form of expression. But where Ray and Cassavetes emphatically part ways is in Ray's willingness to accept alienation from society as a possible social stance for a character and as an adequate, final imaginative relation to experience. Which is to say, while Ray's films invariably propel their characters outside community and family and encourage them to formulate an imaginative alternative to it, Cassavetes' films do the opposite. They drive their characters deeper and deeper into the hearts of their families, apart from which, they suggest, there can be no possibility of an adequate or satisfying life. If Ray is the great American poet of alienation and estrangement, of an eccentric imaginative and social centrifugality away from homes past and present, Cassavetes is the poet of essential imaginative and social centripetality—of the necessity of always moving even further into the bosom of the family as the only possible cure for imaginative disturbance.

Because it is interested in individuals insofar as they are members of groups, the central scenes in *A Woman Under the Influence* could never be simplified into the one-, two-, and three-shots, and shot–reverse shots of orthodox Hollywood technique. (Even *Minnie and Moskowitz* depends heavily on two-shots of the title characters and on occasional foreground-background separations of them from the world from which they are fleeing.) What Cassavetes offers instead in *A Woman Under the Influence* is a cinematic style that never frames or separates one or two central characters apart from the fields of influences continuously present around them—a style capable of registering over-

lapping circles of influence and competing planes of interaction between three, four, five, or more different characters at once in any one
scene, with each participant deserving and getting studiously equal
treatment from the camera. When Nick (cowardly and shamefacedly)
brings his co-workers home for breakfast the morning after he has
stood Mabel up, Cassavetes gives full measure to each participant in
the obligatory ceremony of introductions that precedes the meal; and
once everyone has met everyone else, he moves his camera leisurely up
and down the double row of faces seated at the table between Nick and
Mabel. The adjustments and corrections of relationship required of
individuals in groups such as this are the subject of this film. Even as
Mabel exchanges playful winks, nods, and squints of affection with
Nick, seated at the other end of the table, Cassavetes' camera refuses
to frame either of them in isolation, and chronicles the rippling effect
of their tiny love signals on the construction workers sitting between them.

All of the important moments in the film are moments when groups
of characters are present, each one vying for attention and dramatic
influence on the direction and course of a scene. Scenes become three-
ring circuses of competing attractions in which each of three, four, or
five characters solicits our attention and that of Nick and Mabel, complex fields of forces that each actor simultaneously contributes to and
is swayed by. (Pinter and Chekhov provide examples of something like
this strange, competitive play of rival fields of influence and relationship on stage, but never before has it been rendered with such
intensity in film.)

In the central scene of the film, one of the most affecting moments
in all of Cassavetes' work, Mabel is not even allowed to have her
nervous breakdown in private. Nick, her mother-in-law, Dr. Zepp, the
family physician, and the children (whom we do not see in the frame
but hear upstairs in their bedroom) all jockey for positions, parts, and
lines in her "scene." Just at the instant our sympathies go out most
poignantly to Mabel, Cassavetes cuts to another character's part of the
room and the expression on his face, his preparation for his entrance
once Mabel has provided his cue. When Mabel is delivering her most
touching lines, Cassavetes mixes in another character's comments, advice, or reaction to her. We see or hear Mama Longhetti herding the
children together in their room upstairs and shouting stage directions
to Dr. Zepp; Nick circling around Mabel trying to calm her down and
keeping the doctor away from her; Dr. Zepp chasing away the med-

dling mother-in-law, giving instructions to Nick on how to handle Mabel, and furtively opening his black bag and filling a hypodermic to sedate her when he can get near enough. In place of the close-ups that show us the aftermath of Maria's attempted suicide in *Faces*, Cassavetes deliberately holds his camera low and away from Mabel and repeatedly intercuts shots of the others to keep us continuously aware of the contexts around her. Characters keep appearing in the borders of the frame, behind, in front of, or to one side of her. They circle around Mabel like planets searching for proper distances at which to establish orbits, each perturbed by the gravitational fields of the others and forced into repeatedly recalculated course corrections.

It is in the editing of scenes such as this one that one feels how carefully Cassavetes has studied Capra's work—Capra being one of the most subtle and complex cutters in film, who makes the editorial effects of a so-called master of montage like Eisenstein seem crude, heavy-handed, and manipulative in comparison. As one watches Cassavetes' cutting around, in front of, and behind Mabel during *A Woman Under the Influence*, one cannot help being reminded of Capra's photography and editing in his story of "a man under the influence"—*Meet John Doe*, which stars Gary Cooper in a role strikingly similar to Mabel's in many ways (and even more similar to Cosmo Vitelli's in Cassavetes' next picture, *The Killing of a Chinese Bookie*). Unlike some of Capra's other central figures, Cooper's dramatic predicament is precisely his lack of a "character"—in every sense of the word. Others around him attempt to "dictate" a self for him—to give him a new identity, to script lines for him to say, actually to rename him—in a way that can only make one think of Mabel's dramatic situation. If the analogy between the two characters is a fair one, Mabel's mad scene, when all of the influences in her life come together to conspire simultaneously against her, has its rough equivalent in the four or five minutes in *Meet John Doe* immediately before and during Cooper's radio speech to the nation, one of the greatest scenes in all of Capra's work. Capra's editing brilliantly captures the emotional, social, and intellectual blackmail to which Cooper is subjected, with forty or fifty intercuts of all of the influences, bribes, and coercions around him, until Cooper's own identity becomes only an extension of the influences around him. Cooper (like Mabel) "breaks down" in the course of it all by going through with the speech he had intended to abort, and by becoming, for the rest of the film, the fiction that has been passed on him. He becomes "John Doe."

There is no privacy or isolation in Cassavetes' moral universe. (One can count on the fingers of one hand the number of times Nick and Mabel are actually alone, or alone together, in the course of the film.) But *A Woman Under the Influence* defines interpersonal influence less as a problem to be overcome than as a condition of all creation. It is the stimulation of love. Man is necessarily and exhilaratingly a social animal, and Cassavetes can no more imagine a solo performance in life than he can in love. A fugitive and cloistered virtue is by definition no virtue at all. The genius of the long lenses and distant camera set-ups that give *A Woman Under the Influence* its particular richness is that even as they reveal more of the constraints on an individual performance, they at the same time give the actor the room to maneuver, the free margin for performance in response to those influences, that was unavailable to characters in *Faces.*

With a conscientiousness that some audiences have mistaken for technical incompetence, Cassavetes keeps pulling focus from foreground to middleground to background and back again during the film, making slices through the yards of depth in any one shot, each slice no more than two or three faces deep at a time. Cassavetes has commented on the technical reasons for such repeated focus pulling during the shooting:

We set it all up with such an extremely long lens that I knew it would be technically impossible to do it all in focus. The operator and the focus puller couldn't possibly be in concert because there'd be no way of knowing where the actors would be at any one moment. It had to be a natural thing: certain things would come and go in focus because there were so many points of interest switching back and forth all the time.[4]

Regardless of the particular technical situation that gave rise to it, Cassavetes' willingness to allow "so many points of interest [to switch] back and forth" is inseparable from the larger stylistic concerns of *A Woman Under the Influence*. Omniscience is as impossible as neutrality or objectivity in this world. The slides and shifts of focus force a viewer, like an ideally responsive character, to juggle two, three, four, or more perspectives at once in any one scene, no one of which is more definitive or final than the others.

Pulling focus and changing perspectives might be metaphors for the experience of the film. Cassavetes provides an unending series of "refocusings"—an experience of the competing, shifting, and over-

lapping planes of relationship surrounding, threatening, and ultimately linking Nick and Mabel in love. Several times in the course of
the film, Nick refers to their home as a sanctuary and escape from the
pressures and influences of life, but every scene of the film denies them
that luxury. Nick and Mabel are no sooner alone at home than there is
a knock at the front door, the telephone rings, a mother-in-law intrudes
unannounced, a neighbor visits, or the children gather round to remind
them of unavoidable obligations incurred, responsibilities to live up to,
social and biological promises to keep. Even less than in *Minnie and
Moskowitz* can a particular scene be staged without the hazards of interruption, disruption, or the encroachment of complications beyond the
control of any one of its principal actors.

Mabel is the character Cassavetes' films have been waiting for. She
is the culmination of the most sensitive and interesting female performers in the previous films—a Lelia much matured, a Jeannie Rapp
shouldering the burdens of being a parent and a wife, a Minnie converted from swinging single to both mother and daughter in an extended family. But she incorporates these newly incurred entanglements of relationship without giving up any of the imagination,
creativity, and responsiveness the earlier performers showed. The multitudinous influences in the Longhetti family matter so intensely to her
and to us because she is a character on whom none of them are lost.
Cassavetes has created a heroine of Jamesian sensitivity on whom none
of the Jamesian subtleties of relationship will be wasted.

Or, to shift the comparison to contemporary performers, and to take
up the balletic metaphor Cassavetes offers in the film, one might say
that Mabel's qualities of performance only find their equal in the performances of the greatest contemporary ballerinas in the most interesting recent dance. In her willingness, on the one hand, to make
herself completely responsive to the immensely powerful, syncopated,
competing rhythms and choreographic influences on her, and, on the
other hand, in her simultaneous determination not to enslave herself to
those forces, but to find a way to chart an eccentric, continuously
adjusted, free course among them, Mabel displays the off-centered
poise, the unbalanced power, and the daring improvisational abandon
of Suzanne Farrell or Patricia McBride on stage. (Or an apt analogy
might be made between Mabel's capacities of comic performance and
the puckish wit and zany poise of the sculptural dance figures of Joel
Shapiro.)

It goes without saying that there is no ideological stereotyping of Mabel or of the characters around her. One of the things that confused so many of the initial reviewers of the film, feminists and antifeminists alike, is that there are no villains, ideological signposts, or psychological "placements" of characters, and therefore no way to exempt oneself from the continuous act of attention the film asks of a viewer. Audiences anxious for a "key" to unlock the experience of the film, a clue to explain the mystery of a particular character, got nothing but movement through complex experiences that defied such simplifications. In the case of Mabel in particular, there is simply no way to place her offered in the film. She is a performer in many respects as clever, creative, and responsive as her creator, and a character whose sureness and delicacy of response are incapable of being embarrassed or caught out by the most searching cinematic scrutiny.

To a greater or lesser extent each of the characters of the previous films "succeeds" by denying or ignoring certain truths about themselves or their situations. (Even Seymour and Minnie survive by sorting out and disposing of certain influences in their lives.) But Mabel does the opposite; she survives through acts of inclusion. To list the roles and parts she plays in the course of the film—mother, daughter, wife, cook, housekeeper, lover, patient, entertainer, hostess, psychological therapist—is only to hint at her capacities of inclusion. These roles and parts do not mesh easily and the attempt to keep them all in balance is what makes Mabel's life so difficult, but there is no option of avoiding the struggle. Mabel does not collapse or wither under her burdens and responsibilities. Quite the contrary. She thrives under them. They stimulate her. They are oppressive, confining, or overwhelming only to the extent that one is incapable of creative response to them, is incapable of being stimulated to new, more inclusive performances under the pressure of them. In the course of A Woman Under the Influence, Mabel plays off, parodies, mocks, cajoles, and generally tries to "make something" of every influence around her. (Interestingly, the original screenplay makes Mabel even more of a master parodist than the final version of the film does.) Her capacity to improvise and make scenes out of whatever material comes to hand is, in fact, what most of the other, less imaginative characters around her call her "craziness." To remain as vulnerable, as available, as sensitive to influences as she is, in the middle of this high-voltage force field of relations, is to court a kind of insanity. Mabel's insanity, indeed, might be defined as her refusal to close the door on the influences around her, her effort to remain responsive to all of them, to hold simultaneously in mind every possible promise to keep.

In the central tradition of American performance from Hawthorne and Twain to Faulkner and Pynchon, Mabel raises again the question of what it is to shape a free self out of all the stylistic, historical, and biographical "influences" that beset an individual. And, as in that tradition, her capacity to play with, and against, the styles arrayed around her becomes evidence simultaneously of her attempt to clear a space for her own free performances and of the sway alien styles hold over her imagination. Mabel's long mad scene at the center of the film is thus paradoxically both her freest and her most enslaved moment, as she plays off and parodies one after another the tones and mannerisms of her husband, her mother-in-law, and her doctor while they close in around her in her living room.

Cassavetes' achievement in *A Woman Under the Influence* is that as a writer, director, and editor he shows himself to be as cinematically sensitive and delicately responsive to these influences, interpersonal pressures, and networks of relations as Mabel herself is. It is not to disparage his earlier work to assert that nowhere else does he show the sure, delicate sensitivity to the complexities of mature adult relationships that he does here. The previous films did not require that. The stasis and emotional paralysis of the T-groups of *Faces* were wonderfully captured by Cassavetes' own visual and narrative style in that film, as overwrought, intense, and confining as the situations he was describing. The camera on the *qui vive* and narrative breathlessly on the move in *Minnie and Moskowitz* were suited to the desperate, vehicular quality of the ever-changing emotional and social transactions in that film. But only in *A Woman Under the Influence* does Cassavetes show the capacity to register fully mature, sophisticated, and creative social relations.

If Mabel is the film's heroine, her director is its true hero. Her consciousness is simply a specific instance of the consciousness Cassavetes brings into existence in his cinematic style. And to the extent that a viewer comes up to the standards of attention and sensitivity the film expects, his consciousness of the complexity of these situations becomes an extension of Mabel's and Cassavetes' consciousnesses as well. The film is an educative experience for the ideal viewer. It circulates him through situations with Mabel, guiding his eye and training his ear. "Circulation" is an especially appropriate word to describe this process insofar as what Cassavetes has discovered is the possibility of endless movement (as in *Minnie and Moskowitz*), within strict constraints (as in *Faces*). The discovery of the possibility of freedom within severe limitation is essential to the effect of *A Woman Under the Influence* and the secret of its implicit solution to the felt problems in both of the previous films. If, as he did in *Faces*, Cassavetes typically chooses to have scenes run their course in one fairly confined location or set, he sees an escape here out of the static gatherings of that film by providing Nick and Mabel with a continuously changing, complicating, and cross-fertilizing audience for their performances. If the five or six principal scenes typically begin and end with Nick and Mabel alone together in a room (like Richard and Maria Forst), those moments are only temporary pauses or punctuation marks in a continuous circulation of neighbors, friends, and relatives through the Longhetti home in endlessly changing positions, roles, and relationships.

But the most interesting process of narrative circulation in *A Woman Under the Influence* is not spatial or social, but tonal. Only Billy Wilder among directors and the early Neil Simon and Harold Pinter among playwrights comes to mind as doing something comparable to Cassavetes in this respect. It is as if he had too many attitudes toward any one moment or scene to be willing to screen out the shifts of tone for the sake of an artificial artistic consistency. All of Cassavetes' films swing and lurch across different tones and attitudes in this way. Sometimes the effect takes the form of a sudden and unexpected glissade from one tone to another. In *Minnie and Moskowitz*, in one of the strangest and most memorable moments in Cassavetes' work, Seymour, distraught and desperately in love with Minnie, puts a pair of scissors to his throat and threatens to kill himself to prove his love. We do not really expect suicide, but it is a serious, highly charged dramatic moment in a film of sudden, explosive eruptions of violence. What actually follows is precisely what we would never have expected. Gesticulating with the scissors, Seymour accidentally cuts off half of his huge mustache by mistake, and the scene slides in a split second from the sublime to the ridiculous. Or consider the even more complex movement in the scene in *Husbands* when Harry briefly returns home from his wake cum binge to find his wife and mother-in-law waiting up for him. After asserting his freedom to do whatever he pleases and threatening his wife but failing to intimidate her emotionally, Harry suddenly begins throttling her mother in revenge, because as he says, he knows that "will get to her." What is the viewer to make of such a scene? When

Harry is strangling his mother-in-law or forcing his wife at knife-point onto her knees to say that she loves him a moment later, we don't know whether we are watching tragedy, melodrama, or farce.

But *A Woman Under the Influence* seems to go even beyond *Faces*, *Husbands*, or *Minnie and Moskowitz* in its operatic shifts and confusions of tone. Humor and pathos, slapstick and brutality, silliness and sincerity, the ridiculous and the sublime keep bumping elbows. How, for example, is one to understand the strange scene of the backyard party when Mabel tells her children to "die for Mr. Jensen," a neighbor, as she plays the music from *Swan Lake* on the radio? In one camera angle Cassavetes frames the skeptical Mr. Jensen (who by this point believes Mabel is crazy); Mabel sincerely trying to make a good time for the children and Mr. Jensen (but having the opposite of the intended effect on him); the little girls making elegant, touching little "dying swan" balletic gestures; and the boys absurdly and incongruously miming a cowboy gunfight at the O.K. Corral (since that is all "dying" means to them). Of course, one starts by viewing it as a "comic" scene. But it is much more than that. "Comic" does not come close to doing it justice. First, there is Mr. Jensen's annoyed, embarrassed, and far from humorous presence, reminding us of the construction workers' incomprehension of Mabel in the scene that immediately preceded this one. Then one cannot help noticing how the merely "comic" difference between the little boys and the little girls here is a summary of the whole failure of understanding between Mabel and Mr. Jensen or Mabel and Nick throughout the film. One cannot help remembering, too, that the last time we saw Mabel playing the radio and listening to music like this was the night Nick stood her up, the night she went to bed with a strange man. The scene will drop out of our consciousnesses altogether until the next time we hear Mabel humming the same music and mimicking the gestures of the dying swan. How are we supposed to feel about this "comic" dying swan pantomime then—when we watch Mabel going through the same motions the little girls are performing here, in her suicide attempt?

Or how are we to understand the weird scene of Nick's beach excursion with his children, when he gets the kids absurdly, comically, rip-roaring drunk in the back of his panel truck and chooses that moment to tell them how he "didn't want to send [their] mother away"? Or, what are we to make of one of the most affecting scenes in all of Cassavetes' work when, during Mabel's suicide attempt, his camera follows Nick and the children upstairs to their bedroom, and lingers on their bouncing on their beds, while Mabel is bleeding on the couch downstairs?

The only conclusion one can draw about such scenes is that our inability to sort out the tones and moods within them is exactly Cassavetes' goal. He is interested in teasing us (just as he teases his characters) out of our knowingness, and making exploration and discovery possible. These scenes enact the tonal equivalents of the narrative techinques of discovery in his plots and the visual techniques of the exploration of possible relationships in his framing, focusing, and editing. The lurches of feeling, the tonal instabilities and mixtures force a viewer to suspend judgment, to become aware of the complexly conflicting contexts, points of view, and relationships present in any one moment.

Mabel's success in the course of the film (to the extent that she does succeed) is her ability to keep from being "known" or "understood" by any of the characters around her. And here one needs to emphasize the irreducible mystery and unknowability of all of Cassavetes' most interesting characters. There is a density to his characters' lives and situations that makes the viewer repeatedly aware of how much more to them and their relationships with others there is than we can see in any one shot or scene. As in the "contrapuntal" shooting and editing patterns of *Faces*, Cassavetes' shots repeatedly refer us as much to all the material they cannot comprehend as to the bits and pieces of relationships they do comprehend. One thinks of André Bazin's brilliant description of Renoir's "révolution du découpage" in *The Rules of the Game*:

For the structure of images in the anecdotal or theatrical film inherited both from painting and the theatre, for the plastic and dramatic unity of the "shot," Renoir substitutes the stare of his camera, which is at once idealized and concretized. Henceforth the screen will not try to offer us a sense of reality, but will deliver it to us in the manner of a cipher grid moving across a coded document.

This revolution is not without analogies to Impressionist painting. Until Impressionism the "composition" of a painting was also theatrical or decorative: it depended on the structure of the frame. . . . After Manet, and above all Degas and Renoir, the frame was no longer a stage. If it still sometimes played a role in the composition, it was negatively, through its discordance with reality. By interrupting the continuum of reality, the frame suggested what lay beyond it.[5]

Similarly, any one shot or scene in a Cassavetes film gives us only one thread in a vast hidden web of relationships, the tug and pull of each of which is continuously felt by the characters. It gives us one local, limited view of a situation too complexly interesting to yield itself to anything that might be called a comprehensive or total view. Furthermore, as in the characters in Renoir's films of the thirties, there is an interiority to Nick and Mabel, as there was to Harry, Archie, and Gus, and will be to Cosmo and Myrtle, that defies our knowing them (or even Cassavetes' knowing them) in any ultimate sense, as much as it frustrates their fellow characters' knowingness. Cassavetes seems almost to make a joke of this secret at the center of things at the end of *Husbands* when in two successive moments he has Gus whisper a joke in Harry's ear that convulses Harry with laughter and changes the whole tone of the scene up to that point, and then has Gus follow up the joke with a Jerry Lewis style "cigarette trick" for the group in Harry's room, but in both cases "forgets" to let the audience in on the joke or the trick. We cannot hear the one and the other is blocked by Gus's head in the camera position from which Cassavetes chooses to photograph it. But these are comparatively trivial secrets. Most of the time the effect is much more like the essential mystery at the heart of the work of Hawthorne, James, or Pynchon. Hawthorne's characters hide within their unexplainable symbolic visions and ineffable silences, James's late characters are cloaked and protected by the muffling cadences and qualifications of his style, and Pynchon's figures elude our deepest scrutiny through the pretence of their feigned reality and inscrutable historicity, but all are working as much in the fear of themselves and their characters being found out as is Cassavetes.

It is this that Cassavetes suggested in response to an interviewer's question about whether he "created a moral universe" in his films:

> I am a moralist in that I believe the greatest morality is to acknowledge the freedom of others; to be oneself and not to be in judgment of others who are different from you. . . . I absolutely refuse to judge the characters in my films and it is imperative that the characters neither analyse themselves nor others during the course of the filming. I refrain from leading people by their noses by not imposing a stereotyped moral vision on my work.[6]

It is a dream of the free self in a free society as old as America, but the tough-minded recognition of *A Woman Under the Influence* is just how hard it is "to be oneself" amid all the clutter of influences that impinge upon any individual. Mabel's most difficult task in the film is to attempt to free herself from the well-meaning "understanding" of those who love and care about her. "Tell me what you want me to be. . . . I can be anything you want," she says more than once to her husband, but her accomplishment (as well as the source of her dramatic problems) is that she has a "self" too richly responsive and creative to be simply "anything" once and for all for anyone.

"Be yourself" is the advice Nick gives Mabel throughout the film. "We're on your side," her relatives and friends keep repeating. (It is the same refrain the three husbands of *Husbands* occasionally cheer one another up with.) But the strength of *A Woman Under the Influence* is the extent to which its study of influences takes us beyond all such simple definitions of "selfhood" and beyond analysis of experience into alternative "sides," opponents, or obstacles. Cassavetes' mixed-up tones, characters, and relationships teach us to appreciate the confusion of selves, roles, and relations that go into the making of any one "self"—especially one as sensitive and imaginative as Mabel. This is what makes Mabel not only Cassavetes' most interesting character, but a figure qualitatively different from anyone else in the film. Each of the other characters futilely tries to assert the authority of a unitary, fixed self over the complexities of feeling and relationship, and (like a more humane version of Zelmo Swift) ultimately falls back on an assertion of personal authority in order to try to contain the mess and confusion of experience.

Nick, who rattles off a series of orders and instructions to anyone within shouting distance of him every time he is faced with uncertainty or confusion, is only the most comically well-intentioned of the lot. If one regards him as a kind of frantic film director who thinks he can direct every scene through an act of will and personal authority, it is only because so much of *A Woman Under the Influence* seems to be a parable about the hazards of acting, writing, and directing, and of the simplifications of certain kinds of role-playing and scene making, such as those Mama Longhetti indulges in. Each of the principal characters around Mabel makes the mistake of trying to build a scene around himself and his own desires, but as all of Cassavetes' work is devoted to showing, no adequate actor (or director) can hope to exempt himself from the continuous give-and-take of an evolving relationship in order unilaterally to direct or control the progress of a scene.

Nick and Mabel Longhetti are, like most of the other principal characters in Cassavetes' films, alter egos for the filmmaker himself. As parents in an extended ethnic family, they function, in an entirely

296 DR. ZEPP comes in, a man in his fifties, serious, kind, an old fashioned general practitioner, carrying a black bag.

297 Mama Longhetti comes out of the children's bedroom and down the stairs.

Everything stops.

298 Mabel looks at Dr. Zepp, back to Nick, back to Mama Longhetti who hovers by the staircase.

> MABEL
> Who's sick? I had the hiccups earlier -- I got rid of them. I don't need a Doctor any more. What's up?

> DR. ZEPP
> (to Nick)
> Has she been drinking?

> MABEL
> Sure I've been drinking. What the hell you think this is? This...
> (pointing to her glass)
> is a drink.

> DR. ZEPP
> Mabel, did you take a pill? Have you been taking any pills?

> MABEL
> Is morphine a pill? Sure, I take pills. I take vitamin pills, I take sleeping pills, uppers, downers, inners, outers... What's up? What's he want me to do, Nick? Walk a straight line? What did you tell him? That I drink? Dr. Zepp, I am very upset, therefore, I look upset and I act upset. Occasionally, I calm down. I have anxieties. I don't like this woman in my house guarding the staircase. She's guarding the staircase from me. Up above are my children in my home and she is the kiss of death.

299 Dr. Zepp goes to the table and starts undoing his bag.

> DR. ZEPP
> Mabel, what seems to be the trouble?

(CONTINUED)

124.

551 CLOSEUP - ANGLE ON NICK

552 ANGLE ON MABEL

553 Nick walks over to Mabel. They embrace, he gives her a
    long extended kiss. She hugs him and won't let him go.

554 Dr. Zepp walks over.

                         DR. ZEPP
                    (separating Nick and
                     Mabel)
               You're overdoing it, Mabel, you just
               calm down and relax. Calm... have to
               be calm.
                    (touching her hand)
               You be calm. Can you be calm?

                         NICK
               All right, enough with this. Come
               with me.

555 He takes Mabel by the hand and leads her to the stairs.

556 NEW ANGLE - THE STAIRCASE

    He takes her halfway up. They are relatively alone.

                         NICK
               I'm with you Mabel. There's nothing
               you can do wrong. I want you to be
               yourself. This is your house. You
               can be you. Your own personality.
               No fears. You understand? Just
               yourself.

557 CLOSEUP - MABEL

    She looks at him.

558 CLOSEUP - NICK

559 CLOSEUP - MABEL

                         MABEL
               I don't know what you want. How do
               you want me to be?

                         NICK
               Yourself.

                         MABEL
               You mean funny or sad or happy or
               shy, or what? Which self?

                                        (CONTINUED)

Performing oneself into or out of existence
—The near indistinguishability of endlessly inventive self-creation
and dangerously self-jeopardizing self-destruction in Cassavetes' world

Two non-sequential pages from the original script of A Woman Under the Influence, *completed in 1972. Page 75: during Mabel's breakdown. Page 124: shortly after her return home.*

practical and unmetaphorical sense of the terms, as actor-directors in their own independent productions—scripting, casting, organizing, blocking, staging, and editing scenes with large groups of people. *A Woman Under the Influence* is a study of the capability of the individual actor-director, in this practical sense of the term, to succeed as both an actor and a director: to succeed as an actor in playing with, and off, the various groups in which he is involved, in a sufficiently sensitive, tactful, and creative way; and to succeed as a director in making humanly complex, interesting, and moving scenes.

To watch Nick and Mabel interacting with each other and the groups of people who circulate through their home is to watch two opposed styles of acting and direction. Where Nick is the master of the large command—of the direct, blunt assertion of authority, Mabel is the mistress of winks, nods, and sly encouragement. Where Nick, confronted with potential confusion or uncertainty, takes refuge in shouting orders from headquarters and tyrannizing over the actors around him, Mabel's directing strategy is one of gentle, playful, oblique interaction with those around her, not to make them speak her lines, but rather to encourage them to dare to express the best in themselves. Nick and Mabel as it were repeat in a finer tone the parable about acting and directing in Capra's *Pocketful of Miracles*, in which Peter Falk also appeared and of which so much of his performance in this film reminds us. In *Pocketful of Miracles* Capra compares the balletic with the elephantine by contrasting Bette Davis's capacities for fluid, magical metamorphoses of roles, styles, and tones with Peter Falk's Damon Runyon–ish awkwardness, bluntness, and flat-footed literalism. (Incidentally, the scene in *A Woman Under the Influence* in which Falk gives ridiculously clumsy stage directions to guests at the welcome home party for Mabel after her return from the mental hospital is a direct reprise of the famous scene in *Pocketful of Miracles* in which Falk as Joy Boy utters his immortal "Alright, nobody sweats!" line to the mugs he is rehearsing for Apple Annie's house party.)

Nick is imperative, forceful, and direct; Mabel is comically, wryly oblique. Nick craves planning, organization, order, and control. Mabel thrives on spontaneity, improvisational opportunity, and continuously sensitive repositionings and revisions of relationship. Nick needs and wants structure; Mabel plays with and against structures. If all of Cassavetes' other work were not an implicit warning against drawing such a conclusion, one might regard *A Woman Under the Influence* as a definitive statement of distinctively "male" and "female" ways of organizing experience and making art, with Nick and Mabel representing the two sexual possibilities. Since Mabel represents a capacity of performance contrasted in every way with the Faustian, structure- and power-hungry need to arrange and control experience represented by Nick, her range of performance would then represent not only a particular human strategy of survival, but perhaps more importantly, Cassavetes' exploration of the creative possibilities of a unique "feminist aesthetic" offering itself as an alternative to "masculine" modes of artistic manipulation, domination, and arrangement.

A Woman Under the Influence (like the subsequent Gloria) would then be a feminist film in a much more profound sense than that of merely offering an ideological analysis of social and psychological differences between men and women. It would be a definition of the feminist position not in terms of ideological conflicts between men and women, and even less in terms of the need for women to adopt male positions and points of view, but in terms of truly alternative forms of consciousness and performance. In Mabel, Cassavetes would be offering a capacity of performance that is a full-fledged alternative to Nick's male range of performance. Where the male stance is marked by its need for definition, domination, and fixity, Mabel (and later Gloria) display a power of wit, parody, slyness, and mercurial movement that can totally out-class and out-maneuver the male position. If interpreted in this way, A Woman Under the Influence and Gloria would be defining and exploring a feminist power of performance and quality of consciousness for their central characters that cut beneath ideological differences in beliefs and attitudes between men and women, and make such more superficial differences almost unimportant. (In the writing of women such as Eudora Welty, Elizabeth Bishop, and Arlene Croce one can perhaps detect an analogue in literature to what Cassavetes is doing in film, according to this view. If one is capable of reading between the lines to hear the play of tones, styles, and meanings these women writers perform with, one can trace the outlines of what such a feminist aesthetic—as distinguished from a feminist ideology— would look like in writing.)

But the shortcoming of this strictly sexual reading of the film is that notwithstanding all of the obvious and undeniable sexual resonances of Nick's and Mabel's rival capacities of performance, Cassavetes' other films tell us that he does not see their performative differences as intrinsically identified with sexual differences. Not only are there female characters in abundance in his work (Maria in Faces, for example) whose qualities of performance are more like Nick's than Mabel's, but in *Minnie and Moskowitz* Cassavetes, in effect, reverses the sexual polarity that I have just described, allowing Seymour a capacity of performance very similar to Mabel's as he plays off others of the same and of the opposite sex in the course of the film. Which is to say that Cassavetes perceives that the differences in consciousness and performance in our culture are only adventitiously parceled out generally along sexual lines and are not the exclusive property of either sex.

The point of Cassavetes' juxtaposition of Nick's and Mabel's ways of staging scenes is not to force a viewer to take sides for or against one character or another, but the contrary: to keep the film from locking itself into any one style of relationship, to keep the scenes, the characters, and their relationships sufficiently in motion in relation to one another to prevent any absolute or definitive choices from being made. The film is structured out of contrasts of styles both within and between scenes that emphasize the differences between Nick's and Mabel's alternative styles of improvisational scripting, acting, directing, and editing the interactions of the people around them. It contrasts Mabel's performance as mistress of ceremonies at the spaghetti breakfast with Nick's performance as master of ceremonies at the homecoming party for Mabel. It contrasts Mabel's wacky, spontaneous, and disorganized party for Mr. Jensen, herself, and their children with Nick's over-structured, over-planned, and over-serious attempt to entertain the children at the beach when Mabel is in the hospital. And the contrasts and juxtapositions of style and sensitivity built into the film extend beyond those embodied in the figures of Nick and Mabel. One of the most sublime and affecting effects in the film is the implicit contrast between the two major dinner gatherings around the Longhetti table over which Nick and Mabel both jointly preside in their disjointed ways: the spaghetti meal for the construction workers near the beginning of the film, and the welcome home dinner for Mabel with her family near the end of the film. The touching irony of the juxtaposition is that Nick's rough and clumsy construction worker friends show a sensitivity to Mabel's powers of performance and a respect for her feelings that her own family lacks. At the end of their respective scenes, the construction workers know when to leave, while the family excruciatingly and voyeuristically lingers on around the table beyond all bounds of tact or human decency.

But Cassavetes is interested in condemning no one. *A Woman Under the Influence*, like his other work, is about the creative differences that arise from the interplay of rival styles of acting and relationship—differences that initiate creative acts of performance, differences that create possibilities of social and biological creation. Cassavetes is always interested in heightening dramatic contrasts, not in lessening them, and in some weird way Nick and Mabel represent the couple his work has been waiting for, not in spite of their inexhaustible differences, but because of them. The free play of these creative differences is the impulse of life, love, and drama for Cassavetes. They are something never to be wished away, eliminated, or compromised out of existence (as a certain kind of feminist ideology would mistakenly insist), but to be robustly explored and muscularly worked through, as vigorously as Nick and Mabel work through their relationship to each other and to the characters around them in this film.

Mabel is a much better actor and director than Nick is, but not because she finds a way of being superior to him, or beyond him. She is more sensitive and alert than he is precisely because she finds ways of including him and his feelings and attitudes in her performances—parodically, playfully, satirically, and lovingly—just as Cassavetes himself finds ways of including both of them in his film. Drama, as Mabel the brilliant ballerina, perfect party hostess, and ideal film director realizes, is, like making love, always a collaborative venture. It is a process of partnering and creative interplay that can neither be imposed upon nor originate entirely within a single individual.

Husbands and *Minnie and Moskowitz* were able to free their central characters only by a subtle series of narrative repressions that at certain key moments backed away from some of the problems raised in the films. Cassavetes' accomplishment in *A Woman Under the Influence* is that in it, for the first time, he is able to see his central characters through all of his narrative complications without a final loss of will for him or them. To say that *A Woman Under the Influence* brings back home the problems the previous films had to wall out is more than a metaphor: the self-dramatizations of *Shadows*, the marital infidelity of *Faces*, the gawking groups of spectators of *Husbands*, the moments of sexual violence and brutality that were finally pushed away into the outside world by the ending of *Minnie and Moskowitz* are discovered to have been present in the living room, bedroom, and dining room all along. They are all brought back home; nothing is avoided, elided, or repressed. Mabel, Nick, and we live through it all, and the miracle is that we survive with love. In place of confrontations or resolutions, *A Woman Under the Influence* offers muddles of involvement, confusions of caring, and entanglements of relationship. In place of prospects of escape or transcendence, it sketches toils of responsibility, influence, and affection that make individual freedom more, rather than less, problematic as it goes along.

The entire film is as tough and unsentimental as its relentless final few minutes, when, after the awkward and painful gathering of friends and relatives, Mabel's suicide attempt, and the putting of the children to bed, Cassavetes forces Nick and Mabel to return to the mess downstairs. Subdued, weary, and (as Mabel says) eager to get into bed together, alone, at last, they are spared nothing. They have to go through the ceremony of reestablishing a superficial order in the household, tidying up the room, and taking care of Mabel's wounds. No words pass between them for the last five minutes of film time as Cassavetes holds his camera on them with a neorealist patience and contentment with the ordinary sloppy rituals of life. Nothing is cut, nothing elided, nothing forgotten. They turn off the lights, close the sliding doors to the bedroom, and as Cassavetes' now static camera holds and holds, through the curtains we can dimly make out the bed being pulled out and Nick beginning to unzip Mabel's dress. We are in the final seconds of the film, and we know it not only because of the music, but because the credits are already rolling on the screen. All a viewer wants is that, after all the pain and turmoil they have gone through together, Nick and Mabel should finally get to bed together without another problem, without another interruption. The lights are coming up in the theatre and the audience is rising from its seats, but if you are listening very carefully, you hear the hall telephone begin to ring, the telephone that has been associated throughout this long, painful film with nothing but problems, crises, and interruptions.

So where has it all gotten Nick, Mabel, or us? We have negotiated an obstacle course, traced our way through a tangled web of influences, and come to only the most momentary respite, a tender, caring, moment of love in which we perhaps understand a little better what Cassavetes' publicity material called "the dilemmas of love," but in which no end, resolution, or solution to the "dilemmas" is expected or offered. In place of a portable philosophy, A Woman Under the Influence provides only a doctrine of the unceasing work of adjustment and arrangement, a belief in the necessary labor of all loving relations, and the inevitability of personal differences and conflicts of allegiance.

But lest this sound too bleak, A Woman Under the Influence also demonstrates how the labor of love is also a kind of play, with all the stimulation, excitement, and exhilaration of the most serious and mature playing. That is in fact the metaphor Cassavetes used to describe his own real-life marriage to Gena Rowlands in his interview with *Playboy*:

I enjoy Gena because she enjoys some of the things I do, because she hates some of the things I like, and because I hate some of the things she likes. We keep learning how to play together so that I can step on her toes gently and she can step on mine gently and we can make a lot of noise. Our kids understand it to the point where we've all become some sort of team, a group of people who really enjoy each other.[7]

Jumbled together under the rubric of "playing together" in this passage are the different metaphors for friendship, love, and the family that run through all of Cassavetes' films, all of them present and pulling against one another in this film. "Playing together" is a group of noisy musicians learning how to perform together; a team of athletes learning how to compete together and with one another; a couple learning how to dance together and partner each other; and, the metaphoric sense that subsumes all of the others, a group of actors learning how to play a scene together, watching themselves play together, functioning as players, audiences, critics, and directors of their own performances.

The metaphor of the dance is a natural one for Cassavetes to draw upon in this statement, and a scene involving dancing occurs in almost all of the films as a literal event. That is because the central subject of all of these films is the process of emotional, social, and imaginative choreography that takes place between two or more people, and not some doctrine or meaning excepted from it. The films offer the viewer the invigorating spectacle of an eccentric pattern of personal performance, a life-affirming course of action and survival that is tested against every resistance Cassavetes can apply to it. Furthermore, in Cassavetes' moral universe it always, as the saying goes, "takes two to tango." Dancing values the individual performer, just as Cassavetes' films do, only insofar as his individuality is compatible with, and expressible in, a relationship with at least one other performer. And, like a dance performed against the continuous resistance of gravity, the inherent limitations of the human body, and the alien movements of a partner, the complex interpersonal negotiations of Cassavetes' characters playing together in performance are as exciting and inspiring to watch on the second or tenth viewing as on the first.

If the labor of love is imagined to be a process of dancing or playing together in *A Woman Under the Influence*, then the inadequacy of my previous metaphor of the film as an obstacle course is apparent.

Cassavetes' films are a course to be run without a finish line, a victor, or a reward at the end. In Cassavetes' universe, there are no winners and no ends, no morals, lessons, or ideological statements offered. There is only the challenge and exhilaration of endless and endlessly adjusted playing or dancing together as its own reward. Nothing is made, achieved, or affirmed by the end of *A Woman Under the Influence* except Nick's, Mabel's, and our own having lived through all that has been played out, and remaining both vulnerable to, and undaunted by, all the influences we have been subjected to. If Nick and Mabel never get anywhere, it is not because they are standing still, but because even in the very final seconds of the film, their lives are still on the move. We and they have nothing to show for it all but an enriched awareness, a consciousness greater to the extent that we have suffered together, been forced to see more and to respond to more than we would otherwise have guessed we were capable of.

If we are wiser in the end, it is only because we have fewer illusions about love and complacencies about the assertion of freedom. We are no more confident or hopeful about Nick's and Mabel's futures together than they themselves are. We have simply succeeded in running a course of events, tested ourselves to the extreme against a series of influences and interruptions, and, if we have been worthy, managed through all the difficulties and pressures, like Nick and Mabel, to keep alive a belief in the possibilities of love and responsiveness, even as we have not blinked or evaded the hazards of the course. That is not much by the standards of worldly success, and it is certainly no guarantee for the future, but in Cassavetes' moral universe it is everything, and sufficient reason for him to regard this film as a supreme affirmation of the power and value of the human spirit, and to allow him to call this profound, exhilarating tragedy, in his own sincere opinion, his "most optimistic film."[8]

CHAPTER VIII

SELF-DEFENSE, SELF-SUFFICIENCY, AND SELF-ANNIHILATION
The Killing of a Chinese Bookie

To divorce oneself from society, to exist without roots, to set out on that uncharted journey into the rebellious imperatives of the self . . . to explore that domain of experience where security is boredom and therefore sickness, and one exists in the present, in the enormous present which is without a past or future, memory or planned intention, the life where a man must go until he is beat, where he must gamble with his energies through all those small or large crises of courage and unforeseen situations which beset his day, where he must be with it or doomed not to swing. *Norman Mailer*

The great man is he who in the midst of the crowd keeps with perfect sweetness the independence of solitude. *Ralph Waldo Emerson*

A Woman Under the Influence is John Cassavetes' "most optimistic" film, his paean to the power of an individual to survive, even to thrive, in the midst of every influence into which he can plunge him. But in another respect, it is the opposite of optimistic. It is a film in some ways darker, more bleak, and more disturbing than anything that precedes it. Never before has the embattled individual been in such an exposed and precarious position. Never have so many and such powerful forces been massed against him. If Mabel is in a sense a grown-up, matured Lelia—an imaginative, parodic role-playing improvisor of the fullest maturity—how much more difficult has performance become for Mabel than it was for Lelia. It is all very well to celebrate Cassavetes as the poet of saving eccentricity and unpredictability, but the unremitting pain of *A Woman Under the Influence* is evidence of Cassavetes' own awareness of how far from hospitable the world is to a performative aesthetic. Indeed, the film is testimony more to the unsustainable psychic cost of such an aesthetic than to its profits.

I called *Minnie and Moskowitz* a turning point in Cassavetes' career insofar as it was in that film that he was first able to imagine a society hospitable to the creative and fully alive self. It was the smallest possible society, one made up only of Minnie and Seymour, a marginal group comically disengaged from the larger, harsher world of the film, but a significant positive accomplishment nonetheless. But *Minnie and Moskowitz* is also a turning point in a negative sense. Minnie and Seymour are threatened as no previous characters in Cassavetes' films are. They are less powerful, less confident, and more hedged round by threatening forces. That is why their performances seem less a positive overflow of spontaneous energies (as Lelia's or Chet's were) and more a scrambling, half desperate reaction to forces outside their control or purview.

Minnie summarizes her difficulties with men early in the film in a drunken monologue addressed to her girlfriend Florence:

The world is full of silly asses who just crave your body. I mean not just your body. . . I mean they want your soul, your heart, your mind, your everything. They just can't live until they get it. And then they get it and you know, Florence, they don't really want it.

But her statement might stand as a summary of the newly harried and embattled position of the individual in all of the films that follow *Minnie and Moskowitz* as well. She is describing the situation Seymour and she face, but she is also describing the predicament of Mabel Longhetti, Cosmo Vitelli, Myrtle Gordon, and all of Cassavetes' most interesting performers in the films that follow. They are all forced to become performers literally or metaphorically on the run.

That is to say, even as *Minnie and Moskowitz* shows Minnie and Seymour successfully piecing together a relationship of love, understanding, and comically creative inventiveness, it also affirms with extraordinary vigor the presence and power of a world hostile to every possibility they represent, a world that wants nothing more than to annihilate the free individual and the delicate network of personal relations and sensitivities around him. Of course, the earlier films—*Shadows, Too Late Blues, A Child Is Waiting, Faces,* and *Husbands*—refer repeatedly to impersonal realms of business and commerce, the mechanicalness and insensitivity of which corrode personal relations. But there is still the faith that a purely personal style of relationship might be established outside of, and separate from, these harsh, insensitive patterns of behavior.

The early films were attempts to define the boundaries of such independent and separate personal spaces. It is no accident that almost all of the significant drama of *Shadows, Too Late Blues, A Child Is Waiting, Faces,* and *Husbands* is assertively personal, or that almost all of the important scenes in *Shadows, Faces,* and *Husbands* are set in homes and apartments (when they are not set in environments even more buffered and protected from the world, such as the clubs, bars, and hotel rooms of *Husbands*—places of recreation, fantasy, and games, separated from the worlds of business and finance). The characters in these films need to be protected in such spaces in order that the bloom not be rubbed off their personal explorations. In the films before *Minnie and Moskowitz,* Cassavetes protects and shelters his characters with a clear conscience. The contrasting styles of business and pleasure, public and private life, impersonal and personal relations may still frequently be confused (and one subject of these films is their frequent confusion), but ideally they are distinguishable and separable, and there is no doubt whatever about which of the styles of behavior Cassavetes considers more important and central to life.

But something happens to shake that confidence around the time of *Minnie and Moskowitz.* That film attempts to continue along the lines of the previous work; it attempts to exorcize public, mechanical, impersonal styles of relationship comically in order to affirm the value of private, personal, conversational forms of relationship in bedrooms and restaurants. Indeed Cassavetes may even believe that that is the story he is telling—the story of the independent integrity of the private space Minnie and Seymour clear for themselves in the course of the film. But if we trust the tale and not the teller, an entirely different story emerges. The schizophrenia of the plot, the jarring lurches from one setting to another, the continuous spatial movement, and the fugitive quality of the relationship Minnie and Seymour finally achieve, all tell how difficult it has suddenly become to affirm and cordon off a sacrosanct private world of personal relations for his central characters. But perhaps the greatest change in the structure of *Minnie and Moskowitz,* and the one with the most radical ramifications for the work that follows it, is that the pacings of the scenes have altered. Scenes are not as long, or as conducive to intimate personal explorations as they were in the earlier films. The editorial timings are no longer in the service of the characters' personal needs; they have become as clipped, hectic, and relentless as the rhythms of the public world the film supposedly wants to exorcize. That is why "lyrical" interludes that try to affirm the sovereignty and superiority of merely personal styles, relations, and pacings—such as the *2001* space-capsule sequence or the "green world" coda—suddenly feel artificial, contrived, and limited. Time and the breathless rush of events become the ultimate threats to a character's existence. He must now learn how to live with these mechanical, in-human rhythms. Without shutting them out, he must create the possibility of acceptable, comfortable human rhythms of relationship once again.

One might say that Cassavetes' attempt in *Minnie and Moskowitz* backfired on him and his characters. In a daring attempt to free Minnie and Seymour (or Jeannie and Chet) in one blow, he knocked down all the walls that hem in the characters of *Faces*, only to discover to the discomfort of the film's comic premise that he had let in too many distractions, too much worldly confusion, too many alien styles, pacings and entanglements, which he then had to attempt to wall out again in some of the film's lyrical interludes in order to give his central pair a chance to fall in love. But *A Woman Under the Influence* is denied even the ambivalence about walling in and walling out of the film before it. The aliens have scaled the walls and the world of strangers, professionals, brusque, hostile, indifferent, or insensitive others is discovered within the Longhetti home. There is not even a pickup truck or shrub-filled back yard into which to retreat. (The family station wagon is jammed to the roof with children, toys, and an uncomprehending mother-in-law, and the back yard is watched over by the insensitive Mr. Jensen.) Nick and Mabel do not even have the chance to stage a leisurely, uninterrupted scene within the walls of their own home—something the callow adolescents in *Shadows* or the doomed "dinosaurs" in *Faces* could take for granted.

The harrowing recognition of Mabel's mad scene is that there is, even in one's own home, a world of categories (such as "insanity"), relationships (such as her patient-doctor relationship with Dr. Zepp and her daughter–mother-in-law relationship with Mama Longhetti), and events (such as a nervous breakdown) in which merely personal feelings and intimacies are beside the point, during which personal values such as sensitivity, tact, and kindness are irrelevant. From a filmmaker whose career has been built around the importance of personal relations comes the recognition of how little personal relations may sometimes count. No scene more eloquently summarizes the changed facts of life in Cassavetes' films than Mabel's long breakdown scene in the bosom of her family. The family, that place of retreat and protection in the previous films, is useless to her. The individual is alone in her own home; she faces a threatening, indifferent, and un-comprehending world in the form of her own family.

There is a sober maturity in these later works in comparison with which even a film as tragic as *Faces* seems almost innocent and youthfully idealistic. (Though it should be clear that this is in no sense a limiting judgment on the previous films, any more than one must dismiss the earlier, simpler work of Dreyer or Capra in order to appreciate the peculiar strengths of their later achievements.) *Shadows*, *Too Late Blues*, *Faces*, and *Husbands* hold out possibilities of personal fulfillment through personal effort. However much particular characters fail in their efforts, it is always theoretically possible to create a free space and style for a fresh, unfettered relationship with another character. There is uninterrupted time and space (if no more than a few hours on one or two sets) in which to explore the possibilities of freedom with another sensitive human being. Even Richard and Maria Forst have that much available to them. But Mabel is trapped, surrounded, and under the tyranny of scrutiny in the heart of her family in ways that even they are not. There is no "world elsewhere" of love and understanding to which to flee, and no free, unfettered, purely exploratory relationship even imaginable for her.

The greatness of the two films that follow *Minnie and Moskowitz* (which seem Cassavetes' two supreme achievements and among the most extraordinary of recent films) is attributable to Cassavetes' recognition of the limitations of merely stylistic arrangements of reality, or to put it another way, to his cinematic realization of forces (such as time) that assertively refuse to yield to emotional blandishments or personal suasion. It is instructive to notice how even the meaning of "craziness" has shifted between *Minnie and Moskowitz* and *A Woman Under the Influence*. Considered strictly in terms of words and actions, Seymour is "crazier" than Mabel ever is guilty of being, yet he is never for one instant in danger of being locked up or committed to a mental institution. His craziness is treated as a creative response to society's pressures; hers is a pathology. His is allowed to be an attractive and powerful *style* of behavior in a world where *style* is everything; hers is a clinical event defined by medical categories that are not susceptible to negotiation or interpersonal redefinition. That is to say, personal style is still powerful in *Minnie and Moskowitz*. But there can be no merely stylistic escape route from society's ultimate pressures, influences, and judgments for Mabel. Family, friends, strangers, and unnegotiable, inescapable definitions of sanity, insanity, and selfhood hedge her round at every point.

The characters in the three films after *A Woman Under the Influence* are in an even less enviable position than Mabel. They must function within bureaucracies of relations, tangled webs of personal and impersonal involvements that defy their personal powers of rearrangement, and from which even a temporary release is impossible. There is no such thing as a merely personal relationship or a merely personal style in these films. Everyone and everything in them is always already interpreted, understood, and surrounded by others. No longer does a character have the luxury of negotiating the rhythms, terms, or locations of a relationship. Under these conditions selfhood itself becomes a problematic entity. Characters are so surrounded and interpreted that merely holding on to a "character" becomes an effort. ("Tell me what you want me to be. I can be anything"—Mabel's desperate formulation of her predicament, might be an epigraph for any of these films.)

In a world in which the person is so threatened and embattled, the personality so enmeshed in alien entanglements, and the expression of personality so difficult, the very preservation of the self becomes an issue. No longer, as in earlier films, is a performance merely the exuberant, unplanned bubbling over of an unpremeditated personal style. Performances are forced to become oblique, furtive, or calculated for special effects and results. Disguises, schemes, and secret, private strategies for survival become necessary if a successful performance is to be staged at all against these multitudinous resistances. Silence, exile, and cunning become necessary tactics of survival.

One of the most telling changes in Cassavetes' work in *A Woman Under the Influence* and the films that follow it is the profound alteration in the nature of the musical scoring. Both the first and the revised versions of *Shadows* (like Robert Frank's *Pull My Daisy*, which is profoundly indebted to the first version of *Shadows*—released one year before it—for both its form and its content), have syncopated, unbalanced, jazz soundtracks that echo the uninflected, asymmetrical, ever-permuting forms personal relationships take in them. The same is true of *Too Late Blues*. *Faces* and *Husbands* are, with the exception of a few songs, unaccompanied by music. The soundtrack of *Minnie and Moskowitz* returns to the jazzy rhythms of *Shadows*, especially when Seymour is on screen, but adds extensive layerings of worldly noise that the characters can never wall out or escape from, and a small number of lyrical interludes at special moments in the flowering of Minnie and Seymour's relationship. But nothing changed radically in

Cassavetes' soundtracks between *Shadows* and *Minnie and Moskowitz;* the jazz syncopations only got more elaborate and complex.

But with *A Woman Under the Influence, The Killing of a Chinese Bookie, Opening Night,* and *Gloria* the soundtracks change dramatically. The films suddenly become melodramas (in both senses of the word; but let me confine myself here only to the strictly musical meaning of the term, originally used to describe plays with musical accompaniment). For the first time in his career, Cassavetes chooses to back his films with a virtually independent and, for long stretches, continuous musical score, used at crucial moments to enhance or explain the dramatic action. In effect, in local instances, Cassavetes returns, astonishingly enough, to classic academy scoring techniques, as they were used in Hollywood melodramas of the forties. Bo Harwood's extraordinary musical scores for the first three of these films and Bill Conti's (much inferior) score for *Gloria* revisit the musical world of Hollywood melodrama. Now one may reasonably object to making such a point of the importance of this in Cassavetes' career, since after all this sort of orchestration is only what every ordinary Hollywood film utilized unthinkingly for twenty or thirty years, and why should it matter so much in this case? But it does matter, if only because Cassavetes' work has in so many respects been at odds precisely with the melodramatic bent of this traditional Hollywood aesthetic. The effect of the music in these films is that, for the first time in Cassavetes' work, certain emotional experiences have become incommunicable (to other characters as well as to the movie audience) in other than musical terms. Specific emotional moments become expressible not in the give-and-take of a social or dramatic interchange, but only in musical accompaniments that back frequently silent, solitary, or socially estranged figures such as Cosmo, Myrtle, and Gloria. Cassavetes' use of such musical backing to his stories is only the outward and audible evidence of a troubling isolation, loneliness, and emotional privacy that has suddenly appeared in the films and their central characters, and is different from anything in his earlier work.

Though the change in orchestration occurred most decisively with *A Woman Under the Influence,* it may in fact be traced back to the musical interludes in *Minnie and Moskowitz.* The lyrical interludes in that film function in the same way the melodramatic scoring does in the subsequent films. Minnie and Seymour wrap themselves in music in the cab of Seymour's truck in the *2001* sequence and the film score itself wraps them in music in a bushy backyard in the coda, in situations in which musical plangency substitutes itself for the pains and difficulties of social performance. But if *Minnie and Moskowitz* is irregularly punctuated by occasional moments in which social discourse becomes irrelevant or inadequate, *A Woman Under the Influence* is assembled of one such moment after another. Melodrama has triumphed over all more public and social forms of understanding and expression. (Since *A Woman Under the Influence* has far and away been Cassavetes' most successful film, it is tempting to attribute its popularity to this aspect of it. As crowd-pleasing politicians, evangelists, authors, journalists, prime-time television producers, and Hollywood directors all understand, we live in a culture at this point in history in which the forms of melodrama dominate the human imagination.)

More specifically, *A Woman Under the Influence* locates the viewer (and its characters) in the world of Italian opera—from the opening choric strains accompanying shots of laborers working on a flooded pipeline to the minor key orchestration of the ending. It is not accidental that Cassavetes makes Nick Italian, that the construction workers hold a contest to see who can sing an aria from *Aida* at breakfast, or that as Mabel waits at home alone for Nick to return, she plays on the radio the great "Addio, sognante vita" duet that Mimi and Rodolpho sing at the end of the third act of Puccini's *La Bohème*. To my emphasis on the operatic aspects of the film, it might be replied that as early as *Shadows*, Cassavetes' Lelia has a consciousness almost as grandly operatic in the imaginative possibilities it entertains as does Mabel. And that is true. But the vaulting faith of *Shadows* (which must in retrospect seem just a little youthfully naive to anyone who has sat through the horrors of *A Woman Under the Influence*) was precisely that this operatic richness of consciousness and intensity of desire was expressible in the eminently nonoperatic forms of life and love in the real world. Cassavetes, like Lelia, then believed that the actual structures of social intercourse could be made responsive to the most idealistic requirements of individual consciousness. (The same optimistic assumption informs *Too Late Blues*, *Faces*, and *Husbands*, even if Cassavetes' characters prove its reality more in their failures than in any success they achieve.) But that confidence has gone from Cassavetes by the time of *A Woman Under the Influence*.

He is a filmmaker whose earlier work was premised on his previously unquestioned faith in the value of the cultivation and refinement of public performances and on the study of the expression of feeling (or the failures of the expression of feeling) between characters in social situations. But the music in these late films now communicates emotions that have no other form of expression, emotions experienced by characters who, in their solitude and estrangement (like Mabel sitting alone waiting for Nick) have no possible social resources or forms of expression. Their feelings cannot be spoken, performed in front of an audience, or dramatically expressed in any other way; they exist only in the music of the soundtrack and the isolated consciousness of one individual. In the scene after Cosmo has lost everything in gambling debts early in *The Killing of a Chinese Bookie* and is riding back to the club that is no longer his, slouched over in a rented limousine and photographed in profile, Bo Harwood's music tells everything he has no words for and no one to whom to express them if he had. With this music and these central figures, we have moved into a world of irreducible, incurable inexpressivity, inscrutability, and loneliness, a world where no public, social performance of a character's experience is adequate or possible.

All of which is to say that Cassavetes' work has moved into the world of melodrama in the other unpejorative sense of the word as well. The melodramatic strain in his later work is indicative of an imaginative and expressive crisis that also afflicts the work of James, Twain, Mailer, Pynchon, and many other American artists. It occurs when the attempt to move beyond particular social forms and structures of meaning is enlarged (or contracted) into an attempt to move beyond all social forms and structures. In the work of all of these artists, what began as a strategy of criticism or parody of the adequacy of certain forms of expression is gradually transformed into a repudiation of all such forms of expression. The style of their work takes on a metaphorical or metaphysical insistence, a melodramatic heightening, or a gestural inarticulateness that, in what it cannot or will not express in more orthodox ways, poignantly communicates how imagination has been cut off from any possible social form of expression or realization. Like the consciousnesses of their creators, characters' consciousnesses have become too rich and strange for any more publicly intelligible form of communication or performance.

An image that appears throughout *The Killing of a Chinese Bookie* is that of its central character, Cosmo Vitelli, surrounded by a sea of other faces asking him questons, dictating instructions to him, scrutinizing his responses. It is an image that echoes Mabel's wrenching mad scene as she stands in her living room encircled, coached, hectored, and watched over by her husband, children, mother-in-law, and family doctor, and her similarly exposed suicide scene at the end of *A Woman Under the Influence*. But Cosmo is in an even more exposed, more put upon, and more vulnerable position than Mabel. After all is said and done, she at least has her family, with whatever small consolation they can offer her. In her moments of direst need, she can turn to her husband, her children, her relatives, and friends, no matter how inept, uncomprehending, or insensitive they may be in their efforts of love and support. Cosmo has no legitimate biological or social family. Worse yet, he has three surrogate "families" making distinct, irreconcilable, and mutually exclusive claims on him. He is a "father" and boss of a sleazy, smalltime nightclub; he is a sometime "lover" and "husband" to one of the girls he employs and perhaps to her mother as well; and he is an obedient "son" to the brutal family of Mafia heavies who own him and his club. But to say that Cosmo has three families is only to say that he has no family at all in the way Cassavetes' earlier characters do. None of the characters in the three films that follow *A Woman Under the Influence* have families even of the flawed sort Mabel does. The concept of the family itself as a support system for the individual, as a private place of shelter and love, troubled as it is in the immediately previous films, ceases to exist entirely in *The Killing of a Chinese Bookie* and the later work.

The Killing of a Chinese Bookie is Cassavetes' excursion into *film noir*, and never has that hard-boiled, perilous world of constant threat been translated with more authority into the medium of color film stock. It is a world of garish colors and gaudy costumes that camouflage more than they disclose; of glaring brightnesses that blind instead of illuminating; and of shadows too deep for any eye or camera to penetrate that perfectly mirror the film's moral world of betrayal, deceit, and inexorable menace outside all of the codes and orders of daylight society. The drama of the film is Cosmo's solitary attempt—not entirely different from Mabel's—to hold onto a "home," a "family" of sorts, and a power of performance amid the hostile, destructive, person- and personality-withering entanglements into which he is thrust. But unlike Mabel, Cosmo, this man under the influence (played by Ben Gazzara in what is certainly the performance of his life, and one that in its range and subtlety can only be compared with Gena Rowland's performance in the previous film) is under the influence of much more than the emotional tugs of love and family. The Mafia is out to take over his club; he is being set up as a murderer in a Mob war, and subsequently, in a double cross, to be murdered by the Mob; his club is on the brink of bankruptcy; his personal and romantic life is a shambles; and his whole dream of personal style, class, and distinction—the dream that drives his life—is a sham.

The closest Cosmo comes to having a physical home anywhere in the film is the sleazy, tawdry strip joint and nightclub he runs called the Crazy Horse West. It is more than a physical location for him, it is his life and his whole world, the supreme imaginative and stylistic achievement of his existence, his momentary stay against the confusion around him. As Cassavetes' publicity material for the film explained:

> The Killing of a Chinese Bookie is the story of Cosmo Vitelli, an ordinary man who has constructed his life as many American men do. He has defined himself in terms of his work; it is more than a way to make a living, it is his entire existence—paid for in monthly installments [to the Mob]. . . . The Crazy Horse West is his world, a world he re-creates every night: he writes, directs, choreographs, and announces [its acts].

Cosmo is an artist and the Crazy Horse West in its trashy, tawdry way is the masterwork of his life. "Class" and "style" are everything to Cosmo (he has nothing else), and at the Crazy Horse West the bartenders and waitresses wear cowboy and cowgirl costumes; the strippers don't just strip, but do artistic numbers like "The Gunfight at the O.K. Corral" and "An Evening in Paris"; and the whole show is emceed by an overweight, epicene master of ceremonies, a doppelganger for Cosmo, called "Mr. Sophistication," who has his own appreciation of the importance of style and class and wouldn't be caught dead on stage in anything less classy than a silk-screened tuxedo T-shirt and a sequined top hat. But Cosmo is the real master of ceremonies at the Crazy Horse West and no detail is too small or unimportant for him to supervise. He is there every waking minute, circulating, greeting rare visiting Mafia dignitaries, making sure they get a good table close to the stage, and pouring them a complimentary glass of Dom Pérignon when he is feeling especially flush.

As the film begins we see Cosmo making the final payment on seven years of "protection" and "licensing" money to Marty Reitz, a gangster important enough to be thought to be paying Cosmo a compliment in personally collecting the money from him. It is the happiest day in Cosmo's life—although even this extreme emotional fact will take us the next twenty or thirty minutes of the film to realize, so poker-faced and emotionally restrained are these characters. (Cosmo is forced to be as controlled, withdrawn, and repressive of his own feelings as Mabel was exuberant, outgoing, and expressive.) In this *film noir* world of icy self-control and cold-blooded self-preservation, the mere expression of emotion is dangerous. In fact, Cosmo's egregious error (and evidence for his extreme emotional state) is that he actually dares to speak his mind for one moment near the end of his meeting with Marty:

Marty: Cosmo, you're a prince. Now you can go out and work for yourself.
Cosmo: Marty, you're a low life. No offence, but you have no style. I do business with you, but you have no style.
Marty: Cosmo, any time you need some help come to me.
Cosmo: I don't ever want to see you again.
Marty: Don't push it.
Cosmo: (*to himself, as he walks away*) Asshole.

It is a dialogue that defines the issues of the rest of the film: what it means to be a low life; what it means to lack style (or to have it); and, above all, what it means to survive in a world where even the momentary expression of one's true feelings is dangerous to one's existence. Notice how Marty, despite Cosmo's candor, does not lose his cool. And yet it is not in the least a coincidence that it is Marty who orders Cosmo's death halfway through the film. But in this world even the decision to have someone murdered is not an act of passion.

Cosmo himself, to anyone who does not know him, might be thought the "low life" who lacks "style." He is the proprietor of a tacky, tasteless, financially foundering strip joint that has been in hock to the Mob for the past seven years, who, the day after this payoff scene, will again lose his club in gambling debts at a Mob-operated casino. He is a man cut off from any normal, healthy system of sexual or social relationships, who struggles for the two and a half hours of the film simply to keep himself and his club going against the overwhelming pressures that accumulate to do him and it in. And yet it is the beauty of this film to define what this all-round loser is able to make of his life and of these diminished things. For it is the genius of Cosmo (and his creator) that in the course of the film he does achieve a weird sort of style, class, and distinction—within the limits of his own ignorance, clumsiness, and mistimings, as he hurries toward the destruction of his club and his own death.

If Cosmo were asked what his "style" consisted in, there is no doubt that he would reply it was the Crazy Horse West itself. We are made aware of all the things the Crazy Horse West is to him in the scene that immediately follows the payoff with Marty. When Cosmo goes off to "celebrate" in the nearest corner bar, it is a doubly revealing scene. In the first place we see how radically alone and bereft of normal human ties and supports he is. At this moment of all moments, he has no one to celebrate with, no family to tell the news to, and no friends beyond the employees of his own club (who are all at work on the Sunday evening shift) who even care about him. He tells the cabbie who drives him to the bar and who comes briefly inside with him, whom he has met only half an hour before, as much about his life as we will ever learn. It is an almost total emotional and personal desolation, and Cosmo's predicament might be merely pathetic if it were not for the other point of the scene: that Cosmo is not really homeless and lost as long as he has his club. The bar that he has wandered into is a model of all that the Crazy Horse West would be if it lacked him: dreary, dingy, dull, and devoid of imagination. The woman barkeep wears a dirty smock; the drink she hands him is dripping wet; and the jukebox is the only entertainment.

But it is important to an understanding of the full complexity of Cosmo's situation to recognize how marginal is his reign even in his own home and castle, the Crazy Horse West. For seven years he has had to make illegal payments to hold onto it, and even as they have accepted his cash, the Mob have never taken their eyes off his "valuable spot." If his club is an extension of his own marginal, ragtag, im- provised existence, it takes every drop of his life's blood to keep it going. The sad, touching joke that runs through the film is that every time the Mob take Cosmo away from his club, if only for an hour, to harass, to threaten, and, finally, to kill him, the place starts to fall apart.

Even now, in the first few minutes of the film, and before the real pressures have started to mount, Cosmo no sooner pays off the last of his debt to the Mob, spends an hour "celebrating," and returns to the Crazy Horse, than he finds the bartender out of uniform, the boy who parks the cars gone, and the waitresses who are supposed to be on duty downstairs, goofing off upstairs in the strippers' dressing room. Cosmo is forced to be an improvisor long before the Mob starts putting pres- sure on him. As he returns to the club and begins to sort out the muddle, we feel the precariousness of all that he has built at the Crazy Horse West. Cosmo clears the piano player and the waitresses out of the girls' dressing room, and Cassavetes' camera speaks volumes about the mess, clutter, and improvisatory imperatives of his world.

He sits down, makes some small talk and tries to tell a funny story to Teddy (Mr. Sophistication) and the girls as they get ready for the evening show. But Cassavetes' framing and soundtrack communicate how tenuous the reign of this club owner, impresario, artistic director, and choreographer is even over his own employees. They ignore him, interrupt him, and keep up their own competing stream of conversation, which prevents him from telling his story. One girl even makes him stand up and move out of Cassavetes' fixed frame so that she can retrieve her costume from the chair behind him. Cassavetes deliberately breaks every rule of compositional focus in the photography and framing of the scene, to the point of having Sherry, the most voluptuous of the strippers, mirrored just behind and to one side of Cosmo the whole time he is on camera. All the time he is telling his pointless and banal anecdotes, she is adjusting her scanty costume over her bare breasts so that even the best intentioned of viewers may find it hard to give Cosmo and his words full attention. The visual and verbal distractions, the unfocused framing, the confusingly mirrored background, and the clutter of this scene and the dressing room in which it takes place are the point of it. Cassavetes has moved us into a world where even a character's capacity to hold attention on himself, to organize a visual or verbal space around himself, to make a scene (even a scene as simple and prosaic as the telling of a funny story) has been called into question.

It is an investigation of the difficulty of scene making that Cassavetes could have learned from any number of Capra's films, films such as *Mr. Deeds Goes to Town, Mr. Smith Goes to Washington*, or *Meet John Doe*, which raise explicit questions about what it is to be the star of a scene. Not accidentally, *Deeds, Smith*, and *Doe* are all about weak or reluctant stars (like Cosmo), stars who cannot seem to fill the dramatic space allowed them. And Capra's camera in all three films seems to find every excuse possible to pan or cut away from his central figures to the audiences watching them and reacting to them, or behind the scenes to the manipulators using them or scheming against them. What does it mean to be a star if one cannot dominate the space of the frame at a dramatic moment in one's own movie? What does it mean to be a star if the context of one's words and actions is more interesting than the text? What, above all, does it mean to be a star in a democracy, in both a cinematic and social world where all men are supposedly created equal?

There is an interestingly similar moment to this one in *Too Late Blues*. Instead of Cosmo in his girls' dressing room, we see Ghost Wakefield in his own dressing room at a moment of crisis in the film. He makes a dramatic speech to his manager, but rather than shooting the con-

ventional and expected close-up of Ghost, Cassavetes chooses to photograph his manager, a visiting starlet, Ghost's sponsor (the Countess),
and Ghost all together in one long-shot, with Ghost himself the smallest and most distant figure in the frame, holding forth in the background of the shot. Ghost makes his dramatic speech, but the point is
that he cannot make his presence felt more powerfully to the people in
the dressing room with him than he can to a viewer in the theatre
audience. But the difference between Ghost and Cosmo is that this
condition of dramatic and cinematic powerlessness is a temporary one
in Ghost's life. The compositional and acoustic clutter in this particular
scene in *Too Late Blues* comunicates a momentary social, psychological,
and dramatic aberration that will be addressed and corrected in the
course of the film. Ghost's task will be to learn how to be a true star and
how to organize a dramatic space. But for Cosmo this muddle is the
condition of all existence, one of the dramatic facts of life that he lives
with in *The Killing of a Chinese Bookie*.

For all the democratic evenhandedness of Cassavetes' framing and
editing in *A Woman Under the Influence*, Mabel was at least guaranteed
the capacity to make a "scene" out of the depths of her despair, however much pain it cost her, or resistance it met with from those around
her. She could at least count on the attention, however insensitive or
uncomprehending, of her family as an audience to her performance.
But in this alternately threatening and indifferent *film noir* environment
Cosmo cannot take for granted even the attention of an audience. He
is all too close for comfort to his own buffoonish, effete, and emascu-
lated master of ceremonies, Mr. Sophistication, whose own stage
"scenes" with his girls invariably degenerate into confusion, nonse-
quiturs, pointless banter with his intended audience, and hurt feelings
for himself.

The mortifying similarity between the well-meaning, but hopelessly
clumsy, creator in the wings and the character who is his dramatic
double on stage is too obvious and painful to be lost on Cosmo (short
for Mr. Cosmopolitan?). Mr. Sophistication is a fun-house–mirror
mockery of everything Cosmo aspires to be, but a mockery all too
touchingly, heart-rendingly close to Cosmo's reality. Cosmo costumes
himself in a tuxedo (with a clip-on bow tie!) for his meetings with Mafia
heavies; Mr. Sophistication dresses up for big performances in his
tuxedo T-shirt. Cosmo fights for his life against the mob in a scene that
could be out of a Hollywood western, while Mr. Sophistication fights
for his life on stage in a skit called "The Gunfight at the O.K. Corral."

Embarrassment and confusion about what is in the script and what is not, and an inability to improvise a free performance in the margin
—*Cosmo's double, Mr. Sophistication, and his girls*

Uttering platitudes that are intended to pass for philosophies of life and ad-libbed gaucheries that are supposed to be witty, both Cosmo and Mr. Sophistication are in the same affecting way fundamentally unable to get their respective acts together sexually, socially, or theatrically. It is ironically fitting that, with everything else conspiring against him, Cosmo's own artistic creation should backfire on him and become a running parody of his own dreams of sophistication, style, and masculine self-sufficiency. It is an irony all the more excruciating in that it is apparent not only to the viewer of the film, but to Cosmo himself, acutely aware that he is in over his head trying to make it so far from home.

Cosmo is not, however, the only creator in a potentially embarrassed and chagrined relation to his creation. The similarities between John Cassavetes, the creator of the film, and Cosmo Vitelli, his creation, are as striking as those between Cosmo and Mr. Sophistication. Both are former New York boys struggling as independent artists and entrepreneurs to hack a path through the artistic and financial jungle of L.A. Both, with more or less dubious results, are managers of theatrical repertory companies. Both are up against bureaucratic forces and commercial systems that make any success problematic and marginal at best. And both keep plugging away in defiance of all reasonable odds. A little inside joke for the knowledgeable filmgoer points up Cassavetes' explicit identification with Cosmo: the casting of Al Ruban as the character Marty Reitz, Cosmo's financial backer, the gangster who holds the mortgage on Cosmo's club, and the one to whom he makes the final payment at the start of the film. Ruban is, not coincidentally, Cassavetes' own long-time money man—a financial backer for his film projects, the producer of the movie we are watching, and a man to whom Cassavetes has been mortgaged financially and spiritually for even longer than Cosmo has been to Marty. But before one further equates Cassavetes with Cosmo, one needs to consider how this ruefully disarming artistic self-portrait is something of which Cosmo would never have been capable. Cassavetes' witty, self-deprecating capacity to see himself in this small businessman, his willingness to expose himself to artistic view in this way, in this lovingly ironic and wry portrait of a shabby, struggling independent artist so very similar to himself, is finally proof not of his similarity to Cosmo, but of their vitally important difference. Cosmo's Mr. Sophistication is a different kind of creation, and one that suggests a much less favorable judgment of its creator's capacities of self-reflection.

But Cosmo is in a much more painful and difficult position than even his foppish and confused master of ceremonies. The audience he performs in front of is much tougher and less forgiving than that which Teddy and the girls face, and the pressures on Cosmo much more than artistic. He is no sooner free from his seven-year indenture to the Mob, than he goes out for an evening of pleasure with three of his girls at a Mob-run casino and loses $23,000 in one night of gambling. The gangsters he must deal with would regard a movie such as *The Godfather* as a sentimental period piece. For all of its bloodthirstiness, Coppola's Mafia functions with the codes of honor and personal loyalty of an extended Italian family. But in this world, the family has fallen apart even for the Mafia. Cassavetes brings the Mob into the decade of computerized record keeping, boardroom politics, and tax deductible dinners for out-of-town guests. The mobsters who call Cosmo into a back office at the casino and require him to sign a "Form 223" and a "Form 17" perform less with the gusto of blood brothers, than the mechanical efficiency and impersonality of the Small Business Loan Department at Chase Manhattan or a cold-blooded group of venture capitalists assessing an investment opportunity. Displays of emotion or personality would only get in the way of their work. (In a harrowing scene cut from the first print of the film, but restored to the second, we see a doctor and his wife getting worked over before Cosmo arrives. What makes the scene most frightening is that the mobsters are utterly uninterested in the doctor's paying them money in order to square his debt. They are interested in the "files" on his presumably illustrious patients. They realize that money is only the loose baggage of power. These gangsters deal not in dollars but in bureaucratic power, symbols, and forms of control, like the CIA or the corporate conglomerates their operations so much resemble.)

But the pressures on Cosmo, the small businessman, are not merely from the outside. After the fiasco in the casino, as he is taking his girls back home, and even before he has had a chance to gather himself together after the working over the Mob have given him, one of his girls starts to put pressure on him about whether she should begin looking for a new job (since he has apparently been wiped out and, as she is at pains to remind him, she is "two inches under the height limit"). The absurdity and near comedy of having to deal with a problem as trivial as this at a time like this is the essence of Cosmo's predicament (and an epitome of Cassavetes' studiously evenhanded attention to all of the pressures around him).

The Killing of a Chinese Bookie is an exploration of the possibilities of performance in such a relentlessly demanding world. In a larger sense, it is an examination of the possibilities of retaining a personal style and being able to make a scene when thirties, forties, and fifties conventions about how to make scenes are no longer available. It is an exploration Cassavetes has been conducting in one way or another in all of his work, but Cosmo is deprived of dramatic resources, impoverished and isolated, threatened and endangered in ways that Seymour, Minnie, and Mabel never are. And yet out of this imperiled condition, out of this poverty of resources and conflict of alliances, emerges Cosmo's marginal but undeniable success, thrown back on his own private, personal resources against all adversity. His achievement is little more than his ability to hold on to a shred of personality and individuality in the midst of all these assaults and pressures. Cosmo is never for a minute of the film free to write or direct his own performance (as he writes and directs the shows his girls put on), but in the course of the film he learns to live with the alien pacings, rhythms, and styles that are thrust upon him and to make something of them.

In exchange for his debt, the Mob forces him to murder "an obscure Chinese bookie." But it is a setup. The Mob intends Cosmo (who has not held a gun since he did duty in Korea) to be killed in the attempt (since then his club reverts to them), and the "Chinese Bookie" (of the title of the film and the instructions they give to Cosmo) is not really a Chinese bookie at all, but "the heaviest man on the West Coast" (as one of the gangsters explains to Cosmo after the deed has been done). He is the Los Angeles equivalent of the Godfather, protected around the clock by armed bodyguards. Cosmo, the small businessman who wants nothing but to be left alone, is tangled in the bureaucracy of the Mob. This self-reliant, self-sufficient entrepreneur with the nineteenth-century values of Andrew or Dale Carnegie is thrust into the bureaucratic realities of twentieth-century corporate America.

At first he refuses to do the killing, but in the middle of a show at his club one evening, he is suddenly called out onto the street, beaten up in an alley (to indicate that his financial backers are in no mood for stylish games), and wedged into the front seat of a car between four gangsters. They give him a gun, a hot-wired car, and five minutes of the most disorientingly detailed directions on how to do the murder. It is a scene that would be comic if it were not so absurdly pathetic and frightening. In one long take looking into the darkened car at the stunned figure of Cosmo surrounded by these heavies, Cassavetes shows the gangsters giving him a bewildering crash course in Mob assassination that covers everything from how to release the safety on the gun they force into his hands and how to drive to the Chinaman's house to how to get around his watchdogs with a dozen hamburgers with "no ketchup, no relish, no onions."

Improvisation becomes an imperative of survival in Cosmo's comic, pathetic struggle to keep alive, keep moving, and keep his club going for the next hour of the film. The car he is given no sooner gets going down the freeway than he has a blowout, which of course he cannot repair since he doesn't have a key to the ignition, let alone the trunk. (Nor would a friendly state trooper's help be especially desirable.) Cosmo ends up taking a series of cabs to the scene of the murder. Never has the hallmark of *film noir*, grace under pressure, been more brilliantly and weirdly demonstrated. At one point while waiting for a cab to arrive, he even has the presence of mind to call back to his club from a pay phone to check on how the show is going (having left that evening under rather unusual and unexpected circumstances). The scene that follows, in which Gazzara ends up singing, "I Can't Give You Anything But Love, Baby"—the theme song repeated throughout the film—to a bartender at the club in order to try to identify which act is then on stage, is as incongruously comic as anything Cassavetes has ever done. And what makes it both bizarre and comic is that at a time like this—in a phone booth under the neon glare of a deserted gas station off the freeway, on his way to the scene of a murder he doesn't want to, but will have to, commit—Cosmo succeeds in making a coherent, recognizable, poised, controlled "scene" at all. (A scene funnier and more touching than anything his comedian Teddy does on stage in the whole course of the film.) As the world goes to pieces, maybe a Bob Newhart monologue is the only adequate and appropriate response.

Cosmo has to improvise another comic routine only a few minutes later when he goes into a bar to get the dozen hamburgers to take with him. Of course, the waitress insists on wrapping them individually and Cosmo has to make up an absurd story about how he wants them just thrown together in a bag because his "wife hates waste. She can't stand garbage." As he then has to stand listening to the stories the waitress and bartender tell about *their* spouses, we are reminded of just how radically alone Cosmo is, how far he is from having a home and a wife, even one who hates garbage.

Cosmo may be unable to stage a scene in the girls' dressing room, or to choreograph an elegant one on the stage of his club (and the shows there are as sleazy and tasteless as can possibly be imagined), but before *The Killing of a Chinese Bookie* is over, he has choreographed the final hours of his life and staged the scene of his death with an awkward aplomb and composure that makes the professional gangsters and killers massed around him, stalking and watching his every move, look like rank amateurs. Silence, exile, and cunning are his only resources, but Cosmo is never more masterful than in his final showdown with the Mob in a deserted warehouse where they have brought him to bump him off. When Cosmo gets away from the gangsters and hides, Mickey, a professional killer, comes gunning for him, crouching down with both guns blazing like something out of *Gunfight at the O.K. Corral*. But what Mickey does not reckon with is that Cosmo is an old hand at theatrical choreography. He will not allow himself to be typecast in Mickey's scenario of a shoot-out. Never one to rely on someone else's artistic conventions, Cosmo improvises his own script and dramatic blocking. He breaks the first rule of gangland combat by declining combat altogether, and simply remaining perfectly still in a dark corner until Mickey has used up all of his big lines and heavy ammunition. It is not surprising that this stage manager understands the uses of light and shadow, the possibilities of dramatic change of pace, and the limits of artistic conventions better than the thugs around him. In fact, Cosmo, the duke of dark corners and glaring spotlights, never seems more comfortable and less worried than when he is performing under the lights, on stage or off. Negotiating the intersections of blinding light and velvety darkness in the warehouse, walking up the center of the Chinaman's stage-lighted driveway, phoning from under the glaring neon of the service station, or moving across the back of the stage at the Crazy Horse West, Cosmo maintains a glacial imperturbability in a sea of noise and confusion. Situated halfway between Mr. Sophistication, the parody of his dreams, and the Chinese Godfather, the apotheosis of his dreams, Cosmo outdoes the first in poise under pressure and the second in inscrutable self-possession. (The stoical subtlety of Gazzara's face and the slightly mysterious oriental cast of his features have never been used before in film with such dramatic effect to suggest so many depths beyond depths of self-control, self-composure, and self-sufficiency.)

It is his gunfight (or his avoidance of it) in the warehouse that is his masterpiece of timing, choreography, and lighting, and not "The Gunfight at the O.K. Corral" he mounts on his stage. It is his evening in Los Angeles—shuttling between the house of Rachel and Betty, his lovers, his club, the Chinaman's, and the deserted warehouse, without missing a beat—that counts finally as his most daring voyage of the imagination, and not his "An Evening in Paris." Like Mabel Longhetti at the center of the storm of relationships that is her family, or like the title character in Barbara Loden's *Wanda* (a film that has striking similarities with the overall pacing, plotting, and development of Cassavetes' film), Cosmo manages to display an eccentric, off-beat, off-center, nonverbal poise precisely at the dramatic moments other characters would go to pieces.

Cosmo Vitelli lives up to the Latin and Greek resonances of his name—"beautiful, orderly, deftly moving life force"—as his timings get sharper and sharper the more pressures he finds himself under. His capacities for beautifully flexible, lithely responsive movement are never more thrillingly demonstrated than in his flight from the scene of the murder he is forced to commit. In one of the very few strict "action" sequences of his work, Cassavetes uses a masterly matched series of eleven rapidly dovetailed shot–reverse shots to communicate how

Weaving an eccentric course between the mob's and his own
interpretation of how he should play his part
—*Cosmo signing away his club and part of himself to the mob*

finely tuned the timings in Cosmo's life have become. Cassavetes'
editing is exhilarating in its finesse as he shows Cosmo running for a
bus, changing to a cab, and hopping into a second cab in a series of
split-second movements and counter-movements from one vehicle to
another. The sequence is a beautiful summary of the mastery over
space and time that Cosmo achieves in the second half of the film.
Faced with the inhuman pressures and the mechanical rush of the
events in which he becomes enmeshed, he converts these very pressures into opportunities for cool, calm performance. Like an ideal film
director, he turns the chaos and the confinements of sets, personalities,
and schedules into creations, not by denying or repressing their energies, but by converting them into occasions for disciplined action.
Cosmo converts the insane pressures placed on him and the cramped,
poorly lighted "sets" within which he must perform into opportunities
for achievement; he translates the potentially brutalizing rush of show
time into the comfortable rhythms of a humane, human performance.

Cosmo's most exciting performances are significantly not social or
verbal, as were those of Cassavetes' earlier characters, but spatial and
temporal, as a process of learning how to move alone in the real space

and time of a city and through the corridors of his club. But even in the earlier, more social films a character's capacities of movement in space and time functioned as visual metaphors for his social powers of performance. In this sense Cosmo is the culmination of a long line of Cassavetes' heroes, who, since *Faces*, have been exploring the possibilities of physical, temporal, and psychological movement. A character's relation to real physical spaces and his capacities of moving within them are central to the experience of these films. The enormous and insatiable imaginative appetites of the characters are almost always directly expressed in terms of their appetites for movement and mastery over space and time. A character's imaginative and performative mobility (or lack of it) invariably shows up in his capacity for meaningful physical mobility (or lack of it).

Cassavetes' films are a little like works of dance in the ways they express themselves through forms of movement. It is expressively significant that the characters in *Faces* and *Husbands* in their desires for escape and freedom, keep shuttling frantically from one space to another, only repeatedly to discover that what they thought would be a freer, larger space for performance is, in fact, a space at least as emotionally and socially confining as that from which they originally fled. *Husbands* is virtually an extended essay on the capacity (or incapacity) of individuals to move gracefully within, and therefore to humanize, various sizes and sorts of institutional spaces, from gyms to grand hotels. It is not an accident that the opening scenes of *Minnie and Moskowitz* give us a Seymour lithely and deftly negotiating the sinuous ramps of parking garages and moving easily from place to place across busy city intersections and crowded sidewalks; or that the contrasting scenes introducing Minnie show her enclosed and sedentary, confined within the spaces of a bus, a movie theatre, and Florence's and her own apartments. The plot of the film, in large part, amounts to Minnie's exploring the possibilities of Seymour-like movement, while Seymour simultaneously is forced to entertain the possible values of sedate domesticity. The "green world" coda of the film may be understood in these terms as Cassavetes' attempt to reconcile the two alternatives: to find a space in which Minnie and Seymour can sit still, and yet not be confined or have space close in around them as it repeatedly does in the earlier scenes in the bars and restaurants in which they are each unable to sit still for any amount of time.

Cassavetes' characters have an appetite for movement in space and time more like the passionately energetic figures of modern dance created by Taylor, Balanchine, Tharp, and Joffrey than those of most other movie directors. Their energy, speed, and capacity to fill up and control space and time are direct indexes of their imaginative capacities of performance. In the later films, as the social traps and threats to personal freedom become more pervasive, a character's capacities of sheer movement become increasingly important (even, as I will argue in my discussion of *Gloria*, as the value of movement as an end in itself becomes increasingly problematic).

But it is obvious that much has changed between the earlier films and *The Killing of a Chinese Bookie*. In his ability to articulate his own unorthodox "style" of action and movement, his "class," his talents as an artistic improvisor and *bricoleur*, his redemption of time, mess, and pressure, and his ability to make the alien sets and pacings within which he is forced to move his own, Cosmo resembles Seymour. And yet there is a radical difference in the situations of the two characters. There is something disturbing, even horrifying, about Cosmo's capacities of unending movement and consummate performance. For all the success of Cosmo's self-defense, it becomes increasingly indistinguishable from self-annihilation. *The Killing of a Chinese Bookie* and the films following it raise the same questions about Emersonian self-reliance that the late novels of Henry James do: when does self-reliance become self-renunciation? When does self-sufficiency become alienation? When does radical independence become radical loneliness? When does the strategy of performing one's self into being become the ultimate strategy of self-withdrawal? When does consummate self-presentation become a form of self-dissipation and self-erasure?

Cosmo becomes so good at playing parts and improvising roles that it becomes increasingly difficult to tell where he is—or if there is a Cosmo—under the stoic mask and the poised performance. He masterfully plays husband, boss, son, father, or lover as he shuttles between his three homes and families. But there is a vacuum at the center of each role. In none of the "homes" or roles can he simply be himself at home; which is why this genial mixer, club owner, and master of all ceremonies is paradoxically the most profoundly isolated and horrifyingly lonely of all of Cassavetes' characters.

Cassavetes offers a disturbing reversal of the exuberant celebrations of the power of performance and the fascination with role-playing in his earliest films (just as James's late novels question the optimistic exuberances of performance in his earliest work). As Cosmo gradually works himself free of influences and pressures, he becomes progressively less visible to those around him. Instead of expressing it, performance becomes a means of concealing or erasing the self. As Cosmo becomes an increasingly voluble, confident, and consummate actor, he becomes increasingly illegible, inscrutable, and unreachable. How are we to square his final peroration to his performers, in which he tells them he believes, above all, in always "being comfortable," with the bullet in his side that makes him wince while he talks? How are we to understand his final speech to the audience at his club? He gets up on stage and speaks to them directly, for the first time in the film apparently presenting himself to them in full view, not hiding behind his creations, not ventriloquizing through his characters. But it is a sham and a lie. His promiscuous visibility is only his final strategy of concealment. His lively buoyancy is only a way of hiding the fact that he has only minutes to live. Above all, how are we to understand his final visit to Betty and Rachel, the only individuals in his life who really care about him personally and offer him unconditional love? He is dying, and they know it. We might expect that he would speak personally to them at least, but the dramatic pull of focus that Cassavetes uses to announce Cosmo's "entrance" into their house, and his carnation-boutonniered "costume" tell us how completely theatrical his visit is. Cosmo, the man who has staged his life with rented chauffeurs, limousines, tuxedos, girls, and leftover bottles of Dom Pérignon, is staging his death. It is all theater, where "style" and "class" masquerade as reality, and where Cosmo, the stoic *film noir* hero, is also the ultimate *film noir* con man. As even the idealist Emerson came to realize by the time he wrote his late essay "Fate," "there is something that cannot be talked or voted away," and the sad recognition of *The Killing of a Chinese Bookie* is that no degree of "style" or "class" can alter or delay Cosmo's appointments with the unarrangeable realities of his life and his oncoming death.

There are similarities between *The Killing of a Chinese Bookie* and both Ken Hughes' *The Small World of Sammy Lee* and Arthur Penn's *Mickey One*, but one might note in passing Gazzara's role and much of the essential dramatic situation evolved out of Cassavetes' work with Peter Falk on Elaine May's *Mikey and Nicky* two years earlier. *Mikey and Nicky* is another of those neglected small masterpieces of American filmmaking and is the record of Cassavetes' most important acting performance in a production other than his own to date. It would be worth extended discussion if there were space for it here, but suffice it to say that it is another *doppelgänger* film in which an expressive theatrical character is doubled with an inexpressive, undemonstrative one and all reality is thereby made ghostly. (Just as Mr. Sophistication's act on stage and its similarity to what Cosmo is doing in life off stage strangely and misleadingly make what Cosmo is doing seem like a form of theater too.) Furthermore, *Mikey and Nicky*, like *The Killing of a Chinese Bookie*, is a film in which the protagonists use their considerable powers of performance not as vehicles, however imperfect, of self-exploration and tentative self-expression (as, for example, Mabel did), but as strategies of self-concealment and self-protection. Such characters deliberately cultivate the fatal illusion that the world can be transformed into a stage, that life can become a mere matter of donning a series of masks and costumes, of playing a succession of parts and scenes that can protect one from the potential pain of true emotional exposure and shelter one from the difficulties of authentic personal contact.

Cosmo's farewell to Betty and Rachel is made particularly poignant by Cassavetes' decision to show us Rachel at home with her mother in a run-down, seedy apartment, entirely off stage and out of costume for the first time in the film. We see her coming out of the shower naked, upset and anxious about Cosmo's well-being, and her body and face look younger, more frail and vulnerable than they ever have on stage. For the first time, we see that she has been wearing a wig in all of the previous scenes as well, something we never even imagined. We don't recognize her or her manner until it suddenly dawns on us that the apparent stripping of her clothes and baring of her body on stage has all along only been a form of covering herself up and hiding herself (as she is revealed here) from view. Like Cosmo's calculated morale-building "confidences" and "confessions" to his girls in their dressing room, and his "personal" appearances on the stage of his club in front of his audience, a "strip show" is only another, even more consummate, act of concealment. In this film about acting, stripping is not an act of revelation, but an "act" in the other sense of the word, an act of withdrawal into conspicuous invisibility.

We have only once before in the film been allowed to follow one of Cosmo's girls off the stage, out of the dressing room, and back into her home like this, in an earlier scene with an effect similar to this one. In the scene in which Cosmo takes three of his girls out to celebrate the paying off of his Mob license early in the film, he walks into Sherry's house to pick her up, and inadvertently (and typically clumsily) barges in on her in her bedroom while she is still putting on her gown. Sherry, who bares her breasts over and over again every night on Cosmo's stage, and whom we see nonchalantly getting dressed in front of Cosmo in the dressing room at the beginning of the film, is upset and embarrassed because Cosmo has seen her partially undressed. She acts not like a "professional stripper" (whatever that is), but like a teenager getting picked up for a big date, and we suddenly realize that that is what she is too in a film that so strenuously refuses to simplify complex human identities into the unlifelike forms of mere movie characters.

The effect is similar in the scene with Rachel. We realize that we have not seen this personal side of her until this moment. The shabbiness and drabness of the room in which she and her mother live, as well as the anxious solicitousness of her voice (her worried tones so different from the aplomb she shows on stage) as she asks her mother to stay off the telephone so that Cosmo can get through to them if he has to, suddenly, touchingly make us aware of how much everything we have seen up until then was only illusion, stagecraft, and "style."

What occurs at Betty's is not any final disclosure, but only the most polished stage farewell Cosmo can pull off. He makes his dramatic entrance in tuxedo and carnation, tanned, handsome, and still poised (with a bullet in him). He talks to Betty and Rachel with the same stock set of jokesy bromides he uses to get through his other stage performances in the film. It is not accidental that the cluttered walls of Betty's kitchen, where she and Cosmo have their final conversation, remind us of the cluttered walls of the dressing room where we first saw Cosmo talking to his girls, or that the high-key lighting is equally stagey. There is no off-stage space left, no merely personal physical or psychological space remaining in Cosmo's life. Betty's home is only a slightly more cramped stage for a performance in front of a slightly smaller audience than usual. There is no free space left for mere "life" or "feeling."

Cosmo lets slip his stoical, sphinxlike mask for the briefest explosion of anger and the one other reference to his personal life and family background in the film (other than the moment with the taxi driver earlier). It is a momentary loss of control and composure that necessarily reminds us of the scene with Marty that began the film, and that in effect began all of Cosmo's problems. But it lasts only a few seconds, and Cosmo quickly regains his poise, a poise behind which he will strut toward his death.

He has mortgaged everything, finally even his life. Cosmo is both the master and the master parodist of *film noir*, of the rhythms of flight and pursuit, and of stylish behavior. He is an American master performer and master parodist, but the one role he seems unable (or unwilling) to master is any that would require him to call his self-reliant mastery of all possible styles and roles into question, any role that would ask him to make himself vulnerable to a particular human being in a form of intimacy that cannot be stylistically controlled or staged. All of life has become a matter of styles and surfaces. Cosmo is the perfect post-modern personality, and in a sense (though Cassavetes undoubtedly would not have intended it) *The Killing of a Chinese Bookie* is Cassavetes' deconstruction of deconstructionism. It is his analysis of the insufficiency of a merely stylistic understanding of expression. The Derridean view of art as all a matter of surfaces is not all that different from the Los Angeles view of life as all a matter of "style" and "form." Cosmo is the Derridean hero. He has decentered his entire life and cut all roots that might impede free movement (roots to his Lower East Side ethnic upbringing, to his family and friends, to permanent human commitments). He is the ideal self-made American entrepreneur and opportunist, skating on the infinitely thin ice of the Los Angeles scene, safe from breaking through the surface as long as he can keep himself perfectly unencumbered and perpetually on the move.

Cosmo plays all the roles of family man, but nowhere is he willing to dare to put them together into a real biological family, or to let himself become vulnerable to the appeals of Rachel and Betty that he do so. To commit himself to a family in this sense, and not just to a series of familial roles, would, of course, be to sacrifice his absolute self-control, his coolness under pressure, and his perfect mobility and freedom. But it would also be to come into possession of an authentic self for the first time.

Cosmo stages four separate and successive exits in the four final confrontations of the film—in the warehouse, at Rachel's and Betty's, upstairs in the dressing room at the Crazy Horse West, and on the stage under the lights. Or perhaps it is only one exit rehearsed and polished in front of four successively larger audiences. He takes charge; he manages the scenes like a pro; he pays his final farewells, forgetting no one—no one but himself, that is. The paradox of Cosmo's mastery is that it is also an abdication.

But there is one final exit after those four, and since there is no audience present to see it (except the audience in the movie theatre), we get a glimpse of the Cosmo that Cosmo would not show to an audience. In his final exit from the film itself, standing alone out in front of his club, as he looks down at the pocket full of his own blood and the blood stain on the side of his dapper blazer, Cosmo frowns. It is something he would never do if there were anyone there to see him. (One wonders why he frowns: is it because he has ruined a classy jacket; because blood is messy and hard to get out at the dry cleaners; because he realizes that someone in the club's audience might have seen it and noticed that his grooming tonight was less than impeccable? Or is it because he is dying? The first three explanations seem strangely equivalent to the fourth.) He looks down at his wound and at himself with a sideward glance as if he had up to this point even managed to separate himself from his own body, and only now remembers that he has one, and that a body is something one cannot control stylistically. A self-sufficient, self-made man living out the American dream of success and comfort, he has done everything to put all of life in order, masterfully arranged his personal relations and business affairs, paid all his final farewells. By giving up everything, even himself, he has sought to be free at last of all the messy emotional and biological confusions, compromises, and pressures that impinge on him. But the mess won't go away.

CHAPTER IX

BUREAUCRACIES
OF THE IMAGINATION
Opening Night

You have to fight sophistication. Sophistication comes to anybody [who] has been doing [his] job for a while. You have to fight knowing, because once you know something, it's hard to be open and creative; it's a form of passivity—something to guard against.   *John Cassavetes*

Organization tyrann[izes] over character. . . . Every spirit makes its house, but afterwards the house confines the spirit.
Ralph Waldo Emerson

It would be hard to conceive of films less star-struck than *Shadows* or *Faces*. The essence of those films is their egalitarian aesthetic of democratic interaction, which is at the furthest remove from the star-system scene making of traditional Hollywood films. Cassavetes' earliest work reminds the individual performer that he is a member of a group no one can dominate or control. The individual is required to negotiate the entanglements of group life and pass his private, personal dreams through the force fields of friends, family, and society. That is what makes it all the stranger and more significant that—for all their continuing willingness to lavish time and space on the performances of minor characters in a spirit of democratic respect for each of the figures in the world of the film—Cassavetes' films should increasingly, starting with *Minnie and Moskowitz* and *A Woman Under the Influence*, become star vehicles focusing on the consciousness and performative power of one more and more isolated and alienated figure.

It goes without saying that in these later films Cassavetes is not simply attempting to play to an audience that buys tickets on the basis of star appeal. Mabel Longhetti, Cosmo Vitelli, Myrtle Gordon (of *Opening Night*), and Gloria Swenson (of *Gloria*) play starring roles in their respective films, and the actors who play them are stars as no previous figures in Cassavetes' films were, but they are not merely a regression to the old-fashioned Hollywood sense of stardom. They are stars in situations where stardom has itself become questionable and troubling. They are stars who are not fully qualified for stardom, who do not want to be stars, or to accept the responsibilities of stardom. They are reluctant stars, who would prefer to be left alone or ignored. Compare Mabel Longhetti's desperate plea to Nick:

Tell me . . . don't be afraid to hurt my feelings, tell me what you want me to be. How do you want me to be? I can be that. I can be anything. You tell me, Nicky.

with Cosmo's peroration to his girls at the end of *The Killing of a Chinese Bookie*, his design for living comfortably with a bullet in the side:

I'm only happy when I'm angry, when I'm sad, when I can play the fool, when I can be what people want me to be rather than be myself. . . . You under-stand? . . . And that takes work . . . you got to work overtime for that . . . . Doesn't matter who you are, what personality you choose. Choose a person-ality. . . . Let's go down there and we'll smile, we'll cry big glistening tears that pour onto the stage. We'll make their lives a little happier . . . so they won't have to face themselves. They can pretend to be somebody else. Come on. Be happy. Be joyous.

They are the statements of figures who cast themselves as stars of their own shows, but they are stars in a paradoxical sense. They would use their stardom to erase themselves, to disappear into the communal fantasies of the audience they perform in front of. Performance for these characters is not a way of expressing the self, but of hiding it from dangerous or threatening scrutiny. In the American tradition of con-spicuous anonymity, they have chosen to conceal themselves behind a parade of roles, voices, and disguises rather than expose the weak, vulnerable self behind it all.

But for all their strategies of self-protection, their desires for ano-nymity and invisibility, there is no getting off stage for any of these later characters. They are at one and the same time the most exposed and visible of Cassavetes' characters and the most radically alone, secretive, and private. Characters in the early films exist so entirely as members of social groups that Cassavetes simply felt no need to show them outside of those groups. But from *A Woman Under the Influence* on, characters start appearing on screen alone. It is the sort of thing that would be unremarkable in the work of another director, but it is un-precedented for Cassavetes. The loneliness has become so pervasive in *The Killing of a Chinese Bookie* that it is hard to say that Cosmo is ever other than alone in that film, no matter how large the group assembled around him. He and Myrtle Gordon in the next film are never more isolated and inscrutable than when they are in a crowd, or on stage in front of one. The very possibility of holding onto a free and independent self—a self other than the postures and disguises a star controls and manipulates on stage and off—is called into question. Is there any room left for mere persons in this world of impersonal pressures and dehumanizing influences?

Opening Night is an even more difficult, dark, and disturbing film than *The Killing of a Chinese Bookie*. And if one decides finally that it is flawed and unsatisfactory in a way the film that preceded it was not, it is at least evidence of the depths Cassavetes is unblinkingly exploring, and of his refusal to retreat from the confusing complexities of his explorations. Myrtle Gordon, both the star of the film and the star of the play that takes place within it, is a woman weaker and more vulnerable than Cosmo, and more subtly threatened by the pressures accumulated around her than Mabel. She is an aging, but still talented and respected, actress going through a crisis of confidence in her talent, her personal and professional relationships, and her capacity to give and receive love. Most of the film is ostensibly set in New Haven (actually shot in Pasadena), where the play she stars in is going through rehearsals and out-of-town tryouts prior to the New York "opening night" with which the film concludes (actually shot in Los Angeles).

Mabel has to juggle the influences of the half-dozen or so individuals who constitute her extended ethnic family. Cosmo has to balance the conflicting roles, pressures, and imperatives of three different kinds of "families." But Myrtle Gordon is in an even more demanding situation. As an unmarried, childless, loverless actress, she must negotiate professional bureaucracies, none of which offer even the minimal emotional protection and sustenance of a family. Her home is the theater, but it is a house of mirrors in which it is impossible to tell sincerity from falsehood, role-playing from reality, characterization from character, and family from work.

Complicating it all is the fact that Myrtle Gordon is a professional performer. It is not for nothing that Cassavetes' most recent work is increasingly interested in the situation of professionals. Mabel Longhetti is the first in the sequence. Mabel, of course, would, if asked, deny that she is a professional performer, as would most of her family. They would insist that her only profession is that of housewife and mother, but in fact, the whole drama of *A Woman Under the Influence* would not arise if Mabel were only a housewife and a mother. Her problem, put most starkly, is that she is an entertainer, a performer, trapped in the role of a housewife and mother. As the events of the plot make abundantly clear, Mabel's true genius is as a party giver, a joke teller, a game player, and a general purpose performer at each of the many gatherings the film depicts. Her dramatic predicament, in short, is that no one will recognize that fact. Cosmo Vitelli is a professional; Myrtle Gordon is a professional; and the star of the following film *Gloria*, Gloria Swenson, is a former showgirl and professional. A professional performer is someone who is never off stage, never not acting, someone who is at the farthest remove from the performative innocence of Hughie and Tony, Richard and Maria, or Harry and Archie. The performers in the later movies can see themselves with almost the same perceptiveness with which we and the characters in their films see them. Role-playing, acting, and performing in group situations are ways of life for them.

Myrtle Gordon is an actress who has played roles on stage in front of audiences comparable to the roles in Cassavetes' earlier films. She has studied the timings and rhythms of temper tantrums and emotional breakdowns. She has learned how to cry or collapse on cue. She has already played in the theater the part she suddenly realizes she is cast to play in her life. Moreover, everyone around her knows it. A sigh, a cry, or a wave of the hand from her can never be a merely personal gesture; it is something they have seen her mastery of on stage too often. They themselves are professionals—actors, stagehands, and rehearsal coaches—who cannot be innocent or naive about the scenes she makes.

One way to try to get through the house of mirrors in *Opening Night* would be to attempt to sort out the real from the virtual images, to try to say when Myrtle or those around her are acting and when they are not, when they are performing on stage and when off. But it would be as wrong an approach to *Opening Night* as it is to *Hamlet*, because the very point of the situation is that these performers are never off stage. There is no simpler, more innocent self underneath these various gestures, stances, and roles. These are their characters' selves. The boundary lines between the play Myrtle is in and the rest of her life are meant to be impossible to draw. There can be no parcelling of experience into theatrical and nontheatrical compartments. *Hamlet* and *Opening Night* are equally tours through haunted mansions in which it has become impossible to separate the ghostly from the actual presences.

Myrtle Gordon is an aging actress undergoing a crisis of confidence in herself playing a woman in the play *The Second Woman* who is undergoing the same crisis. (To appreciate the effect this doubling has on the basic story, consider the difference between the situations of a Maria Forst of *Faces* undergoing a crisis in the privacy of her home, and an actress undergoing a crisis like Maria's being forced to play a character like Maria's on stage in front of the rest of the cast of *Faces*. The "plots" of the two stories may be similar, but the doubling changes the nature of the drama entirely. The drama is social in the first version, and psychological and inward in the second.) The actor to whom Myrtle is linked on stage is Maurice Adams, a former lover in real life and on stage, who as Marty on stage is as cool, cynical, and distant to Myrtle as he is to her as Maurice in real life. Myrtle, the actress, secretly wonders if she should have set aside her career to have had children, a family, and a "real life" outside the theater, just as Virginia, the character she plays, secretly wonders if she should have stayed married to her first husband in the play, a man whose life is crowded with children and family connections.

But as the awkwardness of this delineation of Myrtle's "real" life as distinct from her life in the play already suggests (like the clumsiness of this use of quotation marks around "real"), it is just these sorts of discriminations that *Opening Night* makes it difficult to believe in or keep track of. (During the rehearsals, the scriptwriter, Sarah Goode, does suggest to Myrtle that she should just "read her lines and keep her personal feelings out of the play," as if an absolute separation were possible. But Myrtle's inability to follow Sarah's advice is sufficient proof of its inadequacy.) To the extent that it succeeds at all—and in many ways it fails to do this and therefore fails to be completely satisfying—what *Opening Night* does is to sufficiently complicate our awareness of both "reality" and "acting" so that the terms lose their separateness from each other. Professional, calculated role-playing and posturing, bureaucratic expediency, and psychological manipulation are aspects of these character's realities. There is no alternative pastoral self underneath all these masks, roles, and postures.

Opening Night is Cassavetes' most obviously Pirandellian film, but it is important to remember that though the performances of the central characters in *Opening Night*, *The Killing of a Chinese Bookie*, and *A Woman Under the Influence* take on a new level of complexity beyond those in the earlier films, in no sense are acting, role-playing, and performance new events in Cassavetes' work. Mabel, Cosmo, and Myrtle are the most vulnerable, threatened, confused, lonely, and deeply troubled of Cassavetes' characters, but the challenges and confusions confronting the self bringing itself into existence through performance have all along been the central dramatic events in Cassavetes' work. Myrtle and Cosmo are professional performers whose on-stage lives literalize the metaphor of performance as survival in Cassavetes' work, but the imperative of performance is at the heart of each of the earlier films as well. The characters who interest Cassavetes exist only by virtue of their performative capacities, their abilities to play with, and against, the audiences around them. For Cassavetes it is only in this process of performance that the truly interesting self is created, held in existence, dissipated, or lost.

This is not a minor point, and it suggests one of the possible reasons Cassavetes' "characters" and the "scenes" in which they engage have been so consistently misunderstood by most film reviewers of the past two decades. Roughly speaking, there have been two dominant schools of film reviewing in this country over the past twenty or thirty years.[1] Stanley Kauffmann may be taken to be the current nominal head of the realistic school, and Pauline Kael of the other, which I will call the impressionistic school, for lack of a better term. Kael's kind of criticism actually was created in explicit reaction to realistic criticism. In place of the literal-minded, factual evaluation of films according to their fidelity to historical, social, or psychological realities, the Kaelian school of criticism—following the lead of Susan Sontag and the suggestion of several early-1960s aesthetic theories—pursues "uninterpretable" shocks, thrills, and *frissons* in the experience of a film and praises the primitive, fragmentary, visionary moments within it.

It should be obvious, even from this perfunctory account, why the Kaelian school of criticism should be relatively indifferent to the values offered by Cassavetes' films. With its emphasis on the visionary, the extractable, and the thrilling, it could not be further from Cassavetes' sensibilities and sense of the possibilities of human life. But what will take more explanation is why the realistic school of criticism (which both predominates in our culture and has been much harder on Cassavetes' work, since he certainly aspires to be a realistic filmmaker, the argument runs) is equally unsuited to a proper appreciation of his films.

At its simplest, the realistic school of criticism looks for the presence of particular kinds of naturalistic ornamentation in the sets, costumes, plot, and dialogue of a film. In its more complex manifestations, it demands well-defined forms of psychological coherence and articulation in characterization, acting performances that deepen and "develop" psychologically in the course of a film, and a narrative composed of a series of discrete, progressively arranged confrontations, climaxes, and resolutions. All of which is to say that filmic "realism," and the criticism based on it, in its simple or complex manifestations, is not intrinsically any more "realistic" than any other standard of expression. "Realistic" films are as complexly coded and rule-governed as any other cinematic style of expression, and "realism" is a style of understanding like any other style.

Realistic criticism is perfectly adequate to deal with the postwar films of Wyler, Zinnemann, Lumet, Pakula, Ritt and those of other filmmakers whose assumptions about expression essentially go hand in glove with its assumptions about well-made, psychologically coherent drama, but the problem is that no set of critical or filmic assumptions is less appropriate to an adequate appreciation of Cassavetes' work. In fact, probably the most damaging confusion that pervades discussions of his work is the mistaken impression that he is a realistic director (which his *cinéma vérité* techniques have, needless to say, encouraged viewers and critics to assume). But the disruptive energies of imagination and desire and the unsystematic extravagances of performance are deliberately put at war with the apparently realistic forms of experience in his work. It is just the structures of social and psychological organization that filmic and critical realism takes for granted that Cassavetes' work is designed to disrupt and bring into question.

In place of the coherent character types, well-defined psychological motivations, and monotonic patterns of behavior and development demanded by realism, Cassavetes' films offer mercurial, oblique, and unpredictable potentialities of performance where almost nothing is determined or structured in advance of the particular opportunity of performance. Or to be more precise, one might say that Cassavetes frequently seems to begin his films with realistic character types and structures of behavior and motivation in mind, only almost immediately to depart from them by encouraging his characters (and the actors who play them) to play with, and against, such structures. The characters and actors are encouraged to move beyond simpler identities into a larger appreciation of the many roles, stances, and identities that can become possible under the pressure of imagination and desire. The sheer excessiveness, extravagance, and gratuitousness of the performances in these films communicate personal energies and intensities of feeling that cannot be expressed in less theatrical, or more realistic, ways.

Lelia may begin *Shadows* (and Lelia Goldoni may have approached the role at the beginning of her work with it) as the realistic expression of a fairly simple social and psychological type of character—the adolescent girl awakening to the power of her own sexuality—but as the film progresses she becomes something richer, stranger, and more mysteriously interesting than that. In the opening minutes of *A Women Under the Influence*, we may take Mabel Longhetti to be a standard stock modern dramatic type that extends from at least *A Doll's House* through *Mildred Pierce* and beyond—the frustrated, misunderstood housewife. But in the middle of one of her weirdly parodic performances, she makes any such simple characterization of her role entirely inadequate. If Lelia and Mabel were meant, in the "realistic" way, to be well-made characters who are presented and developed in a coherent, continuous psychological trajectory in the course of their narratives, they would be the dramatic failures many critics have charged them, and most of Cassavetes' other characters, with being. But these crude psychological typologies and narrative structures are only the pretexts for much more complex performative texts, which move the characters excitingly and energetically beyond the pigeonholes of naturalistic characterization and description and are, in fact, meant to repel such formulatable ways of knowing and responding. Indeed, to the extent that a character in one of Cassavetes' films is reducible to being a "character" in this realistic conception of the concept, he is fundamentally flawed and uninteresting to Cassavetes. The films are punctuated with brilliant cameo "character" parts. There is an unending procession of tidy, well-made, coherent, "realistic" characters marvelously rendered in Cassavetes' films—extending from Benny Flowers and Frielobe in *Too Late Blues* through Morgan Morgan and Zelmo Swift in *Minnie and Moskowitz* to the figures of the gangsters in *The Killing of a Chinese Bookie*. But these characters are significantly the lost ones in their films. They are the figures in whom Cassavetes has given up hope. The performances of Lelia, Ghost, Chet, and Mabel will never be comprehended by the realistic structures of psychology and motivation that can explain these others. Those very structures would box in the free energies of imaginative and social exploration that Lelia, Ghost, Chet, and Mabel (and the actors who play them) devote themselves to releasing. Their selves are too complexly interesting to ever be comprehended by the ordinary conception of a fixed, stable "self."

All of which is to argue that Cassavetes' films offer the viewer irreducible, bottomless complexities and indirections of performance, and not anything like naturalism or realism. While naturalistic acting and plotting is centripetal—directing attention to some central, unitary motive for behavior or focusing point for a scene—the performances Cassavetes elicits are centrifugal displays of energies too complex and powerful to be traced back to any simple psychological origin or projected ahead to a unitary goal. In place of superficial, realistic correspondences between objects and events in the film and the world, or simplistic, centripetal assumptions that life can be articulated into a series of discrete psychological intentions, origins, motives, and goals, Cassavetes presents characters and relationships that cannot be reduced beyond the centrifugalities, excesses, eccentricities, and exfoliations of performance. Thus the performative obliquity, elusiveness, and extravagance of his scenes are not to be apologized for, they are what is most valuable in his work. There is no going behind these energetic, always somewhat mysterious characters and the scenes in which they engage to descriptions of simpler selves and relationships. The social and imaginative reality Cassavetes is most interested in exploring is irreducibly stylized in these respects.

The characters in whom Cassavetes is most interested—Lelia, Hughie, Tony, Ghost, Jeannie, Chet, Gus, Seymour, Minnie, Mabel, Cosmo, Myrtle, and Gloria—have a fluidity and flexibility of identity more like actors acting than like conventionally well-defined characters reacting. Their selves and their mutual relationships are not things fixed or constituted in advance, but are made up of an inexhaustible and endlessly inventive succession of roles, postures, tones, stances, and styles. That (and not because of inadequate scripting or rehearsal) is the reason the scenes they enact so frequently look like the improvisations of actors. They remind us of actors creating and revising their characters, roles, and relationships, making and unmaking scenes as they go along, responding improvisatorily to the forces around them. Not only do they perform like actors improvising, but long before the figures of Cosmo in *The Killing of a Chinese Bookie* or Myrtle in *Opening Night*, Cassavetes' characters perform explicitly in the roles of actors. When, early in *Faces*, Richard and Freddie do some of their old college routines for Jeannie after they go to her apartment, as a way of getting through the awkwardness of introductions, and then invite her to get up and do something for them, all three are playing the roles of actors experimenting with material, trying out bits of stage business on each other, and attempting to top one another's performances in the strictly theatrical sense of the terms. The husbands of *Husbands* do the same thing. As old friends who have heard one another's routines before, they function as a well-polished improvisatory ensemble, taking turns doing "turns," letting one or another of the group generate a bit of stage business, watching and appreciating it as long as they can, and then stepping in at just the right (or wrong) moment when the first performer's energy or inspiration begins to flag, in order to continue the scene, turn the impulse in a new direction, or try to top or cap the previous performance by going it one better. It is in the competing and accumulating energy of such successive "turns" that Cassavetes' most powerful scenes develop, and not in any rising or falling curve of confrontation, crisis, and resolution.

What such sheerly performative pacings and forms of personal relationship indicate is not what hostile critics contend—that Cassavetes turns on the lights and camera and allows actors to improvise scenes as they go along—but a profound and liberating vision of one possible form of human relations and identities. Life at its most interesting, daring, and challenging (which is not to say all of life, but only the life Cassavetes is most intensely interested in exploring on film) is made up of the possibility of such free, unsystematized, unfettered, individual performances and relationships between people. Though comparisons could be made between this vision and the drama of Chekhov and Pinter, the most significant connection is with the uniquely idealistic vision of Henry James, whose figures are freed to respond to the movements of imagination and desire in a similar way.

For both James and Cassavetes, the self is interesting and worth studying precisely to the extent that it is at least momentarily capable of staging a performance of this sort, a performance that liberates itself temporarily from psychological, social, and intellectual structures of organization and understanding and launches it on a daring and imaginative adventure. But though one wants to take nothing away from James, it is interesting to notice that Cassavetes chooses as his performers figures who are in many respects in a more complex predicament than those in James's work. James deliberately chose as his ideal performers figures who were to some extent freed from certain complications of involvement with prosaic, worldly affairs. It was the idle rich leisure class, and within this group especially the figure of the young, sexually appealing woman with all the possibilities of the world before her and relatively few constraints on her choices—the marvelous heroines of his novels from *The Europeans* to *The Golden Bowl*—that most powerfully suggested such free possibilities of performance for James.

But Cassavetes not only shows none of James's imaginative bias toward the already halfway liberated, but seems, on the contrary, positively stimulated by socially and biologically encumbered lives of the sort James seemed to see few possibilities in. That is to say, Cassavetes is as excited by the performative possibilities of an over-the-hill hippie like Seymour Moskowitz, a beach bum and gigolo like Chet, and a harried, married, middle-aged housewife like Mabel, as he is by more obviously imaginatively alluring and performatively unencumbered figures like Jeannie and Lelia.

But however different the particular performers in their works may be, the origins of the performative impulse are the same for both artists. Both Cassavetes and James depart from what I have been calling realism precisely to the degree that their allegiances are to the overwhelming authority of the forces of desire and imagination and not to the authority of social and psychological structures that would limit or circumscribe the play of such energies. For both artists, the deforming, disorganizing pressures of desire and imagination are always at work gratuitously, excessively, and sometimes dangerously distorting what would in a more realistic work be the tidy, inviolate package of "character" and the clear contours of the artistically well-defined relationship. Imaginative energies break the bundle of character and erupt into scenes in the form of the stylization, the gratuitousness, and the excessiveness I have been calling performance, for lack of a better term, all the way through this book.

For both James and Cassavetes, the result of depicting characters and scenes so open to the deforming, distorting pressures of desire and imagination, and figures so fascinatingly unfinished with the ultimately unfinishable process of figuration, is a text that assertively cannot be discussed or understood in strictly realistic terms. Like the three husbands' bullying and indefensible badgering of the female singer in the bar scene in *Husbands*; like Mabel's endless, self-pleasuring (but literally pointless and often audienceless) transformations and reconstitutions of herself in *A Woman Under the Influence*; like Ghost's self-destructive and interminable displays of undirected, useless energy in *Too Late Blues*; like the clowning, mugging, and preening Lelia engages in in *Shadows*, such performances are always and by definition in excess of all merely "realistic" facts, motivations, or justification. They run on too long, they are too intense, and they invariably result in "scenes" and pain and misunderstanding by others, but that is their essence. These performances are evidences of imaginative and passional energies literally in excess of anything answerable to, or accountable in terms of, "realistic" structures of social and psychological organization. (Just as the final artistic texts of both James's and Cassavetes' works are everywhere themselves stylistically deformed in the same ways by the pressures of their own otherwise inexpressible and unappeasable imaginative impulses that can find no more "realistic" form of expression.)

But texts liberated from the repressive artistic codes of realism and so open to such stylistic distortions, and characters vulnerable to such powerful imaginative deformations, create large and significant artistic problems with which both James's and Cassavetes' work must come to grips. A world of such potential imaginative plasticity and flux, and scenes so susceptible to the deformations of desire and the pressures of imagination can be bewildering for a character to function in (as Myrtle Gordon in *Opening Night* will most plangently demonstrate). A text of this sort can be as bewildering an experience for its author and its audience as it is for its characters. Parallel to the increasing imaginative confusions the characters in these later films undergo, one senses Cassavetes' own impending and encroaching authorial confusions about the situations with which he is trying to deal. Though I have only occasionally alluded to it in my previous discussions of the films, there is an ominous and disturbing imaginative problem that surfaces from time to time in all of Cassavetes' work and that becomes increasingly troubling in the later films. It surfaces in what a flippant or unsympathetic critic might call a pop-Pirandello way at the moments when fantasy or dream states start to replace reality in the films, especially the later ones. But more generally, the problem might be described as how at key moments dreams, hallucinations, fantasies, fictions, and private imaginations seem not so much to enrich and enlarge our sense of reality, as to displace it and the rest of experience in the films. (It is an imaginative problem all the more interesting insofar as it has surfaced in so many instances in American fiction—from *The Marble Faun, The Confidence Man,* and *The Sacred Fount* to more recent works—in some of the same ways it appears in Cassavetes' films.)

Let me give three examples from three different films of this strange and upsetting aspect of Cassavetes' work (though the artificial or dreamlike endings of most of his later films might be cited generally in illustration of the phenomenon.) The first is the problematic film-within-a-film opening of *Faces*, where Richard Forst and the executives around him sit down in the opening scene to view a promotional movie and Cassavetes match-cuts from the shot of the projector light and the beginning of the film they are viewing to the credit sequence of *Faces* itself. A similar effect occurs in the final scene of *Husbands*. Cassavetes deliberately includes a "bad take" in the final print of the film in a notorious long shot in which the sound boom and mike are clearly visible across the top of the frame for the entire duration of the take. The presence of the boom was cited at the time of *Husbands'* release as evidence of Cassavetes' general *cinéma vérité* indifference to production values, or as proof of his casualness or sloppiness about filmmaking. But what that ignores is that the inclusion of this bad take was obviously one of the most uncasual and deliberately calculated moments in all of *Husbands*. It is a moment almost strictly parallel to the opening moment in *Faces*, a scene in which Cassavetes is deliberately calling attention to his film *as film*. Both are moments in which Cassavetes, as if to shake the "realistic" treatment of his films, is reminding the viewer of the assertive factitiousness and stylization of the experience in which he is participating. The third example is the bizarre and wonderful sequence early in *Minnie and Moskowitz* in which Cassavetes edits back to back what are obviously two successive takes of the same shot of Jim preparing to leave Minnie's apartment.

Now all three instances could simply be dismissed as being arty, cute, or coy, and the few critics who noticed such moments and did not simply write them off to sheer incompetence on Cassavetes' part generally took that line with them—chastising Cassavetes for the incompatibility of his *cinéma vérité* techniques and such games with the boundaries of art and reality (defined by them in the special sense used above). But, as I have been arguing, for Cassavetes this is to define both art and reality too narrowly. His work is an attempt to capture moments when art, style, or performance transform reality beyond these simpler definitions of it. The artificial endings and the factitious moments in Cassavetes' films are not meant to be hermetic, self-regarding displays of the power of art separated from reality, but the opposite. They are celebrations of the ways art and performance make reality memorable, interesting, and, at times, glorious. They exist in gratitude and acknowledgement that it is only in the excesses of performance and the artificialities of art that the dream of freedom can be momentarily liberated and expressed, and in admission and apology that it is in the impotence of art and performance that it ends. For a filmmaker for whom imagination counts for so much, these moments are humble, awed recognitions of both the power and the weakness of acts of dreaming in art and in life.

But there is also a darker side to all this. These moments represent the surfacing of a potential imaginative problem that haunts all of Cassavetes' work (just as it did the similarly idealistic work of James, Hawthorne, Emerson, and many kindred spirits). In a vision of the world that gives so much authority to desire and imagination, the world is always on the verge of being converted into a virtually Pirandellian dream-event. The actual experience of social life is always in danger of being replaced by fantasy or dream life. That is to say, the films, like the dazzling imaginative performances of the actors and characters in them, are always on the brink of transforming themselves into self-satisfying, self-contained imaginative performances that acknowledge nothing outside of their own fictional arrangements of styles and events.

The scenes I have singled out in *Faces* and *Husbands* are fortunately not typical of the films as such, but they are telling inasmuch as they momentarily verge on turning *Faces* and *Husbands* into Chinese boxes of fictions within fictions. Each seeks temporarily to suspend the film experience in a purely fictional world of its own, separate from the refractory, dream-resistant world outside the movies. In effect, each escapes from the unmanageable realities of social life into a self-contained, self-sufficient fiction within a fiction.

But Cassavetes' wrestling with the relationship between fiction and reality in his work does not always result in such unsatisfactory and unfortunate effects. The double take of Jim's farewell in *Minnie and Moskowitz*, and in fact all of that film, might be cited as evidence of how stimulating Cassavetes' experiments with the interpenetration of style and reality can be at their best. *Minnie and Moskowitz* is Cassavetes' most stylized and dreamlike film up to *Opening Night*. As I've already noted, characters in the film artificially repeat one another's lines, pick up and mimic gestures from one another's scenes, and take turns playing one another's parts. Furthermore, as the director and editor of the film, Cassavetes adds still more stylization with his own imposition of additional editorial, narrative, and photographic patternings. But *Minnie and Moskowitz* succeeds not in spite of its stylizations, but because of them. Unlike the false moments cited from *Faces* and *Husbands*, the stylizations it exposes us to are the stylizations of experience, not of the world of movie-making. The repetitions, fictionalizings, and patternings of *Minnie and Moskowitz* are those the movies and other forms of mass communication have made an unavoidable part of American life. The film takes as its subject the inescapable stylization of human relationships in the modern world.

The falsity of the two moments in *Faces* and *Husbands* is that there Cassavetes' games with art and reality momentarily insulate the experience of the film in a special world in which movies refer only to moviemaking. The success of the rest of those films and all of *Minnie and Moskowitz* is that the stylizations and artistic arrangements direct our attention outside of the artistic experience to the ways art shapes life.

Educated by the experience of these films, the viewer approaches *Opening Night* with the question of whether its stylizations, in many respects much more bewildering and pervasive than those of the earlier films, are going to be like those of the two scenes in *Faces* and *Husbands*, or like those in *Minnie and Moskowitz*. Is the play-within-a-play structure of the film going to educate a viewer to an increased awareness of the stylistic forces at work in everyday life, or is it going to be a way for Cassavetes to insulate his characters in a shadow world of dreams, delusions, and artistic arrangements of their own, and his own, making, from which no escape is imaginable or possible? To some extent *Opening Night* seems to be doing both things at once, which is one of the reasons that it is certainly Cassavetes' most maddening and frustrating film.

It puts Myrtle in a much more difficult position than that of Lelia, Gus, Archie, or Seymour. Her audiences are more tyrannical and more demanding; and since she is a professional performer who must face the pressures of rehearsals, scripts, and interaction with fellow performers on stage, there is little or no room for the eccentric expression of merely personal feelings and attitudes in her performance. That is Myrtle's problem: her effort to find or make a free social, psychological, and imaginative space within which she can stage a free, personally expressive performance. *Opening Night* is the first film in which Cassavetes incorporates explicit moments of fantasy and hallucination into the plot (though there were scenes of the same sort in the initial script of *A Woman Under the Influence*, subsequently deleted). Perhaps that is because hallucinations and daydreams are the one imaginative space that Myrtle can indisputably call her own, free from the scrutiny and encroachment of the theatrical bureaucracy around her. But it is, of course, a sad situation when nightmares and delusions are one's only imaginative escape hatch.

In her waking life it seems impossible for Myrtle to find a free space within which to stage a free performance in front of a receptive audience. That is why at key moments in the film, just when a viewer might think that he is seeing a free, unfettered expression of the self, Cas-

Trapped in roles and unable to get off stage
—*Maurice, Manny, and Myrtle*

savetes pulls the rug out from under him. It is impossible to cordon off separate spaces for scenes of "acting" on the one hand, and "sincerity" or "honesty" on the other. Even on stage, when we might expect to be able easily to tell the dancer from the dance, Myrtle, Maurice, and Gus (Virginia's first husband) improvise, interrupt, and play with the script of the play in which they are acting so much during rehearsals and performances that it is impossible to be certain at any one moment whether we are hearing "them" or their lines. During the middle of a scene in rehearsal, Myrtle turns to Maurice and speaks to him so sharply or plangently that we are sure she has left her character behind, only to have the scene continue from that point and make us suddenly realize that those particular lines were in the script of the play. At other moments, Maurice, or Manny, or another man speaks love lines to

Myrtle in the privacy of her apartment, lines that are intended to be sincere statements of passion, but they sound more wearily rehearsed and dispassionately memorized (and they probably were) than anything that takes place on stage. Cassavetes' camera and editing, likewise, are continuously working to prevent our parceling experience into easy categories of "on stage" versus "off stage" events. During rehearsal of the play, he holds his camera low and away from Myrtle up on stage until we are convinced that we are sitting in a seat in the auditorium watching her go through a well-rehearsed display of passion only to discover seconds later that she is at that very moment interrupting the play with a personal statement of her feelings about her character. At another moment he suddenly cuts to a hand-held close-up of a character's face agitated with violent emotion, only abruptly to switch perspectives and show us that we are watching a scene from the play performed in front of an audience.

Each time we try to establish a final or definitive perspective or focus on an event, Cassavetes deliberately disrupts it. The pre-credit sequence of the film establishes the style. The opening medium-shot of the film shows Myrtle chain-smoking back stage, standing beside her wardrobe mistress and a prop man, who offers her a drink. She takes a drink from his bottle and, with a cut to a shot of the stage lights and the curtain coming up, and the sound of applause swelling on the soundtrack, Cassavetes suddenly reveals that what might have been presumed to have been a relaxed and private moment, with the three figures perhaps all alone in an empty theater after a rehearsal, is actually the emotionally charged instant prior to Myrtle's initial stage entrance in front of a packed house. Cassavetes then cuts to a shot of the applauding audience from something like Myrtle's view of it on stage. But before we can comfortably reorient ourselves to this perspective, he suddenly cuts to a view of the stage from the audience's point of view.

From a seat in the audience, we would have been unable to see or even imagine the three shots that preceded it. In fact, the precise view of the stage that Cassavetes provides us with in the fourth shot is one in which we cannot even see Myrtle on stage. The scene she is playing in has already begun, and we hear her voice and the excitement of the rest of the audience at seeing her, but the back of a head in front of us blocks her from our view.

Opening Night is a film about such potentially conflicting "angles" or "perspectives" on experience, never allowing us to forget that each of them is only partial, isolated, and limited. Cassavetes has come full circle from his earlier protestations about the unimportance and insignificance of editing and camerawork. They are the opposite of invisible and self-effacing here. Cassavetes is interested in reminding us of the presence of the camera and of the editing of the film. The head that blocks our vision of the stage in that first view from the audience is not there by accident. Cassavetes is interested in our remembering the specificity and incompleteness of any particular viewpoint.

Much of *Opening Night* is deliberately assembled out of a series of wrenchingly abrupt 90 and 180 degree changes of camera position that make the focus pullings of *A Woman Under the Influence* seem gentle and humane in comparison. *A Woman Under the Influence* traces a complex network of pressures and influences around Mabel and Nick, but an ideally vigilant and sensitive observer (as Mabel sometimes is, and a member of the audience of the film may be imagined to be) could still manage to hold all the lines of influence in mind at once. Such an observer would only have to be capable of psychologically "pulling focus" and shifting his social "field of view" as subtly and continuously as Cassavetes' photography and editing does in the film. But all that changes in *Opening Night* (though *The Killing of a Chinese Bookie* went a long way in the direction of *Opening Night*). As in the opening sequence, Cassavetes' shifts of camera placement represent not the sensitively shifting and adjusted perspectives and focuses of an ideally responsive observer or participant to a scene, but a series of irreconcilably conflicting points of view from the perspectives of many different audiences or participants. The camera is not a surrogate for an ideally sensitive human eye. It is not a stand-in for a perfect, invisible observer. No human observer could occupy the different points of view of this camera or synthesize them into a single comprehensive one. That is to say, the different views do not add up or cohere as they did in the earlier films. Instead, the photography and editing becomes, as it were, an extension of the process of bureaucratic categorization and relationship that it documents. The viewer of the film is circulated through plane after plane of limited perspective. There are views from in front of the stage, from on stage, from the wings, from the back of the theater, from outside the theater, from the perspective of an actor, from the perspective of the producer, from the perspective of the audience. We are made aware of layer after layer of personal perspective, theater technology, and commerical bureaucracy as we move through a series of disorientingly different and irreconcilable positions.

Cassavetes even makes extensive use of the point-of-view shot and the shot–reverse shot techniques his previous films had generally avoided. But he does not use reverse shots merely to identify a speaker or to take up the dramatic slack in a long conversation, but genuinely to explore the two or more different points of view that make up any conversation. These camera movements (like the frequent mirror shots in the film) are used not to add "visual interest" to otherwise visually dull scenes, but to explore the psychological issues of different personal perspectives that are at the heart of them. Like the cubist fragmentations of face and torso in Picasso's work, they function to juxtapose two or more alternative ways of "reading" a scene, two or more ways of "seeing" oneself or someone else.

Just as it enlarges our awareness of possible perspectives on a scene, *Opening Night* radically expands the context of an event (as the title itself suggests with its allusion to a context that affects the course of the entire film, although not occurring until the very end of it). The context of an action or scene in *Shadows, Faces, Husbands,* and *A Woman Under the Influence* is, in almost every case, defined by, and limited to, the particular group of individuals gathered together in a room at any one moment. That is to say, the relevant context of a performance was personal and social. But *Opening Night* (like *The Killing of a Chinese Bookie*) forces its characters to recognize contexts and obligations distinctly beyond the personal interests and control of the individuals involved. There are bureaucratic networks of relation to be taken into account (such as the formal, codified professional relationships of directors, actors, writers, and producers). There are vast, impersonal deadlines and schedules that must be met (such as the fact that dominates the entire film, that while Myrtle is trying to understand her feelings, an opening night for which tickets have been sold and publicity arranged is drawing nearer day by day). There are biological and biographical contexts and realities (like Myrtle's age and the failure of her past love affairs) that will not yield to stylistic or emotional suasion. There are a host of financial, commercial, and professional considerations that sensitivity, kindness, and consideration (the cardinal virtues required of Cassavetes' earlier characters) have nothing to do with. They are not sufficient to get Myrtle through this experience; as she demonstrates, they may only get in the way of a producer's, writer's, and director's interests. There is a play to be mounted, deadlines have to be met, and financial backers and an audience perhaps indifferent to the personal crises of the play's leading lady have to be pleased.

The complexities of the different bureaucracies in which Myrtle is embedded are suggested by the first three scenes in which we see her. As already described, in the first scene we see her about to go on stage, flanked by stagehands in the wings on one side, actors performing on stage on the other, and a live audience in front of her. In the next scene we see her in an apparently private moment leaving her dressing room with her wardrobe mistress, only to open a door and instantly have to compose herself publicly again against the onslaught of a noisy crowd of autograph hunters, whose illusion is that they are now seeing her off stage and in private. Only seconds later, in the third scene, we see an entirely different Myrtle Gordon, tired and discouraged inside the protective armor of a curbside car into which she is whisked to escape the crowd and in particular one overeager young fan who paws at the steamed-up window. (This shot of the fan trying to touch Myrtle Gordon through the window cannot help but remind the viewer of the scene shot from the same angle in *Meet John Doe* in which Barbara Stanwyck does the same thing to a car Gary Cooper rides away in. These strikingly similar films both use automobiles to summarize the insulating shields erected around their central characters.) In these first three scenes, *Opening Night* immediately confronts us with the question of where the "real" Myrtle Gordon is among all these performances.

Opening Night is Cassavetes' most difficult film, but if these disorienting enlargements of context and alternations of perspective were only part of a tiresome, audience-teasing effort to make things as complicated as possible it would not be worth sitting through. Cassavetes, it goes without saying, is utterly uninterested in intellectual woolgathering on grand, abstract themes such as art versus life, illusion and reality, or the individual versus bureaucracy. On the contrary, one feels that he would have done anything in his power to simplify the camera placements and the role confusions in this film. But almost against his own desires, he found that there was no easier way to communicate the complexity and density of these characters' lives. There was no simpler way to express the individual's predicament.

Myrtle Gordon's problem is precisely her refusal to face the full complexity of the relationships in which she is involved. Her implicit plea throughout the film is that other characters recognize her as a human being in trouble, a person in need of love. Now coming from Maria Forst or Jeannie Rapp that would be a modest and reasonable request, but what does it mean in Myrtle's world? She can no more divorce herself from the crowds around her, the roles she has played, and the mythology that has made her what she is, in order to be a mere woman, than Marlene Dietrich, Greta Garbo, or Marilyn Monroe could. When Myrtle asks Maurice why they can't be lovers again, he replies:

"You're a big star. I've got a small part. The audience doesn't like me. I can't afford to love you." His tone is as chilly and cynical as ever, but that makes his words no less true at this time and place. Myrtle can never be a mere woman again, if she ever was one in the first place.

She collapses on stage after being slapped by Maurice during a rehearsal, and David Samuels, the play's producer, calls from the audience, "Bravo!" thinking (or pretending) it is an inspired addition to her performance. She breaks into tears in her dressing room during an argument over her difficulties with the play, and Manny Victor, her director, comments to the group at large, "Here come the tears again!" Are these cruel, abusive, or heartless remarks? Hardly. No character's performance in a "scene" of this film can exempt itself from possibilities of interpretation. David's and Manny's interpretations of what they see may be more or less charitable and generous, but there is nothing inappropriate about the activity of interpretation in itself in this world. Within the contexts and perspectives of *Opening Night*, treating Myrtle's faint merely as a faint, and her tears only as tears would be fatuous. There can be no pristine experiences, no simple acts of self-expression between these characters, and Myrtle knows it as well as anyone else. She has gotten where she is by striking postures and making scenes, on stage and off. There is no private space left in her life within which simple expression can occur.

Middle-aged Manny Victor summarizes the situation when confidentially telling Myrtle about an affair he had with a nineteen-year-old admirer several years before. She was not in love with "him," he says. "She went to bed with everything I had ever done." The point is that there is no "him" apart from these things; or rather that the "him" who did physically exist apart from these things only got in the way of their relationship. After a short time, "She told me, very politely, that I was too old for her, that I made her uncomfortable when we went out." But the deeper dramatic point of this embarrassing, touching, apparently private confidence is that it is no sooner over than Cassavetes lets us see that, looked at from another perspective, it is not a private confidence at all. Manny is only doing what his producer pays him to do. He is a hard-working, conscientious director naturally worried about his leading lady only a few days before his play's opening night. It is his job to comfort his star. His story about his affair with the young girl is not a personal revelation; it is intended to console Myrtle and encourage her to see her own doubts about herself as normal. His conversation with Myrtle is not a moment of personal disclosure and intimacy; it is a working lunch.

But this is not to call Manny a hypocrite or a charlatan either. No relation or revelation can be merely personal or private in this world, and to expect otherwise would be only naive. Myrtle's private doubts and fears have public consequences whether she wants them to or not; and Manny's personal relationship to Myrtle can never be separated from his professional relationship to her. Early in the film, there is a scene in which Myrtle calls Manny at three in the morning to ask him to tell her that he loves her (they have in the past been lovers). He tells Myrtle, "There's no one I love more than you at this moment," in front of his wife, and then cradles the receiver and whispers to Dorothy, his wife: "You know I love you, honey." Is one expression of love more or less sincere than the other? Myrtle is the star of the most important production Manny has ever mounted, and even Dorothy is not just his wife. The moment before Myrtle calls him, Manny has just asked Dorothy to attend all the rehearsals in order to help him to work on the female roles in the play. That is to say, even Dorothy does not stand in a merely personal relationship to him. She is part of the company, too, and needs to be begged, bribed, and cajoled into doing her best.

Later on in the film, Manny and Myrtle spend the night together. (Is it love? Morale building? Is there any difference?) The next morning, we see Myrtle and Manny coming into the theater together for a rehearsal, and it is significant that Cassavetes photographs their entrance from two radically opposed perspectives. First, he sets up the shot from eye level directly in front of them, watching them enter the theater together from over someone's shoulder. Then, in a reversal, he shifts his camera 180 degrees to show their point of view as they walk in together and we discover that it is Manny's wife who has been watching them come in. It is a characteristically jolting reversal of perspective, but what is more interesting at this moment is that Manny shows no shame and Dorothy no reproach or despair. Manny has done his ultimate duty by his star. Dorothy understands the complexity of the moment.

Myrtle has been protected all her life by a bureaucracy of institutionalized compliments, professional lovers, supportive stagehands and pampering directors. She has been protected additionally by her youth, her beauty, and her enormous talents from ever having had to face biological realities such as aging, the loss of love, or the failure of talent. Doormen have held endless doors and umbrellas for her. Stagehands have always been ready with a bottle of something or other to tide her over the rough spots in a performance. Kelley, her obliging wardrobe mistress, has saved her the trouble of having to dress or pick up after herself. Her director, her producer, and her writer have always offered her endless "love," "friendship," and "understanding." She is obviously a star who has taken full advantage of all the emotional and professional narcotics that have been dispensed for the last thirty years.

Opening Night ends, as noted, with a theatrical "opening," but it begins with a more important and personal "opening night," a night on which Myrtle first recognizes the bureaucracy that has swaddled and protected her all these years. She witnesses the accidental death of a young, passionately adoring fan and her own long-suppressed feelings well up. In comparing her own state of passivity and protection (bureaucratically, physically, and psychologically) with the young fan's state of exposure and vulnerability, something "opens" in Myrtle's heart and soul after many years of professional dormancy. She cries out to be treated as a woman in pain, a lover in need of love, a human being in distress, but the bureaucracy within which she has flourished up to now is designed to prevent just such recognitions. The question of the film is whether Myrtle can pull herself out from under the rubble of her collapsed illusions now that the bureaucratic protections that still surround her no longer comfort her, but threaten her personal existence. The rest of the film is a testimony to the pervasiveness of these forces of social, psychological, and imaginative bureaucratization. How can Myrtle free herself to be like the young girl she so much envies? Even to her adoring fans, Myrtle is not a mere woman, but a star, a character on stage, a packaged product.

Myrtle visits the family of Nancy, the girl who has died, in their run-down apartment. She tries to be a mere mourner, a temporary member of this ordinary Jewish family, but the attempt is absurd. She is "Miss Gordon," the famous actress, and only disrupts the family gathering. There is no way to demythologize the self. Marilyn Monroe had to be Marilyn Monroe even in the bedroom, and there is no way for Myrtle to separate her love affairs with Manny, David, and Maurice from her business affairs with her director, her producer, and her co-star. Myrtle can never again be (and probably never has been) a Nancy. Even love is part of the bureaucracy.

It is at this point that I part ways with Cassavetes. There is every reason to believe from the publicity material he released with *Opening Night* that he intended that Myrtle succeed in extricating herself from the deadening bureaucratic insulation that muffles her cries. Her putative success seems to involve a fairly subtle adjustment of her on-stage and off-stage relationships during the second hour of the film and, more importantly, the growth of a relationship with Dorothy Victor, Manny's wife, another "second woman." Furthermore, Myrtle goes through a complete exorcism of the specter of her younger self that has haunted her throughout the film, finally confronting and killing her delusions about her lost youth in a scene in which she goes berserk in public and undergoes the equivalent of a nervous breakdown. Then she goes on a drunken bender and shows up on the play's opening night only in time to sleepwalk through her role on stage and perform a weird improvised scene with Maurice at the end of the play and a few minutes from the end of the film. It seems that Cassavetes intends us to see in her desperate fight for her life and her sanity, and in the weird self-abasements and humiliations she undergoes in the last twenty minutes of the film, that Myrtle has broken free of the star system in which she has been swaddled and liberated herself from her own delusions about her past. But her success seems schematic and contrived; her freedom seems unconvincing and false; and the viewer is unpersuaded.

The problem with the ending of *Opening Night*, and the larger problem Cassavetes confronts at this point in his career, is that he seems so much better at describing the bureaucracies of experience than the free, creative, imaginative movements of the individual, that he seems simply unable to get Myrtle out of the situation in which he has imagined her. Of Cassavetes' films, *Opening Night* is most like one of Ingmar Bergman's, and, like a Bergman character, Myrtle is trapped by her society, her past, and her imagination and is virtually powerless to change or improve her situation. Given the forces that hedge her round and limit her possibilities of redefinition, there is almost no way she can meaningfully improvise a new self or new possibilities of creative performance for herself. However desperately she tries, she is unable to find a style or form with which to express herself apart from the imaginative bureaucracies in place around her. Again like a Bergman character, her only truly personal or unique form of imagination and expression is her bizarre hallucinated conversation with the young girl she has seen killed. It is as if the self has become so threatened and trapped at this point in Cassavetes' work that the only escape route he can imagine for it, the only authentically personal form of experience and expression he can give Myrtle, is that of her horrifying, nightmarish hallucinations. Incommunicable, unshareable, eccentric private fantasies, visions, and dreams are the only alternative to bureaucratic entrapment, and yet they are an alternative upon which no larger community of feeling and relationship can be established. The self is threatened, isolated, and alone.

It is the opposite of the imaginative situation in the earlier films. There Cassavetes was so much better at depicting healthy eccentricity, idiosyncracy, and play, and robust small societies organized around the unfettered free play of the individual impulse, than at depicting worldly or imaginative bureaucracies that critics charged him and his characters with self-indulgence and irresponsibility. Perhaps it is his fate to oscillate from one imaginative extreme to the other without ever finding a comfortable midpoint between the two. And perhaps a midpoint is not desirable. Certainly it could not produce such energetic works of art.

The story and situation for *Opening Night* were, surprisingly enough, conceived with the encouragement of Gena Rowlands when Cassavetes was working on *Husbands*. To a degree *Opening Night* is a remake of *Husbands*, with a woman in the lead as a replacement for the three husbands. It is a film about the need to keep the child in the woman alive, the need for this actress, like the husbands, to remain in touch with fantasy and dreams. But the extraordinarily different texture of the two films tells how much had changed in the seven years intervening between *Husbands* and the time *Opening Night* was made. Myrtle's position is much more difficult than was, say, that of Gus (the most accomplished and poised performer in the earlier film). To the very conclusion of *Opening Night*, there is a pervasive and withering bureaucracy of relations and understandings so completely in place around Myrtle that in no sense can she be said to escape it, or to score a personal victory over it, except through the quirky privacy of her self-destructive hallucinations, or in the perversity of the humiliating, embarrassing, and absolutely awful improvised performance Maurice initiates on stage with her at the end of the film. But if *Shadows*, *Faces*, and *Husbands* tell us anything, it is that freedom is not a matter of mere improvisational eccentricity, iconoclasm, or escapism, but the result of a fine and delicate knowingness and sensitivity. Cassavetes' inability to find a way out of the bureaucratic labyrinths of *Opening Night* for Myrtle in any warmer, more loving way than through a cranky, improvised, performance on stage in front of an indifferent audience is what makes *Opening Night* the darkest and most disturbing of his films. *The Killing of a Chinese Bookie* and, to a greater extent, *Opening Night* (and *Gloria* after it) bring Cassavetes' work to the point of crisis, to the point of doubting the power of the increasingly isolated and beleaguered self to survive the vast impersonal forces massed against it. The protagonists can only retreat into the secrecy, silence, and privacy of public performance as a refuge for their sovereign consciousnesses, and that is why the victory with which each of these films ends is indistinguishable from failure.

CHAPTER X

BEATING THE SYSTEM
Gloria

> I can understand the feeling that certain people would like a picture
> to have a more conventional form, so that they can borrow it, much like
> the gangster movie. It's an art form in America. So everything is under-
> stood within the gangster form. . . . But if you deal with [characters and
> events in an unconventional way], then it's very hard for people to get
> with the film because of their expectations. Once it gets going, they think,
> "Okay, now let's get going." It may be going [already], however, in some
> area they're not aware of. *John Cassavetes*

In commercial terms, both *The Killing of a Chinese Bookie* and *Opening
Night* were unmitigated disasters. In a desperate attempt to bring the
earlier film to the public, Cassavetes actually edited two entirely distinct versions of *The Killing of a Chinese Bookie,* one after the other. The
original print (which is clearly superior and is the basis of all of my
discussion) got only a brief and limited national distribution in 1976,
and lukewarm, or less than lukewarm, reviews. So Cassavetes went
back in 1978 (after completing *Opening Night*) and extensively reedited
the film to make the narration shorter, simpler, and easier to follow. But
that version has yet to receive any national release at all in this country,
and *The Killing of a Chinese Bookie* in either version remains a great,
neglected masterpiece.

The inauspiciously titled *Opening Night* got even shorter critical and
commercial shrift, virtually opening and closing on the same night the
few times it has been shown. It received its first public screening at the
Fox Wilshire on 21 December 1977. Cassavetes' goal was that it be
technically eligible for Academy Award consideration that year—
consideration that, needless to say, it did not get. Five years later, it had
still not been given a general release. After a few additional press and
festival screenings, this film, too, was withdrawn from circulation.
Cassavetes speaks occasionally about rereleasing it in the near future,
but considering its length, difficulty, and density, there is no reason to
think it will fare any better a second time around.

Cassavetes was at a commercial, professional, and critical dead end only comparable to the point his career had reached after the failure of his foray into Hollywood with *Too Late Blues* and *A Child Is Waiting*. But *The Killing of a Chinese Bookie* and *Opening Night* are terminal works in more than the commercial and financial senses. Like *Faces*, which documented that previous period of doubt and despair, they are dark, problematic, and pessimistic works. Whether Cassavetes intended it or not, their characters are trapped in situations from which they cannot be extricated. After the technical, logistical, and bureaucratic problems of filming *Opening Night* (with its director's and producer's nightmares of work in front of live audiences on real stages in actual theaters), and his utter inability to get a distributor for the film, Cassavetes found himself early in 1978 at a point of artistic crisis different in origin from, but only slightly less acute than, that felt by Myrtle Gordon in the film he had just made.

At this moment of creative enervation, chance came to Cassavetes' aid. After seventeen years of strenuous independence from Hollywood studios and studio executives, he was unexpectedly invited by a major studio to make a picture again. The film that resulted, *Gloria*, is one of Cassavetes' less interesting films, and in many ways not a true Cassavetes film at all, but it gave him the breathing-space and opportunity he needed to avoid stagnating after the crisis of the two previous projects.

Over the years, in addition to acting, Cassavetes has written many uncredited scripts in order to finance his own productions. He wrote the original script of *Gloria* not to film but "to make a little money" to take care of the considerable debts he had incurred after the financial debacle of *Opening Night*. MGM commissioned it to feature their tow-headed tyke Ricky Schroder. As Cassavetes recalled: "I wrote the story to sell, strictly to sell. It was no great shakes." However, while the script was being prepared, MGM lost its child prodigy to Disney Productions, and Cassavetes' script subsequently got passed along to Columbia Pictures. Columbia then astonished Cassavetes by buying the script on the condition that he direct it. As he tells it, his agent called up to say, "'I've got good news and bad news. Columbia loves the picture, and they want Gena in it.' 'What's the bad news?' I said. 'They want you to direct it.'"[1]

After a few months of tinkering with the script and trying to make the best of a less than ideal situation, *One Summer Night* (the production title) went into filming in the summer of 1979. The result is a children's movie for adults who like gangster films. Caught halfway between a Warner Brothers thriller and a Walt Disney fairy tale, *Gloria* will probably satisfy neither children nor adults, but it could never be confused with the work of any other director.

If *Gloria* is simpler, less serious, less engaged (and ultimately much less engaging) than Cassavetes' other work, it seems a small price to have paid to escape the imaginative entrapments and dead ends of the earlier films. Cassavetes seems almost to be toying with his obsessions, stretching and exaggerating elements of the previous films, playing dramatic games with their plots. Some of the same imaginative disturbances and problems are present that were in *The Killing of a Chinese Bookie* and *Opening Night*, but in *Gloria* Cassavetes finds a way to dally with his previous predicaments, to tease and mock his own earlier seriousness in a way that can only be called healthy. It is not for nothing that Yankee Stadium is prominently visible in the background of many of the scenes (which were shot on location in Manhattan and the Bronx). There is a gamelike, sporty quality to the entire film.

Gloria Swenson (Gena Rowlands) is a retired showgirl, gun moll, and gangsters' paramour getting on in years who, as the film begins, is blissfully content and self-contained. She was obviously a classy number in her prime and has prudently saved her pennies and devoted years to preparing to nestle into a quiet, luxurious retirement, free of encumbering relationships and compromising alliances. Within the decaying shell of a run-down apartment house near Yankee Stadium, she has made herself a comfortable, secure home—a small, cozy nest of old photographs, show business memorabilia, personal bric-a-brac, and dozens of luxurious, billowy, silk dresses and kimonos, which she will wear throughout the film. Her chubby, taffy-colored cat is the only love in her life now, a lover who makes no psychological demands whatever on her. Gloria feels safe and unthreatened. She has walled herself and her emotions into a tidy island of comfort in her decaying Bronx neighborhood.

Cassavetes has more than once found inspiration for aspects of his films in the work of Billy Wilder, and the similarities to Wilder's *Sunset Boulevard* are not accidental. In the period immediately before Cassavetes' own work, Wilder was one of the greatest cinematic explorers of the American identity, and of the processes of creating (or pretending to create) a personal identity through the power of performance. It was natural that Cassavetes would watch his films carefully. The name of Cassavetes' heroine, Gloria Swenson, is an allusion to the star of Wilder's film, Gloria Swanson (whose name was originally Swensen). More importantly, Wilder's and Cassavetes' heroines make identical attempts to build homemade worlds in which to ensconce and protect themselves. They have spun self-protective cocoons woven out of pieces, parts, roles, and images of themselves in the past in which to live. They would reign as queens in picture palaces built out of personal photographs, memorabilia, and artifacts in which the only image visible is their own image mirrored, multiplied , magnified, and projected larger and clearer than life. In short, they aspire to make the Hollywood star system a design for living. They would make their lives dramas in which every other character's part will be subservient to their own. All roles will be typecast, with bit players always in their control. The performances of others will be fully scripted and blocked out in advance. Well-defined identities will never be put in doubt. Tidily formulated selves will never be put in jeopardy.

One does not need to be told at this point in a study of Cassavetes' work that this is the most dangerous and self-destructive aspiration a character can have. Richard and Maria Forst, Archie, Harry, and Gus, Cosmo, and Myrtle each started out with the same confidence that performances and identities could be scripted, arranged, and controlled in that way. Like film stars or directors terrified by departures from the script, each thought identities could be typecast and performances programmed in advance. Each thought the self could be organized to keep out the mess of unplanned emotions, personal contingencies, and untidy relationships. Like a lighter version of *Faces*, *Husbands*, *The Killing of a Chinese Bookie*, or *Opening Night*, the rest of *Gloria* is devoted to reexposing Gloria to all of the emotional, social, and psychological dangers she had thought she could wall out of her life and retire from. Like so many of Cassavetes' other films, *Gloria* begins with a sudden and irreversible dislocation and rupture. All of the cozy certainties and securities in Gloria's life are disrupted and called into question.

Gloria's mistake is to walk down the hall of her apartment building one sunny summer morning to borrow some coffee from a Puerto Rican family on her floor, a family on the other side of the tracks from her in every imaginable way. The father (Buck Henry) is a Mafia accountant who has been tactless enough to squeal about some of his accounts to the FBI. As a result, the whole family—mother, father, mother-in-law, and three children—are about to be murdered as an example to others by a team of Mafia hit men. The wife has recognized one of them lurking down in the lobby, and Gloria, little knowing what she is letting herself in for, walks in on a scene of complete panic. A few minutes later, persuaded by his father to hide the youngest child in her apartment, she leaves with six-year-old Phil in tow. The other children refuse to go with her at all, and even Phil goes only reluctantly and grudgingly. Only seconds after they arrive in her apartment, Phil's family is wiped out and a two-hour chase across New York begins, as the odd couple, more comically mismatched than Minnie and Seymour, flee to avoid the pursuing mobsters.

Cassavetes playfully turns every convention of the traditional gangster movie upside down. Phil, the scared, six-year-old Puerto Rican boy trying to buck up and "be a man" in front of this strange woman, is a parody of every tough-talking Cagney or Muni character on the lam. And Gloria, fighting off gangsters right and left with her chrome-plated thirty-eight, is the feminist inversion of every comic book and movie G-man ever invented. In the process of trying to survive, Phil and Gloria spout half the clichés of tough-talking male-female relations from thirties movies: "Take a walk"; "You're a nice girl, Gloria, but you're not for me"; "We can't go on like this"; "These lights are driving me crazy" (this last from little Phil leaning out of a flop-house window, his face alternately illuminated and darkened by the pulse of a neon light, in a shot that must be in half the gangster films ever made).

The joke, of course, is that Hollywood Central Casting would not have considered these two characters for bit parts in that sort of film. Their predicament is, in fact, that they are each cast in the wrong movie—a movie neither of them wants to be in any more than the other. Gloria wants nothing more than to be left to herself, and pint-sized tough guy Phil wants a little playmate, a mother, a wife, anything but the street-wise gun moll the genre dictates as the proper companion for a man. The result is that for most of *Gloria* what we end up noticing is all the ways Phil and Gloria refuse to be reduced to gangster movie typologies, all the ways in which their particular, incongruous humanity keeps them from fitting into the normal, predictable contours of the genre in which they appear to be trapped.

They are as miscast as the star of *Chinese Bookie*, mild-mannered, generous, entrepreneurial Cosmo, who would make a better president of the local Rotary Club than he does a Mafia hit man. In casting against character types, Cassavetes is encouraging his actors and characters to free themselves from the roles they find themselves playing. As always, he is most interested not in the way individuals fulfill the impinging and regularizing structures of plot, characterization, and form, but in the ways they break out of them. The artistic predicament of his characters is thus analogous to their psychological predicament: they must explore the possibilities of breaking free of the compromising, homogenizing, repressive structures and systems both of the society in which they live and of the film in which they are cast, just as the plots of the films force them to make their ways against the resistance of indifferent, alien, or hostile others who would deny them any right to exist outside of their systems of understanding and influence.

That is why the local events in a Cassavetes film are so surprising and unpredictable. The tones of a scene, the expectations of the genre, and the contours of a predictable plot sequence exist only to be repeatedly fractured by the characters. Consider the tonal shifts in the scene already mentioned, at the beginning of *Gloria*. It begins with the portentousness of shots of the three Mafia hit men gradually closing in with mechanical efficiency around the Rodriguez apartment. Those shots are dovetailed with others of Mrs. Rodriguez upstairs arguing with her husband, calling him names, absurdly gesticulating, and berating him for doing something so stupid as to get them into trouble with the Mob. Then the mother-in-law starts screaming at both the husband and the wife for one of them to call the police to stop it all (which, it goes without saying, would be futile). In one cinematic glissade, we have moved from *film noir* to a shouting match in a Marx Brothers movie. And then the children start crying in fear and confusion, and we are in still another, sadder, more tender world. At this point, Gloria, knowing nothing of what is going on, saunters in and casually lounges against the door jamb, asking if she can borrow some coffee. With her still visible in the background, apparently indifferent to it all, Buck Henry starts kissing, hugging, and crying over little Phil, saying good-bye to him forever, giving him advice for the rest of his life. How many different movies are we in? Gangsters ominously and inexorably closing in; a nearly comic Puerto Rican family argument; a casual, carefree visitor; a father's tears over his son. Is there any director with a more pervasive and life-affirming faith in the power of personality to swerve away from the forms (artistic, narrative, and social) that would attempt to predict it, limit its possible range of responses, or tyrannize over it, here even in the face of death?

One can never predict where a scene will go in any of Cassavetes' films, but perhaps because of the simplicity and starkness of our expectations within this particular genre, life has never seemed so ex-

plosively, jauntily, and encouragingly open to possibility. In her first
confrontation with the Mob after the murder of Phil's family, Gloria
faces a carfull of gangsters who have pulled up alongside her and Phil
on the street. She is asked quite politely to turn over Phil and the Mob
account book his father gave him. She resists, but the gangsters know
her, she knows them, and the whole conversation takes place on a
friendly first-name basis. As one of the well-dressed mobsters starts to
get out of the car, the scene seems predictable enough. Perhaps Gloria
and Phil will run away down the street. More likely there will be the
sort of tugging and shouting contest that other gangster pictures have
taught us is the only kind of resistance women are capable of putting
up. But the one thing we never expect is what happens—that Gloria
should open up on the car at point blank range with her revolver. As
the car screeches away from the curb, as if to rub in the shock of the
scene, Cassavetes cuts to a close-up shot of the faces of the men sitting
in it, looking as stupified as we feel. They slump one by one in their
seats as she continues firing. Then, in a spectacular stunt scene all the
more unexpected from a director who never uses stunt scenes, their car
goes out of control, careens off parked cars and rolls over upside down,
its occupants all dead. As if to top this, Cassavetes cuts to Gloria
making her escape by nonchalantly yelling "Taxi" and hopping into a
passing cab with Phil, and has the driver (who apparently has not seen
what we have) blandly point it out to her with the comment, "That's
some accident."

But the roles Phil and Gloria must work out a free relation to are
more than those of the gangster movie genre. More important and
more limiting than the roles the movies cast them in are the human
roles in which they typecast themselves and each other. They each
begin in emotionally sheltered and falsely secure situations: Phil—the
youngest child in a tight-knit Puerto Rican family; Gloria—cozily ensconced in her apartment with her cat, her paintings, her photographs,
and her memories. As in all of Cassavetes' work, the process of the film
is the enforced movement from innocence to experience, in this case
the process of stripping Phil and Gloria of their protective emotional
coverings as inexorably as the rooms in which they sleep together in
their flight are progressively denuded of comforts and comforting associations. They are stripped physically—Phil to his jockey shorts and
Gloria to her bathrobe—but the important stripping down is social and
psychological. Gloria and Phil gradually open up to each other as they
allow themselves to become vulnerable to each other and their tough

guy and tough girl patinas are peeled away. (It is this process of authentic emotional excavation, incidentally, that makes *Gloria* so much more interesting than a superficially similar film such as *Little Miss Marker*, in which Shirley Temple's coy, cocky audacity only masquerades as the exploratory innocence of childhood.)

It is always difficult for a child actor to achieve any significant emotional range or depth, but under his stone-faced exterior Phil (played by seven-year-old John Adames) develops in the course of the film into both more of a boy and more of a man than one might have expected at its start. Gena Rowlands turns in the sort of tour de force of emotional expressiveness that can be called routine only of her. Like a lesser Mabel, Cosmo, or Myrtle, Gloria must explore the possibilities of responsiveness to wildly conflicting influences and expectations. She shows what can be made of these rival forces—playing sassy, tough, sweet, sexy, maternal, sarcastic, and tender roles one after another in the film. She is a person breaking the boundaries of psychological and emotional typecasting as relentlessly as the character she plays breaks the boundaries of cinematic genre casting.

Gloria's achievement is to successfully "outplay" the Mob in every sense of the word. She proves that anything these rigid, rule-bound men can do, she can improvise better (and more gleefully). The terms of the conflict are explicitly those of the difference between the sexes. In this sense, *Gloria* is one of the few "feminist" films in which the woman is not forced to identify implicitly with the male oppressor. Far from renouncing or suppressing her femininity in order to compete in the all-male world of gangsterdom, Gloria uses it to surprise and bewilder her would-be captors. Rather than regarding her femininity as a handicap in the battle, her billowy, silk chorus girl costumes, her brassy good looks, and her refusal to play by the rules of ladylike behavior are turned into tacit taunts and reproaches that paralyze her stolid, flat-footed opponents. (And her feminist taunts and reproaches are not always tacit: "Sissies . . . you let a woman beat you!" she shouts to the thugs she has trapped on a subway train.)

Gloria camps up her adopted gangster role with a prankish, parodic glee that one cannot help admiring, but at the same time her sheer playfulness, the way she casually tries out and uses up one role after another is the weakest aspect of the film. The problem is that it seems all too easy and too painless. Gloria lands us back where Lelia began in *Shadows*—posturing, preening, and showing off. And yet even Lelia, one of Cassavetes' simplest characters, had to face the confusing psy-

The crisis of the post-modern personality and the de-centered self
dispersed into a fluidly shifting succession of roles
—*Ghostly, mercurial Gloria, the quick-change artist, outplays
the gangsters and perhaps plays herself out of personal existence as well*

chological and social consequences of role-playing in a way that Gloria
never has to. Gloria embodies the joys and excitements of experimentation, improvisation, and exploration without paying any of the
prices Lelia, Ghost, Gus, Harry, Archie, Mabel, and Cassavetes' other
characters had to. That is why, though it is undoubtedly to take the film
too seriously, especially in the light of Cassavetes' protestation that it
was done as work for hire from a script he considered far less than
ideal, one must call it a psychologically and socially irresponsible film.

Perhaps one feels the inadequacies of *Gloria* all the more acutely in
that it follows so closely on the heels of achievements like *A Woman
Under the Influence, The Killing of a Chinese Bookie*, and (the less satisfactory) *Opening Night*, films that take the complexities and hazards of
role-playing as their very subject. They each document the difficulties
of juggling conflicting roles and the extraordinary social and psychological cost of an adequate performance. *The Killing of a Chinese Bookie*
and *Opening Night* indeed darkly suggest that the cost of negotiating
the influences that surround an individual may be exorbitant, in excess
of any conceivable benefit to oneself or others. They suggest that the

price of performance may be ultimate estrangement, isolation, and loneliness.

And with that aspect of the two previous films in mind, perhaps one can find faint traces of their outlines in *Gloria*. For *Gloria*—once one looks beyond its gleeful love of parody and playful succession of costume changes—is a film, like the ones immediately preceding it, of profound individual isolation and loneliness. Not only is there no society of which Gloria and Phil can be contributing members, but there is no relationship by which they can be linked to each other without giving up the identities that make them distinctive and interesting in the film. Like Minnie and Seymour before them, Gloria and Phil are on the run from a hostile and threatening world. But the later couple lacks the earlier one's escape route to the realms of marriage, the family, and suburbia. Gloria and Phil are denied any possible destination for their frantic flight and must take whatever chilly comfort they can in the pleasures of sheer movement.

The increasing pace of movement in the films from *Minnie and Moskowitz* on, a pace that quickens and climaxes in *Gloria*, is the most disturbing stylistic development in Cassavetes' recent work. From cruising down Wilshire Boulevard in Seymour's truck, to shuttling with Cosmo between his club and the precincts of the Mob in *The Killing of a Chinese Bookie*, to negotiating the Byzantine backstage corridors and spaces of *Opening Night*, to the sensuous swoop of the helicopter around Yankee Stadium during the opening credits of *Gloria* and the endless cab rides that carry Phil and Gloria around the five boroughs of New York, movement has increasingly, desperately, become an end in itself. Movement has become the last remaining expression of personal freedom and independence. It has become a last-ditch strategy of survival under fire. Characters move not to immerse themselves in new experiences, but to disengage themselves from the past, to escape the potential bondage of static social relationships. As pressures have accumulated, and characters have become more psychologically and socially constrained in the later films, it is as if they have chosen to escape into the only certain freedom and independence remaining—the joy of pure motion. Certainly, Cosmo's cosmic balancing act with his three families, his endless, clockwork shuttlings from one to the other and back again, had this quality.

None of Cassavetes' films more exuberantly celebrates the sheer sensuousness and excitement of movement through space (on the part of both its camera and its characters) than *Gloria*, and yet in none of the films does movement seem more mechanical, more purposeless, more an end in itself. "Stop and you're dead. A moving target is harder to hit. Keep on the move and at least the future is open to possibility," might be Cosmo's philosophy of life, or Gloria's, as it was at moments Minnie's and Seymour's. It is a philosophy whose only consolation is the prospect of endless change through endless repositioning. The tick-tock of time that dogs most of these recent characters can at least be kept at bay if they can synchronize their movements to the mechanical pressure and rush of the world that is besetting them. The appetite for space and time in Cassavetes' most recent films brings his work round full circle. This is the filmmaker who seemed so indifferent to cinematic pacings in his earliest work that he annoyed critics and audiences with his willingness to let his scenes run on long past normal cinematic durations. This is the filmmaker who was so uninterested in mere mechanical movement in his early work that he would not hesitate to limit the setting of an entire film to two or three rooms of a house or apartment. This is the filmmaker who, for all the travel his characters were ostensibly engaged in, cut out almost all of the scenes of mere walking, driving, or riding in *Shadows, Too Late Blues, Faces,* and *Husbands.* But that is obviously not to suggest that Cosmo and Gloria and Phil are freer and less fettered than the earlier characters, but just the opposite—that they are perhaps even more trapped and hemmed round. The prospect of endless frantic flight and hectic movement is no different from the prospect of endless immurement and immobility. Gloria and Phil endlessly on the run are paradoxically not very different from the trapped, immobilized figures of *Faces.*

But this is probably to freight too heavily this easy, fairy-tale-like movie, and to interpret it too darkly. Movement is not inevitably a negative condition. The most important positive fact about Cassavetes' own career is that it has successfully kept on the move. Almost alone among contemporary filmmakers, he has shown that the dream of artistic freedom can be kept alive and on the move amid compromising and constricting technical, bureaucratic, and commercial entanglements—if, as he has done, one is willing to venture away from the securities, comforts, and stabilities of the studio system and the orthodoxies of acting and directing. Cassavetes' philosophy has always involved unceasing motion, adjustment, and correction of course as he goes along.

If there is a single, unequivocally positive statement that these films make, even in their most tough-minded and darkest moments, it is of the inestimable value of free movement and the imperative that we all dare to sally forth from our states of protection and security as Cassavetes himself has done, and as Gloria, Myrtle, Cosmo, and each of the central characters in the films are forced to do. The movement in these films is the visual and spatial expression of the endless renegotiations of new experiences and relationships that Cassavetes has always asked of himself and his characters. For it is only in free movement—in leaving illusory comforts and certainties behind and in running the hazards of the course—that exploration, discovery, and growth is possible.

Only in coming down from our ivory towers of retirement and security to jostle with the mess and muddle and risks of life on the street, as Gloria is forced to do, is there the possibility of a new, life-affirming relationship to others and to ourselves. It is in this sense that Cassavetes' films are documents not of transcendence but of immersion, not of escape but of profounder involvement, not of security but of exposure to the mess and confusion in which life must be lived.

It is a doctrine of baptism by immersion that D. H. Lawrence eloquently described in the conclusion to his *Studies In Classic American Literature* in trying to account for the particular robustness and energy of the greatest American art. And though Lawrence was thinking of writers such as Whitman, Hawthorne, and Melville, it is interesting that the metaphor he uses to describe the strength of the American tradition is almost identical to the one Cassavetes chooses to work out in his films—the metaphor of the traveller daring to venture outside of the theoretical, social, and psychological "mansions," homes, and apartments that shelter and protect him, and being forced "to go down the open road" of experience without the comfort of either security or destination:

The Open Road. The great home of the Soul is the open road. Not heaven, not paradise. Not "above." Not even "within." The soul is neither "above" nor "within." It is a wayfarer down the open road.

[The soul accomplishes herself only] through the journey itself, down the open road. Exposed to full contact. On two slow feet. Meeting whatever comes down the open road. In company with those that drift in the same measure along the same way. Towards no goal. Always the open road. . . .

"In my Father's house are many mansions."

"No. . . . Keep out of mansions. A mansion may be heaven on earth, but you might as well be dead. Strictly avoid mansions. The soul is herself when she is going on foot down the open road."

It is the American heroic message. The soul is not to pile up defenses around herself. She is not to withdraw and seek her heavens inwardly, in mystical ecstasies. She is not to cry to some God beyond, for salvation. She is to go down the open road, as the road opens, into the unknown, keeping company with those whose soul draws them near to her, accomplishing nothing save the journey, and the works incident to the journey, in the long life-travel into the unknown, the soul in her subtle sympathies accomplishing herself by the way. . . .

This is [the] message of American democracy.

The true democracy where soul meets soul, in the open road. Democracy. American democracy where all journey down the open road.

It is a belief in salvation through democratic interaction that helps explain why there are so few lyrical interludes, and no privileged points of view, in Cassavetes' films. In place of Hollywood's escapes into exalted or insulated subjectivity, Cassavetes offers only arduous, time-bound transits and transactions between characters.

The preceding quotation does justice to the breathless breeziness of *Gloria*, but that is just the problem. Surely Lawrence makes "going down the road" sound all too easy and painless. His own novels and Cassavetes' earlier films are the best counter-arguments to the blitheness of his position. They are extended lessons in the social and psychological hurdles that make "going down the road" more often arduous, painful, and discouraging than exhilarating.

It is significant that Lawrence was writing about Walt Whitman, that happy loafer with the universe, at this point in his book. Gloria is a Whitmanesque character, and *Gloria*, with its love of movement and the great outdoors and the two combined in energetic flights across the cityscape, is Cassavetes' most Whitmanesque film. Ever on the move, alternately manic and insouciant, it glories in its gleeful play with a succession of outrageous postures and roles. But, as Whitman's own career and the careers of those—such as Kerouac and Ginsberg—who followed him down that artistic road illustrate, the Whitmanesque position is not without potentially grave psychological, emotional, and artistic dangers. That is to say, Cassavetes' three most recent films are Whitmanesque in a thoroughly disturbing way. The particular aesthetic problems of *Gloria* make explicit what was implicit in the two previous films. The central characters in all three have become (or been forced to become) such consummate quick-change artists that in some more personal sense they have ceased to exist as unique, private individuals. They have been forced to become so chameleonlike in response to the forces impinging on them that they may be said to have given up the possession of any controlling identity separate from the one they have adopted for the moment. In an upsetting way, Cosmo, Myrtle, and most of all Gloria remain invisible and in hiding beneath their truly spectacular powers of performance, inscrutable and in retreat from the societies of which they are a part, strangely absent from their own films.

Like Norma Desmond, whom she so much resembles in this respect, Gloria has so gloriously and energetically distributed herself into a succession of stylized roles, stances, and parts and has become such a mercurial mistress of social ceremonies, parodies, and postures that she has, in effect, given up the possibility of holding on to any merely personal relationship or form of expression. That is why, for all of her star presence and her domination of the screen space during *Gloria* (the film is virtually a one-woman show in which Gena Rowlands is almost never off camera), we know as little about Gloria as an individual at the end of the film as we did at its start, and much less about her in general than we do about any of Cassavetes' earlier principal characters. Her truly awesome performative powers and capacities of energetic movement allow her endlessly to defy the gravity of the predicaments she finds herself in, but the result is that she is morally, psychologically, and epistemologically almost weightless. (Is it any wonder that throughout she seems half in love with death, or that in the end death makes for so little change in her condition?) As in the writing of Whitman, Pound, and much subsequent American literature in the line of Whitman, embracing the universe at moments becomes almost indistinguishable from withdrawing from it. Cosmic inclusiveness and imaginative fluidity become little different from cosmic reclusiveness and imaginative fugitiveness. Whitman sometimes seemed unaware of the possible irony, but Cassavetes is closer to Henry Adams in his nightmare recognition that to disperse one's self in such an abundance of *personae*, styles and stances, to display such protean plasticities of selfhood, is perhaps not to gain one's soul, but to lose it: to give up a personal claim on any identity and become a semiotic function of one's environment.

For all of the superficial sprightliness and the maniacal glee of the film, Cassavetes' discomfort with the situation of his heroine and the "going down the road" philosophy she enacts must have been extreme. Perhaps that is why *Gloria* ends with a reminder that we have after all, only been watching a movie. It concludes with a kind of apology for the whole preceding film, and a scene that attempts to deny all of the imaginative disturbances that came before it. *Gloria* ends with a dream-like wish-fulfillment coda that recalls the one at the end of another on-the-road film, *Minnie and Moskowitz*, and that is perhaps Cassavetes' confession of his distress with its Whitmanesque qualities.

After Gloria is apparently killed by thugs in an elevator as she leaves the apartment of the Mob boss, Phil flees to Pittsburgh as she has instructed him to do. Arriving there, he goes to a cemetery to pray, as he has done once before in the film. It is a scene of utter bereftness, until unexpectedly a black limousine silently glides up the driveway, a mysteriously veiled woman in mourning gets out, lifts her veil to reveal that she is Gloria, and she and Phil embrace in the final seconds of the film. It is the final, consummate costume change in a film about role-playing and quick changes of costume, and one so unexpected and outrageous (since we have every reason to believe that Gloria has been killed in the immediately preceding shoot-out) that it seems almost a parody of the earlier ones. But what is even more telling is that Cassavetes films the reunion in slow motion (in the test prints the film even more joltingly switched from color to black and white at this point).

This fantasy-fulfillment ending may be defended as self-consciously admitting its own artificiality and unreality. But that seems to be too easy on Cassavetes and his film. However fashionable unreliable endings may be, there is a coyness in this act of insulating the ending from criticism and an evasiveness in this cute retreat into a fiction within a fiction that is entirely uncharacteristic of Cassavetes' most engaged and engaging work. *Sunset Boulevard* is another film that ends with a slow motion, dreamlike fantasy. Norma Desmond descends grandly down a staircase in front of the lights and cameras of the newsreel photographers she imagines to be making a movie starring her. But the difference between the endings of *Sunset Boulevard* and *Gloria*, to the disadvantage of Cassavetes' film, is that Wilder makes it clear that Norma's fantasy is only a fantasy, and as such an evasion of life. The crucial problem with the ending of *Gloria* is that it does the opposite. It tries to make fantasy substitute for life, replacing the real difficulties of human communication and community that the film has previously documented with the dreamlike ease of a fantasized community, something against which the entire preceding film has been powerfully marshalling evidence.

Dreams and dreaming have always been metaphorically central to Cassavetes' work, as this whole book argues, but from *Minnie and Moskowitz* on, there has been a disturbing change. Fantasies, reveries, and even momentary hallucinations (as in *Opening Night*—and here one should also remember that the initial script of *A Woman Under the Influence* contained an extended dream sequence, not to mention the hallucinatory dreamlike sequences Mabel lives and acts out during the course of the film) increasingly threaten not to enrich, but to displace, waking reality. Cassavetes allows fantasies of imagined community and communication to substitute for actual failures of true human society. In fact, all of *Gloria* could be considered an extended dream sequence in this escapist sense. From its first lingering swoop over the Bronx skyline in the opening of the film to the artifice of the coda that concludes it, *Gloria* announces that it will entertain a special fictional relationship to ordinary reality. That is the true significance of the fact that Cassavetes chooses to people his film predominantly not from the world of real gangsters, but from the world of Hollywood gangsterdom and the forms of experience films have given to it.

In the introduction to *The Scarlet Letter*, Hawthorne defined "romance" as "a neutral territory somewhere between the real world and fairy-land, where the Actual and the Imaginary may meet, and each imbue itself with the nature of the other." Cassavetes may be said, in Hawthorne's sense of the word, to have been writing romances all along and not known it. That is to say, like Hawthorne and many other major American artists, he is interested in testing the conditions under which the imagination may be kept alive, mobile, and free in the face of oppressive actualities. But to appreciate the vigor with which the imagination is kept alive in a hostile environment in the earlier films is to realize how far *Gloria* has left behind Hawthorne's "neutral territory somewhere between the real world and fairy-land" where the equal but opposite attractions of both imagination and actuality are equally felt. *Gloria* has moved over the boundary into fairyland. In the phrase of Henry James, another geographer of the possibilities of life in that land where the rival claims of the imaginary and the actual are both staked, the balloon of Cassavetes' fiction in this most recent film seems not tightly enough tethered to the ground. *Gloria's* gorgeous photography, frequently elegant compositions, and aerial perspectives make it at times Cassavetes' most beautiful and visionary visual experience. The viewer of the film is frequently lifted above the level of the pedestrian on the street and magically, enchantingly transported into a dreamlike cinematic world. Especially in the film's ending, he is offered the experience of escaping the complications of human society and living through the eye in a dream world—inhabiting the realm of the American sublime. It is a powerfully tempting prospect, but as all of the films before *Gloria* are devoted to demonstrating, such a flight from the mess of reality always represents more of a loss than a gain.

In Cassavetes' defense, the problem of balance between the rival claims of imagination and society has haunted the work of almost every great American artist, most notoriously that of Hawthorne himself. Many a previous American novelist, poet, and filmmaker before Cassavetes has been seduced into letting out the tether and willing himself into a dreamlike fairyland of fiction promising ultimate release from the complex pressures of actuality. Given the special conditions under which *Gloria* was made, and the fact that he was persuaded to use a gorgeous color ending in place of his original choice of a more realistic and harsher black and white, one hopes that it is premature to say that Cassavetes is perilously close to becoming the Wallace Stevens, the Henry Thoreau, or, much worse yet, the John Ford of the contemporary American experience, retreating into gorgeous fictions, escaping into the simplified social world of romance, or finding solace in dreamed societies of the imagination wherever the real waking world fails to live up to his ideals of a healthy, robust society of free and expressive men.

CHAPTER XI

WORRYING THE DREAM

Maybe there never was an America . . . maybe it was all Frank Capra.

I adore Frank Capra. He was and still is, in my opinion, the greatest filmmaker that ever lived. . . . At the same time I don't emulate Capra. The characters in my films display a lack of comfort and find themselves in petty and embarrassing situations, but this is only because they haven't come to grips with their emotional natures. I am a tough and deeply cynical person. Capra didn't care about his cynicism. I wish I could . . . really express the beautiful ideas he could without feeling perhaps that these ideas are not truthful. . . . [My] films are a road map through emotional and intellectual terrains. . . . By affording the spectators a glimpse into ideas that confuse, rock, and disturb them, I offer the mind food for thought. An aesthetic experience that leaves the spectator vacant is no form of art. *John Cassavetes*

The danger of an extended study of an artist's work is the illusion it fosters that the individual works have been "placed"—that they have been bundled, tied up, and tagged, and can now be filed away and effectively dismissed under a particular set of categories and attitudes. It would be a mistake to think that this could be done to any work of art worth the effort of investigation, but all the more grievous a mistake when dealing with work as aggressively mobile and unstable as that of Cassavetes. In approaching work whose essential strength is its exploratory, adventuresome quality, it becomes crucial that the observer avoid cutting the experience down to sizes and shapes that fit his critical schemes. That is why I have repeatedly taken pains in the preceding pages to emphasize not tidiness in Cassavetes' work but mess and muddle, not its coherence, unity, and clarity, but the swerves and oscillations of feeling in any one film, the contradictory attitudes present in any one scene, the diversity of impulses informing each moment.

Consider, for example, the ambivalences and contradictions in *Husbands*. It is no accident that Cassavetes the director casts himself as a confused character, a mixed-up husband, a boyish explorer in the film. As both director and character, he is unable to make up his mind between the value of excursions and the necessity of returns. He is unable to choose between the freedom and excitements of romantic adventure and the stability and stimulation of commitments to home and family. The film ends up pleading in favor of both social husband-hood and psychological bachelorhood, even as it recognizes the irrec-oncilability of the two alternatives in its plot—after all, one cannot be in Long Island and London at the same time; there is no happy middle ground between being at home with one's family and being on a wild weekend binge with a call girl. Likewise, in *Minnie and Moskowitz* Cas-savetes is absolutely unable to choose between Seymour's jaunty, devil-may-care iconoclasm and Minnie's conservative, home-centered domesticity.

But to recognize this is to recognize that Cassavetes and his films are almost completely out of step with reigning methods and values of criticism in this century. Twentieth-century academic criticism of both film and literature has traditionally extolled "poise," "irony," "control," and, above all, "balance" in the work of art. And no set of attitudes is less appropriate to an appreciation of these films. Rather than culti-vating a state of aesthetic balance, Cassavetes' works throw themselves and their viewers into deliberate tailspins of imbalance. Rather than aspiring toward an artistic stasis and suspension of attitudes, his works aggressively put rival positions and attitudes at war with each other.

The enormous energy of Cassavetes' films comes precisely from the fact that their attitudes are not decided and worked out in advance, and presented to the viewer in a fait accompli of intricate visual patterns, metaphors, or structures. Cassavetes is not somewhere anterior to or outside of his text like Stephen Daedalus's (and James Joyce's) God of creation, ironic and detached, looking down on his work, "paring his fingernails." He is not removed from the films, poised above them, at an aesthetic distance from their events, emotions, and characters. His personal passions, confusions, explorations, doubts, and questions are embedded and embodied everywhere in them.

The result of this is that the films themselves are not in the least otherworldly, self-sufficient aesthetic objects. They do not artfully jux-tapose or analytically compare rival rhetorical strategies. They do not conduct experiments with fictions, or tease a viewer with an infinite regress of fictions within fictions. They do not "deconstruct" them-selves. They do not merely "play" with signifiers, signs, or semiotic codes. Nor, as in the now old dream of the New Criticism, are their meanings suspended (and neutralized) in a stable solution of tensions, ambiguities, or alternative "points of view." All of which is to say that they are not (in the terminology of the latest fad in critical jargon) "texts" cut off from an engagement with the contexts of society, history, biography, and the particularities of adult human life at this time and place in our culture. In the face of the passionate commitments and human engagements of these films, such a critical vocabulary—alternately scientific, philological, and mechanical—should fall silent with embarrassment at the blithe irresponsibility of its disengagement from the realities of ordinary life and feeling.

These films everywhere pulse with the pressures of the human desires that created them and which they take as their subjects. And the result is necessarily an entirely different sort of work from the kind usually postulated by academic criticism, a text ultimately much more passionately personal, mobile, energetic, exciting, and unresolved. While the ideal works of art described by most critics stand still and resonate around a fixed pattern of images, or are frozen into a series of structural choices or mimetic strategies, these films never stop moving. Their scenes, plots, and characters never stop changing, adjusting their course, and lunging away from past positions. To stop reacting, adjusting, and correcting their courses would be to stop living for these characters and their creator.

That is why one repeatedly has to describe these films (and the characters in them) not in terms of positions, but in terms of movements, oscillations, and reversals of direction. And despite the physical limitations of their one- or two-set situations, like their director, the most interesting characters in these films never seem to stop moving, physically, socially, or imaginatively. Cassavetes is as energetically, anxiously American in his appetite for movement as Nicholas Ray. And that is probably why both filmmakers are so addicted to settings with stairways. Compare the sets in Ray's *Rebel Without a Cause* or his *Bigger Than Life* with the stairways, hallways, and corridors in the houses and apartments of *Faces, Minnie and Moskowitz, A Woman Under the Influence, The Killing of a Chinese Bookie, Opening Night,* or *Gloria.* In both directors' films stairways and passages between public and private spaces, between living rooms and bedrooms, or between theatrical stages and backstage makeup and dressing rooms represent possibilities of social, psychological, and imaginative movement that are at the very heart of the filmmakers' and their central characters' explorations. They come to stand for the possibilities of imaginative transit that the films value much more than any conceivable position or stance.

Cassavetes is not somewhere poised halfway between balanced alternatives; nor does he somehow dramatically subsume or harmonize rival positions into a final synthetic resolution. He and his works live in these imbalances, these denials of the possibility of stasis or poise. As much as his characters, he is torn between contradictory perceptions and impulses; and the very narrative swerves and oscillations in these works are proof of his refusal to deny or compromise these unresolved counter-pulls. It is in this sense that Cassavetes can be said to be his own best critic. He is certainly ahead of any of the critics who have come to his films so far. But his criticism is not in interviews and publicity statements to the press; it is in the films themselves. He has been in them from the beginning, already questioning the impulses each of his critics has only later and more superficially questioned.

The films test his own and his characters' impulses by passing their performances through the environments that most resist them, by passing their imaginative impulses through the personal, social, and narrative contexts most hostile to them. In *A Woman Under the Influence*, Mabel's "madness" begs us to treat it as a state of Laingian transcendence, a visionary superiority to the prosaicism of ordinary life. Pauline Kael and many other critics noted as much in negative reviews of the film, which generally spent more time attacking Laingian psychology than attending to the complexity of Cassavetes' use of (and implicit criticism of) the Laingian point of view in the film. What Kael and others failed to see was how Cassavetes' relentless pulls of focus and shifts of perspective deliberately embed Mabel's Laingian madness in a world of family, friends, and relatives who absolutely deny her the luxury of a transcendent stance. In other words, Cassavetes' photography and editing already criticize the Laingian impulse of the film (even while honoring it and exploring it) more stringently and rigorously than any of his critics could. Minnie and Seymour, shell-shocked and battle-scarred as they are from the wars of love, are two more potential runaways. They would gladly insulate themselves from the shocks and jars of a world that has caused them so much pain (and one can hardly blame them). But it is Cassavetes who prevents them from escaping into either misanthropic reclusiveness or a fairy-tale movie romance and courtship. It is his narrative that prevents their withdrawal from the world, either as lovers or as strangers. His narrative compels them into engagement with the world, and makes possible their eventual engagement with each other. In the largest sense, it was not hostile critics who first criticized the ending of *Minnie and Moskowitz*, but the whole tough-minded film that comes before it. *Minnie and Moskowitz* is, as are most of Cassavetes' other films, a dream movie daring to dream of the most idealistic and passionate possibilities of personal relatedness and romance. But, as its stylistic lurches testify, it is a dream film that works at waking itself up at the same time that it desperately struggles to hold onto its dream.

Similarly, in the later films, the explorations of the complexities of "stardom" represent an examination and worrying of the premises of democracy and principles of democratic interaction upon which the films are organized. The "stars" and would-be "stars" in these films attempt to control a dramatic space and unilaterally dictate the course of interactions, but Cassavetes' photography, editing, and scripting deliberately educate them, and us, into recognizing the necessity of democratic interplay with non-stars, with all the bit players and bit parts of life.

The films are less interested in making an abstract statement about the forms of contemporary American experience than in bracingly, delicately negotiating the counter-pulls and conflicts of that experience. They do not merely choose as their subject matter the paradoxes inherent in the American dream of life, liberty, and the pursuit of happiness, but as discernibly as in the work of Emerson, Hawthorne, William James, and Henry James, in their very forms and rhythms, they embody those divisions of allegiance and conflicts of interest. They enact the tug-of-war between the free expressive needs and desires of the individual, and the responsibilities exacted by a society in which the individual is at best only democratically equal to everyone else. The individual's effort to withdraw from the compromises and pressures of democratic social life into some transcendent freedom and visionary independence is pitted against his inevitable suction back into the force field of society. His attempt to imagine himself an exception to all predetermined categories of relationship and systems of understanding comes into conflict with his discovery of his relentless embeddedness in them. His urge to abandon himself to the vagaries of personal impulse is put in competition with his discovery of his inability to escape fundamental and enduring social, temporal, and structural commitments.

In short, the films (like the characters in them) no sooner dream the dream of individual freedom, adventure, and self-sufficiency than they passionately proceed to question their own dream. As powerfully as these works embrace the imaginative sovereignty, importance, and freedom of the individual, they chasten his individualism by passing him through cinematic and social environments that trouble his dreams. That is why, in the final analysis, though they are populated with escapist, irresponsible, or self-indulgent characters, the films themselves are the opposite of escapist, irresponsible, or self-indulgent. The critics who charge them with this failure cannot tell the dancer from the dance. Cassavetes' characters indeed repeatedly veer off in escapist and individualistic directions, only to have his photography, editing, and soundtrack continuously reimplicate them in the very web of influences, pressures, and contexts from which they thought they could flee.

Characters can never remove themselves from the society of others even for the time of a dream of freedom. (That is why even the films in which there are relatively few principal characters—such as *Faces* or *Husbands*—feel more crowded with human relations than a contemporary blockbuster with a cast of thousands.) These family men and women on the run from the social restrictions and performative limitations of family life are inevitably forced back into the bosoms of their families (or like Harry in *Husbands* are doomed unconsciously to construct a surrogate family outside the home). There is nowhere to run to. Like an earlier cartographer of the counter-pulls of the American dream, Cassavetes realizes that no matter how "lovely, dark and deep" the prospects of escape, transcendence, and vision are, the individual and the individual work are always and everywhere restrained by formal, narrative, social, and psychological "promises to keep."

In my chapter on *Shadows* I described Cassavetes' characters as "figures unfinished with the process of figuration," and, overlooking the difference between the tone of *Shadows* and that of the later films, the phrase might suffice to denote the essential quality of all of Cassavetes' characters. The clowns, the con men, and the hustlers in these films, the emotional babies and the most mature adults—all are figures of desire and would-be free imagination searching for some adequate form of expression for their inchoate, inarticulate dreams. Yet Minnie, Seymour, and Zelmo, Richard, Maria, Chet, and Jeannie, Gus, Harry, and Archie, Nick and Mabel, and all the others are doomed to express themselves in the distorting or repressive forms of ordinary social discourse. To paraphrase Cassavetes' characterization of Minnie Moore's predicament in *Minnie and Moskowitz*, they have all the values, emotions, and ideals in the world but no place to put them. Or, to adapt a line from *The Killing of a Chinese Bookie*, they are perpetually "all dressed up with no place to go." In an Emersonian sense, Cassavetes' characters are spirits with a virtually infinite imagination of personal freedom and expressive intimacy looking to find or make a human community hospitable to their desires. They are lonely souls whose infinities of desire invariably can find no finite form of free expression but who refuse to give up on their quest or abandon hope in its complete fulfillment in the real world of space, time, and society.

This quality shared by all of Cassavetes' characters is what makes Cassavetes' films feel so different from most other contemporary film, theater, fiction, or poetry, even as it affiliates his work most profoundly with the great American tradition of Emerson, Hawthorne, and William and Henry James. The formal, psychological, and social constraints of space, time, family, and society are acknowledged and detailed exhaustively in the films, only to be exploded into irrelevance and unimportance by even more powerful forces of individual desire and imagination. Compared to Cassavetes' work, most other films and twentieth-century American works of art ultimately subjugate their characters to a "reality"—however defined—more powerful than themselves. Individual power is sacrificed to the stability of a system; eccentricity is traded in for consistency and coherence. But in every unpredictable turn and excess of their performances, Cassavetes' characters, like their creator, pay ultimate allegiance not to the virtue of formal stability, but to the adventure of instability and the perpetually deforming and untameable energies of desire and imagination.

Not that they consciously choose to do so. They acutely feel the perilousness of their adventure of insecurity and do everything in their power to avoid it. They struggle desperately to stop the frightening oscillations—once they have almost accidentally released them—that make of their lives an unstable balance. Like Mabel pleading with Nick to "tell me what you want me to be. I can be anything," or Cosmo in his death speech telling his girls to "pick a role . . . be someone else," the characters recoil from the precarious, exhilarating career of freedom Cassavetes propels them, and himself, into. Like the husbands of *Husbands*, they run away from the insights they stumble upon. Like Cosmo, they attempt to hide from their freedom, to repress knowledge of it, or even to deny that there has been any adventure at all or that the life and the death of the soul are at stake in the oscillations of their lives. But the luxury of avoiding the struggle with instability is one that

Cassavetes denies them and denies himself in creating them and in following the tortuous paths of their eccentric careers to the end—the luxury of relaxing into prefabricated identities, inherited forms of expression, and the easy subordination of the putatively free self to formal and social forces. Even to fail is to make a choice in these films. There is no escape from the terrible burden of individual responsibility.

Value is achieved in the moment-by-moment career of a personal performance. In William James' phrase, it grows up *within* experience, and not by reference to preexisting or predetermined forms of meaning or relationship. That is the American, pragmatic adventure of these films—the endless challenge offered to their central characters. But the burden of freedom is also the source of the quiet hysteria and endless anxiety of all of Cassavetes' characters. Their predicaments are potentially as painful and frightening as they are stimulating. They are suspended between vaulting Romantic ideals of freedom and self-expression and an American faith that such ideals only matter in, and can be expressed in, the real world. They are caught in mid-stride between the extraordinary, almost unspeakable dreams and desires of Dreyer's Joan of Arc or Gertrud and an all-American attempt to convert them into practical designs for living and schemes for self-improvement and self-expression like those in a movie by the Marx Brothers or Jerry Lewis.

But why call this an essentially American understanding of experience, and illustrate it with examples from James, Frost, and Capra as I have been doing? I hope the preceding chapters have already suggested several possible reasons. But at the very least one does it to emphasize the fundamental difference between Cassavetes' films and the superficially similar work of certain important contemporary European directors. If Antonioni's, Bergman's, Fassbinder's, or Fellini's films also involve explorations of styles of personal freedom for their central characters, it is with a radically different point of view from Cassavetes. These European directors are in search of escape routes out of the entrapments and paralyses of society, bureaucratic institutions, and certain social relationships, and to that extent their works can be thought to originate in impulses toward freedom similar to those of Cassavetes. But where they differ from him is in the trajectory and end point of those initial impulses. The old, idealistic American dream of making a new society and a new world of new men and women is still alive in Cassavetes' work as it never is in the work of these European filmmakers, for whom the weight of the old world is so tangible and oppressive. The romantic dream of creating a world answerable to the needs of the imagination is still alive in America in Cassavetes' work. For whatever complex historical and cultural reasons, it died long ago in Europe, if it ever existed there. Cassavetes' dream, as exalted as that of the founding fathers, is one that actually aspires to envision a new world of new men and new relationships congruent with the most idealistic conceptions of the freedom and free expression of the individual, not merely (as in Antonioni's work, for example) to escape the old world in the evanescent transcendency of vision, rapture, or the apotheosis of death. Society constrains and limits Antonioni's, Bergman's, Fassbinder's, or Sautet's characters so that on the other side of their impulses toward freedom are, at the most, only the most fleeting and isolated experiences of rapturous vision, apocalyptic apotheosis, or atavistic passion, rather than the *novus ordo seclorum* that is dared to be dreamed at the most exalted moments in Cassavetes' work.

Contrast the destinies of Maria Braun in *The Marriage of Maria Braun*, Guido in $8\frac{1}{2}$, and the Jack Nicholson reporter in *The Passenger* with those of Lelia, Richard Forst, and Cosmo, characters in many respects similar to one another. For all of Cassavetes' stringent criticisms of his characters (and the last two are doomed in any sense of the word), no viewer of the films in which they are featured can avoid seeing that Cassavetes astonishingly enough believes that each of them just might have succeeded in assembling a brave new self free from the fetters and traps of the past if only their performances had been bold and creative enough. Cassavetes is not wearily or cynically criticizing these failed characters for their imaginative audacity. He is not treating their dreams of freedom and ideal community as if they were merely ideals and impossible aspirations, unrealizable in the real world (as Fassbinder does). He is not nostalgically regretting the absence or unattainability of truly visionary possibilities in ordinary life (as Antonioni does). He is not even treating idealistic dreams as special or evanescent events, as unique stylistic, fictional, imaginative, or spiritual achievements (as even visionary filmmakers such as Fellini and Jacques Rivette do). With an unjaded faith that Antonioni, Bergman, Fassbinder, and even Rivette and Fellini lack, that dreams count in the real world of space, time, and society, Cassavetes is enthusiastically endorsing and cheering on the attempts of his characters to start utterly afresh, to remake their identities anew, and to build a society answerable to the most exalted claims of their imaginations. The extraordinary hope of Cassavetes' work, as contrasted with the nostalgia, resignation, or melancholy that pervades most of the work of these other directors, originates in Cassavetes' real belief each and every time that his characters just may succeed in their outrageous imaginative claims on reality. The exhilarating, impossible Emersonian dream just will not die.

The radical difference between two films as superficially similar as Cassavetes' *Husbands* and Rivette's *Céline et Julie Vont en Bateau* is instructive and typical. The similarity of the impulse behind each film is undeniable. Both films are essentially (and explicitly) about the possibilities of "keeping alive the child in the adult." For Céline and Julie, as for Archie, Harry, and Gus, the goal is to keep alive the possibilities of play, creative zaniness, and unpredictability in life. And both films explicitly use the metaphor of improvisation as a technique of survival. But the difference is telling. *Céline et Julie* defines freedom as a state of consciousness estranged from a larger society, while the essence of *Husbands* is to explore the possibility of creating in the real world a society that will answer the requirements of the imagination and the liberated consciousness. That is to say, Cassavetes is interested in forging a "world elsewhere" precisely where Rivette suggests there is nowhere. Rivette is playing games with fictions, with assertively artistic restructurings of consciousness, while Cassavetes is exploring the imaginative possibilities of an actual society of real men.[1] The intractably social side of Cassavetes' work—the public nature of its personal transactions, the incessant meetings, introductions, and farewells, and the seemingly unending talk—is of the essence of his vision of realizing the dream of freedom not merely as a matter of consciousness, style, or art but as a social reality in the real world.

At several points earlier in my discussion I've compared Cassavetes' scenes with those of Harold Pinter. If one enlarges the genre of drama to include film, I take them to be the two major dramatists in the English language to have emerged during the past twenty-five years. They are the dramatists whose characters are situated in social matrices of the greatest density and extensiveness, and the two preeminent contemporary masters in the depiction of the intricate, oblique ways characters negotiate such social matrices and jockey for positions within them in the continuous play of their talk, their glances, their pauses, and their silences.

For all of their similarity, however, there is an essential difference between Cassavetes' work and that of Pinter that helps to define Cassavetes' emphatic Americanness. Compare *Faces*, Cassavetes' most Pinteresque drama in its social density, psychological enclosure, and physical confinement, with Pinter's *The Homecoming*. Many aspects of the two works are related, but while Pinter is obviously engaged in criticizing particular social, familial, and sexual structurings of power and personal relations, he is utterly British in his refusal to do what Cassavetes does in *Faces*, which is to suggest the possible inadequacy or irrelevance of *all* merely social structures and arrangements of experience. The extreme, unappeasable energies of personal idealism and emotion registered in *Faces* (which are completely absent from *The Homecoming*) act as a radical criticism not simply of the particular forms of social relationship embodied in the work, but of the adequacy of all possible and conceivable social structurings and expressions of desire and imagination. Cassavetes' films (like Chaplin's, Capra's, or Ray's) expose us to extravagances and intensities of idealism and feeling that carry us beyond the particularities of a local criticism of the social matrix to an interrogation of its adequacy in *any* conceivable form to answer to the truths of the human spirit and our needs of self-expression. For all four American filmmakers there may be an unbridgeable gap between the dreams of the imagination and the expressive possibilities of all actual society and all forms of self-expression. There may be, and then again there may not be; they cannot make up their minds. For all four that doubt is not, however, reason to abandon the dream, but justification for embracing it all the more firmly.

It is at this point that Cassavetes' work departs most decisively from that of most other contemporary American filmmakers as well. Richard Poirier has brilliantly argued that the tradition of American literature split in the twentieth century into two lines, the one a vestige of the original visionary strain, and the other a turning away from the Jamesian faith in the power of desire and the imagination to transform reality, in order to grovel in the realities of Wharton and Dreiser. The same split may be said to have taken place in American film.

In discussing *Minnie and Moskowitz*, I alluded to one manifestation of this split in American filmmaking, in terms of the two distinct forms of romantic comedy created during the 1930s and 1940s—the "idealistic" comedies in the Chaplin-Capra line and the socially "pragmatic" or utilitarian comedies of Van Dyke, Hawks, and Sturges. But the split is even more visible in the serious films of the 1940s and later. Especially after the Second World War (and coincident with Capra's own abandonment of the visionary impulse in his work) most American film took the path of Wyler, Zinnemann, Kramer, Ritt, Pakula, Pollack, and Lumet to social relevance and reconciliation, acknowledging no higher imaginative aspiration than the integration of the individual into society. It is from that tendency that Cassavetes departs, to hearken back to the visionary strain that virtually ended in this country with Capra's populist works. That is what makes Cassavetes' films stand out as being so radically different from most of the American work of the past thirty years. Far from compromising the individual imagination in an attempt to find a local habitation and a name for it, or embracing the overriding postwar goal of integrating the individual into society, Cassavetes' films cry out for the unappeasability and absolute sovereignty of imagination and desire.

And as in the great tradition of American literature from Hawthorne and Emerson to James, Faulkner, and West, the result of the discrepancy that the work opens up between the imagination and the world, the gap between uncompromising desire and any possible object of its fulfillment, is manifested in the excessiveness, gratuitousness, and mysteriousness of style. One must, therefore, reverse Cassavetes' protestation that he is a filmmaker without a style, and argue that it is almost all other American films that are styleless (notwithstanding their "obsession with technique and camera angles"), and his that are the most stylistically anxious and aware. Other films tacitly deny style any power to transform reality, but in Cassavetes' work the old dream of changing reality through style is still alive. The excesses, the repetitions, the longueurs, the loose ends, and the mysteriousness of his films are the most eloquent registrations in contemporary film of the vaulting dreams of perfect self-expression and democratic community that cannot find any other outlet or expression than in this violence (some would say crudity) of style.

But what keeps Cassavetes from floating off into the solipsistic heaven of the avant-gardists is precisely the yoking of the most extreme claims of the imagination to the most mundane events and worldly settings. Imagination is never able to escape the obstacle course of reality. To put it in terms of the Puritan imagination, which it so much resembles, there is what one might call a "work ethic" in Cassavetes' films. It is an ethic of reimmersion in the forms and obligations of society that shapes the major works in the American artistic tradition and counteracts the visionary tendencies present in the same works. There is a requirement that the hero or saint negotiate the ultimate refining fire of social forms and relations. For Cassavetes, as for Emerson, there can be no self-sufficient escape into a dream of personal transcendence, however tempting the prospect. The vision must always be brought back to the world of social responsibilities; it must always be forced to negotiate the styles and tones of social intercourse. The individual must return to the bosom of the family from his excursion into the wilderness.

There is, needless to say, a visionary impulse at the heart of the American experience from Cooper to Frost, but if characters run off to construct and temporarily inhabit imaginative "worlds elsewhere," they and their creators only care about their experience insofar as it can be brought back home to those who stay at home. That the American sublime can be domesticated is indeed the dream of America. Like the literary heroes who precede them, Cassavetes' characters are only momentarily able to entertain the ideal of leaving society behind and giving unfettered expression to themselves. (In Twain and James it is those ersatz Europeans the Duke and the Dauphin and the Pateresque artist Gilbert Osmond who aspired to such self-possessed self-sufficiency. The goal of Huck Finn and Isabel Archer—or even a paragon of self-reliance such as Thoreau—is not visionary escape or radical individualism, but the opposite of these things: participation in a truer community and fuller membership in a larger and more extended family than is available to them when they begin their individual excursions.)

Cassavetes can, on these grounds, and especially in contrast with filmmakers such as Antonioni and Fassbinder, be accused of cultural and imaginative conservatism (just as Robert Frost, William Carlos Williams, Elizabeth Bishop, or Anton Chekhov can be accused of the same thing when compared with more visionary or more apocalyptic writers). His films, after all, offer not even the most temporary possibilities of transcendence or of release from the most minor excruciations of life for his characters. A character can never remove himself from a family in these films—whether the particular family in the film is biological, social, professional, or imaginative: the extended ethnic family of the Longhettis; the suburban circle of acquaintances around the Forsts; or the economic, bureaucratic, and professional tangles of influence within which Cosmo, Myrtle, and Gloria explore the possibilities of movement. But Cassavetes' aesthetic is less a repressive political or ideological stance than a tough-minded recognition of certain unavoidable realities of the family-centered, domestic, work-a-day world his characters (like most of his viewers) inhabit.

For Cassavetes' family men and women, dreams of adventure, freedom, and escape inevitably have social consequences. Influences and pressures can never be escaped, wished away, or transcended; they can only be lived through. For a member of an actual family, success can never be defined through strategies of repudiation, flight, or withdrawal, but only through acts of loving inclusion, accommodation, and the enlargement of sensibilities and responsiveness. Whatever may be the case in the financial and commercial attainment of the American dream (where a get-rich-quick scheme may conceivably allow one to strike it rich with practically no investment of time, money, or effort), in the realms of marriage, the home, and the family, there can be no visionary or imaginative shortcuts to happiness. If Cassavetes' films are conservative, it is in recognition of the conservative realities of adult emotional life and all long-term human relationships.

But lest this sound too oppressive, lest the individual seem too hedged round with responsibilities and networks of obligation in this world, several facts about Cassavetes' vision of the family and of the role of the individual within it should be remembered. In the first place, the individual performer as Cassavetes imagines him is fully equal to the task before him. There are few artists with a more exalted and exalting sense of the potential strength and inventiveness of their characters, and of their nearly infinite capability to creatively reshape their identities under pressure of the forces around them.

Unlike the characters in Altman's or Antonioni's films, Cassavetes' characters are, with all their flaws and foibles, exhilaratingly capable of holding their own against the best (and the worst) to which their director can subject them. Unlike the characters in Hawks's, Ray's, or Scorsese's films (the last being a director whose work is often bracketed with that of Cassavetes because of the tremendous admiration of the younger man for the older), the improvisational eccentricity and energy of Cassavetes' characters, to the extent that they interest him, is always a form of creative engagement with the social world, never an escape from it or a form of irresponsibility, alienation, or neurosis. Hawks, Ray, and Scorsese, in effect, define the possibilities of life and drama in terms of contrasted, mutually exclusive, alternatives. On the one side is the play of desire and imagination expressed in performative excess, eccentricity, and theatricality. On the other, are the quotidian social responsibilities of family, wife, children, society, and friends. But for Capra and Cassavetes the two realms are not alternatives. Dreams are not evasions, or saving escapes, or temporary comic or neurotic aberrations, but are, if they are valuable at all, the enrichment of all of life. Capra and Cassavetes believe fervently that our actual social roles and identities are not something defined in advance, independent of our desires and separate from our capacities of performance, something to which we must either yield or against which we must rebel, but are up for continuous imaginative reappropriation and redeployment. Compare the heroines of Antonioni's *The Red Desert* and Cassavetes' *A Woman Under the Influence*. Both are women driven half-crazy by their feelings of isolation and the failures of communication in their lives. But how different and much bleaker is Antonioni's sense of the possibilities available to Guiliana from Cassavetes' vision of the possibilities for Mabel. Both women begin in the same state. But while Guiliana is, in effect, trapped throughout her film in an old, outmoded self, Mabel is free to remake herself and her relations with others in a nearly infinite variety of ways. While Guiliana is stuck in her failed dreams and the memories of her past, Mabel can remake her identity in endlessly inventive performances of her self.

Erik Erikson said that the central problem of the American personality is the unending and ever-revised quest for identity, and Cassavetes' films take as their subject crises of identity at least as profound as those Erikson described. But even Erikson did not have a greater confidence in the power of the self to reform itself in exhilarating, life-affirming performances under the pressure of the influences it must negotiate. It is not an exaggeration to say that American art and John Cassavetes' films in particular empower the individual performer as has not been done since the drama of the English Renaissance. The idealism of Cassavetes' films is, in this context, only his supreme faith in each character's capacities to improvise himself creatively into productive relatedness with those around him, while at the same time not sacrificing his free and mobile imagination.

The family becomes the model for all performative relations in Cassavetes' work. The family is simultaneously the stage, the audience, the arena, and the troupe of actors in these films. That is why, as prosaic as they may seem at first glance, the central events in most of these films—learning how to be a mother, father, husband, wife, lover, or friend—have nothing to do with mastering a fixed set of rules or roles. As Cassavetes imagines it, the family, with its endless adjustments, transactions, and shifts of roles and relationships, is the essential testing ground for the greatest and most challenging performances of life and art.

And the corollary of that is that the family, far from being the enemy of the individual, is the place where his true freedom is brought into existence, tested, and sustained. That was the ideal of the robustly ethnic family in which Cassavetes was raised, the ideal of the family he and Gena Rowlands have created with their children, and the ideal of these films. The family is the place where the most exciting energies of performance are stimulated and released, not repressed. An individual does not exist in his full potentiality except in a family (in the largest imaginative sense of the word); to leave the family behind would be to leave part of himself behind. As Nick and Mabel Longhetti most eloquently demonstrate, it is only in negotiating all of the influences and pressures of family life, in the labor of loving adjustment to all of the others around a character, that the individual is stimulated into the fullest existence. To escape the tug and pull of family influences, however painful they may be to live with, is to become one of the hopeless drifters or derelicts in these films.

Finally, and perhaps most importantly, what is implicit in this performative aesthetic is that the family within which the individual makes his identity is not a fixed entity, a social structure he must take or leave, or with which he is forced to come into slavish congruence. Basic to Cassavetes' work is the proposition that the families, societies, and relationships in which his characters are involved are made by the individuals themselves. They are not something imposed upon the characters by forces beyond their control, but something always up for rearrangement, renewal, and reappropriation. The society of these films is not something determined in advance, prefabricated before the individual enters into a contract with it, but something improvised into existence and continually revised by the particular individuals who are its members.

The vision of the relationship of the individual to others in this society is one that is present in Cassavetes' work as early as *Shadows*. Cassavetes' goal is that individual differences be brought into their fullest and most robust play in the competition of as many different styles, tones, and performances as possible. In this healthily competitive society, the individual is not levelled into neutrality or homogenized into blandness, but is brought into his fullest, freest and most independent identity through the play of differences. That is the source of the distinctively American optimism and pragmatism of these films.

To emphasize the "optimism" (or what would better be called the "life-affirming" qualities) of these films is, obviously, not at all to suggest that they are callow or simplemindedly positive (that should be abundantly clear from the preceding discussion). Indeed, the performances Cassavetes offers for our inspection are more often than not as painful and troubling as anything in twentieth-century art. And yet it is still necessary to insist that while Antonioni, Altman, Kubrick, Bergman, and Coppola offer essentially negative stances on the prospects for meaningful human communication and relatedness at this time and place in civilization, Cassavetes, for all his tough-mindedness and what he calls his cynicism, stands almost alone in making films (however excruciating) that testify to the power, and not the weakness, of the human spirit and to the potential stimulation, and not the necessary frustration, of all human society. In fact, it is precisely to the extent that he convinces us that he and his characters have looked into the abyss and still managed to keep buoyantly alive the possibilities of love and generosity that one is so moved and elated by Cassavetes' affirmations. One might argue that the supreme works of art in the Western tradition are always just such bracing acts of affirmation. Needless to say, this runs against all of the cults of fashionable nihilism in the criticism of the arts today and for most of this century. Shakespeare was another such idealistic dramatist, who for all of his tough-mindedness was as (anachronistically) romantic as Cassavetes in this respect. During the darkest scenes in *Hamlet, Lear,* or *Antony and Cleopatra,* great tragedies though they are, there is still communicated his almost breathless wonder at the indominability and incorruptible nobility of the human spirit. Overcoming all the dread, there is a still stronger feeling of exhilaration at the performative range, freedom, and power of the individual actor. It is a feeling not unlike the strange exhilaration bordering on joy communicated during even the saddest, most tragic and painful moments in *Faces* and *A Woman Under the Influence.* This is not to deny the inordinate pain, but to recognize that one watches the painful beauty and nobility of the performances of these actors, these characters, and their creator with an awed sense of exaltation that such things are possible. That is why Cassavetes' tragedies can paradoxically, in the very depths they plumb, like the tragedies of all the greatest playwrights from Shakespeare to Chekhov, leave one feeling more refreshed and inspired by the greatness of the human heart than other artists' rose-colored visions.

It has been the argument of these pages that John Cassavetes is, even in the most painful of his films, for these reasons our noblest, most inspiring, and truest historian of the American experience. He is our greatest dreamer, dreaming the dream of America as it has been dreamed by generations since the beginning. Both as a filmmaker and as an artist, he is an American dreamer attempting to beat the system and trying to keep alive his own extravagant, idealistic dream of the possibility of personal freedom and individual expression in the repressive bureaucratic, social, and stylistic environments of modern film-making; just as the characters in his films are American dreamers trying to keep alive their middle-class dreams of life, freedom, and self-expression in the challenging emotional, psychological, and familial environments in which he situates them. His films are chronicles of the yearnings, excitements, and frustrations of daring to dream that American dream, and of the conflict between the ideals and the realities of the contemporary American experience inside and outside of Hollywood.

His is the impossible, exalted dream of making a world and a society hospitable to the unappeasability of human imagination and the insatiability of desire. It is the dream of being able to improvise a new self and an original performance for a new world, free from alien styles and artificial restrictions. It is the dream of being able to make one's own homemade society and identity, and to be free to remake and revise them as often as necessary, and to be able to find one's truest freedom in the process. The bold, idealistic settlers and immigrants who came to this country, like John Cassavetes' own father, came not in quest of individual autonomy, independence, and isolation, but in the dream of building a community of families and relationships within which the individual would not sacrifice his freedom, but come into the fullest possession of it for the first time. That was the American dream of life, liberty, and the pursuit of happiness. These films worry that dream all over again—the possibility of personal freedom amid the responsibilities of democracy; the possibility of inhabiting a society answerable to one's most excessive ideals of independence and self-expression; the possibilities of fashioning "star" performances within the person-withering bureaucracies of modern culture. The worry, for anyone who cares as passionately about the American experience as John Cassavetes does, is inseparable from the dream.

NOTES

The epigraph from John Cassavetes on p. vii is from an interview with J. Stevenson, "John Cassavetes: Film's Bad Boy," *American Film* 5 (January–February 1980): 48; the epigraph from Emerson is the opening sentence in his essay "Experience," reprinted in *Selected Writings of Ralph Waldo Emerson* (New York: New American Library, 1965), p. 327.

INTRODUCTION

The epigraph is quoted from a discussion of *Faces* in Joseph Gelmis, *The Film Director as Superstar* (Garden City, N.Y.: Doubleday, 1970), p. 80.

I. FREEDOM FROM STYLES AND STYLES OF FREEDOM

The epigraph from Henry James is from an unsigned review of *Azarian: An Episode* in *North American Review* 100 (January 1865): 276; the epigraph from Cassavetes is from Joseph Gelmis, *The Film Director as Superstar* (Garden City, N.Y.: Doubleday, 1970), p. 82.

[1]Two books deserve mention as notable exceptions to the general neglect. Diane Jacobs in *Hollywood Renaissance* (South Brunswick: A. S. Barnes, 1977) and James Monaco in *American Film Now* (New York: Oxford, 1979) both recognize Cassavetes as a major director, though neither has space or opportunity to discuss his work in the detail it deserves.

[2]Gelmis, p. 79.

[3]See my discussion of this "high-tech" phenomenon in modern literature in my essay on John Ashbery, in *American Poets Since World War II,* ed. Donald Greiner (Detroit: Bruccoli-Clark, 1980).

[4]Gelmis, p. 82.

[5]Gelmis, pp. 82–83.

[6]Colin Young and Gideon Bachmann, "New Wave or Gesture?" *Film Quarterly* 14 (Spring 1961): 7.

[7]"*Playboy* Interview: John Cassavetes," *Playboy* 18 (July 1971): 70.

[8]Young and Bachmann, p. 7.

II. MAKING SCENES AND FORGING IDENTITIES:
THE MAKING OF *SHADOWS*

The chapter epigraph from Henry James is quoted from his *Autobiography,* ed. Frederick W. Dupee (New York: Criterion Books, 1956), pp. 106–7; the epigraph on page 56 is from "John Cassavetes Goes for the Edge," in Grover Lewis, *Academy All the Way* (San Francisco: Straight Arrow Books, 1974), p. 115.

[1]John Cassavetes, ". . . and the Pursuit of Happiness," *Films and Filming* 7 (February 1961): 7.

[2]Ibid.

[3]Clara Hoover, "An Interview With Hugh Hurd," *Film Comment* 1, no. 4 (1963): 25–26.

[4]John C. Waugh, "A Director's Hopes," *Christian Science Monitor*, 14 February 1961, p. 6.

[5]Joseph Gelmis, *The Film Director as Superstar* (Garden City, N.Y.: Doubleday, 1970), p. 83.

[6]Pauline Kael, "The Corrupt and the Primitive," in *Going Steady* (New York: New American Library, 1970), p. 239.

III. CHILDREN, CLOWNS, AND CON MEN: WORKING FOR HOLLYWOOD ON *TOO LATE BLUES* AND *A CHILD IS WAITING*

The epigraph is from the introduction to the published screenplay of *Faces* (New York: New American Library, 1970), p. 7.

[1]"*Playboy* Interview: John Cassavetes," *Playboy* 18 (July 1971): 70.

[2]John Cassavetes, "What's Wrong With Hollywood," *Film Culture* 19 (April 1959): 4–5.

[3]"*Playboy* Interview," p. 211.

IV. FIGURES OF DESIRE: *FACES*

The epigraph from Cassavetes is taken from André S. Labarthé, "A Way of Life: An Interview with John Cassavetes," *Evergreen*, March 1969, p. 47.

[1]Jonas Mekas, "Movie Journal," *Village Voice*, 23 December 1971, p. 63.

[2]Labarthé, p. 46.

[3]This as well as all of the quotations in the following paragraph are taken from Cassavetes' introduction to the published screenplay of *Faces* (New York: New American Library, 1970) pp. 7–9. Cassavetes is quite casual about dates in his statements about his films and I have silently corrected the dates in this quotation. For the record, *Faces* was written between October and December 1964. After a month of rehearsals and some rough blocking, filming began on 2 January 1965 and was completed in July of that year. John Cassavetes' home was used as the set for the Forst home; the home of Lady Rowlands, Gena Rowlands's mother, was used as the set for Jeannie Rapp's apartment. The film was in editing from July 1965 to March 1968 at which point a 220-minute print was shown to enthusiastic audiences in Beverly Hills, Toronto, and Montreal. By August, the 129-minute version of the film as it presently exists was arrived at and screened in several locations abroad. *Faces* received its official American premiere in September at the New York Film Festival, and was nationally distributed in November 1968.

[4]"*Faces*: A New Film by John Cassavetes," *Cinema* 4 (Spring 1968): 25.

[5]Max Lerner, *America as a Civilization* (New York: Simon and Schuster, 1957), p. 691.

[6]Ibid., p. 585.

[7]In fact, Cassavetes' attempt to have "everything lean on something and the whole lean on nothing" accounts for the only false moment in the film, the initial match-cut between the first scene and the title of the film. When Richard Forst sits down in his corporate screening room to preview the film his advertising people are trying to sell him, and Cassavetes cuts from a shot of the blank screen and the glare of the projector light in Richard's office to the title of the movie we are watching, the effect is merely artsy and arch. The shortcoming of this particular ironic juxtaposition is that the match is purely a formal one and has no important human significance in the film. But this is the only false moment in a marvelously braced and bracing series of matchings. Fortunately, the connection at this moment is so hollow and merely theoretical that we forget it seconds after it occurs. The strength of the other match-cuts in *Faces* is that they contextualize, and therefore comment upon, the contents, and not merely the forms, of the scenes they join.

[8]Joseph Gelmis, *The Film Director as Superstar* (Garden City, N.Y.: Doubleday, 1970), p. 84.

[9]Gautan Dasgupta, "A Director of Influence: John Cassavetes," *Film* (England) no. 26 (May 1976), p. 5.

[10]J. Stevenson, "John Cassavetes: Film's Bad Boy," *American Film* 5 (January–February 1980): 46.

[11]Gelmis, pp. 80–81.

V. IN DREAMS BEGIN RESPONSIBILITIES: *HUSBANDS*

The first epigraph is taken from Lynn Bloom, "Cassavetes, Falk, Gazzara," *Girl Talk*, May 1971, p. 32; the second is from Joseph Gelmis, *The Film Director as Superstar* (Garden City, N.Y.: Doubleday, 1970), p. 86.

[1]Andrew Sarris, "Some Strange Movies Have Slipped By," *Village Voice*, 1 March 1976, pp. 115–16.

[2]Ann Guerin, "Dead-On Dialogue as the Cash Runs Out," *Life*, 9 May 1969, pp. 54–55.

[3]George Plimpton, ed., *Writers at Work: The Paris Review Interviews, Second Series* (New York: Penguin, 1977), pp. 346–47. See my brief discussion of cinematic superficiality in a review of David Thomson's *Overexposures* and *A Biographical Dictionary of Film* in *Chicago Review* 34 (Summer 1983): 111–16.

[4]Ralph Appelbaum, "Crucial Culture: An Interview with John Cassavetes," *Films* 1 (January 1981): 16.

VI. LOVE ON THE RUN: *MINNIE AND MOSKOWITZ*

The epigraph is from the introduction to the published screenplay of *Minnie and Moskowitz* (Los Angeles: Black Sparrow Press, 1973).

[1]"Playboy Interview: John Cassavetes," *Playboy* 18 (July 1971): 70.

[2]Andrew Bergman, *We're in the Money: Depression America and Its Films* (New York: New York University Press, 1971), pp. 133–34.

[3]Wylie Sypher, *Comedy* (Garden City, N.Y.: Doubleday, 1956), pp. 241–42.

[4]All quotations from this scene are for convenience of reference taken from pages 45–49 of the published screenplay of *Minnie and Moskowitz*, which, in this

scene, differs only slightly from the phrasing of the finished film and is somewhat more complete.

[5]Jonas Mekas, "Movie Journal," *Village Voice*, 23 December 1971, p. 64.

[6]Gavin Millar, "Cassavetes," *The Listener* (England), 11 January 1973, p. 61.

[7]Toni Kosover, "It's What's Going on Behind the Faces That *Faces* Is All About," *Women's Wear Daily*, 19 November 1968, p. 4.

[8]Gautan Dasgupta, "A Director of Influence: John Cassavetes," *Film* (England), no. 26 (May 1976), p. 5.

[9]William James, from the chapter "Pragmatism and Humanism," in *Pragmatism*, reprinted in *Pragmatism and Other Essays* (New York: Washington Square Press, 1963), p. 115.

[10]Ibid., p. 114.

VII. MASTERING THE INFLUENCES: *A WOMAN UNDER THE INFLUENCE*

The epigraph is from Gautan Dasgupta, "A Director of Influence: John Cassavetes," *Film* (England), no. 26 (May 1976), p. 5.

[1]Judith McNally, "*A Woman Under the Influence:* An Interview with John Cassavetes," *Filmmaker's Newsletter* 8 (January 1975): 25.

[2]Andrew Kopkind, "Mabel's Mad Againe," review of *A Woman Under the Influence*, *The Real Paper*, 19 February 1975, p. 15.

[3]See the discussions of Ozu's "classicism" and Dreyer's "romanticism" in my essays on Dreyer's *Ordet* and *Gertrud* and Ozu's *Tokyo Story*, *Late Autumn*, *Equinox Flower*, and *The Flavor of Green Tea Over Rice* in *Magill's Survey of Cinema—Foreign Language Films*, ed. Frank Magill (Englewood Cliffs, N.J.: Salem Press, 1984).

[4]McNally, pp. 24–25.

[5]André Bazin, "*The River:* A Pure Masterpiece," in *Jean Renoir* (New York: Simon and Schuster, 1973), pp. 107–8.

[6]Dasgupta, p. 5.

[7]"*Playboy* Interview: John Cassavetes," *Playboy* 18 (July 1971): 62.

[8]Dasgupta, p. 4.

VIII. SELF-DEFENSE, SELF-SUFFICIENCY, AND SELF-ANNIHILATION:
THE KILLING OF A CHINESE BOOKIE

The epigraph from Norman Mailer is from the essay "The White Negro," reprinted in *Advertisements for Myself* (New York: G. P. Putnam's Sons, 1976), p. 301; the epigraph from Emerson is from "Self-Reliance," reprinted in *Selected Writings of Ralph Waldo Emerson* (New York: New American Library, 1965), p. 262.

IX. BUREAUCRACIES OF THE IMAGINATION: *OPENING NIGHT*

The epigraph from John Cassavetes is from Russell Au Werter, "A Talk with John Cassavetes," *Action: The Director's Guild of America* 5 (January–February 1970): 14; the epigraph from Emerson is from "Fate," reprinted in *Selected Writings of Ralph Waldo Emerson* (New York: New American Library, 1965), p. 382.

[1]For a more extended discussion of contemporary film criticism, see my "Film Criticism," *Raritan Review* 1 (Fall 1981): 89–106, and "Writing in the Dark," *Chicago Review* 34 (Summer 1983): 89–110.

X. BEATING THE SYSTEM: *GLORIA*

The epigraph is from Tony Galluzzo, "Movie Making: An Interview with John Cassavetes," *Modern Photography* 36 (June 1972): 111.

[1]J. Stevenson, "John Cassavetes: Film's Bad Boy," *American Film* 5 (January–February 1980): 46.

XI. WORRYING THE DREAM

The initial epigraph is quoted in Jeanine Basinger, "America's Love Affair with Frank Capra," *American Film* 7 (March 1982): 81; the second is from Gautan Dasgupta, "A Director of Influence: John Cassavetes," *Film* (England), no. 26 (May 1976), p. 6.

[1]See my discussion of Rivette's *Céline and Julie Go Boating* in *Magill's Survey of Cinema—Foreign Language Films*, ed. Frank Magill (Englewood Cliffs, N.J.: Salem Press, 1984).

FILMOGRAPHY

Shadows (1958, 1959)

Script and Direction	John Cassavetes (based upon a drama workshop improvisation)
Assistant Director	Al Giglio
Lighting	David Simon
Lighting Assistant	Cliff Carnell
Photography	Erich Kollmar (16 mm/black and white)
Assistant Cameraman	Al Ruban
Sound	Jay Crecco
Music	Charlie Mingus
Saxophone Solos	Shafi Hadi
Songs	Jack Ackerman ("Beautiful") Hunt Stevens Eleanor Winters
Sets	Randy Liles Bob Reeh
Editor	Maurice McEndree
Supervising Editor	Len Appelson
Production Manager	Wray Bevins
Production Assistants	Maxine Arnolds Anne Draper Mary Ann Ehle Ellen Paulos Leslie Reed Judy Kaufman
Producers	Maurice McEndree and Nikos Papatakis (for Gena Production)
Associate Producer	Seymour Cassel
Distribution (USA)	Lion International Films Ltd., and subsequently by Faces International Films, Inc.
Running Time	60 minutes (1958 print in 16 mm); 87 minutes (1959 print, enlarged to 35 mm from 16 mm)

CAST

Ben	Ben Carruthers
Lelia	Lelia Goldoni
Hugh	Hugh Hurd
Tony	Anthony Ray
Dennis	Dennis Sallas
Tom	Tom Allen
David	David Pokitillow
Rupert	Rupert Crosse
Davey	Davey Jones
Vickie	Victoria Vargas
Piano Player	Pir Marini
Jack, director of dance studio	Jack Ackerman
Jacqueline	Jacqueline Walcott
Three girls in restaurant	Joyce Miles
	Nancy Deale
	Gigi Brooks
Girls at party	Lynne Hamelton
	Marilyn Clark
	Joanne Sages
	Jed McGarvey
	Greta Thysen
and featuring also	Cliff Carnell
	Jay Crecco
	Ronald Maccone
	Bob Reeh
	John Cassavetes

Too Late Blues (1961)

Direction	John Cassavetes
Script	John Cassavetes and Richard Carr
Photography	Lionel Lindon (black and white)
Editing	Frank Bracht
Music	David Raksin
	(seventeen original pieces by Shelley Manne, Red Mitchell, Benny Carter, Uan Rasey and Jimmy Rowles)
Art Director	Tambi Larsen
Dialogue Coach	Jud Taylor
Production Manager	William Mull
Assistant Director	Arthur Jacobson
Costumes	Edith Head
Producer	John Cassavetes for Paramount
Running Time	103 minutes

CAST

John "Ghost" Wakefield	Bobby Darin
Jess Polanski	Stella Stevens
Benny Flowers	Everett Chambers
Nick	Nick Dennis
Baby Jackson	Rupert Crosse
Tommy	Vince Edwards
Frielobe	Val Avery
Skipper	J. Allen Hopkins
Reno, the barman	James Joyce
Countess	Marilyn Clark
Billie Gray	Allyson Ames
Girl at bar	June Wilkinson
Charlie, the saxophonist	Cliff Carnell
Red, the bassist	Seymour Cassel
Shelley, the drummer	Dan Stafford
Pete, the trumpet player	Richard Chambers

A Child Is Waiting (1963)

Direction	John Cassavetes
Script	Abby Mann
	(based on his original story and teleplay)
Photography	Joseph LaShelle (black and white)
Production Designer	Rudolph Sternad
Editor	Gene Fowler, Jr.
Music	Ernest Gold
Sound	James Speak
Assistant Directors	Lindsley Parsons, Jr., and Douglas Green
Production Manager	Nate H. Edwards
Associate Producer	Philip Langner
Producer	Stanley Kramer. A Larcas Production for United Artists
Running Time	102 minutes

CAST

Dr. Matthew Clark	Burt Lancaster
Jean Hansen	Judy Garland
Sophie Widdicombe	Gena Rowlands
Ted Widdicombe	Steven Hill
Reuben Widdicombe	Bruce Ritchey
Mattie	Gloria McGehee
Goodman	Paul Stewart

Miss Fogarty	Elizabeth Wilson
Miss Brown	Barbara Pepper
Holland	John Marley
Mrs. McDonald	June Walker
Dr. Lombardi	Mario Gallo
Dr. Sack	Fred Draper
Douglas Benham	Lawrence Tierney
Mrs. Phillips	Ruby Dandridge
Dr. Mazer	Tiger Joe Marsh
Others	Billy Mumy, Brian Corcoran, Jay Phillips, Butch Patrick, Michael Stevens, Kenneth Carter, David Markowitz, Marilyn Clark, George Dunn, J. Allen Hopkins, James Rawley, David Fresco, Noam Pitlik, Kelly O'Hara, Tony Maxwell, David Ocnoff, Sighle Lancaster, Moria Turner, Ted Jacques, Amy Bade, Ruth Clark, and the children of the Pacific State Hospital in Pomona.

Faces (1968)

Script and Direction	John Cassavetes
Photography	Al Ruban (16 mm/black and white)
Camera Operator	George Sims
Musical Director	Jack Ackerman
Song	Charles Smalls ("Never Felt Like This Before")
Art Director	Phedon Papamichael
Editors	Al Ruban and Maurice McEndree
Sound	Don Pike
Associate Producer	Al Ruban
Producer	Maurice McEndree
Distribution	Walter Reade, Inc. and subsequently by Faces International Films, Inc.
Running Time	A 220-minute print was shown to various audiences in March 1968; a final 129-minute print was completed in August 1968.

CAST

Richard Forst	John Marley
Jeannie Rapp	Gena Rowlands

Maria Forst	Lynn Carlin
Chet	Seymour Cassel
Freddie	Fred Draper
Jim McCarthy	Val Avery
Florence	Dorothy Gulliver
Louise	Joanne Moore Jordan
Billy Mae	Darlene Conley
Joe Jackson	Gene Darfler
Stella	Elizabeth Deering
Anne	Anne Shirley
Nita	Nita White
Harry Selfrine	Erwin Sirianni
Jim Mortensen	Jim Bridges
Edward Kazmier	Don Kranz
Judd Lang	John Hale
J. P.	John Finnegan
Comedian	O. G. Dunn
Bartender	George Sims
Others	Dave Mazzie
	Julie Gambol

Husbands (1970)

Script and Direction	John Cassavetes
Director of Photography	Victor Kemper
Production Supervisor	Fred Caruso
Supervising Editor	Peter Tanner
Assistant Editor	Tom Cornwell
Post-production Editor	Jack Woods
Assistant Editor	Robert Heffernan
Production Coordinator	James Joyce
Production Controller	Bert Schneiderman
Color	by Deluxe
Producer	Al Ruban and Sam Shaw for Columbia Pictures
Running Time	154 minutes at its initial screening in San Francisco; 140 minutes in the revised release print.

IN NEW YORK:

Art Director	Rene D'Auriac
Production Manager	Robert Greenhut
Script Continuity	Nancy Norman
First Assistant Director	Alan Hopkins
Camera Operator	Richard Mingalone
	Mike Chapman

First Assistant Cameraman	Edward Gold
Sound	Dennis Maitland
Gaffer	Richard Quinlan
Dialogue Supervisor	Fred Draper
Composition Artist	Edith Shaw

IN LONDON:

First Assistant Director	Simon Hinkley
Second Assistant Director	Phillip Mead
Camera Operator	Jeff Glover
First Assistant Cameraman	Edward Gold
Sound	Barrie Copland
Gaffer	Len Crow
Props and Effects	Henry Newman
Script Continuity	Peggy Lashbrook

CAST

Harry	Ben Gazzara
Archie	Peter Falk
Gus	John Cassavetes
Mary Tynan	Jenny Runacre
Pearl Billingham	Jenny Lee Wright
Julie	Noelle Kao
Leola	Leola Harlow
Annie	Meta Shaw
Red	John Kullers
The Countess	Delores Delmar
Diana Mallabee	Peggy Lashbrook
Mrs. Hines	Eleanor Zee
Stuart's Wife	Claire Malis
Annie's Mother	Lorraine McMartin
Ed Weintraub	Edgar Franken
Sarah	Sarah Felcher
"Jesus Loves Me"	Antoinette Kray
"Jeannie"	Gwen Van Dam
"Happy Birthday"	John Armstrong
"Normandy"	Eleanor Bould
Susanna	Carinthia West
Margaret	Rhonda Parker
Minister	Joseph Boley
Stuart's Grandmother	Judith Lowry
"Shanghai Lil"	Joseph Hardy
Barmaid	K. C. Townsend
Nurse	Anne O'Donnell
Nurse	Gena Wheeler
Stuart Jackson	David Rowlands

Minnie and Moskowitz (1971)

Script and Direction	John Cassavetes
Photography	Alric Edens
	Arthur J. Ornitz
	Michael Margulies
Sound	Melvin M. Metcalfe, Sr.
Film Editor	Robert Heffernan
Post-production Supervisor	Fred Knutsen, Jr.
Costume Designer	Helen Colvig
Musical Supervisor	Bo Harwood
Script Supervisor	Dalonne Jackson
Assistants to the Producer	James Joyce
	Elaine Goren
Assistant Directors	Kevin Donnelly
	Lou Stroller
Associate Producer	Paul Donnelly
Producer	Al Ruban
Distribution	Universal
Running Time	115 minutes

CAST

Minnie	Gena Rowlands
Moskowitz	Seymour Cassel
Zelmo Swift	Val Avery
Jim	John Cassavetes
Hobo (Morgan Morgan)	Tim Carey
Mrs. Moskowitz	Katherine Cassavetes
Girl	Elizabeth Deering
Florence	Elsie Ames
Georgia Moore	Lady Rowlands
Kelly	Holly Near
Wife	Judith Roberts
Dick	Jack Danskin
Mrs. Grass	Eleanor Zee
Ned	Sean Joyce
Minister	David Rowlands
Others	Kathleen O'Malley
	Jimmy Joyce
	Santos Morales
	Chuck Welles

A Woman Under the Influence (1975)

Script and Direction	John Cassavetes
Photography	Caleb Deschanel

Camera Operators	Mike Ferris and David Nowell
Additional Camera Operator	Gary Graver
Camera Assistants	Tony Palmieri, Fred Elmes, Leslie Otis, and Larry Silver
Key Grip	Cliff Carnell
Gaffer	David Lester
Lighting Crew	Christ Taylor, Bo Taylor and Merv Dayan
Lighting	Mitch Breit
Music	Bo Harwood
Sound	Bo Harwood
Boom	Nick Spaulding
Sound Mix	Mike Denecke
First Assistant Director	Jack Corrick
Second Assistant Director	Roger Slager
Art Director	Phedon Papamichael
Production Secretary and Wardrobe	Carole Smith
Script Continuity	Elaine Goren
Props	Kevin Joyce
Graphics	Steve Hitter
In Charge of Post-production	Robert Heffernan
Supervising Editor	Tom Cornwell
Editors	Elizabeth Bergeron, David Armstrong and Sheila Viseltear
Producer	Sam Shaw for Faces International Films, Inc.
Running Time	146 minutes

CAST

Mabel Longhetti	Gena Rowlands
Nick Longhetti	Peter Falk
Tony Longhetti	Matthew Cassel
Angelo Longhetti	Matthew Laborteaux
Maria Longhetti	Christina Grisanti
Mama Longhetti	Katherine Cassavetes
Martha Mortensen	Lady Rowlands
George Mortensen	Fred Draper
Garson Cross	O. G. Dunn
Harold Jensen	Mario Gallo
Doctor Zepp	Eddie Shaw
Vito Grimaldi	Angelo Grisanti
Bowman	James Joyce
Clancy	John Finnegan
Aldo	Cliff Carnell
Muriel	Joanne Moore Jordan
Willie Johnson	Hugh Hurd

Billy Tidrow	Leon Wagner
Joseph Morton	John Hawker
James Turner	Sil Words
Angela	Elizabeth Deering
Tina	Jacki Peters
Principal	Elsie Ames
Adolph	Nick Cassavetes
Dominique Jensen	Dominique Davalos
Adrienne Jensen	Xan Cassavetes
John Jensen	Pancho Meisenheimer
Eddie the Indian	Charles Horvath
Aldo	Sonny Aprile
Gino	Vince Barbi
Adolph	Frank Richards
Nancy	Ellen Davalos

The Killing of a Chinese Bookie (1976, 1978)

Script and Direction	John Cassavetes
Production Designer	Sam Shaw
Art Director	Phedon Papamichael
In Charge of Post-production	Robert Heffernan
Supervising Editor	Tom Cornwell
Sound/Music	Bo Harwood
In Charge of Lighting	Mitchell Breit
Associate Producer	Phil Burton
Production Manager	Art Levinson
Camera Operators	Fred Elmes
	Mike Ferris
Camera Assistants	Michael Stringer
	Catherine Coulson
	M. Todd Henry
	Robert Hahn
Lighting Crew	Donald Robinson
	Chris Taylor
	Bruce Knee
Sound Editor	Jack Woods
Sound Mixer	Buzz Knudson
Music Conductor/Arranger	Anthony Harris
Assistant Editors	Terri Messina
	Frank Morgenstern
	Neal Meisenheimer
Graphics/Titles	Richard Upper
Production Secretary	Teresa Stokovic
Script Supervisor	Sandra King
Director's Secretary	Lanie Heffernan

Props	Miles Ciletti
Wardrobe	Mary Herne
Second Assistant Director	Nate Haggard
Accounting	Connie McFeeley
Associate Art Director	Bryan Ryman
Set Construction	Verna Bagby
	Robert Vehon
	Bruce Hartman
Cinemobile Driver	Stephen Brooks
Producer	Al Ruban for Faces Distribution Corporation
Running Time	135 minutes (1976 version)
	108 minutes (1978 version)

CAST

	Cosmo Vitelli	Ben Gazzara
The Gangsters:	*Flo*	Timothy Agoglia Carey
	Mort Weil	Seymour Cassel
	Phil	Robert Phillips
	John the Boss	Morgan Woodward
	Eddie-Red	John Red Kullers
	Marty Reitz	Al Ruban
The Family:	*Rachel*	Azizi Johari
	Betty (the mother)	Virginia Carrington
The Entertainers:	*Mr. Sophistication*	Meade Roberts
	Sherry	Alice Friedland
	Margo	Donna Gordon
	Haji	Haji
	Carol	Carol Warren
	Derna	Derna Wong Davis
	Annie	Kathalina Veniero
	Yvette	Yvette Morris
	Musical Director	Jack Ackerman
Characters:	*Lamarr*	David Rowlands
	The Waitress	Trisha Pelham
	1st Cabbie	Eddie Ike Shaw
	Sonny	Salvatore Aprile
	Commodore	Gene Darcy
	Bartender	Benny Marino
	Waitress	Arlene Allison
	Vince	Vince Barbi
	Blair Benoit	Val Avery
	Lavinia	Elizabeth Deering
	The Chinese Bookie	Soto Joe Hugh
	The Bookie's Girl	Catherine Wong
	2nd Cabbie	John Finnegan
	Mickey	Miles Ciletti

Scooper	Mike Skloot
Flo's Friend	Frank Buchanan
Parking Lot Attendant	Jason Kincaid
Poker Players	Frank Thomas
	Jack Krupnick

Opening Night (1978)

Script and Direction	John Cassavetes
Director of Photography	Al Ruban
Camera Operators	Frederick Elmes and
	Michael Ferris
Camera Assistants	Catherine Coulson and
	Jed Skillman
Gaffers	Donne Daniels
	Joseph L. Rezwin
	Donald Robinson
	Richard Ross
Graphics/Still Photographer	Richard Upper
Sound	Bo Harwood
Boom Operator	Crew Chamberlain
Sound Assistant	Joanne T. Harwood
Sound Mixer	Bill Varney
Composed Music	Bo Harwood
Arranged and Conducted Music	Booker T. Jones
Musical Consultant	Lee Housekeeper
Editor	Tom Cornwell
Assistant Editors	Kent Beyda
	Nancy Golden
	Hal Bowers
Sound Editor	Joe G. Woo
Production Managers	Foster H. Phinney
	Ed Ledding
Second Assistant Director	Lisa Hallas
Production Coordinator	Teresa Stokovic
Assistant to the Producer	Sharon Van Ivan
Art Director	Brian Ryman
Chief Set Construction	Abraham Zwick
Prop Man	Robert Vehon
Costume Designer	Alexandra Corwin-Hankin
Wardrobe Masters	Miles Ciletti and
	Charles Akins
Men's Wardrobe	Gangi of Rome
Location Supervisor	Jack Krupnick
Script Supervisors	Tom Cornwell and
	Joanne T. Harwood

Stunt Drivers	Victor Paul and
	Charles Ticerni
Stunt Double	Donna Garrett
Casting	Prometheus Patient
Post-production Secretary	Kathleen Barker
Teacher/Welfare Worker	Adria Licklider
Production Assistants	Carol Roux
	Robert Bogdanoff
	Raymond Vellucci
Publicists	Esmae Chandlee and
	Eve Siegel
Secretaries	Arlene Harris and
	Michelle Hart
Accounting	Susan Howell
Representative of Local 33	Pat Don Aroma
Stagehands	Larry Baughman, Larry Dean,
	Dave Walker and Emmett O'Connell
Location Equipment	Cinemobile
Sound	Goldwyn Studios
Laboratories	MGM
Associate Producer	Michael Lally
Executive Producer	Sam Shaw
Producer	Al Ruban
Distribution	Faces International Films, Inc.
Running Time	144 minutes

CAST

Myrtle Gordon	Gena Rowlands
Maurice Adams	John Cassavetes
Manny Victor	Ben Gazzara
Sarah Goode	Joan Blondell
David Samuels	Paul Stewart
Dorothy Victor	Zohra Lampert
Nancy Stein	Laura Johnson
Gus Simmons	John Tuell
Jimmy	Ray Powers
Kelly	Louise Fitch
Leo	Fred Draper
Prop Man	John Finnegan
Vivian	Katherine Cassavetes
Melva Drake	Lady Rowlands
Shirley	Sharon Van Ivan
Doorman	Jimmy Christie
News Stand Operator	James Karen
Bell Boy	Jimmy Joyce
Bartender	Sherry Bain
Bar Maid	Sylvia Davis Shaw

Maitre d'	Peter Lampert
Lena	Briana Carver
Charlie Spikes	Angelo Grisanti
Carla	Carol Warren
Eddie Stein	Meade Roberts
Sylvia Stein	Eleanor Zee

Gloria (1980)

Script and Direction	John Cassavetes
Music	Bill Conti
Photography	Fred Schuler
Art Director	Rene D'Auriac
Costume Designer	Peggy Farrell
Miss Rowland's Clothes by	Emmanuel Ungaro
Paintings by	Romare Bearden
Editor	George C. Villasenor
Casting	Vic Ramos
Production Manager/ *Associate Producer*	Steve Kesten
1st Assistant Director	Mike Haley
2nd Assistant Director	Tom Fritz
Assistant Editor	Lori Bloustein
Sound Effects	Pat Somerset, Jeff Bushelman Burbank Editorial Service, Inc.
Music Editor	Clifford C. Kohlweck
Camera Operator	Lou Barlia
1st Assistant Cameraman	Sandy Brooke
2nd Assistant Cameraman	Ricki-Ellen Brooke
Sound Mixers	Dennis Maitland, Sr. Jack C. Jacobsen
Rerecording Mixers	Wayne Artman, C.A.S. Tom Beckert, C.A.S. Michael Jiron, C.A.S.
Boom	Tod Maitland
Sound Recordists	Danny Rosenblum James Perdue
Script Supervisor	Nancy Hopton
Chargeman Scenic	Bill Lucek
Property Master	Wally Stocklin
Music Scoring Mixer	Dan Wallin
Special Effects	Connie Brink Al Griswald Ron Ottesen
Set Decorator	John Godrey
Wardrobe	Marilyn Putnam

Hairstylist	Verne Caruso
Makeup	Vince Callahan
Saxophone	Tony Ortega
Guitar	Tommy Tedesco
Key Grip	Dennis Gamiello
Best Boy	Tom Volpe
Dolly Grip	John Mazzoni
Gaffer	Rusty Engels
Best Boy	Ken Connors
Second Unit Director	Gaetano Lisi
Location Manager	Tom Lisi
	Jim Foote
Still Photographers	Jessica Burstein
	Adger Cowan
Publicity	Ann Guerin
Production Assistants	Harvey Portee, Chip Cronkite
	Liz Gazzara, Jed Weaver
	Mark Sitley, John Thomas
Production Office Coordinator	Eileen Eichenstein
Assistants to Producer	Larry Shaw and
	Robert Fieldsteel
Assistant to John Cassavetes	Kate Barker
Field Man	John (Red) Kullers
DGA Trainee	Penny Finkleman
Transportation Captain	Jim Giblin
Aerial Photography	Peter Gabarini
Dialogue Coach	Richard Kaye
Auditor	Susan Hoffman
Title Design	Sam Shaw
Producer	Sam Shaw
Distribution	Columbia
Running Time	110 minutes

CAST

Jeri Dawn	Julie Carmen
1st Man/Gangster	Tony Knesich
Kid in elevator	Gregory Cleghorne
Jack Dawn	Buck Henry
Phil Dawn	John Adames
Margarita Vargas	Lupe Garnica
Joan Dawn	Jessica Castillo
2nd Man/Gangster	Tom Noonan
3rd Man/Gangster	Ronald Maccone
Heavyset Man	George Yudzevich
Gloria Swenson	Gena Rowlands
Irish Cop	Gary Klar
TV Newscaster	William E. Rice

Riverside Drive Man #5	Frank Belgiorno
Riverside Drive Man #4	J. C. Quinn
Riverside Drive Man #7	Alex Stevens
Riverside Drive Man #8	Sonny Landham
Riverside Drive Man #6	Harry Madsen
Car Flip Cabbie	Shanton Granger
Bank Teller	John Pavelko
Assistant Bank Manager	Raymond Baker
Ron/Vault	Ross Charap
Clerk/Adams Hotel	Irvin Graham
Uncle Joe	Michael Proscia
Desk Clerk/Star Hotel	T. S. Rosenbaum
New York Cemetery Cabbie	Santos Morales
Hostess	Meta Shaw
Waitress	Marilyn Putnam
Frank	John Finnegan
Mister	Gaetano Lisi
Penn Station Hood #3	Richard M. Kaye
Penn Station Hood #5	Steve Lefkowitz
Penn Station Hood #4	George Poidomani
Broadway Bartender	Lawrence Tierney
E. 104th Street Cab Driver	Asa Adil Qawee
Boy in Bitch Mother's Apartment	Vincent Pecorella
Bitch Mother #1	Iris Fernandez
Bitch Mother #2	Jade Bari
Subway Person #2	David Resnick
Men in Newark Station	Thomas J. Buckman
	Joe Dabenigno
Bellman	Bill Wiley
Greek Cashier	John M. Sefakis
Sill	Val Avery
Newark Cabbie	Walter Dukes
Lincoln Tunnel Cabbie	Janet Ruben
Aldo	Ferruccio Hrvatin
Guillermo D'Antoni	Edward Wilson
Tony Tanzini	Basilio Franchina
Milt Cohen	Carl Levy
Pat Donovan	Warren Selvaggi
The Baron	Nathan Seril
Tonti	Vladimir Drazenovic
Desk Clerk/Newark Hotel	Edward Jacobs
1st Traveler	Brad Johnston
Pittsburgh Cabbie	Jerry Jaffe

RENTAL SOURCES FOR THE FILMS

Shadows, Faces, A Woman Under the Influence, The Killing of a Chinese Bookie, and *Opening Night* are available from John Cassavetes, c/o Ms. Esmae Chandlee, 9021 Melrose Avenue, Los Angeles, CA 90069.

Too Late Blues is available from Films Incorporated and Paramount Theatricals.

A Child Is Waiting is available from Films Incorporated, Budget Films, United Artists 16, Westcoast Films, and Wayne Ewing Films.

Husbands is available from Twyman Films, Swank Motion Pictures, and Corinth Films.

Minnie and Moskowitz is available from Clem Williams Films, Swank Motion Pictures, and Twyman Films.

Gloria is available from Kit Parker Films and on videotape from RCA/Columbia Video.

INDEX

Designer: Lisa Mirski
Compositor: Interactive Composition Corporation
Text: 10/13 Palatino
Display: Palatino
Printer: The Murray Printing Company
Binder: The Murray Printing Company